Contents

KT-468-317

Acknowledgements

We have been particularly fortunate in having had a larger than usual group of advisors to help produce this new edition. Some of the names listed below have been involved before, indeed Ian Baillie helped us from the very first edition and both Carolyn Huckfield and Bob Sharpe for nearly as long.

Copies of **Who Else Writes Like ...?** are to be found in many Australian public libraries and so therefore we were delighted that professional staff members from the Bayside District Libraries of Melbourne happily agreed to help with the 6th edition.

As always our most grateful thanks are extended to all the people who assisted in this latest edition. They are:-

Fiona Allison	Kingston-upon-Thames Borough Council
Ian Baillie	West Dunbartonshire Council
Malcolm Batten	Westminster City Council
Jennie Bolitho & colleagues	Bayside Libraries, Melbourne, Australia
Lindsay Casseldon	South Tyneside Council
Jill Craven	Barnsley Council
Timothy Davies	Rotherham Borough Council
Sue Goult	Leicestershire County Council
Carolyn Huckfield	Herefordshire County Council
Dennis Malley	
Jack Meadows	Loughborough University
Julie Potton	Derbyshire County Council
Jeremy Preston	Richmond-on-Thames Libraries
Bob Sharpe	Dorset County Libraries

From the beginning Public Lending Right has been the arbiter for the core collection of authors that form the basis of the book. We therefore greatly appreciate the help we receive from Dr Jim Parker, the Registrar of Public Lending Right, and his colleagues.

We are also most grateful to Viv Green and Mary Yardley, the editors of *Who Next ...? A guide to children's authors,* for their expertise in identifying suitable authors for young adult readers.

Another expert in his own field to whom we are most indebted, Eric Pascal, has ensured that the computer competence at our end has reasonably matched the continued excellence of the staff at LISU. The new Director, Claire Creaser, has given the project her full support while Mary Ashworth and Sharon Fletcher have consistently injected their own personal enthusiasm and expertise into the publication.

Roy and Jeanne Huse

Aldwick
August 2008

Who Else

writes like ... ?

A readers' guide to fiction authors

Sixth edition

Edited by
Roy and Jeanne Huse

LISU Research & consultancy
for performance management
Information, cultural & academic services

Loughborough
University

HUSE, Roy and Jeanne, Editors

Who Else Writes Like ...? A readers' guide to fiction authors

First published 1993, 6th edition 2008

ISBN: 978-1-905499-32-8

Cover design by
Clarissa Musson, Design & Print Services, Loughborough University

Inside pages designed and typeset in Verdana and Arial by
Mary Ashworth & Sharon Fletcher, LISU

Printed by
W & G Baird Ltd, Greystone Press, Antrim, N Ireland, BT41 2RS

Published and distributed by
LISU
Loughborough University, Loughborough, LE11 3TU
Tel: +44 (0)1509 635680 Fax: +44 (0)1509 635699
E-mail: lisu@lboro.ac.uk
Web: www.lboro.ac.uk/departments/dis/lisu

Introduction

Who Else Writes Like ...? was first published under this title in 1993. It is designed to help library users who have read all the books by their favourite authors and are seeking new names to try. Of course, no author writes exactly like another, but the selection of alternatives provided should help to narrow the choices from the hundreds of titles available on the library's shelves. While today's modern technology can produce sophisticated reading lists, the advantage of this guide lies in its simplicity and portability. It can be taken around the shelves by a reader or by a member of the library staff, and for this reason, the editors, advisors and publishers all hope that the guide will be prominently displayed, readily available to encourage maximum use. While this guide is compiled by librarians for librarians, it is of equal value to bookshops and their customers.

The basis for the initial selection of authors continues to be those who are the most borrowed according to the lists compiled by the Registrar of Public Lending Right. These are supplemented with names suggested by a small team of volunteer advisors based in libraries in different parts of the United Kingdom and, in the case of this edition, also in Australia. As a general rule the author should have had three novels published; only in the exceptional circumstance of a first novel becoming a prize-winner or an outstanding publishing success would such an author be included. In total, 1,973 authors are included — including 490 not in previous editions — and they reflect a good cross section of the stock of public libraries across the UK and in Australia.

As always with new editions there are some changes. In general the number of alternative names under each entry has been limited to nine, although there may be up to 12 where an author is extremely popular and in great demand. Many authors now have their own websites; these are included in their entry and were correct at the time of going to press. Details of more general fiction websites, along with further suggested reading material, are to be found at the back of the book. The list of Literary Prizes has been updated with entries included from the year 2000 — earlier winners can be found in previous editions of this guide or online. As social and literary customs constantly change three new genres have been included in this new edition namely: 'Historical Romance'; 'Mature Chick Lit'; and 'Paranormal'. Similarly some minor amendments to subgenre headings have also been made.

A new venture in this edition is aimed at meeting the needs of young adult readers who are in the process of 'crossing-over' from reading books suitable for children to tackling adult novels. To help them, a has been used to identify potentially suitable authors.

As always the aim of this guide is to encourage readers to try the works of new authors and to open up to them the wealth of good reading that is available in their local public library and bookshop.

How to use this Guide

The Reader's Guide - An Alphabetical List

Authors are listed in alphabetical order, followed by a list of suggested alternatives. So pick out an author whose books you like, and see which other writers are recommended underneath. For instance, if you like Philip Kerr, you might also like Geoffrey Archer, Robert Edric and so on.

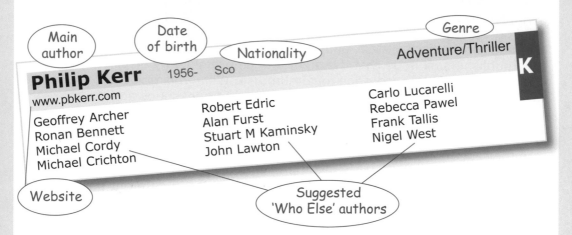

Additional information is given, where known:

- Dates of birth and death
- Nationality (or place of birth) of authors who are not English — see page vi for a list of abbreviations used
- Genre and, in some cases, subgenre, or type of novel (unless 'general')
- Own website
- Pseudonyms
- Characters ⚤ and/or Environment, Occupation
- Prize winners ♛
- Crossover (may be suitable for young adults) ✆
- Also writes for children ☺

Genre

For a list of authors who write in a particular category or genre, such as Crime or Saga, go straight to the Genre listings, beginning on page 302. Some of these are further divided into subgenre, e.g. Crime: Historical - Medieval; Fantasy: Humour.

An increasing number of authors are writing in alternative genres and have separate entries in the main listing for each.

Authors who usually write in one category may occasionally produce a book in a quite different genre, so if genre is important to you, check the jacket details of a book before you read it.

Where there is no genre given, this is because an author's work is considered to be 'general' rather than in a specific genre.

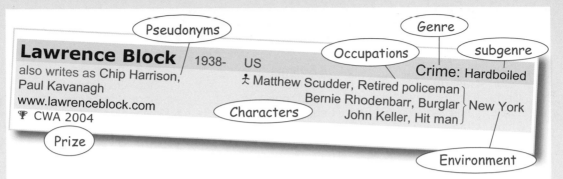

Pseudonym(s) Also writes/wrote as and is/was
Many writers use pseudonyms and some write under several different names. Please go to page 295 for an index of the alternative names used by authors in the main A-Z listing, for which there is no separate entry.

Characters, Series and Families
In the main section these are identified by ⚐. If you know a character's name but have no idea of the author's name, go to page 317 for an alphabetical list of Characters, Sagas, Series and Families, which gives the relevant author.

Literary Prizes and Awards
Where an author has won a literary prize or award, this is shown by ♛ followed by an abbreviated form of the prize and the year(s) won — see page vi for a list of abbreviations used. Most are listed in full, with their descriptions, in the list of Literary Prizes and Awards (pages 338–352).

Crossover Authors
Where authors have written books for children these are indicated with a ☺ as they may offer an easy crossover for readers (although in some cases the children's books are written for a much younger age range). Suggestions for authors to introduce older teenagers to adult fiction are indicated by ⌒. More details and a list of authors are provided on pages 353-355.

Further Reading
There is an increasing number of guides to novelists and their works. Some information about these can be found on pages 356–358.

Websites
Authors' own websites are included in the main A-Z listing but other useful websites can be found on page 359.

Abbreviations

Nationality

Braz	Brazil	Isr	Israel	SA	South Africa
Can	Canada	It	Italy	Sco	Scotland
Carib	Caribbean	Ja	Japan	Sing	Singapore
Chile	Chile	Leb	Lebanon	Spain	Spain
China	China	Malay	Malaysia	Sri Lan	Sri Lanka
Col	Colombia	Mex	Mexico	Swe	Sweden
Cuba	Cuba	Neth	Netherlands	Tah	Tahiti
Den	Denmark	NZ	New Zealand	Tur	Turkey
Fin	Finland	Nigeria	Nigeria	US	United States of America
Fr	France	Nor	Norway		
Ger	Germany	Pak	Pakistan	Ukr	Ukraine
Guy	Guyana	Peru	Peru	Wales	Wales
Ice	Iceland	Pol	Poland	Zam	Zambia
Ind	India	Rus	Russia	Zan	Zanzibar
Ire	Ireland				

Literary Prizes and Awards

Authors	Authors' Club First Novel Award
Black	James Tait Black Memorial Prizes
Booker	Booker Prize for Fiction
British Fantasy	British Fantasy Awards
BSFA	British Science Fiction Association Awards
Arthur C Clarke	Arthur C Clarke Award
Commonwealth	Commonwealth Writers' Prize
Costa	Costa Book Awards (formerly Whitbread)
CWA	Crime Writers' Association
Encore	Encore Award
Faber	Geoffrey Faber Memorial Prize
Guardian	Guardian Fiction Prize / First Book Award
Hawthornden	Hawthornden Prize
Higham	David Higham Prize for Fiction (listed in 4th ed)
Holtby	Winifred Holtby Memorial Prize
IMPAC	International IMPAC Dublin Literary Award
Irish Times	Irish Times International Fiction Prize (listed in 5th ed)
JLR	John Llewellyn Rhys Prize (formerly Mail on Sunday)
Man Booker	Man Booker Prize for Fiction
Man Booker Int	Man Booker International Prize
S Maugham	Somerset Maugham Awards
McKitterick	McKitterick Prize
Nathan	Melissa Nathan Award for Comedy Romance
Ondaatje	Ondaatje Prize (formerly Winifred Holtby)
Orange	Orange Broadband Prize
Pulitzer	Pulitzer Prize for Fiction
Romantic	Romantic Novel of the Year
Saga for Wit	Saga Award for Wit
Sagittarius	Sagittarius Prize
WHSmith	WHSmith Literary Award
Sunday Times	Sunday Times Young Writer of the Year Award
Theakston's	Theakston's Old Peculier Crime Novel of the Year
TGR	Thumping Good Read Book Award
Betty Trask	Betty Trask Awards
Whitbread	Whitbread Book of the Year and Literary Awards
Wingate	Jewish Quarterly / Wingate Literary Prize for Fiction

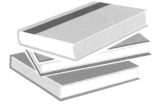

The Readers' Guide
An Alphabetical List

Jeff Abbott   1963-   US   Adventure/Thriller: Legal/financial
www.jeffabbott.com   ☆ Whit Mosley, Judge - Texas

Russell Andrews	Harlan Coben	Elisabeth Hyde
Sam Bourne	Robert Crais	Simon Kernick
Lee Child	James Grippando	George P Pelecanos

Joe Abercrombie   1974-   Fantasy: Epic
www.joeabercrombie.com

Stephen Donaldson	Robin Hobb	Scott Lynch
Raymond E Feist	Tom Lloyd	Karen Miller

Dan Abnett   1965-   Science Fiction: Space opera
www.danabnett.com

Lois McMaster Bujold	David A Drake
Ben Counter	Tanith Lee

Chinua Achebe   1930-   Nigeria
🏆 Man Booker Int 2007

Chimamanda Ngozi Adichie	Khaled Hosseini	Ben Okri
Thalassa Ali	Yasmina Khadra	Markus Zusak
Nadeem Aslam		

Peter Ackroyd   1949-
🏆 S Maugham 1984   Guardian 1985   Whitbread 1985

Martin Amis	Christopher Fowler	Robert Nye
John Banville	John Fowles	Iain Sinclair
Julian Barnes	Maggie Gee	Colm Toibin
Sebastian Barry	James Meek	Jill Paton Walsh

Go to back for lists of
Pseudonyms • Authors by Genre • Characters and Series
Prize Winners • Crossover Authors • Further Reading • Websites

Gilbert Adair 1944- Sco

Julian Barnes	Patrick Gale	Ian McEwan
A S Byatt	Alan Hollinghurst	

Crime: Amateur sleuth
🕴 Evadne Mount, Author • CI Trubshawe, Retired policeman

Catherine Aird	Gyles Brandreth	Christopher Fowler
James Anderson	Agatha Christie	Mark Gatiss
Marian Babson	Carola Dunn	Susan Kandel
M C Beaton	Jasper Fforde	Mike Ripley

Paul Adam 1958- Adventure/Thriller

Paul Carson	Ken Follett	Ken McClure
Robin Cook	Robert Harris	Mark Mills
Len Deighton	Roy Lewis	Eliot Pattison

Douglas Adams 1952-2001 Science Fiction: Humour
www.douglasadams.com
🕴 Hitch-Hikers Guide to the Galaxy Series

Robert Asprin	Neil Gaiman	Sharyn McCrumb
Lois McMaster Bujold	Rob Grant	Robert Rankin
Jasper Fforde	Tom Holt	

Jane Adams 1960- Crime: Psychological
🕴 DI Mike Croft • DS Ray Flowers - Norfolk
Naomi Blake, Blind ex-policewoman

Lisa Appignanesi	Frances Fyfield	Danuta Reah
Hilary Bonner	P D James	Margaret Yorke
Deborah Crombie	Ed O'Connor	

Jessica Adams 1964- Aus Chick Lit
www.jessicaadams.com

Cecelia Ahern	Eve Makis	Melissa Nathan
Susie Boyt	Chris Manby	Alexandra Potter
Serena Mackesy	Carole Matthews	Fiona Walker

Chimamanda Ngozi Adichie 1977- Nigeria
www.halfofayellowsun.com
🏆 Commonwealth 2005   Orange 2007

Chinua Achebe	Kiran Desai	Rohinton Mistry
Thalassa Ali	Will Ferguson	V S Naipaul
Nadeem Aslam	Abdulrazak Gurnah	Helen Oyeyemi
André Brink	Khaled Hosseini	Roma Tearne

Elizabeth Adler

Crime: Romantic suspense

also writes as Ariana Scott
www.elizabethadler.com

Charlotte Bingham	Anita Burgh	Carol Rivers
Rose Boucheron	Elizabeth Edmondson	Penny Vincenzi
Barbara Taylor Bradford	Judith Gould	

Lara Adrian   US

Paranormal

www.laraadrian.com

Keri Arthur	Mary Janice Davidson	Charlaine Harris
Patricia Briggs	Christine Feehan	J R Ward
Mary Higgins Clark		

Cecelia Ahern   1981-   Ire

Chick Lit

www.ceceliaahern.ie

Jessica Adams	Claudia Carroll	Morag Prunty
Susie Boyt	Julia Llewellyn	Célestine Hitiura Vaite
Hester Browne	Sue Margolis	Cathy Woodman
Rebecca Campbell	Sinead Moriarty	Elizabeth Wrenn

Catherine Aird   1930-

Crime: Police work - UK

is Kim Hamilton McIntosh
www.catherineaird.com

DI Sloan & DS Crosby
'Calleshire'

Gilbert Adair	Pauline Bell	Chris Collett
Vivien Armstrong	W J Burley	Roderic Jeffries
A C Baantjer	Agatha Christie	Katherine John
M C Beaton	Ann Cleeves	Robin Paige

Rosemary Aitken   1942-

Saga

also writes as Rosemary Rowe
www.raitken.wyenet.co.uk

'Penvarris', Cornwall

Jessica Blair	Gloria Cook	Susan Sallis
Philip Boast	Winston Graham	Barbara Whitnell
Anita Burgh	Elizabeth Ann Hill	

Boris Akunin   1956-   Rus

Crime: Historical - C19th

is Grigory Chkhartishvillihas

Erast Fandorin, Tsarist agent • Sister Pelagia, Nun

Tom Bradby	George Macdonald Fraser	R N Morris
Gyles Brandreth	Jason Goodwin	Michael Pearce
Arthur Conan Doyle	Michael Gregorio	Barrie Roberts
Ian Fleming	Andrey Kurkov	Frank Tallis

Mitch Albom   1958-   US
www.albom.com

Mary Higgins Clark	Catherine Ryan Hyde	Alice Sebold
Paulo Coelho	Jodi Picoult	Nicholas Sparks
Nicholas Evans		

Maggie Alderson   Chick Lit

Zoë Barnes	Rachel Johnson	Jennifer Weiner
Meg Cabot	Melissa Nathan	Deborah Wright
Jenny Colgan	Freya North	

Brian W Aldiss   1925-   Science Fiction: Space and time
www.brianwaldiss.co.uk
BSFA 1982 & 1985

Isaac Asimov	Joe Haldeman	Kurt Vonnegut
Greg Bear	Robert A Heinlein	John Wyndham
Arthur C Clarke	Brian Herbert	
Harlan Ellison	Frank Herbert	

Alma Alexander   1963-   NZ   Fantasy: Myth
is Alma Hromic
www.almaalexander.com

Arthur Golden	Anchee Min	Amy Tan
Stephen Hunt	Lisa See	Xinran
Ha Jin	Su Tong	

Monica Ali   1967-

Michel Faber	Andrea Levy	Zadie Smith
Roopa Farooki	Arundhati Roy	Meera Syal
Abdulrazak Gurnah	Salman Rushdie	Alex Wheatle
Hanif Kureishi		

Thalassa Ali   US   Historical
www.thalassaali.com   Mariana Givens - C19th India and Afghanistan

Chinua Achebe	Chitra Banerjee Divakaruni	Paul Scott
Chimamanda Ngozi Adichie	Khaled Hosseini	Carolyn Slaughter
Nadeem Aslam	Yasmina Khadra	Carlos Ruiz Zafón
Barbara Cleverly	Rohinton Mistry	Markus Zusak

may be suitable for young adults

Ted Allbeury   1917-2005   Adventure/Thriller
also wrote as Richard Butler, Patrick Kelly

Len Deighton	Colin Forbes	John Lawton
Clive Egleton	Brian Freemantle	Robin White

Conrad Allen   1940-   Crime: Historical - C20th
also writes as Edward Marston, Martin Inigo; is Keith Miles
www.edwardmarston.com

⚐ George Porter Dillman &
Genevieve Masefield,
Ships' detectives, Cunard Line

Barbara Cleverly	Edward Marston	Anne Perry
Carola Dunn	Keith Miles	Jacqueline Winspear

Isabel Allende   ⌒   1942-   Chile
www.isabelallende.com

Gail Anderson-Dargatz	Carlos Fuentes	Tomas Eloy Martinez
Alessandro Baricco	John Galsworthy	Patrick Suskind
Louise Erdrich	Gabriel Garcia Márquez	Mario Vargas Llosa
Laura Esquivel	Shifra Horn	Jeanette Winterson

Catherine Alliott   Chick Lit
www.catherinealliott.com

Cathy Kelly	Tasmina Perry	Fiona Walker
Sue Margolis	Patricia Scanlan	Polly Williams
Carole Matthews		

Karin Alvtegen   1966-   Swe   Crime: Psychological
www.karinalvtegen.com

Ake Edwardson	Anne Holt	Jeff Lindsay
Kjell Eriksson	Arnaldur Indridason	Jo Nesbo
Karin Fossum	Mari Jungstedt	Hakan Nesser
Patricia Highsmith	Jesse Kellerman	Maj Sjöwall & Per Wahlöö

Kingsley Amis   ⌒   1922-95
⚐ Jim Dixon

🏆 Booker 1986

Malcolm Bradbury	Nick Laird	Wendy Perriam
Joseph Connolly	David Lodge	Alan Sillitoe
Michael Frayn	Stanley Middleton	Gore Vidal

☺ also writes children's books

Martin Amis 1949-

Peter Ackroyd	David Flusfeder	Vladimir Nabokov
J G Ballard	Tobias Hill	D B C Pierre
Iain Banks	James Joyce	Adam Thirlwell
Justin Cartwright	Blake Morrison	Virginia Woolf

Niccolo Ammaniti 1966- It

Andrea Camilleri	Jonathan Safran Foer	Ian McEwan
Charles Dickens	Khaled Hosseini	

James Anderson 1936- Crime: Police work - UK
ᵏ CI Wilkins, 1930s - Westshire Constabulary

Gilbert Adair	Carola Dunn	Dorothy L Sayers
M C Beaton	Mark Gatiss	Andrew Taylor
Gyles Brandreth	Susan Kandel	Jacqueline Winspear
Agatha Christie	David Roberts	P G Wodehouse

Kevin J Anderson 1962- US Science Fiction: Space opera
www.wordfire.com

Iain M Banks	Brian Herbert	Alastair Reynolds
Simon Green	Frank Herbert	Kristine Kathryn Rusch
Peter F Hamilton	Larry Niven	Dan Simmons

Lin Anderson Sco Crime: Forensic
www.lin-anderson.com ᵏ Rhona MacLeod, Forensic scientist

Simon Beckett	Gillian Galbraith	Ian Rankin
Benjamin Black	Alex Gray	Manda Scott
Karen Campbell	Nigel McCrery	Louise Welsh

Poul Anderson 1926-2001 US Science Fiction: Space opera

Isaac Asimov	Ray Bradbury	Jack McDevitt
Stephen Baxter	Philip K Dick	Dan Simmons
Gregory Benford	Harlan Ellison	Charles Stross

Gail Anderson-Dargatz Can
www.gailanderson-dargatz.ca

Isabel Allende	Barbara Kingsolver	Ann Patchett
William Faulkner	Alice Munro	John Steinbeck

Lyn Andrews 1943- Saga

is Lynda M Andrews | Liverpool Irish | **A**

Anne Baker
Dilly Court
June Francis

Ruth Hamilton
Joan Jonker
Mary A Larkin

Maureen Lee
Lynda Page
Rowena Summers

Russell Andrews 1952- US Adventure/Thriller

also writes as Peter Gethers; is David Handler

Jeff Abbott
Campbell Armstrong
Harlan Coben

Michael Connelly
Clive Cussler
Humphrey Hawksley

John Katzenbach
Stanley Pottinger
P J Tracy

Virginia Andrews 1923-86 US

also wrote as V C Andrews (with Andrew Neiderman)   ☆ DeBeers Family Series

Susan Hill
Gwen Hunter

Judith Kelman
Nora Roberts

Lisa Appignanesi 1946- Pol

www.lisaappignanesi.com

Jane Adams
Michael Chabon
Helen Dunmore

Jonathan Safran Foer
Clare Francis
Nicci French

Lesley Glaister
Cynthia Ozick
Philip Roth

Diana Appleyard Aga Saga

www.appleyardmedia.co.uk/diana.htm

Charlotte Bingham
Elizabeth Buchan
Victoria Clayton

Annabel Dilke
Sarah Grazebrook
Sandra Howard

Elizabeth Palmer
Joanna Trollope
Jane Elizabeth Varley

Geoffrey Archer 1944- Adventure/Thriller

www.geoffreyarcher.co.uk   ☆ Sam Packer, MI6

Stephen Coonts
Graham Hurley
Philip Kerr

Stephen Leather
Chris Ryan
Julian Jay Savarin

Tim Sebastian
Craig Thomas

Jeffrey Archer 1940- Adventure/Thriller

www.jeffreyarcher.com

Harry Bingham
Nicholas Coleridge
Stephen Coonts

Michael Dobbs
Joseph Finder
Frederick Forsyth

Colin Harrison
Philip Hensher
Sidney Sheldon

Aileen Armitage   1930-   Saga

also writes as Aileen Quigley; is Ruth Fabian   🏃 Eva Bower
www.aileenarmitage.com   Hawksmoor Series - Yorkshire

Jessica Blair	Helen Cannam	Rosie Goodwin
Philip Boast	Catherine Cookson	Kay Stephens
Rita Bradshaw	Glenice Crossland	

Campbell Armstrong   1944-   Sco   Adventure/Thriller

is Campbell Black   🏃 DS Lou Perlman - Glasgow
www.campbellarmstrong.com

Russell Andrews	Stuart MacBride	Julian Jay Savarin
Harold Coyle	Glenn Meade	Tim Sebastian
Colin Forbes	David Morrell	Gerald Seymour

David Armstrong   Crime: Police work - UK

🏃 DI Frank Kavanagh & DC Jane Salt - Shropshire

Marjorie Eccles	J M Gregson	Dorothy Simpson
Kate Ellis	Patricia Hall	Sally Spencer
Geraldine Evans	Louise Penny	Charles Todd

Kelley Armstrong   1968-   Can   Paranormal

www.kelleyarmstrong.com

Keri Arthur	Christine Feehan	Tanya Huff
Patricia Briggs	Laurell K Hamilton	Sherrilyn Kenyon
Poppy Z Brite	Lori Handeland	J R Ward
Mary Janice Davidson	Charlaine Harris	Kim Wilkins

Vivien Armstrong   Crime: Police work - UK

🏃 DI Ian Preston & DS Judith Pullen - Great Yarmouth
DS Roger Hayes & Sgt Prentice - Oxfordshire

Catherine Aird	Ken Bruen	P D James
Lindsay Ashford	Brian Cooper	Susan B Kelly
Stephen Booth	Geraldine Evans	David Lawrence

Jake Arnott   1961   Crime: Hardboiled

🏆 CWA 2005

Glenn Chandler	Ken McCoy	Louise Welsh
Mark Gatiss	David Peace	John Williams
Toby Litt	Mark Timlin	

Keri Arthur   Aus

www.keriarthur.com

Paranormal

♟ Riley Jensen, half vampire

| Lara Adrian | Mary Janice Davidson | Tanya Huff |
| Kelley Armstrong | Christine Feehan | J R Ward |

Sarah Ash

www.sarah-ash.com

Fantasy: Epic

David Bilsborough	Amanda Hemingway	Juliet Marillier
James Clemens	Robin Hobb	Robert Newcomb
David Eddings	Anne McCaffrey	Melanie Rawn

Michael Asher

Adventure/Thriller

North Africa

Tom Clancy	John Fullerton	Chris Ryan
Len Deighton	Andy McNab	Wilbur Smith
Daniel Easterman	Glenn Meade	

Neal Asher   1961-

http://freespace.virgin.net/n.asher

Science Fiction: Near future

Iain M Banks	Peter F Hamilton	Richard Powers
John Birmingham	Sergei Lukyanenko	Alastair Reynolds
Hal Duncan	Richard Morgan	Andrzej Sapkowski
Steven Gould	Larry Niven	Dan Simmons

Jeffrey Ashford   1926-

is Roderic Jeffries

Crime: Police work - UK

| Hilary Bonner | Kate Ellis | Bill James |
| Martin Edwards | J M Gregson | Roy Lewis |

Lindsay Ashford   Sco

www.lindsayashford.co.uk

Crime: Psychological

♟ Megan Rhys, Investigative psychologist

Vivien Armstrong	Tess Gerritsen	Val McDermid
Linda Fairstein	Leonard Goldberg	Sheila Quigley
Frances Fyfield	David Lawrence	Minette Walters

Trisha Ashley

www.trishaashley.com

Aga Saga

Victoria Clayton	Dorothy Koomson	Adele Parks
Lucy Dawson	Gil McNeil	Nicky Pellegrino
Katie Fforde	Jill Mansell	Victoria Routledge
Louise Harwood	Sarah Mason	Linda Taylor

David Ashton
1941-   Sco

Crime: Historical - C19th
♁ Insp James McLevy - Edinburgh

Joyce Holms	James McGee	Amy Myers
Arnaldur Indridason	Edward Marston	Anne Perry
Alanna Knight		

Sherry Ashworth
☌ ☺   1953-

Chick Lit

www.sherryashworth.com

Zoë Barnes	Anne Dunlop	Kathy Lette
Emily Barr	Helen Fielding	Kate O'Riordan
Martina Devlin	Milly Johnson	Arabella Weir

Isaac Asimov
☌   1920-92   US

Science Fiction: Space and time

www.asimovonline.com

Brian W Aldiss	Ben Bova	Robert A Heinlein
Poul Anderson	Arthur C Clarke	Larry Niven
Gregory Benford	Philip K Dick	John Wyndham

Nadeem Aslam
1966-   Pak

♛ Encore 2005

Chinua Achebe	Kiran Desai	Yasmina Khadra
Chimamanda Ngozi Adichie	Margaret Drabble	Caryl Phillips
Thalassa Ali	Khaled Hosseini	Markus Zusak

Robert Asprin
1946-2008   US

Fantasy: Epic

also wrote as Robert Lynn Asprin, and jointly with Peter J Heck

Douglas Adams	Craig Shaw Gardner	Terry Pratchett
Jasper Fforde	Tom Holt	Martin Scott
Alan Dean Foster	Christopher Moore	Freda Warrington

Judy Astley

Aga Saga

www.judyastley.com

Raffaella Barker	Veronica Henry	Charlotte Moore
Anne Doughty	Cathy Kelly	Sinead Moriarty
Rebecca Gregson	Santa Montefiore	Madeleine Wickham

Elizabeth Aston
1948-

Historical

also writes as Elizabeth Pewsey
♁ Darcy Family, C19th
www.elizabeth-aston.com

Jane Austen	Barbara Erskine	Georgette Heyer
Elizabeth Chadwick	Elizabeth Gaskell	Emma Tennant

Kate Atkinson 1951-

www.kateatkinson.co.uk

🏆 Whitbread 1995

Beryl Bainbridge	Liz Jensen	Alice Sebold
Leif Enger	Nick Laird	Ali Smith
Laura Esquivel	Charlotte Mendelson	Roma Tearne
Margaret Forster	Tim Pears	Louise Tondeur

Crime: PI
🏃 Det Jackson Brodie

Giles Blunt	Irene Nemirovsky	Alexander McCall Smith
Arnaldur Indridason	Hakan Nesser	R D Wingfield
Elizabeth McGregor	Peter Robinson	

Margaret Atwood 1939- Can

www.owtoad.com

🏆 Arthur C Clarke 1987   Booker 2000

Joan Barfoot	Gail Godwin	Valerie Martin
Clare Chambers	Nadine Gordimer	Clare Morrall
Robb Forman Dew	Sarah Hall	George Orwell
Miranda Glover	Aldous Huxley	Rachel Seiffert

Jean M Auel 1936- US   Historical

Louise Cooper	Christian Jacq	Edward Rutherfurd
Diana Gabaldon	Juliet Marillier	Manda Scott
Kathleen O'Neal Gear		

Jane Austen 1775-1817

www.janeaustensociety.org.uk

Elizabeth Aston	Elizabeth Gaskell	Emma Tennant
Rachel Billington	Georgette Heyer	Barbara Trapido
Charles Dickens	Alison Lurie	Edith Wharton
Penelope Fitzgerald		

Paul Auster 1947- US

www.paulauster.co.uk

Nicola Barker	Nathan Englander	D B C Pierre
Julian Barnes	Ben Faccini	Thomas Pynchon
E L Doctorow	Jonathan Safran Foer	Geoff Ryman
Dave Eggers	Denis Johnson	Adam Thorpe

> *Go to back for lists of*
> Pseudonyms • Authors by Genre • Characters and Series
> Prize Winners • Crossover Authors • Further Reading • Websites

Steve Aylett   1967-   Science Fiction: Near future
www.steveaylett.com

J G Ballard	Gwyneth Jones	Neal Stephenson
Eric Brown	Ken MacLeod	Tad Williams
William Gibson	Jeff Noon	

Trezza Azzopardi   1961-   Wales
♟ Faber 2001

Stevie Davies	Denis Johnson	Rachel Seiffert
Anne Enright	Ian McEwan	Carol Shields
Maggie Gee	Ann Patchett	Zadie Smith

A C Baantjer   1923-   Neth   Crime: Police work - Netherlands
is Albert Cornelis Baantjer   🚶 Insp DeKok - Amsterdam

Catherine Aird	Marjorie Eccles	Georges Simenon
Colin Dexter	Caroline Graham	Janwillem van de Wetering

Marian Babson   1929   US   Crime: Amateur sleuth
is Ruth Stenstreem   🚶 Trixie Dolan & Evangeline Sinclair, Actresses
                                        Douglas Perkins & Gerry Tate, PR consultants
                                                                          London

Gilbert Adair	Lilian Jackson Braun	Anthea Fraser
Gyles Brandreth	Simon Brett	Alison Joseph

Richard Bachman   1947-   US   Horror
is Stephen King

Douglas Clegg	Dean R Koontz	Dan Simmons
James Herbert	Mark Morris	Peter Straub
Peter James		

David Baddiel   1964-   General

Mark Barrowcliffe	Rob Grant	Matt Thorne
Peter Ho Davies	Andrew Holmes	Nigel Williams
Ben Elton		

Louise Bagshawe   1972-   Chick Lit

Celia Brayfield	Christina Jones	Robyn Sisman
Jilly Cooper	Susan Lewis	Jane Elizabeth Varley
Imogen Edwards-Jones	Lesley Lokko	Fiona Walker
Olivia Goldsmith	Tasmina Perry	Cathy Woodman

Tilly Bagshawe

Chick Lit

www.tillybagshawe.com

Jackie Collins	Jane Green	Jill Mansell
Jilly Cooper	Lesley Lokko	Carole Matthews

Murray Bail 1941- Aus

🏃 Holden Shadbolt

🏆 Commonwealth 1999

Peter Carey	Lloyd Jones	Yann Martel
Maurice Gee	Andrew McGahan	Tim Winton
Kate Grenville	David Malouf	

Elizabeth Bailey

Historical Romance

www.elizabethbaileybooks.com

Lynne Barrett-Lee	Veronica Henry	Jeannie Johnson
Anne Bennett	Anne Herries	Amanda Quick
Donna Hay	Georgette Heyer	Julia Quinn

Beryl Bainbridge 〰️ 1934-

🏆 Guardian 1974   Whitbread 1977 & 1996   Black 1998   WHSmith 1999

Kate Atkinson	Giles Foden	Bernice Rubens
Pat Barker	Linda Grant	Fay Weldon
Penelope Fitzgerald	Simon Mawer	

Anne Baker

Saga

Liverpool

Lyn Andrews	Rosie Harris	Margaret Mayhew
Dilly Court	Audrey Howard	Elizabeth Murphy
Katie Flynn	Maureen Lee	Rowena Summers

R Scott Bakker 1967- Can

Fantasy: Epic

www.princeofnothing.com

Carol Berg	Greg Keyes	Patrick Rothfuss
Steven Erikson	George R R Martin	Brian Ruckley
Guy Gavriel Kay	Anne Rice	J R R Tolkien

David Baldacci 〰️ 1960- US

Adventure/Thriller

www.davidbaldacci.com   🏃 Sean King & Michelle Maxwell, ex-Secret Service agents

🏆 TGR 1997

Linwood Barclay	Brian Haig	Brad Meltzer
Nelson DeMille	Craig Holden	David Morrell
Joseph Finder	Gregg Hurwitz	Michael Robotham
Mark Gimenez	Patrick Lennon	Brad Thor

J G Ballard 1930-

is James Graham Ballard
www.jgballard.com

Martin Amis	Tobias Hill	Edward St Aubyn
Peter Carey	Gunnar Kopperud	Will Self
Romesh Gunesekera		

Science Fiction: Technical

🏆 BSFA 1979   Black 1984   Guardian 1984

Steve Aylett	Michael Jan Friedman	James Lovegrove
Ray Bradbury	William Gibson	Christopher Priest
Philip K Dick	Joe Haldeman	Kurt Vonnegut

Mary Balogh 1944-   Historical Romance: C19th
Regency period

www.marybalogh.com

Anne Barbour	Georgette Heyer	Fenella-Jane Miller
Marion Chesney	Stephanie Laurens	Julia Quinn
Emily Hendrickson		

Melissa Bank US

www.melissabank.com

Mavis Cheek	Alison Jameson	Bella Pollen
Jane Green	Marian Keyes	Curtis Sittenfeld
Wendy Holden	Sophie Kinsella	Jennifer Weiner

Ashok K Banker 1966- Ind   Fantasy: Myth

www.ashokbanker.com

Kate Elliott	Juliet Marillier	Caiseal Mor
Steven Erikson	George R R Martin	Sarah Zettel
Robert Jordan		

Carla Banks   Adventure/Thriller

is Danuta Reah
www.carlabanks.co.uk

Stephen Booth	Daniel Hecht	Danuta Reah
Ken Follett	Tami Hoag	Phil Rickman
Clare Francis	Sarah Rayne	

🏠 may be suitable for young adults

Iain Banks ⌒ 1954- Sco

also writes as Iain M Banks
www.Iain-Banks.net

Martin Amis	Yann Martel	Alan Warner
Douglas Coupland	Will Self	Jeanette Winterson
Ian McEwan		

B

Iain M Banks ⌒ 1954- Sco Science Fiction: Space opera

also writes as Iain Banks
www.Iain-Banks.net
🏆 BSFA 1994 & 1996

Kevin J Anderson	Steven Gould	John Meaney
Neal Asher	Peter F Hamilton	Andrzej Sapkowski
Greg Bear	Sergei Lukyanenko	Charles Stross
Hal Duncan	Ken MacLeod	David Zindell

Russell Banks 1940- US

Louis de Bernières	Charles Frazier	Cormac McCarthy
Pete Dexter	David Guterson	Sue Miller
F Scott Fitzgerald		

Jo Bannister 1951- Crime: Police work - UK

🚶 DI Liz Graham & DS Cal Donovan - 'Castlemere'
Brodie Farrell, PI - South Coast, England
DCI Frank Shapiro • Clio Rees, Doctor

Simon Brett	Liz Evans	Priscilla Masters
Deborah Crombie	Adrian Magson	Peter Turnbull
Marjorie Eccles	Barry Maitland	

John Banville 1945- Ire

also writes as Benjamin Black
🏆 Guardian 1981   Man Booker 2005

Peter Ackroyd	James Hamilton-Paterson	Vladimir Nabokov
Sebastian Barry	Ismail Kadare	William Trevor
Dermot Bolger	John McGahern	Barry Unsworth

Anne Barbour US Historical Romance: C19th

Regency period

Mary Balogh	Emily Hendrickson	Fenella-Jane Miller
Marion Chesney	Georgette Heyer	Julia Quinn
Elizabeth Darrell	Stephanie Laurens	

Alex Barclay 1974- Ire Adventure/Thriller
🏃 Det Joe Lucchesi, NYPD

Mark Billingham	David Hosp	Glenn Meade
Ann Cleeves	J A Kerley	Chris Mooney
Kathryn Fox	Michael Marshall	

James Barclay 1965- Fantasy: Epic
www.jamesbarclay.com

Stephen Donaldson	Greg Keyes	Caiseal Mor
Steven Erikson	Juliet E McKenna	Robert Newcomb
Jude Fisher	John Marco	Stan Nicholls
David Gemmell	George R R Martin	Freda Warrington

Linwood Barclay US Adventure/Thriller
www.linwoodbarclay.com

David Baldacci	Mark Gimenez	Patrick Lennon
Harlan Coben	Gregg Hurwitz	Michael Robotham
Tess Gerritsen	Greg Iles	

Tessa Barclay 1928- Sco Saga
is Jean Bowden 🏃 Craigallan, Corvill & Tramont Families

Emma Blair	Frances Paige	T R Wilson
Pamela Oldfield	Nicola Thorne	Janet Woods

Joan Barfoot 1946- Can
www3.sympatico.ca/jbarfoot

Margaret Atwood	Margaret Drabble	Anne Tyler
Isla Dewar	Carol Shields	

Alessandro Baricco 1958- It

Isabel Allende	Laura Esquivel	Gabriel Garcia Márquez
Paulo Coelho	Carlos Fuentes	Patrick Suskind

Clive Barker ⌒ 1952- Horror
www.clivebarker.com

Jonathan Carroll	Neil Gaiman	Bentley Little
Simon Clark	Richard Laymon	Dan Simmons
Christopher Fowler		

Nicola Barker 1966-

🏆 Higham 1993   JLR 1996   IMPAC 2000   Hawthornden 2008

Paul Auster	Jenny Diski	Lloyd Jones
Julian Barnes	Edward Docx	Marcia Muller
Saul Bellow	Tessa Hadley	J D Salinger

Pat Barker 🌈 1943-

🏆 Guardian 1993   Booker 1995

Beryl Bainbridge	Gunnar Kopperud	Erich Maria Remarque
Louis de Bernières	Valerie Martin	Bernhard Schlink
Linda Grant	Irene Nemirovsky	Charles Todd

Raffaella Barker 🌈 ☺ 1964-

www.raffaellabarker.co.uk

Judy Astley	Kate Fenton	Mary Lawson
Victoria Clayton	Julie Highmore	Isabel Wolff
Louise Doughty	India Knight	

Frank Barnard 1938-

War: Modern

🏃 Kit Curtis, RAF pilot - WW2

F G Cottam	Andrew Greig	Derek Robinson
Elizabeth Darrell	James Holland	Alan Savage
David Fiddimore	Robert Radcliffe	

Robert Barnard 1936-

Crime: Police work - UK

also writes as Bernard Bastable

🏃 Det Supt Oddie & DC Charlie Peace - Yorkshire
Supt Perry Trethowan - London

🏆 CWA 2003

Pauline Bell	Jonathan Gash	Nicholas Rhea
Glenn Chandler	Patricia Hall	Pauline Rowson
Chris Collett	John Harvey	Peter Turnbull
Colin Dexter	Stuart Pawson	R D Wingfield

Julian Barnes 1946-

also writes as Dan Kavanagh
www.julianbarnes.com

🏆 S Maugham 1981   Faber 1985

Peter Ackroyd	Nicola Barker	Rachel Seiffert
Gilbert Adair	Blake Morrison	Graham Swift
Paul Auster	Tim Parks	A N Wilson

☺ also writes children's books

17

Linda Barnes   1949-   US   Crime: PI
www.lindabarnes.com   ⚳ Carlotta Carlyle - Boston, Mass

Stella Duffy	Lauren Henderson	S J Rozan
Janet Evanovich	Marcia Muller	Dana Stabenow
Meg Gardiner	Rick Riordan	Sarah Strohmeyer

Zoë Barnes   Chick Lit
www.zoebarnes.supanet.com   Cheltenham

Maggie Alderson	Donna Hay	Carole Matthews
Sherry Ashworth	Cathy Kelly	Elizabeth Noble
Maria Beaumont	Serena Mackesy	Lesley Pearse

Jill Barnett   US
www.jillbarnett.com

Elizabeth Flock	Tessa Hadley	Mary Alice Monroe
Therese Fowler	Alison Jameson	Laura Moriarty
Nicci Gerrard	Jacquelyn Mitchard	Marcia Preston

Emily Barr   Chick Lit
http://authorpages.hoddersystems.com/EmilyBarr
🏆 WHSmith 2001

Sherry Ashworth	Adele Parks	Fiona Walker
Jenny Colgan	Lisa Tucker	Jennifer Weiner
India Knight		

Nevada Barr   1952-   US   Crime: Amateur sleuth
www.nevadabarr.com   ⚳ Anna Pigeon, Park ranger - National Parks

C J Box	Sue Grafton	Michael McGarrity
Jo Dereske	Tony Hillerman	Margaret Maron
Aaron Elkins	Sharyn McCrumb	Dana Stabenow

Robert G Barrett   1943-   Aus   Crime: Amateur sleuth
www.robertgbarrett.com.au/index.html   ⚳ Les Norton, Bondi Beach lifeguard - Sydney

Peter Corris	Shane Maloney	Ian Rankin
Carl Hiaasen	Armistead Maupin	

Lynne Barrett-Lee   1959-   Chick Lit
www.lynnebarrett-lee.com

Elizabeth Bailey	Harriet Evans	Andrea Semple
Rebecca Campbell	Kate Harrison	Bernadette Strachan
Imogen Edwards-Jones	Sheila Norton	

James Barrington
www.jamesbarrington.com

Adventure/Thriller

🏃 Paul Richter, British agent

Alex Berenson	Frederick Forsyth	Gerald Seymour
Tom Clancy	Gordon Kent	Robin White
Stephen Coonts	Matthew Reilly	

Mark Barrowcliffe   1964-

Lad Lit

David Baddiel	Mike Gayle	Danny King
Matt Beaumont	Sam Holden	Mil Millington
Matt Dunn		

Sebastian Barry   1955-   Ire

Peter Ackroyd	Sebastian Faulks	Joseph O'Connor
John Banville	Damon Galgut	William Trevor
F G Cottam	Andrew Greig	William Wall
Peter Ho Davies	John McGahern	

Beverly Barton   US

Crime: Romantic suspense

www.beverlybarton.com

Allison Brennan	Gwen Hunter	Nora Roberts
Heather Graham	Lisa Jackson	Karin Slaughter
Linda Howard	J D Robb	

Colin Bateman   🏝   1962-   Ire

www.colinbateman.com

🏃 Dan Starkey, Journalist - Belfast

🏆 Betty Trask 1994

Peter Guttridge	Douglas Lindsay	Zane Radcliffe
Danny King	Toby Litt	Mike Ripley
Robert Lewis	Malcolm Pryce	Ian Sansom

Susannah Bates   1970-

Chick Lit

Susie Boyt	Sophie Kinsella	Penny Vincenzi
Julie Highmore	Kathleen Tessaro	Sarah Webb
Lisa Jewell	Rosy Thornton	Liz Young

Stephen Baxter   1957-

Adventure/Thriller: Historical

www.stephen-baxter.com

Conn Iggulden	William Napier	Edward Rutherfurd
James A Michener	Steven Pressfield	Tim Severin

(continues on next page)

Stephen Baxter (continued)   Science Fiction: Technical

🏆 BSFA 1995

Poul Anderson	Wil McCarthy	China Miéville
Ben Bova	Jack McDevitt	Robert Reed
Arthur C Clarke	Ian McDonald	Charles Stross
Susanna Clarke	Sophia McDougall	H G Wells

Greg Bear   1951-   US   Science Fiction: Technical

www.gregbear.com

Brian W Aldiss	C J Cherryh	Wil McCarthy
Iain M Banks	Arthur C Clarke	John Meaney
Gregory Benford	Harlan Ellison	Kim Stanley Robinson
David Brin	Peter F Hamilton	Sean Williams

G S Beard   Sea: Historical - C19th

🚶 John Fury, Midshipman - Nelson's navy

Bernard Cornwell	Jonathan Lunn	Dudley Pope
David Donachie	Allan Mallinson	Peter Smalley
C S Forester	Patrick O'Brian	Julian Stockwin

M C Beaton   1936-   Sco   Crime: Police work - UK

is Marion Chesney   🚶 PC Hamish MacBeth - Scotland
www.agatharaisin.co.uk   Agatha Raisin, Retired advertising executive

Gilbert Adair	Clare Curzon	Patricia Harwin
Catherine Aird	Margaret Duffy	Joyce Holms
James Anderson	Gerald Hammond	Lis Howell
Pauline Bell	Janis Harrison	Susan Kandel

Simon Beaufort   1958-   Crime: Historical - Medieval

also writes as Susanna Gregory   🚶 Sir Geoffrey Mappestone &
is Elizabeth Cruwys   Roger of Durham - C12th England

Alys Clare	Pat McIntosh	Ellis Peters
Paul Doherty	Edward Marston	Candace Robb
Michael Jecks		

Sally Beauman   1944-   Glitz & Glamour

also writes as Vanessa James

Jude Deveraux	Sara MacDonald	Una-Mary Parker
Susan Lewis	Judith Michael	Célestine Hitiura Vaite
Lesley Lokko	Hilary Norman	Penny Vincenzi

Maria Beaumont 1975-   Chick Lit

also writes as **Jessie Jones**
www.letstalkaboutme.com

Zoë Barnes	Milly Johnson	Alexandra Potter
Rowan Coleman	Marian Keyes	Patricia Scanlan
Jane Green	Sophie Kinsella	Sarah Webb

Matt Beaumont   Lad Lit

www.letstalkaboutme.com

Mark Barrowcliffe	Tim Lott	Jonathan Tropper
Matt Dunn	William Sutcliffe	Matt Whyman
Mike Gayle		

Simon Beckett   Crime: Forensic

www.simonbeckett.com   ⚐ Dr David Hunter, Forensic anthropologist

Lin Anderson	Tess Gerritsen	Louise Penny
Benjamin Black	Peter James	Kathy Reichs
Patricia D Cornwell	Keith McCarthy	Nick Stone
Kathryn Fox	Nigel McCrery	Sue Walker

Pauline Bell 1938-   Crime: Police work - UK

⚐ DCI Benny Mitchell - 'Cloughton', Yorkshire
CI Browne & DC Jennie Taylor

Catherine Aird	Brian Cooper	Stuart Pawson
Robert Barnard	Marjorie Eccles	Pauline Rowson
M C Beaton	Patricia Hall	Peter Turnbull

Guy Bellamy 1935-   Humour

Jonathan Coe	Patrick Gale	John O'Farrell
Joseph Connolly	Nick Hornby	Nigel Williams
Michael Frayn	David Nicholls	

Saul Bellow 1915-2005 US

www.saulbellow.org
🏆 Pulitzer 1976

Nicola Barker	David Grossman	Philip Roth
Michael Chabon	Amos Oz	John Updike
Don DeLillo	Frederic Raphael	

Go to back for lists of
Pseudonyms • Authors by Genre • Characters and Series
Prize Winners • Crossover Authors • Further Reading • Websites

21

Gregory Benford 1941- US Science Fiction: Technical

also writes as Sterling Blake
www.gregorybenford.com
🏆 BSFA 1980

Poul Anderson	Ben Bova	Wil McCarthy
Isaac Asimov	C J Cherryh	Brian Stableford
Greg Bear	Paul J McAuley	Sean Williams

Alan Bennett 1934- Humour

Geraldine Brooks	Laurie Graham	Sue Townsend
Jessica Duchen	John Lanchester	Nigel Williams
Stephen Fry	Magnus Mills	P G Wodehouse

Anne Bennett 1949- Saga

www.annebennett.co.uk Birmingham

Elizabeth Bailey	Jean Chapman	Margaret Mayhew
Benita Brown	Hilary Green	Kay Stephens
Julia Bryant	Rosie Harris	Janet Woods

Maggie Bennett 1931- Saga

Emma Blair	Rosie Goodwin	Meg Hutchinson
Philip Boast	Annie Groves	Frances Paige
Margaret Thomson Davis	Evelyn Hood	

Ronan Bennett 1956- Adventure/Thriller

Robert Harris	John Le Carré	Henry Porter
Joseph Kanon	Andrew O'Hagan	Martin Cruz Smith
Philip Kerr	Edna O'Brien	Robert Wilson

Vanora Bennett Historical

www.vanorabennett.com

Tracy Chevalier	Ken Follett	Jane Harris
Barbara Erskine	Philippa Gregory	Alison Weir
Barbara Ewing		

Raymond Benson 1955- US Adventure/Thriller

also writes as David Michaels   🏃 James Bond
www.raymondbenson.com

Tim Binding	Tom Clancy	James Follett
Lee Child	Ian Fleming	

Alex Berenson   US   Adventure/Thriller
www.thefaithfulspy.com   ⚥ John Wells, CIA Agent

James Barrington	Dan Fesperman	Chris Petit
Clive Egleton	Ian Fleming	Henry Porter
Jon Evans	Gayle Lynds	Stella Rimington

Carol Berg   1948-   US   Fantasy: Epic
www.sff.net/people/carolberg

R Scott Bakker	Robin Hobb	Melanie Rawn
Sara Douglass	Mercedes Lackey	Harry Turtledove
Terry Goodkind	Robert Newcomb	

Elizabeth Berg   1948-   US
www.elizabeth-berg.net

Suzanne Berne	Laurie Graham	Jacquelyn Mitchard
Liz Byrski	Ann Hood	Anna Quindlen
Fannie Flagg	Lorna Landvik	Anita Shreve
Patricia Gaffney	Sue Miller	Adriana Trigiani

Suzanne Berne   US   Adventure/Thriller: Psychological
♛ Orange 1999

Elizabeth Berg	Harper Lee	Anita Shreve
Linda Grant	Laura Lippman	Donna Tartt
Kate Grenville	Annie Proulx	Adriana Trigiani
Shirley Hazzard	Julian Rathbone	Minette Walters

William Bernhardt   1960-   US   Crime: Legal/financial
www.williambernhardt.com   ⚥ Ben Kincaid, Defense attorney - Oklahoma

Stephen L Carter	John Hart	Phillip Margolin
James Grippando	John Le Carré	Lisa Scottoline
John Grisham	John T Lescroart	

Steve Berry   1955-   US   Adventure/Thriller
www.steveberry.org   ⚥ Cotton Malone, ex-US Justice Dept,
                                   now antiquarian book dealer - Copenhagen

Sam Bourne	David Gibbins	James Rollins
Michael Byrnes	Katherine John	Paul Sussman
John Case	Chris Kuzneski	James Twining
Michael Cordy	Matthew Reilly	

Mark Billingham

also writes as Will Peterson
www.markbillingham.com
🏆 Theakston's 2005

Crime: Police work - UK
🚶 DI Tom Thorne - London

Alex Barclay	David Lawrence	Chris Simms
Garry Disher	Stuart MacBride	Nick Stone
Joy Fielding	Brian McGilloway	Tony Strong
Peter James	Barry Maitland	Neil White

Rachel Billington   1942-

Jane Austen	Penelope Fitzgerald	Penelope Lively
Rachel Cusk	Margaret Forster	Alison Lurie
Anne Fine	Elizabeth Jane Howard	

David Bilsborough

Fantasy: Epic

Sarah Ash	Raymond E Feist	Karen Miller
David Eddings	Katherine Kurtz	J R R Tolkien
Steven Erikson	Julian May	Tad Williams

Maeve Binchy   ☎ 1940- Ire

www.maevebinchy.com

Aga Saga
Ireland

Sarah Challis	Adèle Geras	Geraldine O'Neill
Anne Doughty	Jan Karon	Imogen Parker
Rose Doyle	Jojo Moyes	Liz Ryan

Tim Binding   1947-

Adventure/Thriller

Raymond Benson	Louis de Bernières	David Lodge
F G Cottam	William Golding	Tim Pears

Charlotte Bingham   1942-

www.charlottebingham.com
🏆 Romantic 1995

Aga Saga

Elizabeth Adler	Elizabeth Buchan	Sarah Harrison
Diana Appleyard	Elizabeth Elgin	Rosy Thornton
Barbara Taylor Bradford	Maeve Haran	

Harry Bingham   1967-

Adventure/Thriller: Legal/financial

Jeffrey Archer	John McLaren	Christopher Reich
Reg Gadney	Steve Martini	Michael Ridpath
John T Lescroart		

Carol Birch 1951-

🏆 Higham 1988   Faber 1991

Louise Doughty	Margaret Forster	Kate Grenville
Helen Dunmore	Lesley Glaister	Deborah Moggach

John Birmingham 1964-   Aus   Science Fiction: Near future

Neal Asher	James Lovegrove	Neal Stephenson
Tom Clancy	Richard Powers	

Benjamin Black 1945-   Ire   Crime: Police work - Ireland

is John Banville   ☖ Quirke, Pathologist - Dublin 1950s • Insp Hackett

Lin Anderson	Alex Gray	Nigel McCrery
Simon Beckett	Peter James	Brian McGilloway
William Brodrick	Matthew Klein	Andrew Taylor
Bartholomew Gill	Laura Lippman	Peter Temple

Cara Black   US   Crime: PI

www.carablack.com   ☖ Aimée Leduc - Paris

Liz Evans	Marcia Muller	Zoë Sharp
Sue Grafton	Sara Paretsky	Cath Staincliffe

Ingrid Black   Ire   Crime: Psychological

☖ Saxon, former FBI agent

Ken Bruen	Mo Hayder	John Sandford
Elizabeth Corley	Theresa Monsour	Erica Spindler
Sarah Diamond	Margaret Murphy	Minette Walters

Emma Blair 1942-   Sco   Saga

is Iain McPhee   ☖ Drummond Family - Scotland
www.emma-blair.com

Tessa Barclay	Christine Marion Fraser	Lesley Pearse
Maggie Bennett	Hilary Green	Eileen Ramsay
Dilly Court	Elisabeth McNeill	Jessica Stirling

Jessica Blair 1923-   Saga

is Bill Spence   C19th Yorkshire
www.jessicablair.co.uk

Rosemary Aitken	Margaret Dickinson	Eileen Ramsay
Aileen Armitage	Iris Gower	Margaret Thornton
Helen Cannam	Annie Groves	Valerie Wood

Victoria Blake

Crime: PI
🏃 Sam Falconer - Oxford University

Alice Blanchard	Grace Monroe	Claire Seeber
Elizabeth Corley	Louise Penny	Paullina Simons
Barry Maitland	Karen Rose	

B

Alice Blanchard   1959-   US   Adventure/Thriller

Victoria Blake	Stuart Harrison	Paullina Simons
Elizabeth Corley	Grace Monroe	Scott Smith
John Gilstrap	Claire Seeber	Boston Teran

Lawrence Block   1938-   US   Crime: Hardboiled

also writes as Chip Harrison,   🏃 Matthew Scudder, Retired policeman ⎫
Paul Kavanagh   Bernie Rhodenbarr, Burglar ⎬ New York
www.lawrenceblock.com   John Keller, Hit man ⎭
🏆 CWA 2004

Raymond Chandler	Elmore Leonard	Robert B Parker
Loren D Estleman	Ross Macdonald	Thomas Perry
Dashiell Hammett	Reggie Nadelson	Peter Spiegelman

Anna Blundy   1970-   Adventure/Thriller
🏃 Faith Zanetti, Journalist

Simon Kernick	Allison Pearson	Tom Sharpe
Sara Paretsky	Alexei Sayle	Carol Smith

Giles Blunt   1952-   Can   Crime: Police work - Canada
www.gilesblunt.com   🏃 Det John Cardinal & Det Lisa Delorme - 'Algonquin Bay', Canada
🏆 CWA 2001

Kate Atkinson	Theresa Monsour	Medora Sale
John Dunning	Jonathan Nasaw	Dana Stabenow
Donald Harstad	Ridley Pearson	Peter Temple
Archer Mayor	Louise Penny	Jess Walter

Philip Boast   1952-   Crime: Historical - Ancient
🏃 Septimus Severus Quistus - Ancient Rome

Margaret Doody	Lynda S Robinson	Marilyn Todd
Lauren Haney	Rosemary Rowe	David Wishart

Saga
🏃 Ben London - London

Rosemary Aitken	Billy Hopkins	Victor Pemberton
Aileen Armitage	Beryl Kingston	Elizabeth Waite
Maggie Bennett		

Dermot Bolger 1959- Ire

John Banville	Patrick McCabe	Edna O'Brien
Roddy Doyle	Colum McCann	David Park
Anne Enright	Brian Moore	Glenn Patterson
James Joyce	Joseph O'Connor	Niall Williams

Hilary Bonner 1949- Crime: Psychological
DCI Rose Piper - Devon

Jane Adams	Robert Goddard	Iain McDowall
Jeffrey Ashford	Gregory Hall	Sarah Rayne
Stephen Booth	Morag Joss	Aline Templeton

Stephen Booth 1952- Crime: Psychological
www.stephen-booth.com *DC Ben Cooper & DS Diane Fry - Peak District*

Vivien Armstrong	Ken McCoy	Ed O'Connor
Carla Banks	Iain McDowall	Louise Penny
Hilary Bonner	Barry Maitland	Andrew Pyper
Robert Goddard	Priscilla Masters	Danuta Reah

Rose Boucheron Saga
www.roseboucheron.com

Elizabeth Adler	Josephine Cox	Beryl Kingston
Julia Bryant	Sarah Harrison	Janet Woods
Anita Burgh	Elizabeth Jane Howard	

Sam Bourne 1967- Adventure/Thriller
is Jonathan Freedland

Jeff Abbott	John Case	Raymond Khoury
Steve Berry	Lee Child	Chris Kuzneski
Dan Brown	Michael Cordy	James Rollins
Michael Byrnes	John Twelve Hawks	James Twining

Ben Bova 1932- US Science Fiction: Space and time
www.benbova.net

Isaac Asimov	Arthur C Clarke	Larry Niven
Stephen Baxter	Greg Egan	Kim Stanley Robinson
Gregory Benford		

Go to back for lists of
Pseudonyms • Authors by Genre • Characters and Series
Prize Winners • Crossover Authors • Further Reading • Websites

Rhys Bowen

Crime: Police work - UK

is Janet Quin-Harkin
www.rhysbowen.com

☶ Constable Evan Evans • Molly Murphy, PI - New York, 1900s
Lady Victoria Georgiana Charlotte Eugenie, Amateur sleuth - 1930s

Clare Curzon	Gregory Hall	Charles Todd
David Dickinson	Peter Lovesey	Jacqueline Winspear
Carola Dunn		

Harry Bowling   1931-1999

Saga

☶ Tanner Trilogy - London

Dilly Court	Elizabeth Lord	Victor Pemberton
Josephine Cox	Kitty Neale	Carol Rivers
Billy Hopkins	Margaret Pemberton	Elizabeth Waite

C J Box   US

Crime: Amateur sleuth

www.cjbox.net

☶ Joe Pickett, National warden - 'Saddlestring', Wyoming

Nevada Barr	Steve Hamilton	Michael McGarrity
James Lee Burke	Donald Harstad	Dana Stabenow
Loren D Estleman	Tony Hillerman	

William Boyd   1952-

www.williamboyd.co.uk

☆ Whitbread 1981   JLR 1982   S Maugham 1982   Black 1990   Costa 2006

Margaret Elphinstone	Matthew Kneale	Simon Mawer
Giles Foden	Nick Laird	Tim Parks
Philip Hensher	Ian McEwan	Richard Powers
Christopher Hope	Alistair MacLeod	James Robertson

Clare Boylan   1948-2006   Ire

Saga

Michael Collins	Edna O'Brien	Patricia Scanlan
Anne Haverty	Wendy Perriam	Sue Townsend

Susie Boyt   1969-

Mature Chick Lit

www.susieboyt.com

Jessica Adams	Julie Highmore	Lynne Truss
Cecelia Ahern	Lesley Pearse	Fiona Walker
Susannah Bates		

Malcolm Bradbury   1932-2000

Kingsley Amis	Howard Jacobson	Paul Torday
Melvyn Bragg	David Lodge	Keith Waterhouse
Michael Frayn	John Mortimer	Evelyn Waugh
Michael Innes	Nicholas Shakespeare	A N Wilson

Ray Bradbury ⌒ 1920- US Science Fiction: Space and time
www.raybradbury.com

Poul Anderson	Robert A Heinlein	Ken MacLeod
J G Ballard	Aldous Huxley	George Orwell
Harlan Ellison		

Tom Bradby Adventure/Thriller

Boris Akunin	Andrey Kurkov	Tim Sebastian
Daniel Easterman	Stephen Leather	Gerald Seymour
Clive Egleton	Robert Ludlum	

Barbara Taylor Bradford 1933- Saga
also writes as Sally Bradford 🏃 Emma Harte
www.barbarataylorbradford.co.uk Ravenscar Series • Deravenel Series

Elizabeth Adler	Una-Mary Parker	Rosie Thomas
Charlotte Bingham	Sidney Sheldon	Nicola Thorne
Jennifer Donnelly	Danielle Steel	Penny Vincenzi

Marion Zimmer Bradley ⌒ 1930-1999 US Fantasy: Epic
www.mzbfm.com

Cecilia Dart-Thornton	Tanith Lee	Caiseal Mor
Barbara Hambly	Holly Lisle	Melanie Rawn
Robert Holdstock	Morgan Llywelyn	Sheri S Tepper
Helen Hollick	Julian May	Liz Williams

Rita Bradshaw Saga
NE England

Aileen Armitage	Hilary Green	Meg Hutchinson
Catherine Cookson	Annie Groves	Freda Lightfoot
Josephine Cox	Ruth Hamilton	Annie Murray
Margaret Dickinson	Una Horne	Lynda Page

Melvyn Bragg 1939-
🏆 WHSmith 2000

Malcolm Bradbury	Sarah Hall	Andrew O'Hagan
A S Byatt	Thomas Hardy	Julian Rathbone
Margaret Drabble	Billy Hopkins	Alan Sillitoe
Sebastian Faulks	Stanley Middleton	Alan Titchmarsh

⌒ may be suitable for young adults

Gyles Brandreth 1948-
www.gylesbrandreth.net

Crime: Amateur sleuth
⚐ Oscar Wilde - C19th

Gilbert Adair	Marian Babson	Arthur Conan Doyle
Boris Akunin	Simon Brett	Peter Lovesey
James Anderson	David Dickinson	

Lilian Jackson Braun 1916- US

Crime: Amateur sleuth
⚐ Jim Qwilleran, Journalist, & Yum Yum & Koko, Siamese cats - 'Moose County', US

Marian Babson	Martha Grimes	Carolyn G Hart
Paula Gosling	Janis Harrison	Margaret Maron

Celia Brayfield 1945-
www.celiabrayfield.com

Glitz & Glamour

Louise Bagshawe	Barbara Delinsky	Katie Price
Jackie Collins	Judith Michael	Victoria Routledge
Jilly Cooper	Hilary Norman	

Chaz Brenchley 1959-
www.chazbrenchley.co.uk
🏆 British Fantasy 1998

Fantasy: Epic

Jim Butcher	Stephen Gallagher	David Martin
Simon Clark	Andrew Klavan	K J Parker
Sara Douglass	Scott Lynch	Patrick Rothfuss

Allison Brennan US
www.allisonbrennan.com

Crime: Romantic suspense

Beverly Barton	Lisa Jackson	Karen Rose
Heather Graham	Theresa Monsour	Sharon Sala
Linda Howard	J D Robb	

Simon Brett 1945-

Crime: Amateur sleuth
⚐ Charles Paris, Actor • Mrs Pargeter - Sussex • Carole Seddon - 'Fethering', Sussex

Marian Babson	Kate Charles	Keith Miles
Jo Bannister	Ruth Dudley Edwards	Catherine Sampson
Gyles Brandreth	Carolyn G Hart	Jill Paton Walsh
W J Burley	Veronica Heley	Stella Whitelaw

Patricia Briggs 1965- US
www.hurog.com

Paranormal
⚐ Mercy Thompson, Car mechanic

Lara Adrian	Christine Feehan	Charlaine Harris
Kelley Armstrong	Lori Handeland	Kim Harrison
		Liz Williams

David Brin 1950- US

Science Fiction: Space opera

www.davidbrin.com

Greg Bear	Brian Herbert	Dan Simmons
C J Cherryh	Frank Herbert	Robert Charles Wilson
Alan Dean Foster	Robert Reed	

André Brink 1935- SA

Chimamanda Ngozi Adichie	J M Coetzee	Nadine Gordimer
Michael Chabon	Jim Crace	Christopher Hope

Poppy Z Brite 1967- US

Horror

www.poppyzbrite.com

Kelley Armstrong	Brian Lumley	Anne Rice
Tanya Huff	Kim Newman	Kim Wilkins
Joe R Lansdale		

Suzanne Brockmann 1960 US

Crime: Romantic suspense

⚑ US Navy 'Seal' teams

is Suzanne Brockmann Gaffney
www.suzannebrockmann.com

Sandra Brown	Nelson DeMille	David Hagberg
John Case	Vince Flynn	Stanley Pottinger

William Brodrick 1960-

Crime: Amateur sleuth

⚑ Father Anselm

Benjamin Black	Nicole Krauss	James Robertson
Andrew M Greeley	Mary Lawson	Andrew Taylor
Alison Joseph	John Le Carré	

Amanda Brookfield 1960-

Aga Saga

www.amandabrookfield.co.uk

Anne Doughty	Kate Long	Robin Pilcher
Adèle Geras	Santa Montefiore	Madeleine Wickham
Erica James	Elizabeth Palmer	

Christopher Brookmyre 1968- Sco

Crime: Humour

⚑ Jack Parlabane, Journalist - Scotland

www.brookmyre.co.uk

Joolz Denby	Carl Hiaasen	Malcolm Pryce
Christopher Fowler	Robert Lewis	Zane Radcliffe
Jack Harvey	Douglas Lindsay	Kevin Sampson
James Hawes	Adrian Magson	Ian Sansom

Anita Brookner 🌣 1928-

🏆 Booker 1984

A S Byatt	Penelope Fitzgerald	Gwendoline Riley
Mavis Cheek	Ian McEwan	Bernice Rubens
Anne Enright	Charlotte Mendelson	Salley Vickers

B

Geraldine Brooks 1955- Aus   Historical

www.geraldinebrooks.com

🏆 Pulitzer 2006

Alan Bennett	Kiran Desai	Melanie Gifford
Tracy Chevalier	Anita Diamant	Christopher Koch
Will Davenport	E L Doctorow	Rose Tremain

Terry Brooks 🌣 1944- US   Fantasy: Epic

www.terrybrooks.net

James Clemens	David Gemmell	Mickey Zucker Reichert
Kate Elliott	John Marco	J R R Tolkien
Raymond E Feist	Elizabeth Moon	Margaret Weis
Maggie Furey	Stan Nicholls	Tad Williams

Benita Brown   Saga

www.benitabrown.com   C19th Tyneside

Anne Bennett	Rosie Harris	Beryl Matthews
Catherine Cookson	Joan Jonker	Elizabeth Murphy
Dilly Court	Margaret Kaine	Mary Jane Staples

Dale Brown 1956- US   Adventure/Thriller

also writes with Jim Felice   🚶 Patrick McLanahan - Aviation
www.megafortress.com   Major Jason Richter, Special Operations Unit, FBI

Richard Herman	Kyle Mills	Julian Jay Savarin
Graham Hurley	John J Nance	James Siegel
Gordon Kent	Patrick Robinson	Robin White

Dan Brown 🌣 1964- US   Adventure/Thriller

www.danbrown.com   🚶 Professor Robert Langdon - Harvard University

Sam Bourne	Michael Crichton	Chris Kuzneski
Michael Byrnes	David Gibbins	Greg Loomis
Lincoln Child	David Hagberg	Douglas Preston
Michael Cordy	Raymond Khoury	Paul Sussman

🌣 may be suitable for young adults

Eric Brown   1960-   Science Fiction: Near future
www.ericbrown.co.uk

Steve Aylett   James Lovegrove   Justina Robson
William Gibson   Adam Roberts   Neal Stephenson
Paul Johnston

Sandra Brown   1948-   US   Glitz & Glamour
also writes as Laura Jordan, Rachel Ryan, Erin St Claire
www.sandrabrown.net

Suzanne Brockmann   Olivia Goldsmith   Harold Robbins
Candace Bushnell   Lisa Jackson   Nora Roberts
Jackie Collins   Jayne Ann Krentz   Penny Vincenzi

Hester Browne   Chick Lit
♁ Melissa Romney-Jones

Cecelia Ahern   Sophie Kinsella   Morag Prunty
Meg Cabot   Nicole Krauss   Olivia Ryan
Marian Keyes   Melissa Nathan   Rosy Thornton

Robert Gregory Browne   US   Adventure/Thriller
www.robertgregorybrowne.com

Lee Child   G M Ford   Alex Kava
Michael Connelly   Mo Hayder   J A Kerley
Thomas H Cook   Jilliane Hoffman   Dean R Koontz

Ken Bruen   1951-   Ire   Crime: Hardboiled
www.kenbruen.com   ♁ DCI Roberts & DS Brant - London
                                  Jack Taylor, Former policeman - Galway

Vivien Armstrong   Barry Eisler   Simon Kernick
Ingrid Black   Allan Guthrie   David Peace
Paul Charles   Patricia Hall   Mark Timlin
Robert Edric   Bill James   Martyn Waites

Julia Bryant   Saga
www.juliabryant-online.com   ♁ Forrest Family - Portsmouth

Anne Bennett   June Francis   Margaret Thornton
Rose Boucheron   Anna Jacobs   Janet Woods
Elizabeth Elgin   June Tate

☺ also writes children's books

Elizabeth Buchan 1948-   Aga Saga
www.elizabethbuchan.com
🏆 Romantic 1994

Diana Appleyard	Eileen Goudge	Mary Stanley
Charlotte Bingham	Angela Huth	Lou Wakefield
Kate Fenton	Anna Maxted	Fay Weldon

B

John Buchan 〰 1875-1940   Sco   Adventure/Thriller
www.johnbuchansociety.co.uk   🏃 Richard Hannay

Jon Cleary	David Dickinson	Robert Goddard
Joseph Conrad	Ian Fleming	Robert Louis Stevenson

Edna Buchanan 1939-   US   Crime: Amateur sleuth
www.ednabuchanan.com   🏃 Britt Montero, Journalist - Miami

Alafair Burke	James W Hall	Laura Lippman
Jan Burke	Denise Hamilton	Liza Marklund
Sue Grafton	Sparkle Hayter	Sara Paretsky

Lois McMaster Bujold 1949-   US   Science Fiction: Space opera
www.dendarii.com   🏃 Lord Miles Vorkosigan

Dan Abnett	Ben Counter	Elizabeth Moon
Douglas Adams	Colin Greenland	Adam Roberts
Orson Scott Card	Peter F Hamilton	Charles Stross
C J Cherryh	Anne McCaffrey	Liz Williams

Edward Bunker 1933-2005   US   Crime: Hardboiled

James Ellroy	George P Pelecanos	Jim Thompson
John Hart	Patrick Quinlan	Don Winslow
Matthew Klein		

John Burdett   Adventure/Thriller: Legal/financial
www.john-burdett.com   🏃 Sonchai Jitpleecheep, Thai American detective

Tom Clancy	John Le Carré	Christopher Reich
Colin Cotterill	Robert Ludlum	Gerald Seymour
Barry Eisler	R N Morris	Martin Cruz Smith

Go to back for lists of
Pseudonyms • Authors by Genre • Characters and Series
Prize Winners • Crossover Authors • Further Reading • Websites

Anita Burgh   1937-   Saga
also writes as Annie Leith
www.anitaburgh.com

Elizabeth Adler	Winston Graham	Carol Rivers
Rosemary Aitken	Shena Mackay	Sue Sully
Rose Boucheron	Una-Mary Parker	Rowena Summers

Alafair Burke   US   Adventure/Thriller: Legal/financial
www.alafairburke.com   ⚘ DDA Samantha Kincaid - Portland, Oregon

Edna Buchanan	Steve Martini	Nancy Taylor Rosenberg
Linda Fairstein	Perri O'Shaughnessy	John Sandford
Sue Grafton		

James Lee Burke   1936-   US   Crime: Hardboiled
www.jamesleeburke.com   ⚘ Dave Robicheaux, Policeman - New Iberia, Louisiana
Billy-Bob Holland, Attorney - Texas, Montana

🏆 CWA 1998

C J Box	James W Hall	Michael Malone
Michael Connelly	Tony Hillerman	George P Pelecanos
James Crumley	J A Kerley	Thomas Perry
Barry Eisler	Jonathon King	James Sallis

Jan Burke   1953-   US   Crime: Amateur sleuth
www.janburke.com   ⚘ Irene Kelly, Journalist - California

Edna Buchanan	Denise Hamilton	Claire McNab
Caroline Carver	Faye Kellerman	Liza Marklund
Meg Gardiner	Laurie R King	Margaret Maron
Sue Grafton	Laura Lippman	Chris Niles

Paul Burke   Lad Lit: Humour
⚘ Frank Dempsey

Matt Dunn	Mil Millington	Kevin Sampson
Stephen Fry	Tony Parsons	Alexei Sayle
Nick Hornby		

W J Burley   1914-2002   Crime: Police work - UK
was William John Burley   ⚘ Supt Wycliffe - Cornwall
www.wjburley.com

Catherine Aird	Kate Ellis	Ruth Rendell
Simon Brett	Caroline Graham	June Thomson
Ann Cleeves	Peter James	

Candace Bushnell   1958-   US   Glitz & Glamour
www.candacebushnell.com

Sandra Brown	Imogen Edwards-Jones	Katie Price
Jackie Collins	Olivia Goldsmith	Nora Roberts
Barbara Delinsky	Jayne Ann Krentz	Plum Sykes

Jim Butcher 1971-   US   Paranormal
www.jim-butcher.com   ☂ Harry Dresden, Wizard - Chicago

Chaz Brenchley	Kim Harrison	Liz Williams
Lori Handeland	J K Rowling	

Gwendoline Butler 1922-   Crime: Police work - UK
also writes as Jennie Melville   ☂ Com John Coffin - London
Major Mearns & Sgt Denny - C18th England

🏆 CWA 1973   Romantic 1981

Paul Charles	Cynthia Harrod-Eagles	Fidelis Morgan
Ann Cleeves	Deryn Lake	Iain Pears
Janet Gleeson	David Liss	David Pirie

Ron Butlin 1949-   Sco

Janice Galloway	A L Kennedy	Ali Smith
A M Homes	Thomas Pynchon	Jonathan Trigell
Denis Johnson	Richard Russo	Alan Warner

A S Byatt   1936-
www.asbyatt.com

🏆 Booker 1990   Irish Times 1990

Gilbert Adair	Robb Forman Dew	Penelope Fitzgerald
Melvyn Bragg	Margaret Drabble	Penelope Lively
Anita Brookner	Patricia Duncker	Marianne Wiggins

Michael Byrnes   Adventure/Thriller

Steve Berry	Dan Brown	Lee Child
Sam Bourne	John Case	James Rollins

Liz Byrski 1944-   Aus
www.lizbyrski.com.au

Elizabeth Berg	Jill Dawson	Monica McInerney
Rachel Cusk	Caro Fraser	Rosie Thomas

Meg Cabot 1967- US Chick Lit

also writes as Patricia Cabot & Jenny Carroll
is Meggin Patricia Cabot
www.megcabot.com

⚐ Princess Mia Diaries Series

Maggie Alderson	Kathy Lette	Andrea Semple
Hester Browne	Chris Manby	Sara Shepard
Sophie Kinsella	Jill Mansell	Paige Toon

Colette Caddle Ire Chick Lit

www.colettecaddle.com

Claudia Carroll	Monica McInerney	Kate O'Riordan
Martina Devlin	Sinead Moriarty	Morag Prunty
Sabine Durrant	Anita Notaro	Kate Thompson

Chelsea Cain US Crime: Police work - US

www.chelseacain.com

⚐ Archie Sheridan, Detective • Gretchen Lowell, Serial killer

Thomas Harris	Jilliane Hoffman	Chris Mooney
Mo Hayder	Paul Johnston	James Patterson
Tami Hoag	Michael Marshall	

Brian Callison 1934- Sco Sea: Modern

James H Cobb	Philip McCutchan	Justin Scott
Alexander Fullerton	James Pattinson	Terence Strong
Duncan Harding	Douglas Reeman	

Claire Calman Aga Saga

Sarah Challis	Christina Jones	Kate Saunders
Victoria Clayton	Sarah Mason	Joanna Trollope
Maeve Haran	Sheila Norton	Isabel Wolff

Andrea Camilleri 1925- It Crime: Police work - Italy

⚐ Insp Salvo Montalbano - Sicily

Niccolo Ammaniti	David Hewson	Arturo Perez-Reverte
Gianrico Carofiglio	Donna Leon	Qiu Xiaolong
Michael Dibdin	Carlo Lucarelli	Georges Simenon
Luiz Alfredo Garcia-Roza	Martin O'Brien	Ronald Tierney

Karen Campbell 1967- Sco Crime: Police work - UK

www.karencampbell.co.uk

⚐ Sgt Anna Cameron

Lin Anderson	Alex Gray	Frederic Lindsay
Gillian Galbraith	Allan Guthrie	Stuart MacBride

Ramsey Campbell   1946-   Horror

www.ramseycampbell.com
🏆 British Fantasy 1991 & 1994

Jonathan Carroll	Christopher Fowler	Whitley Strieber
Simon Clark	Stephen Laws	T M Wright
Douglas Clegg	John Saul	

Rebecca Campbell   Chick Lit

Cecelia Ahern	Lisa Jewell	Shari Low
Lynne Barrett-Lee	Josie Lloyd & Emlyn Rees	Jane Wenham-Jones
Louise Candlish		

Trudi Canavan   🌈 ☺   1969-   Aus   Fantasy: Epic

www.trudicanavan.com

Sara Douglass	Ursula K Le Guin	Garth Nix
Terry Goodkind	Juliet Marillier	Christopher Paolini
Lian Hearn	William Nicholson	

Louise Candlish   Mature Chick Lit

www.louisecandlish.co.uk

Rebecca Campbell	Nikki Gemmell	Dorothy Koomson
Helen Dunmore	Sophie Hannah	Maggie O'Farrell
Sue Gee	Sophie King	Anita Shreve

Helen Cannam   Saga

Aileen Armitage	Elizabeth Elgin	Elvi Rhodes
Jessica Blair	Sheelagh Kelly	Kay Stephens

Stephen J Cannell   1941-   US   Adventure/Thriller

www.cannell.com   🚶 Det Shane Scully - Los Angeles Police Dept

Nelson DeMille	Robert Littell	Martin Cruz Smith
John Lawton	James Long	

Anthony Capella

www.anthonycapella.com

Elizabeth Edmondson	Joanne Harris	Michael Ondaatje
Imogen Edwards-Jones	Sarah Kate Lynch	Lily Prior
Susan Fletcher		

☺ also writes children's books

Lorenzo Carcaterra
1954- US Adventure/Thriller

www.lorenzocarcaterra.com

Massimo Carlotto	Mario Puzo	Boston Teran
Chuck Palahniuk	Sidney Sheldon	John Williams
David Peace		

Orson Scott Card
1951- US Science Fiction: Space opera

www.hatrack.com

Lois McMaster Bujold	Joe Haldeman	Charles Stross
Alan Dean Foster	Dan Simmons	David Zindell

Peter Carey
1943- Aus

www.petercareybooks.com

🏆 Booker 1988 & 2001   Commonwealth 1998 & 2001

Murray Bail	Gabriel Garcia Márquez	Thomas Keneally
J G Ballard	Kate Grenville	Hari Kunzru
Robert Drewe	Tobias Hill	David Malouf
Richard Flanagan	Lloyd Jones	Tim Winton

Massimo Carlotto
It Crime: Hardboiled

🏃 Alligator, ex-con PI

Lorenzo Carcaterra	Robert Ferrigno	Roberta Kray
Alan Dunn	Mandasue Heller	Boston Teran

Gianrico Carofiglio
1961- It Crime: Psychological

🏃 Guido Guerrieri, Lawyer - Bari

Andrea Camilleri	John Grisham	Donna Leon
Michael Dibdin	Patricia Highsmith	Andy Oakes

Roger Carpenter
1937- War: Historical

🏃 Peter Rutland - C19th, Boer War

www.roger-carpenter.co.uk

Bernard Cornwell	Garry Kilworth	Simon Scarrow
George Macdonald Fraser	Allan Mallinson	John Wilcox
Iain Gale	Douglas Reeman	

Irene Carr
1920s-2006 Saga

NE England

Catherine Cookson	Anna Jacobs	Janet MacLeod Trotter
Elizabeth Gill	Denise Robertson	Valerie Wood
Una Horne	Wendy Robertson	Cathy Woodman

Claudia Carroll   Ire   Chick Lit

Cecelia Ahern	Marian Keyes	Morag Prunty
Colette Caddle	Sophie Kinsella	Patricia Scanlan
Maeve Haran	Carole Matthews	Lauren Weisberger

Jonathan Carroll   1949-   US   Fantasy: Dark

www.jonathancarroll.com

🏆 British Fantasy 1992

Ben Counter	Neil Gaiman	Janny Wurts
Stephen Donaldson	Michael Moorcock	

                                                   Horror

Clive Barker	James H Cobb	Graham Joyce
Ramsey Campbell	Christopher Fowler	Peter Straub

Paul Carson   1949-   Ire   Crime: Medical

www.paulcarson.net

Paul Adam	Tess Gerritsen	Ken McClure
Robin Cook	Leonard Goldberg	Michael Palmer
Patricia D Cornwell		

Stephen L Carter   1954-   US   Crime: Legal/financial

William Bernhardt	Craig Holden	Barbara Parker
John Grisham	John T Lescroart	Scott Turow
John Hart	Brad Meltzer	

Justin Cartwright   1945-   SA

🏆 Whitbread 1998   Hawthornden 2005

Martin Amis	Graham Greene	William Nicholson
J M Coetzee	Christopher Hope	John Updike
Damon Galgut	Pamela Jooste	Evelyn Waugh

Caroline Carver   Crime: Amateur sleuth

also writes as C J Carver   🏃 India Kane, Journalist - Australia
www.carolinecarver.com   Jay McCaulay, ex-Army officer

Jan Burke	G M Ford	Adrian Magson
Jodi Compton	Denise Hamilton	Sarah Rayne
Sarah Diamond	Hazel Holt	Peter Temple

Go to back for lists of
Pseudonyms • Authors by Genre • Characters and Series
Prize Winners • Crossover Authors • Further Reading • Websites

C

John Case   1943-   US   Adventure/Thriller
also writes as James Eliot; is Jim & Carolyn Hougan
www.johncase.com

Steve Berry	Michael Cordy	Chris Kuzneski
Sam Bourne	Daniel Easterman	Bill Napier
Suzanne Brockmann	Jean-Christophe Grangé	Gareth O'Callaghan
Michael Byrnes	Raymond Khoury	Alex Scarrow

Michael Chabon   1963-   US

🏆 Pulitzer 2001

Lisa Appignanesi	Nathan Englander	Denis Johnson
Saul Bellow	Ben Faccini	Nicole Krauss
André Brink	Jonathan Safran Foer	Amos Oz
Michael Cunningham	Howard Jacobson	Philip Roth

Mark Chadbourn   1960-   Fantasy: Contemporary
www.markchadbourn.com

Charles de Lint	Terry Goodkind	Katharine Kerr
Stephen Donaldson	Guy Gavriel Kay	David Zindell
David Eddings		

Elizabeth Chadwick   Historical: Medieval
also writes as Nancy Herndon
www.elizabethchadwick.com

Elizabeth Aston	Dorothy Dunnett	Anne Herries
Will Davenport	Barbara Erskine	Georgette Heyer
Christie Dickason	Barbara Ewing	Rosalind Laker
Jennifer Donnelly	Posie Graeme-Evans	Sharon Penman

Sarah Challis   Aga Saga

Maeve Binchy	Patricia Fawcett	Santa Montefiore
Claire Calman	Rebecca Gregson	Jojo Moyes
Marika Cobbold	Julie Highmore	Rosamunde Pilcher
Jennifer Donnelly	Sara MacDonald	Jane Yardley

Clare Chambers   1966-   Aga Saga

🏆 Romantic 1999

Margaret Atwood	Elizabeth Flock	Amanda Eyre Ward
Katie Fforde	Rebecca Gregson	Mary Wesley

Joy Chambers

Aus War: Historical

www.joychambers.com

Elizabeth Darrell	Mark Mills	Kate Morton
Julie Garwood	Di Morrissey	Wilbur Smith
Mary Lawson		

Glenn Chandler

Crime: Police work - UK

🏃 DI Steve Madden - Brighton

Jake Arnott	John Harvey	Priscilla Masters
Robert Barnard	Reginald Hill	Peter Robinson
Deborah Crombie	Quintin Jardine	

C

Raymond Chandler 1888-1959 US Crime: PI

🏃 Philip Marlowe • John Delmas
Los Angeles

Lawrence Block	Luiz Alfredo Garcia-Roza	Reggie Nadelson
James Hadley Chase	Denise Hamilton	Robert B Parker
Peter Corris	Stuart M Kaminsky	James Sallis
Robert Crais	Ross Macdonald	John Shannon

Vikram Chandra 1961- Ind

www.vikramchandra.com

Amit Chaudhuri	Rohinton Mistry	Arundhati Roy
Anita Desai	V S Naipaul	Alex Wheatle
Roopa Farooki	R K Narayan	

Jean Chapman

Saga

Anne Bennett	Una Horne	Denise Robertson
June Francis	Rosalind Laker	Wendy Robertson
Elizabeth Gill	Annie Murray	

Kate Charles 1950- US Crime: Amateur sleuth

is Carol A Chase
www.katecharles.com

🏃 Callie Anson, Female curate
David Middleton-Brown, Solicitor

Simon Brett	Veronica Heley	P D James
Ann Cleeves	Susan Hill	M R D Meek
Andrew M Greeley	Lis Howell	Keith Miles

🌂 may be suitable for young adults

Paul Charles

Crime: Police work - UK

♂ DI Christy Kennedy - London • Insp Starrett - Irish Serious Crime Unit

Ken Bruen	Colin Dexter	Graham Ison
Gwendoline Butler	Georgie Hale	Susan B Kelly
Brian Cooper	Patricia Hall	Maureen O'Brien
Judith Cutler	Graham Hurley	Martyn Waites

James Hadley Chase   1906-85   US   Crime: Hardboiled

also wrote as James L Docherty, Ambrose Grant,
Raymond Marshall; was René Brabazon Raymond

♂ Dave Fenner • Vic Malloy
Steve Harmas • Frank Terrell
Mark Girland • Helga Rolfe

C

Raymond Chandler	Stuart M Kaminsky	Robert B Parker
Dashiell Hammett	Ross Macdonald	

Amit Chaudhuri   1962-   Ind

www.amitchaudhuri.com

🏆 Betty Trask 1991   Encore 1994

Vikram Chandra	Arundhati Roy	Vikram Seth
Rohinton Mistry	Salman Rushdie	Zadie Smith
R K Narayan		

Mavis Cheek   Humour

Melissa Bank	Marina Lewycka	Ben Richards
Anita Brookner	Sue Limb	Lynne Truss
Isla Dewar	Shena Mackay	Arabella Weir
Jane Green	Lily Prior	Nigel Williams

C J Cherryh   1942-   US   Fantasy: Myth

is Carolyn Janice Cherry
www.cherryh.com

Kate Elliott	Tanith Lee	L E Modesitt Jr
Barbara Hambly	George R R Martin	Sheri S Tepper
Stephen R Lawhead		

Science Fiction: Space opera

Greg Bear	Lois McMaster Bujold	Colin Greenland
Gregory Benford	Alan Dean Foster	Peter F Hamilton
David Brin	Michael Jan Friedman	

Marion Chesney   1936-   Sco   Historical Romance

also writes as M C Beaton

Mary Balogh	Elizabeth Darrell	Stephanie Laurens
Anne Barbour	Jude Deveraux	Fenella-Jane Miller
Catherine Coulter	Emily Hendrickson	Julia Quinn

Tracy Chevalier 1962- US Historical
www.tchevalier.com

Vanora Bennett	Ken Follett	Maureen Peters
Geraldine Brooks	Maureen Freely	James Runcie
Will Davenport	Anne Haverty	Jane Stevenson
Stevie Davies	Andrew Miller	Susan Vreeland

Lee Child ☺ 1954- Adventure/Thriller
www.leechild.com ⚐ Jack Reacher, ex-Military policeman - Florida
🏆 TGR 1999

Jeff Abbott	Michael Byrnes	James W Hall
Raymond Benson	Barry Eisler	Graham Hurley
Sam Bourne	Meg Gardiner	Gareth O'Callaghan
Robert Gregory Browne	John Gilstrap	Matthew Pearl

Lincoln Child 1957- US Adventure/Thriller
also writes jointly with Douglas Preston
www.prestonchild.com

Dan Brown	Vince Flynn	Douglas Preston
Daniel Easterman	Andy McDermott	Matthew Reilly

P F Chisholm 1958- Crime: Historical - C16th
is Patricia Finney ⚐ Sir Robert Carey - London
www.patricia-finney.co.uk

Michael Clynes	Fidelis Morgan	Kate Sedley
Patricia Finney	John Pilkington	Peter Tonkin
Philip Gooden	C J Sansom	

Agatha Christie 1890-1976 Crime: Amateur sleuth
also wrote as Mary Westmacott ⚐ Miss Marple
www.agathachristie.com Hercule Poirot

Gilbert Adair	Carola Dunn	Catriona McPherson
Catherine Aird	Kerry Greenwood	Martin O'Brien
James Anderson	Patricia Harwin	Dorothy L Sayers
Natasha Cooper	Susan Kandel	Jacqueline Winspear

Paul Christopher Adventure/Thriller
is Christopher Hyde ⚐ Finn Ryan, Archaeologist

Richard Doetsch	John Twelve Hawks	Kate Mosse
Tom Harper	Tobias Hill	James Rollins
A J Hartley	Greg Loomis	

☺ also writes children's books

Tom Clancy 1947- US   Adventure/Thriller

⚐ Jack Ryan • Net Force Explorers

Michael Asher	John Burdett	Glenn Meade
James Barrington	Duncan Falconer	Kyle Mills
Raymond Benson	Brian Haig	John J Nance
John Birmingham	Gordon Kent	Brad Thor

Alys Clare 1944-   Crime: Historical - Medieval

also writes as Elizabeth Harris   ⚐ Abbess Helewise & Josse D'Acquin - C12th Kent,
www.alysclare.com/home.htm   'Hawkenlye Abbey'

C

Simon Beaufort	Bernard Knight	Mary Reed and Eric Mayer
Paul Doherty	Pat McIntosh	Candace Robb
Margaret Frazer	Ian Morson	Kate Sedley
Cora Harrison	Sharan Newman	Pip Vaughan-Hughes

Lucy Clare 1949-   Aga Saga

Rowan Coleman	Katie Fforde	Rosamunde Pilcher
Patricia Fawcett	Erica James	Kate Saunders
Kate Fenton	Sara MacDonald	

Candida Clark 1970-

Libby Purves	Paul Theroux	Louise Voss
Roma Tearne	Rosie Thomas	Minette Walters

Carol Higgins Clark 1956- US   Crime: PI

www.carolhigginsclark.com   ⚐ Regan Reilly - Missouri

Sue Grafton	Marcia Muller	Rick Riordan
Laura Lippman	Sara Paretsky	Nancy Taylor Rosenberg
Margaret Maron		

Clare Clark   Historical: C18th & C19th

Philippa Gregory	Jane Stevenson
Edward Rutherfurd	Sarah Waters

Mary Higgins Clark 1929- US   Adventure/Thriller: Psychological

www.maryhigginsclark.com

Lara Adrian	Carol Goodman	Hilary Norman
Mitch Albom	Sophie Hannah	Julie Parsons
Thomas H Cook	J A Jance	Liz Rigbey
Joy Fielding	Fiona Mountain	Christina Schwarz

Simon Clark 1958- Horror

www.bbr-online.com/nailed
🏆 British Fantasy 2002

Clive Barker	Douglas Clegg	Gregory Maguire
Chaz Brenchley	Shaun Hutson	Mark Morris
Ramsey Campbell	Bentley Little	Koji Suzuki

Arthur C Clarke 🕮 1917-2008 Science Fiction: Technical

also wrote as E G O'Brien, Charles Willis
www.arthurcclarke.net
🏆 BSFA 1973

Brian W Aldiss	Greg Bear	Robert Reed
Isaac Asimov	Ben Bova	Robert Silverberg
Stephen Baxter	Jack McDevitt	Dan Simmons

Susanna Clarke 🕮 1959- Fantasy

Stephen Baxter	Amanda Hemingway	David Mitchell
G W Dahlquist	Stephen Hunt	Terry Pratchett
Barbara Ewing	Anne McCaffrey	Scarlett Thomas
Neil Gaiman	Yann Martel	J R R Tolkien

James Clavell 1924-94 US Adventure/Thriller

Giles Foden	David Malouf	Laura Joh Rowland
Humphrey Hawksley	Haruki Murakami	Alan Savage
Amin Maalouf	Christopher Nicole	

Victoria Clayton Aga Saga

www.claytons.demon.co.uk

Diana Appleyard	Rowan Coleman	Imogen Parker
Trisha Ashley	Anne Doughty	Rosamunde Pilcher
Raffaella Barker	Elizabeth Jane Howard	Linda Taylor
Claire Calman	Elizabeth Palmer	Mary Wesley

Jon Cleary 1917- Aus Crime: Police work - Australia

🚶 Insp Scobie Malone - Sydney

John Buchan	Hammond Innes	Shane Maloney
Frank Coates	John Lawton	Nevil Shute
Colin Forbes	Claire McNab	

Go to back for lists of
Pseudonyms • Authors by Genre • Characters and Series
Prize Winners • Crossover Authors • Further Reading • Websites

C

Ann Cleeves 1954-

Crime: Police work - UK

www.anncleeves.com

DI Stephen Ramsay • DI Vera Stanhope
George & Molly Palmer-Jones, Ornithologists — Northumberland
Det Jimmy Perez - Shetland Isles

CWA 2006

Catherine Aird	Kate Charles	Matti Joensuu
Alex Barclay	John Connor	Louise Penny
W J Burley	Judith Cutler	Pauline Rowson
Gwendoline Butler	Lesley Horton	Andrew Taylor

Douglas Clegg 1958- US

Horror

also writes as Andrew Harper
www.douglasclegg.com

Richard Bachman	Kim Harrison	John Saul
Ramsey Campbell	Stephen King	Rupert Thomson
Simon Clark	Scott Nicholson	

James Clemens 1961- US

Fantasy: Epic

is James Rollins
www.jamesclemens.com

Sarah Ash	Raymond E Feist	Anne McCaffrey
Terry Brooks	Terry Goodkind	Robert Newcomb
Cecilia Dart-Thornton	Robin Hobb	

Barbara Cleverly

Crime: Historical - C20th

Insp Joe Sandilands - 1920s India

CWA 2004

Thalassa Ali	Martha Grimes	Ngaio Marsh
Conrad Allen	Graham Ison	Michael Pearce
David Dickinson	Laurie R King	Louise Penny
Carola Dunn	Catriona McPherson	Elizabeth Peters

Michael Clynes 1946-

Crime: Historical - C16th

also writes as Vanessa Alexander, Anna Apostolou,
P C Doherty, Ann Dukthas, C L Grace, Paul Harding
is Paul Doherty

Sir Roger Shallot
Henrician England

P F Chisholm	Simon Levack	C J Sansom
Patricia Finney	John Pilkington	Peter Tonkin
Philip Gooden		

Frank Coates Aus

Adventure/Thriller

www.footloose.com.au

Jon Cleary	Judy Nunn
Di Morrissey	Wilbur Smith

James H Cobb
1953- US
Sea: Modern
Com Amanda Lee Garrett - Destroyer USS Cunningham

Brian Callison	Richard Herman	Douglas Reeman
Jonathan Carroll	Christopher Nicole	Patrick Robinson
Duncan Harding	James Pattinson	Justin Scott

Marika Cobbold
Swe
Aga Saga

www.marikacobbold.com

Sarah Challis	Santa Montefiore	Lou Wakefield
Rachel Cusk	Elizabeth Noble	Amanda Eyre Ward
Jessica Duchen	Robin Pilcher	Jane Yardley
Kate Long	Ann Purser	Elizabeth Wrenn

Harlan Coben
1962- US
Crime: Amateur sleuth

www.harlancoben.com
Myron Bolitar, Sports agent - New York

TGR 2003

Jeff Abbott	Michael Connelly	Scott Frost
Russell Andrews	Robert Crais	Gregg Hurwitz
Linwood Barclay	Loren D Estleman	Richard Montanari
Jodi Compton	Brian Freeman	Robert B Parker

Jonathan Coe
1961-
Humour

JLR 1994

Guy Bellamy	Magnus Mills	Tim Pears
Joseph Connolly	David Mitchell	Henry Sutton
John Irving	David Nicholls	Nigel Williams
John Lanchester	Geoff Nicholson	Gerard Woodward

Paulo Coelho
1947- Braz

www.paulocoelho.com.br/engl/index.html

Mitch Albom	Gabriel Garcia Márquez	Audrey Niffenegger
Alessandro Baricco	Mark Haddon	Patrick Suskind
Umberto Eco	Eve Makis	Carlos Ruiz Zafón

J M Coetzee
1940- SA

Faber 1981   Booker 1983 & 1999   Irish Times 1995   Commonwealth 2000

André Brink	Nadine Gordimer	Gunnar Kopperud
Justin Cartwright	Romesh Gunesekera	Doris Lessing
Richard Flanagan	Christopher Hope	Amanda Prantera
Damon Galgut	Pamela Jooste	Gillian Slovo

Martina Cole 1958-

Crime: Hardboiled
DI Kate Burrows - East End, London

June Hampson	Lynda La Plante	Peter May
Mandasue Heller	Kevin Lewis	Hilary Norman
Roberta Kray	Ken McCoy	Sheila Quigley

Rowan Coleman

Aga Saga
Ruby Parker

Maria Beaumont	Patricia Fawcett	Milly Johnson
Lucy Clare	Kate Fenton	Marian Keyes
Victoria Clayton	Jane Green	Sheila O'Flanagan
Jenny Colgan	Kate Jacobs	Rosie Thomas

C

Nicholas Coleridge 1957-

Jeffrey Archer	Rachel Johnson	David Nicholls
Ken Follett	Douglas Kennedy	Harold Robbins
Alan Furst	Jojo Moyes	Sidney Sheldon

Eoin Colfer 1965- Ire

www.eoincolfer.com

Fantasy: Epic
Artemis Fowl

Louise Cooper	William Nicholson	Philip Pullman
Sam Llewellyn	Terry Pratchett	J K Rowling

Jenny Colgan 1972- Sco

www.jennycolgan.com

Chick Lit

Maggie Alderson	Imogen Edwards-Jones	Milly Johnson
Emily Barr	Alison Penton Harper	Tina Reilly
Rowan Coleman	Louise Harwood	Jane Wenham-Jones

Chris Collett

Crime: Police work - UK
DI Tom Mariner - Birmingham

Catherine Aird	Marjorie Eccles	Stuart Pawson
Robert Barnard	Ann Granger	Peter Robinson
Deborah Crombie	John Harvey	R D Wingfield

Catrin Collier 1948- Wales

also writes as Katherine John
www.catrincollier.com

Saga
Heart of Gold Series - Pontypridd, Wales

Elizabeth Daish	Rosie Goodwin	Anna Jacobs
Elizabeth Elgin	Iris Gower	Grace Thompson
Sara Fraser	Rosie Harris	

Jackie Collins 1941-   Glitz & Glamour
www.jackiecollins.com

Tilly Bagshawe	Lesley Lokko	Katie Price
Celia Brayfield	Judith Michael	Harold Robbins
Sandra Brown	Fern Michaels	Madge Swindells
Candace Bushnell	Tasmina Perry	Penny Vincenzi

Max Allan Collins 1948- US   Crime: Forensic
www.maxallancollins.com   ☆ Gil Grissom - Las Vegas

Patricia D Cornwell	Iris Johansen	Kathy Reichs
Lisa Gardner	Keith McCarthy	Karin Slaughter
Tess Gerritsen	Nigel McCrery	

Michael Collins 1964- Ire
www.michaelcollinsauthor.net

Clare Boylan	Richard Ford	Laura Lippman
Michael Cunningham	Alice Hoffman	Tim O'Brien
Louise Erdrich		

Jodi Compton US   Crime: Police work - US
                                 ☆ Det Sarah Pribek - Minneapolis

Caroline Carver	Linda Fairstein	Laura Lippman
Harlan Coben	P D James	John Sandford
Robert Crais		

Michael Connelly 1956- US   Crime: Police work - US
www.michaelconnelly.com
☆ Harry Bosch
Terry McCaleb, Retired FBI Agent } Los Angeles
Mickey Haller, Attorney

Russell Andrews	G M Ford	Dennis Lehane
Robert Gregory Browne	Scott Frost	Reggie Nadelson
James Lee Burke	John Katzenbach	Thomas Perry
Harlan Coben	Thomas Laird	John Shannon

Tom Connery 1944-   Sea: Historical
is David Donachie   ☆ George Markham, Lieut of Marines - C18th

David Donachie	Alexander Kent	Patrick O'Brian
Iain Gale	Allan Mallinson	Dudley Pope

☊ may be suitable for young adults

50

John Connolly   1968-   Ire   Crime: Psychological
www.johnconnolly.co.uk   🏃 Charlie 'Bird' Parker, Retired policeman - New England

Thomas H Cook
Carol Anne Davis
Jeffery Deaver
Robert Ellis

Joy Fielding
Mo Hayder
Jonathan Kellerman
Dennis Lehane

Jefferson Parker
Boris Starling
Nick Stone
P J Tracy

Joseph Connolly   1950-   Humour
www.josephconnolly.co.uk

Kingsley Amis
Guy Bellamy
Jonathan Coe

Charles Higson
Liz Jensen
Geoff Nicholson

Tom Sharpe
Evelyn Waugh
Iain McDowall

Alexandra Connor   Saga
www.alexandra-connor.co.uk   Lancashire

Glenice Crossland
Margaret Dickinson
Ruth Hamilton

Anna Jacobs
Joan Jonker
Freda Lightfoot

Annie Murray
Kay Stephens
Margaret Thornton

John Connor   Crime: Police work - UK
🏃 DC Karen Sharpe - West Yorkshire

Ann Cleeves
Brian Cooper
R J Ellory
Patricia Hall

Lesley Horton
Lynda La Plante
David Lawrence
Iain McDowall

Priscilla Masters
Ed O'Connor
Danuta Reah
Cath Staincliffe

Joseph Conrad   🌂   1857-1924

John Buchan
Louis de Bernières
F Scott Fitzgerald
Abdulrazak Gurnah

James Hamilton-Paterson
Ernest Hemingway
Henry James
Denis Johnson

W Somerset Maugham
V S Naipaul
Robert Louis Stevenson
Virginia Woolf

Pat Conroy   1945-   US
www.patconroy.com

Pete Dexter
Nicholas Evans
Winston Graham

Harper Lee
Larry McMurtry
Anne Rivers Siddons

Paullina Simons
William Styron
Paul Theroux

Go to back for lists of
Pseudonyms • Authors by Genre • Characters and Series
Prize Winners • Crossover Authors • Further Reading • Websites

Storm Constantine 1956-   Fantasy: Dark
www.stormconstantine.com

Mary Gentle	Michael Moorcock	Judith Tarr
Tim Lebbon	Anne Rice	Freda Warrington
Juliet Marillier		

Gloria Cook   Historical
Harvey Series • Pengarron Series
Cornwall

C

Rosemary Aitken	Winston Graham	Susan Sallis
Iris Gower	Elizabeth Ann Hill	E V Thompson

Robin Cook 1940- US   Adventure/Thriller: Medical
♗ Dr Jack Stapleton & Dr Laurie Montgomery - New York

Paul Adam	Kathryn Fox	Ken McClure
Paul Carson	Leonard Goldberg	Michael Palmer
Michael Crichton		

Thomas H Cook 1947-   US   Crime: Psychological
♗ Frank Clemons, PI

Robert Gregory Browne	R J Ellory	Chris Mooney
Mary Higgins Clark	Thomas Harris	John Sandford
John Connolly	Michael Malone	Martin Cruz Smith

Catherine Cookson 1906-1998   Saga
also wrote as Catherine Marchant   ♗ Mary Ann Shaughnessy • Tilly Trotter • Bill Bailey
NE England

Aileen Armitage	Rosie Goodwin	Denise Robertson
Rita Bradshaw	Una Horne	Grace Thompson
Benita Brown	Ken McCoy	Janet MacLeod Trotter
Irene Carr	Sheila Newberry	Annie Wilkinson

Stephen Coonts 1946-   US   Adventure/Thriller
also writes jointly with Jim DeFelice
www.coonts.com   ♗ Rear Admiral Jake Grafton, Naval pilot, &
Tommy Carmellini, ex-Burglar now CIA operative

Geoffrey Archer	Vince Flynn	Chris Mooney
Jeffrey Archer	David Hagberg	Matthew Reilly
James Barrington	Richard Herman	Julian Jay Savarin

Brian Cooper   1919-   Crime: Police work - UK

🏃 CI Mike Tench & DCI John Lubbock - Norfolk

Vivien Armstrong	John Connor	Geraldine Evans
Pauline Bell	Colin Dexter	P D James
Paul Charles		

Jilly Cooper   1937-   Glitz & Glamour
www.jillycooper.co.uk

Louise Bagshawe	Judith Gould	Christina Jones
Tilly Bagshawe	Veronica Henry	Lesley Pearse
Celia Brayfield	Rachel Johnson	Fiona Walker

C

Louise Cooper   ☺   1952-   Fantasy: Epic
www.louisecooper.com

Jean M Auel	Robert Jordan	Melanie Rawn
Eoin Colfer	L E Modesitt Jr	Janny Wurts
Barbara Hambly	Michael Moorcock	

Natasha Cooper   1951-   Crime: Amateur sleuth
also writes as Clare Layton, Kate Hatfield   🏃 Willow King, Civil servant
is Daphne Wright   Trish Maguire, Barrister
www.natashacooper.co.uk   London

Agatha Christie	Susan B Kelly	Veronica Stallwood
Frances Fyfield	Betty Rowlands	Aline Templeton
Joyce Holms	Catherine Sampson	Leslie Thomas

Michael Cordy   Adventure/Thriller

Steve Berry	Michael Crichton	Chris Kuzneski
Sam Bourne	Daniel Easterman	Bill Napier
Dan Brown	Philip Kerr	Douglas Preston
John Case	Raymond Khoury	James Rollins

Elizabeth Corley   Crime: Police work - UK

🏃 DCI Andrew Fenwick - Sussex

Ingrid Black	Val McDermid	Claire Seeber
Victoria Blake	Grace Monroe	Paullina Simons
Alice Blanchard	Karen Rose	

☺ also writes children's books

53

Bernard Cornwell 1944- Historical

also writes as Susannah Kells
www.bernardcornwellbooks.com

Grail Quest Series, C14th
♟ Alfred the Great, C9th • King Arthur, C6th

Michael Curtis Ford	Scott Oden	Pip Vaughan-Hughes
Tom Harper	Simon Scarrow	Jack Whyte
William Napier	Tim Severin	Robyn Young

War: Historical

♟ Richard Sharpe, Napoleonic Wars • Nathaniel Starbuck, American Civil War

G S Beard	C C Humphreys	Steven Pressfield
Roger Carpenter	Garry Kilworth	Patrick Rambaud
Iain Gale	Sam Llewellyn	Edward Rutherfurd
Richard Howard	Allan Mallinson	John Wilcox

Patricia D Cornwell 1956- US Crime: Forensic

www.patriciacornwell.com

♟ Kay Scarpetta, Pathologist
Judy Hammer & Andy Brazil, State Police } Virginia
Winston Garano

🏆 CWA 1990 & 1993

Simon Beckett	Kathryn Fox	Keith McCarthy
Paul Carson	Leonard Goldberg	Nigel McCrery
Max Allan Collins	Lynn Hightower	Peter May
Colin Cotterill	Iris Johansen	Jonathan Nasaw

Peter Corris 1942- Aus Crime: PI

www.petercorris.net

♟ Cliff Hardy - Sydney • Richard Browning • Ray Crawley

Robert G Barrett	Carl Hiaasen	Peter Temple
Raymond Chandler	Gabrielle Lord	Robert Wilson
Robert Crais	Elliot Perlman	

F G Cottam 1957- War: Modern

also writes as Francis Cottam

Frank Barnard	Sebastian Faulks	Daniel Mason
Sebastian Barry	David Fiddimore	David L Robbins
Tim Binding	Andrew Greig	Derek Robinson
Peter Ho Davies	Douglas Kennedy	Robert Ryan

Colin Cotterill 1952- Crime: Forensic

www.colincotterill.com

♟ Dr Siri Paiboun, Coroner - Laos

John Burdett	Kathryn Fox	Peter May
Patricia D Cornwell	Luiz Alfredo Garcia-Roza	Alexander McCall Smith
Garry Disher	Catherine Lim	

Catherine Coulter   1942-   US   Historical Romance

is Jean Catherine Coulter Pogany
www.catherinecoulter.com

Marion Chesney	Victoria Holt	Amanda Quick
Julie Garwood	Judith McNaught	Nora Roberts

Ben Counter   Science Fiction: Space opera

Dan Abnett	David A Drake	Freda Warrington
Lois McMaster Bujold	Tanith Lee	Sean Williams
Jonathan Carroll		

C

Douglas Coupland   1961-   Can

www.coupland.com

Iain Banks	Will Ferguson	Ben Richards
Don DeLillo	Alex Garland	Scarlett Thomas
Bret Easton Ellis	Chuck Palahniuk	Rupert Thomson

Dilly Court   Saga

www.dillycourt.com

Lyn Andrews	Benita Brown	Anna Jacobs
Anne Baker	Josephine Cox	Annie Murray
Emma Blair	Katie Flynn	Kitty Neale
Harry Bowling	Rosie Harris	Janet Tanner

Bryce Courtenay   1933-   Aus   Adventure/Thriller

www.brycecourtenay.com

Eric Van Lustbader	Wilbur Smith
Amin Maalouf	Peter Watt

Josephine Cox   1938-   Saga

also writes as Jane Brindle
www.josephinecox.co.uk

Rose Boucheron	Katie Flynn	Kitty Neale
Harry Bowling	Sara Fraser	Joan O'Neill
Rita Bradshaw	Rosie Goodwin	Wendy Robertson
Dilly Court	Ruth Hamilton	Annie Wilkinson

Harold Coyle   1952-   US   Adventure/Thriller

Campbell Armstrong	Jack Higgins	Douglas Preston
Clive Cussler	Stephen Leather	Matthew Reilly
W E B Griffin	Andy McDermott	Craig Thomas

Jim Crace 1946-

www.jim-crace.com

🏆 Guardian 1986   Higham 1986   Whitbread 1986 & 1997   Holtby 1994

André Brink	Alistair MacLeod	Geoff Ryman
E L Doctorow	Yann Martel	Rupert Thomson
Damon Galgut	David Mitchell	Barry Unsworth

Amanda Craig 1959-   Aga Saga

www.amandacraig.com

Domenica de Rosa	Laurie Graham	Nicky Pellegrino
Janice Galloway	A L Kennedy	Amanda Prantera
Jane Gardam	Allison Pearson	Barbara Trapido

Maggie Craig   Sco   Saga
                                                            Scotland

www.maggiecraig.co.uk

Doris Davidson	Evelyn Hood	Reay Tannahill
Margaret Thomson Davis	Eileen Ramsay	Mary Withall
Meg Henderson	Jessica Stirling	

Robert Crais   1953-   US   Crime: PI

www.robertcrais.com   🏃 Elvis Cole - Los Angeles

Jeff Abbott	Peter Corris	Reggie Nadelson
Raymond Chandler	G M Ford	Robert B Parker
Harlan Coben	Scott Frost	John Shannon
Jodi Compton	Joe R Lansdale	Don Winslow

Candida Crewe   1964-

Kate Grenville	Hilary Mantel	Anne Tyler
Alice Hoffman	Deborah Moggach	

Michael Crichton   ☎   1942-   US

also writes as Jeffrey Hudson, John Lange
www.michaelcrichton.net

Dan Brown	Thomas Harris	Bill Napier
Robin Cook	Philip Kerr	Michael Palmer
Michael Cordy	Ken McClure	Douglas Preston
William Gibson	Richard Morgan	Kim Stanley Robinson

Go to back for lists of
Pseudonyms • Authors by Genre • Characters and Series
Prize Winners • Crossover Authors • Further Reading • Websites

Deborah Crombie
1952- US · Crime: Police work - UK

www.deborahcrombie.com · ⚘ Sup Duncan Kincaid & DI Gemma James - London

Jane Adams	Margaret Duffy	Cynthia Harrod-Eagles
Jo Bannister	Earlene Fowler	Susan Hill
Glenn Chandler	Paula Gosling	Priscilla Masters
Chris Collett	Martha Grimes	R D Wingfield

Neil Cross
1969-

Mark Haddon	Julie Parsons	Lionel Shriver
Sarah Hall	Tony Parsons	Matt Thorne
Tim Lott		

Glenice Crossland
Saga

Aileen Armitage	Pamela Evans	Annie Groves
Alexandra Connor	Katie Flynn	Freda Lightfoot
Margaret Dickinson	June Francis	Margaret Thornton

James Crumley
1939-2008 US · Crime: PI

⚘ C W Sughrue - Texas • Milo Milodragovitch - Montana

🏆 CWA 2002

James Lee Burke	Ross Macdonald	Boston Teran
James Ellroy	George P Pelecanos	Jim Thompson
Robert Ferrigno	Jason Starr	

Charles Cumming
1971- Sco · Adventure/Thriller

www.charlescumming.co.uk · ⚘ Alec Milius, Spy

Len Deighton	Alan Furst	Daniel Silva
Barry Eisler	John Le Carré	Martin Cruz Smith
John Fullerton	Henry Porter	Robert Wilson

Michael Cunningham
☏ 1952- US

www.michaelcunninghamwriter.com

🏆 Pulitzer 1999

Michael Chabon	Richard Ford	Tim O'Brien
Michael Collins	Jonathan Franzen	Jonathan Tropper
Helen Dunmore	Alan Hollinghurst	Virginia Woolf

Clare Curzon
1922- · Crime: Police work - UK

also writes as Rhona Petrie · ⚘ Supt Mike Yeadings & DS Angus Mott - Thames Valley
is Marie Buchanan · Lucy Sedgwick - Early C20th England

M C Beaton	Caroline Graham	Elizabeth Peters
Rhys Bowen	Patricia Hall	Dorothy Simpson
Martin Edwards	Veronica Heley	

Rachel Cusk 1967-

🏆 Whitbread 1993

Rachel Billington	Jill Dawson	Tessa Hadley
Liz Byrski	Anne Fine	Hilary Mantel
Marika Cobbold	Esther Freud	

Clive Cussler 🔖 1931- US   Adventure/Thriller

also writes jointly with Dirk Cussler, Craig Dirgo, Jack Du Brul, Paul Kemprecos
www.cussler.net

🏃 Dirk Pitt
Kurt Austin

Russell Andrews	David Hagberg	Julian Jay Savarin
Harold Coyle	Paul Henke	Justin Scott
Duncan Falconer	Andy McDermott	Brad Thor
Tom Gabbay	James Pattinson	James Twining

Judith Cutler 1946-   Crime: Police work - UK

www.judithcutler.com

🏃 Sophie Rivers, Lecturer • DS Kate Power - Birmingham
DS Frances Harman - Kent

Paul Charles	Hope McIntyre	Catherine Sampson
Ann Cleeves	Priscilla Masters	Michelle Spring
Martin Edwards	Nick Oldham	Cath Staincliffe
Susan Hill	Barrie Roberts	Stella Whitelaw

K O Dahl 1958- Nor   Crime: Police work - Norway

🏃 DI Frank Frølich - Oslo

Karin Fossum	Åsa Larsson	Maj Sjöwall & Per Wahlöö
Anne Holt	Georges Simenon	Fred Vargas

G W Dahlquist   Fantasy

🏃 Miss Temple, Dr Svenson & Cardinal Chang

Susanna Clarke	Anne McCaffrey	Scarlett Thomas
Stephen Hunt	Philip Pullman	Markus Zusak

Janet Dailey 1944- US   Saga

www.janetdailey.com

🏃 Calder Family

Jayne Ann Krentz	Nora Roberts	LaVyrle Spencer
Joan Medlicott	Judith Saxton	Barbara Wood
Belva Plain	Anne Rivers Siddons	

🔖 may be suitable for young adults

Elizabeth Daish

Saga

⚲ Emma - London • Coppins Bridge Series - Isle of Wight

Catrin Collier
Elizabeth Darrell
Lilian Harry

Harriet Hudson
Joan Jonker

Sally Stewart
Sally Worboyes

Elizabeth Darrell

Historical Romance

also writes as Emma Drummond
⚲ Sheridan Family

Anne Barbour
Joy Chambers

Marion Chesney
Elizabeth Daish

Stephanie Laurens
Amanda Quick

War: Modern

⚲ Max Rydal & Tom Black, Royal Military Police

Frank Barnard
David Fiddimore

James Holland
David L Robbins

Alan Savage
Guy Walters

D

Cecilia Dart-Thornton   Aus

Fantasy: Myth

www.ceciliadartthornton.com

Marion Zimmer Bradley
James Clemens
Amanda Hemingway

Robin Hobb
Katharine Kerr
Tanith Lee

Juliet Marillier
Caiseal Mor
J R R Tolkien

Kavita Daswani   Ind

Chitra Banerjee Divakaruni
Manju Kapur

Jhumpa Lahiri
Sharon Maas

Anita Nair
Preethi Nair

Will Davenport

Historical

is James Long

Geraldine Brooks
Elizabeth Chadwick
Tracy Chevalier

Stevie Davies
Margaret George
Matthew Kneale

James Long
Sharon Penman
Susan Vreeland

Doris Davidson   1922-   Sco

Saga

Scotland

Maggie Craig
Margaret Thomson Davis
Elizabeth Elgin

Harriet Evans
Gwen Kirkwood
Elisabeth McNeill

Frances Paige
Eileen Ramsay
Jessica Stirling

Go to back for lists of
Pseudonyms • Authors by Genre • Characters and Series
Prize Winners • Crossover Authors • Further Reading • Websites

Mary Janice Davidson 1969- US · Paranormal

www.maryjanicedavidson.net · Betsy Taylor, Vampire

Lara Adrian	Christine Feehan	Sherrilyn Kenyon
Kelley Armstrong	Lori Handeland	Sara Reinke
Keri Arthur	Tanya Huff	J R Ward

Katharine Davies

Romantic 2005

Margaret Forster	Alice Hoffman	Anna Jacobs
Philippa Gregory	Angela Huth	Joyce Carol Oates
Cynthia Harrod-Eagles		

Linda Davies 1963- · Adventure/Thriller: Legal/financial

www.ex.ac.uk/~RDavies/arian/linda.html · Sarah Jensen, City trader

John Grisham	Mark Mills	Michael Ridpath
Craig Holden	Carol O'Connell	Stella Rimington
Brad Meltzer	Perri O'Shaughnessy	

Murray Davies 1947- · Adventure/Thriller

Peter Ho Davies	Robert Ferrigno	Andy McNab
Brendan Dubois	Andrew Greig	Derek Robinson
Duncan Falconer	Robert Harris	Chris Ryan

Peter Ho Davies 1966- Wales

David Baddiel	Murray Davies	Ian McEwan
Sebastian Barry	Sebastian Faulks	Lionel Shriver
F G Cottam	Andrew Greig	

Stevie Davies 1946- Wales

also writes as Stephanie Davies
www.steviedavies.com

Trezza Azzopardi	Charlotte Mendelson	Salley Vickers
Tracy Chevalier	Michael Ondaatje	Sarah Waters
Will Davenport	Arundhati Roy	

Carol Anne Davis 1976- Sco · Crime: Psychological

www.carolannedavis.co.uk

John Connolly	Carol Goodman	Barbara Vine
Sarah Diamond	Liz Rigbey	Minette Walters
R J Ellory	Jenny Siler	Laura Wilson

D

Lindsey Davis 🌂 1949-   Crime: Historical - Ancient
www.lindseydavis.co.uk   🏃 Marcus Didius Falco - Ancient Rome
🏆 Authors 1989   CWA 1999

Margaret Doody	Rosemary Rowe	Simon Scarrow
Conn Iggulden	Laura Joh Rowland	Marilyn Todd
John Maddox Roberts	Steven Saylor	David Wishart

Margaret Thomson Davis   1926-   Sco   Saga
🏃 Andrina McPherson • Monkton Family • Breadmakers Series
Scotland

Maggie Bennett	Harriet Evans	Alexandra Raife
Maggie Craig	Christine Marion Fraser	Jessica Stirling
Doris Davidson	Meg Henderson	

D

Jill Dawson   1962-
www.jilldawson.co.uk

Liz Byrski	Zoë Heller	Anne Tyler
Rachel Cusk	Liz Jensen	Salley Vickers
Shirley Hazzard	Deborah Moggach	

Lucy Dawson   Chick Lit

Trisha Ashley	Debbie Macomber	Paige Toon
India Knight	Clare Naylor	Jennifer Weiner
Julia Llewellyn	Adele Parks	

Louis de Bernières 🌂 1954-
www.louisdebernieres.co.uk
🏆 CWA 1995

Russell Banks	James Hamilton-Paterson	David Mitchell
Pat Barker	Victoria Hislop	Orhan Pamuk
Tim Binding	Yann Martel	Nicholas Shakespeare
Joseph Conrad	James Meek	Mario Vargas Llosa

Michelle de Kretser   1958-   Aus
🏆 Encore 2004

Arthur Golden	Daniel Mason	Michael Ondaatje
Romesh Gunesekera	Timothy Mo	Salman Rushdie
Kazuo Ishiguro	Haruki Murakami	

🌂 may be suitable for young adults

61

Charles de Lint
1951-   Can   **Fantasy:** Contemporary

also writes as Samuel M Key
www.charlesdelint.com

Mark Chadbourn	Robert Holdstock	Juliet Marillier
Sara Douglass	Guy Gavriel Kay	Caiseal Mor
Neil Gaiman	Morgan Llywelyn	Tim Powers

Domenica de Rosa
1963-   **Aga Saga**

www.domenicaderosa.co.uk

Amanda Craig	Tamara McKinley	Tim Parks
Elizabeth Edmondson	Santa Montefiore	Nicky Pellegrino

Jeffery Deaver
1950-   US   **Crime:** Forensic

www.jefferydeaver.com

🕺 Lincoln Rhyme, Forensic scientist
Rune, Film maker - New York • John Pellam, Film location scout
Kathryn Dance, Interrogator

🏆 TGR 2001   CWA 2004

John Connolly	Michael Marshall	Kathy Reichs
Aaron Elkins	Jonathan Nasaw	Paullina Simons
Brian Freeman	James Patterson	Peter Spiegelman
John Katzenbach	Ridley Pearson	Stephen White

Len Deighton
1929-   **Adventure/Thriller**

🕺 Bernard Samson

Paul Adam	Charles Cumming	John Lawton
Ted Allbeury	Clive Egleton	Stella Rimington
Michael Asher	Alexander Fullerton	Nigel West

Frank Delaney
1942-   Ire   **Saga**

🕺 Kane Family

also writes as Francis Bryan
www.frankdelaney.com

Rose Doyle	D M Purcell	Robert Louis Stevenson
Mary A Larkin	Edward Rutherfurd	William Trevor
Joan O'Neill	Liz Ryan	Jonathan Tropper

R F Delderfield
1912-72   **Saga**

🕺 Craddock Family • Swann Family

John Galsworthy	J B Priestley	E V Thompson
Elizabeth Gaskell	Michael Taylor	Nigel Tranter
Winston Graham		

Don DeLillo   1936-   US
also writes as Cleo Birdwell
🏆 Irish Times 1989

Saul Bellow	Ben Faccini	Chuck Palahniuk
Douglas Coupland	Jonathan Safran Foer	Richard Powers
Dave Eggers	Denis Johnson	Thomas Pynchon
Nathan Englander	Norman Mailer	Tobias Wolff

James Delingpole   Lad Lit: Humour
🚶 Dick Coward, WW2

George Macdonald Fraser	James Holland	Mil Millington
John Harding	Nick Hornby	John O'Farrell

Barbara Delinsky   1945-   US   Aga Saga
also writes as Billy Douglass, Bonnie Drake
www.barbaradelinsky.com

Celia Brayfield	Penny Jordan	Belva Plain
Candace Bushnell	Judith McNaught	Marcia Preston
Therese Fowler	Una-Mary Parker	LaVyrle Spencer
Eileen Goudge	Jodi Picoult	Lisa Tucker

D

Nelson DeMille   1943-   US   Adventure/Thriller
also writes as Jack Cannon, Kurt Ladner, Brad Matthews
🚶 Det John Corey &
www.nelsondemille.net   Kate Mayfield

David Baldacci	Daniel Easterman	Stanley Pottinger
Suzanne Brockmann	Ken Follett	Wilbur Smith
Stephen J Cannell	Robert Littell	James Webb

Joolz Denby   1955-
www.joolz-denby.co.uk

Christopher Brookmyre	Tess Gerritsen	Karin Slaughter
Daphne Du Maurier	David Mitchell	Louise Tondeur

Jo Dereske   1947-   US   Crime: Amateur sleuth
www.jodereske.com   🚶 Miss Zukas, Librarian - Washington State

Nevada Barr	Paula Gosling	Ayelet Waldman
Stephen Donaldson	Hazel Holt	Don Winslow
Earlene Fowler	Jim Kelly	

Anita Desai   ⌒   1937-   Ind

Vikram Chandra	Amitav Ghosh	R K Narayan
Kiran Desai	Ruth Prawer Jhabvala	Salman Rushdie
Chitra Banerjee Divakaruni	Amulya Malladi	Amy Tan

Kiran Desai   1971-   Ind

🏆 Man Booker 2006

Chimamanda Ngozi Adichie	Amitav Ghosh	Helen Oyeyemi
Nadeem Aslam	Kate Grenville	Annie Proulx
Geraldine Brooks	V S Naipaul	Arundhati Roy
Anita Desai	Michael Ondaatje	Vikram Seth

Jude Deveraux   1947-   US   Glitz & Glamour

Sally Beauman	Johanna Lindsey	Nora Roberts
Marion Chesney	Fern Michaels	Danielle Steel
Lucy Diamond	Belva Plain	

Martina Devlin   Ire   Chick Lit

www.martinadevlin.com

Sherry Ashworth	Clare Naylor	Adele Parks
Colette Caddle	Sheila O'Flanagan	Patricia Scanlan
Anna Maxted	Kate O'Riordan	Kate Thompson

Robb Forman Dew   US

Margaret Atwood	Annie Proulx	Carol Shields
A S Byatt	Anna Quindlen	Edith Wharton

Isla Dewar   Sco

Joan Barfoot	Carole Matthews	Zoë Strachan
Mavis Cheek	Anna Maxted	Lynne Truss
Kate Fenton		

Colin Dexter   1930-   Crime: Police work - UK
🏃 DI Morse - Oxford

🏆 CWA 1979, 1981, 1989 & 1992

A C Baantjer	Susan B Kelly	Peter Robinson
Robert Barnard	Iain McDowall	Pauline Rowson
Paul Charles	Guillermo Martinez	Fred Vargas
Brian Cooper	Hakan Nesser	Jill Paton Walsh

Pete Dexter   1943-   US

Russell Banks	Richard Ford	Cormac McCarthy
Pat Conroy	David Guterson	

Anita Diamant 1951- US
www.anitadiamant.com

Geraldine Brooks	Elisabeth Hyde	Salley Vickers
Christie Dickason	Alice Sebold	Susan Vreeland
Jenny Diski	Lisa See	Sarah Willis

Lucy Diamond   Chick Lit
is Sue Mongredien
www.lucydiamond.co.uk

Jude Deveraux	Carmen Reid	Arabella Weir
Wendy Holden	Olivia Ryan	Deborah Wright
Jane Moore		

Sarah Diamond 1976-   Crime: Psychological **D**

Ingrid Black	Babs Horton	Carol Smith
Caroline Carver	Julie Parsons	Gillian White
Carol Anne Davis	Sarah Rayne	Laura Wilson

Michael Dibdin 1947-2007   Crime: Police work - Italy
� ♸ Aurelio Zen

🏆 CWA 1988 & 1990

Andrea Camilleri	David Hewson	Magdalen Nabb
Gianrico Carofiglio	Donna Leon	Barbara Nadel
Dan Fesperman	Carlo Lucarelli	Eliot Pattison
Luiz Alfredo Garcia-Roza	Manuel Vázquez Montalbán	Ronald Tierney

Philip K Dick ☎ 1928-82 US   Science Fiction: Space and time
www.philipkdick.com
🏆 BSFA 1978

Poul Anderson	Robert A Heinlein	Christopher Priest
Isaac Asimov	Michael Moorcock	Kurt Vonnegut
J G Ballard	Tim Powers	John Wyndham

Christie Dickason 1942- US   Historical: C17th
www.christiedickason.com   ♸ Francis Quoynt

Elizabeth Chadwick	Jane Harris	Jean Plaidy
Anita Diamant	Edward Marston	Edward Rutherfurd
Philippa Gregory	Fidelis Morgan	Alison Weir

Charles Dickens ☎ 1812-70

Niccolo Ammaniti	Michel Faber	Iain Sinclair
Jane Austen	W Somerset Maugham	Anthony Trollope
Emma Donoghue	Rohinton Mistry	Tom Wolfe

David Dickinson
Ire　　　　　　　　　　　　　　　　Crime: Historical - C20th

♀ Lord Francis Powerscourt - Edwardian England

Rhys Bowen	Barbara Cleverly	Elizabeth Peters
Gyles Brandreth	Robin Paige	David Pirie
John Buchan	Anne Perry	Barrie Roberts

Margaret Dickinson　　1942-　　　　　　　　Saga
also writes as Everatt Jackson　　　　　　　♀ Kate Hilton - Lincolnshire
www.margaret-dickinson.co.uk

Jessica Blair	Lilian Harry	Mary Mackie
Rita Bradshaw	Elizabeth Jeffrey	Sharon Owens
Alexandra Connor	Jeannie Johnson	Linda Sole
Glenice Crossland	Joan Jonker	T R Wilson

Annabel Dilke　　　　　　　　　　　　　Aga Saga

Diana Appleyard	Elizabeth Jane Howard	Nicola Thorne
Elizabeth Edmondson	Sara MacDonald	Penny Vincenzi
Rachel Hore	Rosamunde Pilcher	Ann Widdecombe

Des Dillon　　1960-　　Sco

Anne Donovan	Laura Marney	Irvine Welsh
James Kelman	Alan Spence	

Garry Disher　　1949-　　Aus　　Crime: Police work - Australia
♀ Insp Hal Challis, Victoria

Mark Billingham	Val McDermid	Martin Cruz Smith
Colin Cotterill	Shane Maloney	Peter Temple

Jenny Diski　　1947-
www.jennydiski.co.uk

Nicola Barker	Maggie Gee	Frances Hegarty
Anita Diamant	Lesley Glaister	Joyce Carol Oates
David Flusfeder		

Chitra Banerjee Divakaruni　　1956-　　Ind
www.chitradivakaruni.com

Thalassa Ali	Sharon Maas	Lily Prior
Kavita Daswani	Amulya Malladi	Meera Syal
Anita Desai	V S Naipaul	Thirty Umrigar
Jhumpa Lahiri		

Michael Dobbs 1948-

www.michaeldobbs.com

⚘ Tom Goodfellow, MP • Francis Urquhart Trilogy, MP
Winston Churchill, MP

Jeffrey Archer	Philip Hensher	Quintin Jardine
Robert Harris	Sandra Howard	Allan Massie

E L Doctorow 1931- US

Paul Auster	F Scott Fitzgerald	Hari Kunzru
Geraldine Brooks	Craig Holden	John Updike
Jim Crace	Thomas Keneally	

Edward Docx 1972-

www.edwarddocx.com

🏆 Faber 2007

Nicola Barker	Philip Roth	Adam Thirlwell
Howard Jacobson	Donna Tartt	A N Wilson
Jhumpa Lahiri		

Richard Doetsch US

Adventure/Thriller

www.richarddoetsch.com

⚘ Michael St Pierre

Paul Christopher	A J Hartley	Kate Mosse
Michael Gruber	Greg Loomis	Douglas Preston
Tom Harper		

Paul Doherty 1946-

Crime: Historical

also writes as Vanessa Alexander,
Anna Apostolou, Michael Clynes,
P C Doherty, Ann Dukthas, C L Grace,
Paul Harding
www.paulcdoherty.com

⚘ Sir Hugh Corbett & Brother Athelstan - C13th England
Alexander the Great & Telamon, Physician -
C3rd BC Greece
Amerotke - Ancient Egypt • The Templars, C11th
Mathilde of Westminster, Physician - C14th England

Simon Beaufort	Susanna Gregory	Simon Levack
Alys Clare	Michael Jecks	Ellis Peters
Margaret Doody	Bernard Knight	Lynda S Robinson

David Donachie 1944- Sco

Sea: Historical

also writes as Tom Connery, Jack Ludlow

⚘ Harry Ludlow, Privateer
John Pearce - Napoleonic Wars

G S Beard	Alexander Kent	Dudley Pope
Tom Connery	James L Nelson	Peter Smalley
C S Forester	Patrick O'Brian	Julian Stockwin

Stephen Donaldson   1947-   US   Crime: PI

also writes as Stephen R Donaldson, Reed Stephens
www.stephendonaldson.com

     Ginny Fistoulari &
Mick Axbrewder

Jo Dereske	Carolyn G Hart	Chuck Palahniuk
James Ellroy	Walter Mosley	Ayelet Waldman

Fantasy: Epic

   Thomas Covenant

Joe Abercrombie	Steven Erikson	Scott Lynch
James Barclay	Ian Irvine	Karen Miller
Jonathan Carroll	Paul Kearney	Robert Newcomb
Mark Chadbourn	Tom Lloyd	Sean Russell

Sara Donati   Historical

is Rosina Lippi
www.saralaughs.com

Daphne Du Maurier	Kathleen O'Neal Gear	Victoria Holt
Barbara Erskine	Susan Hill	Kate Mosse
Diana Gabaldon		

Jennifer Donnelly   ☺   1963-   US   Historical

www.jenniferdonnelly.com

Barbara Taylor Bradford	David Guterson	Kate Morton
Elizabeth Chadwick	Jane Hamilton	Jojo Moyes
Sarah Challis	Haven Kimmel	Ben Richards
Ken Follett	Harper Lee	Meg Rosoff

Emma Donoghue   1969-   Ire

www.emmadonoghue.com

Charles Dickens	Sarah Kate Lynch	Sarah Waters
Joanne Harris	Michèle Roberts	Jeanette Winterson
Anne Haverty	Alice Walker	

Anne Donovan   Sco

Des Dillon	Laura Marney	Alan Spence
Suzannah Dunn	Muriel Spark	Zoë Strachan

Margaret Doody   1939-   Can   Crime: Historical - Ancient

www.nd.edu/~mdoody   Aristotle, philospher, & Stephanos, citizen - Ancient Athens

Philip Boast	Lauren Haney	Marilyn Todd
Lindsey Davis	Rosemary Rowe	David Wishart
Paul Doherty	Steven Saylor	

68

Tim Dorsey 1961- US

www.timdorsey.com

Crime: Humour

☶ Serge Storms - Florida

Kinky Friedman	Elmore Leonard	Malcolm Pryce
Carl Hiaasen	Douglas Lindsay	Donald Westlake
Joe R Lansdale		

Anne Doughty Ire

Aga Saga

☶ Hamilton Family - 'Ballydown', Ireland

Judy Astley	Victoria Clayton	Kate Long
Maeve Binchy	Patricia Fawcett	Joanna Trollope
Amanda Brookfield	Kate Fenton	

Louise Doughty

www.louisedoughty.com

D

Raffaella Barker	Lesley Glaister	Jane Wenham-Jones
Carol Birch	Caroline Graham	Meg Wolitzer
Janet Evanovich	Marge Piercy	Margaret Yorke

Sara Douglass 1957- Aus

www.saradouglass.com

Fantasy: Epic

Carol Berg	Charles de Lint	R A Salvatore
Chaz Brenchley	Terry Goodkind	Harry Turtledove
Trudi Canavan	Gwyneth Jones	Freda Warrington

Clare Dowling 1968- Ire

www.claredowling.co.uk

Chick Lit

Harriet Evans	Marian Keyes	Sheila O'Flanagan
Melissa Hill	Shari Low	Sarah Webb
Cathy Kelly	Monica McInerney	

Arthur Conan Doyle 1859-1930

www.sherlockholmesonline.com

Crime: PI

☶ Sherlock Holmes & Dr John Watson

Boris Akunin	Alanna Knight	Barrie Roberts
Gyles Brandreth	Catriona McPherson	Norman Russell
Peter J Heck	Anne Perry	June Thomson
Laurie R King	David Pirie	M J Trow

Roddy Doyle ☺ 1958- Ire

Humour

☶ Henry Smart

♃ Booker 1993

Dermot Bolger	Niall Griffiths	David Nobbs
Catherine Dunne	Patrick McCabe	Joseph O'Connor
Stephen Fry	Magnus Mills	Irvine Welsh

Rose Doyle
Ire   Aga Saga

www.rosedoyle.com

Maeve Binchy	Mary A Larkin	D M Purcell
Frank Delaney	Joan O'Neill	Elizabeth Wrenn
Jennifer Johnston		

Margaret Drabble
1939-

Nadeem Aslam	A S Byatt	Bernice Rubens
Joan Barfoot	Blake Morrison	Graham Swift
Melvyn Bragg	Ann Patchett	

David A Drake
1945-   US   Fantasy: Epic

www.david-drake.com

Dan Abnett	Ian Irvine	R A Salvatore
Ben Counter	George R R Martin	Margaret Weis
Terry Goodkind	L E Modesitt Jr	Tad Williams

Robert Drewe
1943-   Aus

Peter Carey	Matthew Kneale	Peter Watt
Janette Turner Hospital	David Malouf	Tim Winton
Thomas Keneally	Elliot Perlman	

Daphne Du Maurier
1907-89

Joolz Denby	Susan Hill	Susanna Kearsley
Sara Donati	Joanna Hines	Mark Mills
John Harwood	Susan Howatch	Sue Sully

Brendan Dubois
US   Adventure/Thriller

www.brendandubois.com   🚶 Lewis Cole

Murray Davies	Robert Ludlum	James Siegel
Robert Harris	Kyle Mills	Daniel Silva

Jessica Duchen
Aga Saga

www.jessicaduchen.co.uk

Alan Bennett	Kate Grenville	Santa Montefiore
Marika Cobbold	Elisabeth Hyde	Joanna Trollope

Go to back for lists of
Pseudonyms • Authors by Genre • Characters and Series
Prize Winners • Crossover Authors • Further Reading • Websites

Margaret Duffy   1942-   Sco   Crime: Police work - UK

🚶 Insp James Carrick • Ingrid Langley, Novelist } Bath
Patrick Gillard • Joanna Mackenzie, PI

M C Beaton	Caroline Graham	Adrian Magson
Deborah Crombie	Stuart MacBride	Priscilla Masters

Stella Duffy   1963-   NZ   Crime: PI

www.stelladuffy.com   🚶 Saz Martin - London

Linda Barnes	Lauren Henderson	Marcia Muller
Sparkle Hayter	Claire McNab	Ayelet Waldman

Glen Duncan   1965-

Graham Greene	A L Kennedy	Will Self
Nick Hornby	Andrew O'Hagan	Evelyn Waugh
Denis Johnson	Tim Pears	

D

Hal Duncan   Sco   Fantasy: Contemporary

www.halduncan.com

Neal Asher	Sergei Lukyanenko	Justina Robson
Iain M Banks	Scott Lynch	Andrzej Sapkowski
Steven Gould		

Patricia Duncker   1951-

A S Byatt	Manju Kapur	Salley Vickers
William Golding	Pauline Melville	Jeanette Winterson
Graham Greene		

Anne Dunlop   1969-   Ire   Chick Lit

Sherry Ashworth	Sarah Mason	Kathleen Tessaro
Christina Jones	Anita Notaro	Sarah Webb
Monica McInerney	Carmen Reid	Jane Wenham-Jones

Helen Dunmore   🌈 ☺   1952-

www.helendunmore.com

🏆 McKitterick 1994   Orange 1996

Lisa Appignanesi	Suzannah Dunn	Nell Leyshon
Carol Birch	David Flusfeder	James Meek
Louise Candlish	Nikki Gemmell	Maggie O'Farrell
Michael Cunningham	Christopher Koch	Gillian White

☺ also writes children's books

Alan Dunn

Crime: Hardboiled
🏃 Billy Oliphant, Security consultant - NE England

Massimo Carlotto	Ken McCoy	Catherine Sampson
Robert Edric	Mike Ripley	Martyn Waites
Brian Freeman		

Carola Dunn　1946-

www.geocities.com/CarolaDunn

Crime: Historical - C20th
🏃 Daisy Dalrymple, Journalist - 1920s

Gilbert Adair	Agatha Christie	Catriona McPherson
Conrad Allen	Barbara Cleverly	Robin Paige
James Anderson	Patricia Harwin	David Roberts
Rhys Bowen	Susan Kandel	

D Matt Dunn

Lad Lit

www.mattdunn.co.uk

Mark Barrowcliffe	Mike Gayle	Mil Millington
Matt Beaumont	Nick Hornby	Tony Parsons
Paul Burke		

Suzannah Dunn　1963-

www.suzannahdunn.net

Anne Donovan	Susan Fletcher	Rupert Thomson
Helen Dunmore	Esther Freud	Anne Tyler

Historical: C16th

Posie Graeme-Evans	Jeanne Kalogridis	Robin Maxwell
Philippa Gregory	Katharine McMahon	Alison Weir

Catherine Dunne　1954-　Ire

Roddy Doyle	Jane Hamilton	Joanna Trollope
Anne Fine	Joan O'Neill	Anne Tyler
Susan Fletcher		

Dorothy Dunnett　1923-2001　Sco

Historical

also wrote as Dorothy Halliday
🏃 Francis Crawford of Lymond - C15th England
www.dorothydunnett.co.uk

Elizabeth Chadwick	Margaret Pemberton	Edward Rutherfurd
Margaret Elphinstone	Sharon Penman	Jane Stevenson
Diana Gabaldon	Jean Plaidy	Reay Tannahill
Posie Graeme-Evans	Julian Rathbone	Nigel Tranter

John Dunning 1942- US Crime: Amateur sleuth
www.oldalgonquin.com 🏃 Cliff Janeway, Antique bookseller - Denver

Giles Blunt	Laurie R King	Iain Pears
Earlene Fowler	Marianne MacDonald	Ayelet Waldman
Carolyn G Hart	Keith Miles	Don Winslow

Sabine Durrant Chick Lit
🏃 Connie Pickles

Colette Caddle	Anna Maxted	Andrea Semple
Shari Low	Tina Reilly	Kathleen Tessaro

Jeremy Dyson 1966- Horror

Mark Gatiss	Paul Magrs
Peter James	Haruki Murakami

Daniel Easterman 1949- Adventure/Thriller
also writes as Jonathan Aycliffe; is Denis McEoin

Michael Asher	Lincoln Child	Jack Higgins
Tom Bradby	Michael Cordy	Amin Maalouf
John Case	Nelson DeMille	

Marjorie Eccles 1927- Crime: Police work - UK
also writes as Judith Bordill, 🏃 DI Abigail Moon & Supt Gil Mayo - Midlands
Jennifer Hyde DI Tom Richmonds - Yorkshire

David Armstrong	Pauline Bell	Elizabeth George
A C Baantjer	Chris Collett	Priscilla Masters
Jo Bannister	Geraldine Evans	Betty Rowlands

Umberto Eco 1932- It
www.umbertoeco.com

Paulo Coelho	Andrew M Greeley	Arturo Perez-Reverte
Jostein Gaarder	Amin Maalouf	Jill Paton Walsh
William Golding	Orhan Pamuk	Carlos Ruiz Zafón

David Eddings 1931- US Fantasy: Epic
also writes jointly with Leigh Eddings

Sarah Ash	Ian Irvine	Mickey Zucker Reichert
David Bilsborough	Fiona McIntosh	Robert Silverberg
Mark Chadbourn	Stan Nicholls	Tad Williams
Elizabeth Haydon	Christopher Paolini	Sarah Zettel

Elizabeth Edmondson

Aga Saga

Elizabeth Adler
Anthony Capella
Domenica de Rosa

Annabel Dilke
Rachel Hore
Sara MacDonald

Robin Pilcher
Marcia Willett
Elizabeth Wrenn

Robert Edric   1956-

is Gary Edric Armitage

Crime: PI
⚐ Leo Rivers - Hull

Ken Bruen
Reg Gadney
Kerry Greenwood

Graham Hurley
Simon Kernick

Philip Kerr
Martyn Waites

Historical

🏆 Black 1985

Alan Dunn
Giles Foden

Chris Paling
Tim Pears

Donna Tartt
Barry Unsworth

Kim Edwards   US

www.kimedwardsbooks.com

Miranda Glover
Kate Grenville
Victoria Hislop
Linda Holeman

A M Homes
Barbara Kingsolver
Nicole Krauss
Lori Lansens

Valerie Martin
Kate Morton
Eva Rice
Paul Torday

Martin Edwards   1955-

www.martinedwardsbooks.com

Crime: Amateur sleuth
⚐ Harry Devlin, Solicitor - Liverpool

Jeffrey Ashford
Clare Curzon
Judith Cutler

Bill James
Jim Kelly
Ken McCoy

M R D Meek
Barrie Roberts
Gillian Slovo

Ruth Dudley Edwards   1944-   Ire

www.ruthdudleyedwards.co.uk

Crime: Amateur sleuth
⚐ Robert Amiss & Baroness Troutbeck

Simon Brett
Bartholomew Gill
Veronica Heley

Lis Howell
M R D Meek
Gwen Moffat

Tom Sharpe
Jill Paton Walsh
Patricia Wentworth

Imogen Edwards-Jones   ⌒   1959-

Chick Lit

Louise Bagshawe
Lynne Barrett-Lee
Candace Bushnell

Anthony Capella
Jenny Colgan
Melissa Hill

Tina Reilly
Arabella Weir
Jane Wenham-Jones

⌒ may be suitable for young adults

Ake Edwardson 1953- Swe

Crime: Police work - Sweden

Erik Winter, Detective - Gothenburg

Karin Alvtegen
Anne Holt
Arnaldur Indridason
P D James
Matti Joensuu
Mari Jungstedt
Åsa Larsson
Henning Mankell
Jo Nesbo
Hakan Nesser
Ruth Rendell
Yrsa Sigurdardottir

Greg Egan 1961- Aus

Science Fiction: Near future

www.gregegan.net

Ben Bova
Jon Courtenay Grimwood
Ian McDonald
Ken MacLeod
Robert Reed
Nick Sagan
Neal Stephenson
Sean Williams

Dave Eggers 1970- US

Paul Auster
Don DeLillo
Ben Faccini
Jonathan Safran Foer
Jonathan Franzen
John Harding
Philip Roth

E

Clive Egleton 1927-2006

Adventure/Thriller

also wrote as Patrick Blake, John Tarrant

Peter Ashton

Ted Allbeury
Alex Berenson
Tom Bradby
Len Deighton
Colin Forbes
Frederick Forsyth
Brian Freemantle
Gerald Seymour

Thomas Eidson 1944- US

TGR 1995

Nicholas Evans
Charles Frazier
Kathleen O'Neal Gear
Larry McMurtry
Mark Mills
Stewart O'Nan
Annie Proulx
Jane Smiley
Jane Urquhart

Barry Eisler 1964- US

Adventure/Thriller

www.barryeisler.com

John Rain, Assassin

Ken Bruen
John Burdett
James Lee Burke
Lee Child
Charles Cumming
Ian Fleming
Andy McNab
Jefferson Parker
Robert Ryan

Elizabeth Elgin

Saga

Sutton Family - Yorkshire

Charlotte Bingham
Julia Bryant
Helen Cannam
Catrin Collier
Doris Davidson
Anna Jacobs
Beryl Matthews
Margaret Mayhew
Wendy Robertson
Susan Sallis
Kay Stephens
June Tate

Aaron Elkins   1935-   US   Crime: Forensic

www.aaronelkins.com   ☩ Dr Gideon Oliver, Forensic anthropologist
                                              Chris Norgren, Museum curator

Nevada Barr   Kate Ellis   John Malcolm
Jeffery Deaver   Nigel McCrery   Kathy Reichs

Kate Elliott   1958-   US   Fantasy: Epic

is Alis A Rasmussen
www.kateelliott.com

Ashok K Banker   Maggie Furey   Katharine Kerr
Terry Brooks   J V Jones   Holly Lisle
C J Cherryh   Paul Kearney   Elizabeth Moon

Bret Easton Ellis   1964-   US   Horror

Douglas Coupland   Haruki Murakami   Will Self
Jay McInerney   Chuck Palahniuk   Peter Straub
Graham Masterton   Tim Parks   Tom Wolfe

Kate Ellis   1953-   Crime: Police work - UK

www.kateellis.co.uk   ☩ DS Wesley Peterson - West Country

David Armstrong   Aaron Elkins   Roy Lewis
Jeffrey Ashford   P D James   R D Wingfield
W J Burley

Robert Ellis   US   Crime: Police work - US

www.robertellis.net   ☩ Det Lena Gamble - LAPD

John Connolly   James Patterson   J D Robb
Jonathan Kellerman   Thomas Perry   Nick Stone
Ed McBain

Harlan Ellison   1934-   Science Fiction: Space and time

www.harlanellison.com

Brian W Aldiss   Ray Bradbury   Connie Willis
Poul Anderson   Joe Haldeman   David Zindell
Greg Bear   Audrey Niffenegger

R J Ellory   1965-   Crime: Psychological

www.rogerjonellory.com

John Connor   Karin Fossum   Jeff Lindsay
Thomas H Cook   Jim Kelly   Andy Oakes
Carol Anne Davis   Patrick Lennon   George P Pelecanos

James Ellroy 1948- US

Crime: Hardboiled

♟ DS Lloyd Hopkins - Los Angeles

Edward Bunker
James Crumley
Stephen Donaldson
Loren D Estleman

John Hart
Stuart M Kaminsky
Matthew Klein
Chuck Palahniuk

Jason Starr
Jim Thompson
Joseph Wambaugh
John Williams

Margaret Elphinstone 1948- Sco

Historical

www.margaretelphinstone.co.uk

William Boyd
Dorothy Dunnett
Barbara Erskine

Julie Garwood
Sandra Gulland
Matthew Kneale

Audrey Niffenegger
Margaret Pemberton
James Robertson

Ben Elton 1959-

♟ CWA 1996

David Baddiel
Stephen Fry
Rob Grant

James Hawes
Charles Higson

George Orwell
Keith Waterhouse

Leif Enger 1961- US

Kate Atkinson
Louise Erdrich
Nicholas Evans

Charles Frazier
Haven Kimmel
Jhumpa Lahiri

Adriana Trigiani
Carlos Ruiz Zafón

Nathan Englander 1970- US

www.nathanenglander.com

Paul Auster
Michael Chabon
Don DeLillo

Denis Johnson
Nicole Krauss

Thomas Pynchon
Jonathan Trigell

Anne Enright 1962- Ire

♟ Booker 2007   Encore 2001

Trezza Azzopardi
Dermot Bolger
Anita Brookner

Maggie Gee
Jennifer Johnston
Edna O'Brien

Graham Swift
Gerard Woodward
Louisa Young

Louise Erdrich 1954- US

Isabel Allende
Michael Collins
Leif Enger

Barbara Kingsolver
Alison Lurie
Stewart O'Nan

Annie Proulx
Geoff Ryman
Rebecca Wells

Steven Erikson 1959- Can   Fantasy: Epic
is Steve Rune Lundin
www.tor.com/erikson

R Scott Bakker	Stephen Donaldson	John Marco
Ashok K Banker	Raymond E Feist	Patrick Rothfuss
James Barclay	Jude Fisher	Brian Ruckley
David Bilsborough	David Gemmell	Sean Russell

Kjell Eriksson Swe   Crime: Police work - Sweden
⚤ Insp Ann Lindell

Karin Alvtegen	Matti Joensuu	Ed McBain
Anne Holt	Mari Jungstedt	Henning Mankell
Arnaldur Indridason	Åsa Larsson	Hakan Nesser

Barbara Erskine ⌒ 1944-   Historical
is Barbara Hope-Lewis

Elizabeth Aston	Sara Donati	Kate Mosse
Vanora Bennett	Margaret Elphinstone	Audrey Niffenegger
Elizabeth Chadwick	Helen Hollick	Reay Tannahill

Laura Esquivel 1951- Mex

Isabel Allende	Gabriel Garcia Márquez	Patrick Suskind
Kate Atkinson	Shifra Horn	Célestine Hitiura Vaite
Alessandro Baricco	Lily Prior	Jeanette Winterson

Loren D Estleman 1952- US   Crime: PI
www.lorenestleman.com ⚤ Amos Walker - Detroit • Peter Macklin, Hitman

Lawrence Block	Steve Hamilton	Reggie Nadelson
C J Box	Dashiell Hammett	Rick Riordan
Harlan Coben	Hari Kunzru	Ronald Tierney
James Ellroy	Joe R Lansdale	Don Winslow

Jeffrey Eugenides 1960- US
www.jeffreyeugenides.com
🏆 Pulitzer 2003

Michel Faber	Siri Hustvedt	Donna Tartt
Jonathan Franzen	Rick Moody	John Updike
Andrew Sean Greer	Richard Powers	

Go to back for lists of
Pseudonyms • Authors by Genre • Characters and Series
Prize Winners • Crossover Authors • Further Reading • Websites

Janet Evanovich   1943- US Crime: Humour

also writes as Steffie Hall Stephanie Plum, Bail bondswoman - Newark, New Jersey
www.evanovich.com Max Holt • Alexandra Barnaby & Sam Hooker, Racing drivers
 CWA 1995 & 1997

Linda Barnes   Earlene Fowler   Zoë Sharp
Louise Doughty   Kerry Greenwood   Sarah Strohmeyer
Liz Evans   Pauline McLynn   Valerie Wilson Wesley

Geraldine Evans 1953- Crime: Police work - UK

also writes as Geraldine Hartnett DI Joe Rafferty & Sgt D Llewellyn
www.geraldineevans.com DCI Casey & Thomas Catt

David Armstrong   Marjorie Eccles   J M Gregson
Vivien Armstrong   Caroline Graham   Reginald Hill
Brian Cooper   Ann Granger   Peter Turnbull

Harriet Evans Mature Chick Lit

Lynne Barrett-Lee   Clare Dowling   Alexandra Potter
Doris Davidson   Kate Harrison   Bernadette Strachan
Margaret Thomson Davis   Louise Harwood

Jon Evans Can Adventure/Thriller

Alex Berenson   Gayle Lynds   Tim Sebastian
Dan Fesperman   Chris Petit   Gerald Seymour
Paul Henke   Henry Porter

Liz Evans Crime: PI

is Patricia Grey Grace Smith - 'Seatoun', South Coast, England
www.lizevans.net

Jo Bannister   Sparkle Hayter   Michelle Spring
Cara Black   Joyce Holms   Sarah Strohmeyer
Janet Evanovich   Pauline McLynn   Rebecca Tope
Sue Grafton   Zoë Sharp   Stella Whitelaw

Nicholas Evans 1950-

www.nicholasevans.com

Mitch Albom   Charles Frazier   Paullina Simons
Pat Conroy   Jules Hardy   Nicholas Sparks
Thomas Eidson   Stuart Harrison   Robert James Waller
Leif Enger   Larry McMurtry   Daniel Woodrell

E

Pamela Evans
Saga
London

Glenice Crossland	Elizabeth Lord	Elizabeth Waite
Hilary Green	Victor Pemberton	Jeanne Whitmee
Annie Groves	Carol Rivers	

Barbara Ewing
NZ
Historical

Vanora Bennett	Susanna Clarke	Diana Norman
Elizabeth Chadwick	Deborah Moggach	James Runcie

Michel Faber
1960- Neth

Monica Ali	Alasdair Gray	Jack Kerouac
Charles Dickens	James Kelman	Patrick McGrath
Jeffrey Eugenides	A L Kennedy	W Somerset Maugham

E F Ben Faccini

Paul Auster	Don DeLillo	Jonathan Franzen
Michael Chabon	Dave Eggers	John Updike

Linda Fairstein
1947- US
Crime: Legal/financial
www.lindafairstein.com

Alexandra Cooper, Assistant DA
Det Mike Chapman } New York

Lindsay Ashford	John T Lescroart	Nancy Taylor Rosenberg
Alafair Burke	Steve Martini	Lisa Scottoline
Jodi Compton	Perri O'Shaughnessy	Susan R Sloan
Lisa Gardner	Kathy Reichs	Robert K Tanenbaum

Duncan Falconer
Adventure/Thriller
www.duncanfalconer.com

Tom Clancy	Paul Henke	Chris Ryan
Clive Cussler	Andy McNab	Terence Strong
Murray Davies		

David Farland
1957- US
Fantasy: Epic
is Dave Wolverton

Jude Fisher	Robert Jordan	John Marco
Maggie Furey	Mercedes Lackey	Harry Turtledove
J V Jones	Juliet E McKenna	Jane Welch

Roopa Farooki   Pak

Monica Ali
Vikram Chandra
 Ha Jin
Jhumpa Lahiri

Sharon Maas
Amulya Malladi
Anita Nair
Preethi Nair

Ben Okri
Arundhati Roy
Meera Syal
Thirty Umrigar

John Farris   1936-   US   Horror
also writes as Steve Brackeen

Stephen Gallagher
Stephen King
Richard Laymon

Robert McCammon
Graham Masterton

Peter Straub
Whitley Strieber

William Faulkner   1897-1962   US

Gail Anderson-Dargatz
James Joyce
Cormac McCarthy
Carson McCullers

Toni Morrison
Alice Munro
Joyce Carol Oates
Amos Oz

Tim Pears
William Styron
Alice Walker
Daniel Woodrell

Sebastian Faulks   1953-
www.sebastianfaulks.com

Sebastian Barry
Melvyn Bragg
F G Cottam
Peter Ho Davies

Gunnar Kopperud
Daniel Mason
Simon Mawer
Irene Nemirovsky

Helen Oyeyemi
Chris Paling
Jonathan Raban
Erich Maria Remarque

F

Patricia Fawcett   Aga Saga

Sarah Challis
Lucy Clare
Rowan Coleman

Anne Doughty
Adèle Geras

Charlotte Moore
Rebecca Shaw

Christine Feehan   US   Paranormal
www.christinefeehan.com

Lara Adrian
Kelley Armstrong
Keri Arthur
Patricia Briggs

Mary Janice Davidson
Lori Handeland
Tanya Huff

Sherrilyn Kenyon
Sara Reinke
J R Ward

 may be suitable for young adults

Raymond E Feist
1945- US Fantasy: Epic
www.raymondfeistbooks.com

Joe Abercrombie	Steven Erikson	Scott Lynch
David Bilsborough	Maggie Furey	John Marco
Terry Brooks	Paul Kearney	Karen Miller
James Clemens	Tom Lloyd	Christopher Paolini

Kate Fenton
1954- Aga Saga
www.katefenton.com

Raffaella Barker	Rowan Coleman	Katie Fforde
Elizabeth Buchan	Isla Dewar	Sue Limb
Lucy Clare	Anne Doughty	

Will Ferguson
Can
www.willferguson.ca

Chimamanda Ngozi Adichie	James Meek	John Steinbeck
Douglas Coupland	Alexei Sayle	

Elizabeth Ferrars
1907-95 Crime: Amateur sleuth
was Morna Doris Brown ♴ Andrew Basnett • Felix & Virginia Freer

Anthea Fraser	Maureen O'Brien	Patricia Wentworth
Alison Joseph	June Thomson	Margaret Yorke
Ngaio Marsh		

Robert Ferrigno
1948- US Crime: Hardboiled
www.robertferrigno.com ♴ Jimmy Gage, Reporter - Los Angeles

Massimo Carlotto	James W Hall	Michael McGarrity
James Crumley	Tony Hillerman	Boston Teran
Murray Davies	Jonathon King	

Dan Fesperman
US Adventure/Thriller
www.danfesperman.com ♴ Vlado Petric - Bosnia
🏆 CWA 2003

Alex Berenson	Joseph Kanon	Stella Rimington
Michael Dibdin	Gayle Lynds	Robert Wilson
Jon Evans	Chris Petit	

Go to back for lists of
Pseudonyms • Authors by Genre • Characters and Series
Prize Winners • Crossover Authors • Further Reading • Websites

F

Jasper Fforde

www.jasperfforde.com

1961-   Wales

Crime: Humour

♔ Thursday Next, Literary detective - Swindon
DI Jack Spratt & DS Mary Mary - Reading Police Dept

Gilbert Adair	Mark Gatiss	Terry Pratchett
Douglas Adams	Tom Holt	Malcolm Pryce
Robert Asprin	Robert Lewis	Robert Rankin
Christopher Fowler	Paul Magrs	Connie Willis

Katie Fforde

www.katiefforde.com

1952-

Mature Chick Lit

Trisha Ashley	Therese Fowler	Elizabeth Palmer
Clare Chambers	Debby Holt	Tasmina Perry
Lucy Clare	Debbie Macomber	Alan Titchmarsh
Kate Fenton	Sharon Owens	Lou Wakefield

David Fiddimore

1944-

War: Modern

♔ Charlie Bassett, ex RAF, now spy

Frank Barnard	Andrew Greig	Derek Robinson
F G Cottam	James Holland	Alan Savage
Elizabeth Darrell	Henry Porter	Terence Strong
Alan Furst	Robert Radcliffe	Guy Walters

Helen Fielding

1959-

Chick Lit

♔ Bridget Jones

Sherry Ashworth	Serena Mackesy	Lynne Truss
Joanne Harris	Alexandra Potter	Jennifer Weiner
Veronica Henry		

Joy Fielding

www.joyfielding.com

1945-   Can

Crime: Psychological

Mark Billingham	Sophie Hannah	Margaret Murphy
Mary Higgins Clark	Faye Kellerman	Christina Schwarz
John Connolly	Judith Kelman	

Joseph Finder

www.josephfinder.com

1958-   US

Adventure/Thriller

Jeffrey Archer	Simon Kernick	Michael Marshall
David Baldacci	Matthew Klein	Gareth O'Callaghan
Vince Flynn	Robert Ludlum	Katherine Scholes

F

Anne Fine 🌈 ☺ 1947-
www.annefine.co.uk

Rachel Billington	Zoë Heller	Liz Rigbey
Rachel Cusk	Joan Lingard	Meg Rosoff
Catherine Dunne	Kate Long	Mary Stanley
Nicci French	Libby Purves	Louise Tondeur

Patricia Finney 1958- Crime: Historical - C16th
also writes as P F Chisholm, Grace Cavendish 🏃 David Becket & Simon Ames
www.patricia-finney.co.uk Elizabethan England
🏆 Higham 1977

P F Chisholm	C C Humphreys	C J Sansom
Michael Clynes	Edward Marston	Martin Stephen
Philip Gooden	John Pilkington	Peter Tonkin

Jude Fisher Fantasy: Epic
also writes as Gabriel King; is Jane Johnson
www.judefisher.com

James Barclay	Robin Hobb	Sean Russell
Steven Erikson	Ian Irvine	J R R Tolkien
David Farland	Juliet E McKenna	

Janet Fitch US

Barbara Kingsolver	Christina Schwarz	Jennifer Weiner
Richard North Patterson	Nicholas Sparks	

F Scott Fitzgerald 🌈 1896-1940 US

Russell Banks	E M Forster	Carson McCullers
Joseph Conrad	Ernest Hemingway	Jay McInerney
E L Doctorow	Craig Holden	John Steinbeck

Penelope Fitzgerald 1916-2000
🏆 Booker 1979

Jane Austen	Anita Brookner	Penelope Lively
Beryl Bainbridge	A S Byatt	Emma Tennant
Rachel Billington	Jane Gardam	Edith Wharton

Fannie Flagg 1944- US
is Patricia Neal

Elizabeth Berg	Haven Kimmel	Annie Proulx
Laurie Graham	Lorna Landvik	Adriana Trigiani
Jan Karon	Jojo Moyes	Rebecca Wells

F

Richard Flanagan 1961- Aus

www.richardflanagan.com

🏆 Commonwealth 2002

Peter Carey	Cormac McCarthy	Daniel Silva
J M Coetzee	David Malouf	Peter Spiegelman
Laura Lippman	Salman Rushdie	

Ian Fleming 🌉 ☺ 1908-64 Adventure/Thriller

🏃 James Bond

Boris Akunin	John Buchan	Brian Freemantle
Raymond Benson	Barry Eisler	Stella Rimington
Alex Berenson	James Follett	Daniel Silva

Susan Fletcher 1979-

🏆 Whitbread 2004   Betty Trask 2005   Authors 2004

Anthony Capella	Charlotte Mendelson	Jodi Picoult
Suzannah Dunn	Julie Myerson	Lionel Shriver
Catherine Dunne	Maggie O'Farrell	

Elizabeth Flock US

Jill Barnett	Nicci Gerrard	Marcia Preston
Clare Chambers	Jacquelyn Mitchard	Amanda Eyre Ward
Therese Fowler	Mary Alice Monroe	

F

David Flusfeder 1960- US

🏆 Encore 1997

Martin Amis	Sue Gee	Toby Litt
Jenny Diski	Graham Greene	Glenn Patterson
Helen Dunmore		

Katie Flynn 1936- Saga

also writes as Judy Turner; is Judith Saxton

🏃 Lilac Larkin - Liverpool

www.katieflynn.com

Anne Baker	Rosie Goodwin	Anna Jacobs
Dilly Court	Ruth Hamilton	Elizabeth Murphy
Josephine Cox	Rosie Harris	Kitty Neale
Glenice Crossland	Audrey Howard	Lynda Page

Vince Flynn 1966- US Adventure/Thriller

www.vinceflynn.com

🏃 Mitch Rapp - CIA Washington

Suzanne Brockmann	Joseph Finder	John J Nance
Lincoln Child	David Hagberg	Brad Thor
Stephen Coonts	Brian Haig	

Giles Foden   1967-

🏆 Whitbread 1998   Holtby 1998   S Maugham 1999

Beryl Bainbridge   Robert Edric   Andrew O'Hagan
William Boyd   Pamela Jooste   Paul Theroux
James Clavell

Jonathan Safran Foer   1977-   US

🏆 Guardian 2002

Niccolo Ammaniti   Michael Chabon   Jonathan Franzen
Lisa Appignanesi   Don DeLillo   Nicole Krauss
Paul Auster   Dave Eggers   Richard Powers

James Follett   🌐   1939-   Adventure/Thriller

Raymond Benson   Charles Higson   Justin Scott
Ian Fleming   Alistair MacLean   Craig Thomas
Colin Forbes   Matthew Reilly

Ken Follett   🌐   1949-   Adventure/Thriller

also writes as Simon Myles
www.ken-follett.com

F

Paul Adam   Nelson DeMille   Humphrey Hawksley
Carla Banks   Clare Francis   John Lawton
Nicholas Coleridge   Tom Gabbay   Robert Littell

Historical

Vanora Bennett   Jennifer Donnelly Salley Vickers
Tracy Chevalier   Linda Holeman

Colin Forbes   1923-2006   Adventure/Thriller

also wrote as Richard Raine, Raymond Sawkins   🏃 Tweed, Bob Newman
was Raymond Harold Sawkins   & Paula Grey - SIS

Ted Allbeury   Clive Egleton   Jack Higgins
Campbell Armstrong   James Follett   Charles Higson
Jon Cleary   Frederick Forsyth

G M Ford   1945-   US   Crime: Hardboiled

🏃 Frank Corso, Journalist - Seattle
Leo Waterman, Amateur sleuth

Robert Gregory Browne James W Hall   Jim Kelly
Caroline Carver   Denise Hamilton   Dennis Lehane
Michael Connelly   Steve Hamilton   Kevin Lewis
Robert Crais   J A Jance   Liza Marklund

Michael Curtis Ford   US

www.michaelcurtisford.com

Historical: Ancient

Ancient Greece • Ancient Rome

Bernard Cornwell	William Napier	Mary Renault
Robert Graves	Scott Oden	Steven Saylor
Conn Iggulden	Steven Pressfield	Simon Scarrow

Richard Ford   1944-   US

⚘ Frank Bascombe

🏆 Pulitzer 1996

Michael Collins	Alice Munro	Richard Russo
Michael Cunningham	Tim O'Brien	Jonathan Tropper
Pete Dexter	Richard Powers	Robert James Waller
Garrison Keillor	Jonathan Raban	Tobias Wolff

C S Forester   ⌒   1899-1966

Sea: Historical

⚘ Horatio Hornblower - C18th/19th England

G S Beard	Jonathan Lunn	Dudley Pope
David Donachie	James L Nelson	Peter Smalley
Alexander Kent	Patrick O'Brian	Julian Stockwin

E M Forster   ⌒   1879-1970

F Scott Fitzgerald	Anthony Powell	H G Wells
Henry James	Paul Scott	Edith Wharton
Ruth Prawer Jhabvala	Carolyn Slaughter	Virginia Woolf

Margaret Forster   ⌒   1938-

Kate Atkinson	Sue Gee	Anna Quindlen
Rachel Billington	Linda Grant	Louise Tondeur
Carol Birch	Sarah Hall	Fay Weldon
Katharine Davies	Charlotte Mendelson	Ann Widdecombe

Frederick Forsyth   ⌒   1938-

Adventure/Thriller

Jeffrey Archer	Paul Henke	Kyle Mills
James Barrington	James Long	Alex Scarrow
Clive Egleton	Robert Ludlum	Gerald Seymour
Colin Forbes	Glenn Meade	Daniel Silva

⌒ may be suitable for young adults

F

Karin Fossum 1954- Nor Crime: Police work - Norway
Insp Konrad Sejer & Jacob Skarre - Oslo

Karin Alvtegen	John Harvey	Jo Nesbo
K O Dahl	Arnaldur Indridason	Hakan Nesser
R J Ellory	Mari Jungstedt	Yrsa Sigurdardottir
Jean-Christophe Grangé	Liza Marklund	Maj Sjöwall & Per Wahlöö

Alan Dean Foster 1946- US Science Fiction: Space opera
www.alandeanfoster.com

Robert Asprin	C J Cherryh	Colin Greenland
David Brin	Michael Jan Friedman	Elizabeth Haydon
Orson Scott Card	Simon Green	Elizabeth Moon

Christopher Fowler 1953- Crime: Humour
www.christopherfowler.co.uk Arthur Bryant & John May, Policemen - London

Peter Ackroyd	Jasper Fforde	Malcolm Pryce
Gilbert Adair	Andrey Kurkov	Iain Sinclair
Christopher Brookmyre	Louise Penny	

Horror

British Fantasy 2004

Clive Barker	Graham Joyce	Malcolm Pryce
Ramsey Campbell	Graham Masterton	Michael Marshall Smith
Jonathan Carroll	Kim Newman	

Connie May Fowler 1958- US
www.conniemayfowler.com

Therese Fowler	Carson McCullers	Joyce Carol Oates
Sue Monk Kidd	Sue Miller	Jodi Picoult

Earlene Fowler 1954- US Crime: Amateur sleuth
www.earlenefowler.com Benni Harper, Museum curator - California

Deborah Crombie	Janet Evanovich	John Malcolm
Jo Dereske	Jonathan Gash	Iain Pears
John Dunning	Sue Grafton	Derek Wilson

Karen Joy Fowler 1950- US
www.sfwa.org/members/Fowler

Patricia Gaffney	Jodi Picoult	Anne Tyler
William Kowalski	Anne Rivers Siddons	Rebecca Wells
Elinor Lipman		

F

Therese Fowler   US

Jill Barnett	Elizabeth Flock	Alison Jameson
Barbara Delinsky	Connie May Fowler	Mary Alice Monroe
Katie Fforde	Tessa Hadley	Laura Moriarty

John Fowles   1926-2005
www.fowlesbooks.com

Peter Ackroyd	Alasdair Gray	Robert Nye
Maggie Gee	Thomas Hardy	Graham Swift
William Golding	Victoria Hislop	Rupert Thomson

Kathryn Fox   1966-   Aus   Crime: Forensic
www.kathrynfox.com   ☆ Dr Anya Crichton, Forensic pathologist

Alex Barclay	Colin Cotterill	Richard Montanari
Simon Beckett	Frances Fyfield	Chris Mooney
Robin Cook	Tess Gerritsen	Kathy Reichs
Patricia D Cornwell	Nigel McCrery	Karin Slaughter

Ronald Frame   1953-   Sco

Robert Goddard	A L Kennedy	Allan Massie
Kazuo Ishiguro	Bernard MacLaverty	William Trevor
Robin Jenkins		

F

Clare Francis   1946-   Adventure/Thriller
www.clarefrancis.com

Lisa Appignanesi	Paula Gosling	Hilary Norman
Carla Banks	Sophie Hannah	Christina Schwarz
Ken Follett	John Harvey	

Dick Francis   1920-   Wales   Crime: Amateur sleuth
also writes jointly with Felix Francis   ☆ Sid Halley & Kit Fielding - Horse racing
www.dickfrancis.com
🏆 CWA 1979

John Francome	Robert B Parker	Graeme Roe
Elizabeth George	Jenny Pitman	Lyndon Stacey
Gerald Hammond	Richard Pitman	

June Francis   1941-   Saga
www.junefrancis.co.uk   Liverpool

Lyn Andrews	Glenice Crossland	Sheila Newberry
Elizabeth Bailey	Jeannie Johnson	June Tate
Julia Bryant	Gwen Madoc	Margaret Thornton
Jean Chapman		

John Francome 1952- Crime: Amateur sleuth

also writes jointly with James MacGregor — Horse racing

Dick Francis
Jenny Pitman
Richard Pitman
Graeme Roe
Lyndon Stacey

Ariana Franklin 1935- Crime: Historical - Medieval

is Diana Norman — Adelia Aguiler, Female doctor

CWA 2007

Margaret Frazer
Susanna Gregory
Cora Harrison
Michael Jecks
Sharan Newman
Ellis Peters
Candace Robb
Kate Sedley
Pip Vaughan-Hughes

Jonathan Franzen 1959- US

www.jonathanfranzen.com

Black 2002

Michael Cunningham
Dave Eggers
Jeffrey Eugenides
Ben Faccini
Jonathan Safran Foer
A M Homes
Nicole Krauss
Matthew Pearl
Elliot Perlman
Annie Proulx
Donna Tartt
John Updike

F

Anthea Fraser 1930- Crime: Police work - UK

also writes as Vanessa Graham — DCI David Webb & DS Ken Jackson
'Broadshire', Home Counties • Rona Parish, Author

Marian Babson
Elizabeth Ferrars
Ann Granger
Veronica Heley
Hope McIntyre
Barry Maitland
Catherine Sampson
June Thomson

Caro Fraser Sco

www.caro-fraser.com — Leo Davies, QC
Caper Court Series - London Inner Temple Legal Chambers

Liz Byrski
Cynthia Harrod-Eagles
John McLaren
John Mortimer
Joanna Trollope

Christine Marion Fraser 1945-2003 Sco Saga

Rhanna Series • Kings Series • Noble Series - Scotland

Emma Blair
Margaret Thomson Davis
Gwen Kirkwood
Pamela Oldfield
Sally Stewart
Jessica Stirling
Mary Withall

Go to back for lists of
Pseudonyms • Authors by Genre • Characters and Series
Prize Winners • Crossover Authors • Further Reading • Websites

George Macdonald Fraser
1925-2008   Sco   War: Historical
🏃 Sir Harry Flashman

Boris Akunin	Joseph Heller	Tom Sharpe
Roger Carpenter	Tom Holt	Leslie Thomas
James Delingpole	Garry Kilworth	P G Wodehouse

Sara Fraser
1937-   Crime: Historical - C19th
also writes as Roy Clews   🏃 Thomas Potts, Parish constable - Redditch

Alanna Knight	Amy Myers	Elizabeth Peters
Peter Lovesey	Anne Perry	

Saga
🏃 Tildy Crawford - Midlands

Catrin Collier	Meg Hutchinson	Lynda Page
Josephine Cox	Annie Murray	Janet Tanner

Michael Frayn   ⌒   1933-   Humour
🏆 Whitbread 2002

Kingsley Amis	Patrick Gale	Simon Mawer
Guy Bellamy	Howard Jacobson	Paul Torday
Malcolm Bradbury	David Lodge	

Margaret Frazer   US   Crime: Historical - Medieval
also writes as Mary Monica Pulver; is Gail Frazer   🏃 Sister Frevisse - C15th England
www.margaretfrazer.com   Joliffe Players Series

Alys Clare	Cora Harrison	Ellis Peters
Ariana Franklin	Michael Jecks	Mary Reed and Eric Mayer
Philip Gooden	Sharan Newman	Peter Tremayne

Charles Frazier
1950-   US

Russell Banks	David Guterson	Tim O'Brien
Thomas Eidson	Thomas Keneally	Joseph O'Connor
Leif Enger	Cormac McCarthy	Stewart O'Nan
Nicholas Evans	Larry McMurtry	Daniel Woodrell

Maureen Freely
1952-   US

Tracy Chevalier	Graham Greene	Paul Theroux
Gabriel Garcia Márquez	Orhan Pamuk	Mario Vargas Llosa

⌒ may be suitable for young adults

Brian Freeman
1979- US Crime: Police work - US
www.bfreemanbooks.com ⋏ Det Jonathan Stride & Det Serena Dial - Minnesota

Harlan Coben	Scott Frost	Chris Mooney
Jeffery Deaver	Gregg Hurwitz	John Rickards
Alan Dunn	Patrick Lennon	P J Tracy

Brian Freemantle
1936- Adventure/Thriller
also writes as John Maxwell, ⋏ Charlie Muffin - MI6
Jonathan Evans, Jack Winchester Sebastian Holmes, Son of Sherlock - early C20th

Ted Allbeury	Ian Fleming	Patrick Lennon
Clive Egleton	John Le Carré	James Patterson

Nicci French
1958- Adventure/Thriller: Psychological
is Nicci Gerrard writing with Sean French ⋏ Dr Samantha Laschen

Lisa Appignanesi	Jane Hill	Andrew Pyper
Anne Fine	Joanna Hines	Patrick Redmond
Sophie Hannah	Elizabeth McGregor	Sally Spedding
Frances Hegarty	J Wallis Martin	Sue Walker

Esther Freud
1963-

Rachel Cusk	Terry McMillan	Meera Syal
Suzannah Dunn	Deborah Moggach	Emma Tennant
Alex Garland	Gwendoline Riley	

F

Kinky Friedman
1944- US Crime: Humour
⋏ Kinky Friedman, Country & Western singer - New York

Tim Dorsey	Sparkle Hayter	Rosemary Martin
Dashiell Hammett	Elmore Leonard	Robert B Parker
James Hawes		

Michael Jan Friedman
1955- US Science Fiction: Space opera
Star Trek Series

J G Ballard	Alan Dean Foster	Jay McInerney
C J Cherryh	Barbara Hambly	

Scott Frost
www.scottfrostbooks.com Adventure/Thriller
⋏ Det Alex Delillo - Los Angeles

Harlan Coben	Robert Crais	Gregg Hurwitz
Michael Connelly	Brian Freeman	John Sandford

Stephen Fry 1957- Humour

Alan Bennett
Paul Burke
Roddy Doyle

Ben Elton
Charles Higson
Tim Lott

Geoff Nicholson
Nigel Williams
P G Wodehouse

Carlos Fuentes 1928- Mex

Isabel Allende
Alessandro Baricco

Gabriel Garcia Márquez
Tomas Eloy Martinez

Patrick Suskind
Mario Vargas Llosa

Alexander Fullerton 1924- Adventure/Thriller

♂ Nicholas Everard

Brian Callison
Len Deighton
Duncan Harding

Hammond Innes
Alexander Kent
Philip McCutchan

Allan Mallinson
James Pattinson
Douglas Reeman

John Fullerton Adventure/Thriller

www.johnfullerton.com

Michael Asher
Charles Cumming

Alan Judd
Andy McNab

Henry Porter
Gerald Seymour

Maggie Furey 1955- Fantasy: Epic

Terry Brooks
Kate Elliott
David Farland

Raymond E Feist
Terry Goodkind
J V Jones

Paul Kearney
George R R Martin

Alan Furst 1941- US Adventure/Thriller

www.alanfurst.co.uk

Nicholas Coleridge
Charles Cumming
David Fiddimore
Joseph Garber

Jean-Christophe Grangé
Graham Greene
Philip Kerr
John Lawton

Robert Littell
Stella Rimington
Robert Ryan
Robert Wilson

Frances Fyfield 1948- Crime: Amateur sleuth

is Frances Hegarty ♂ Helen West, Lawyer, & DS Geoffrey Bailey - London
www.francesfyfield.co.uk Sarah Fortune, Lawyer
🏆 CWA 1990, 1991 & 2008

Jane Adams
Lindsay Ashford
Natasha Cooper

Kathryn Fox
Elizabeth George
Joanna Hines

M R D Meek
Margaret Murphy
Robert K Tanenbaum

F

Jostein Gaarder ⌒ ☺ 1952- Nor

| Umberto Eco | Mark Haddon | Iris Murdoch |
| Gabriel Garcia Márquez | Peter Hoeg | Orhan Pamuk |

Diana Gabaldon 1952- US — Historical
Outlander Series

Jean M Auel	Julie Garwood	James Long
Sara Donati	Kathleen O'Neal Gear	Audrey Niffenegger
Dorothy Dunnett	Judith Lennox	Reay Tannahill

Tom Gabbay US — Adventure/Thriller
www.tomgabbay.com
ⵜ Jack Teller

Clive Cussler	Stephen Hunter	Charles McCarry
Ken Follett	John Le Carré	Craig Thomas
Jack Higgins		

Reg Gadney 1941- — Crime: PI
ⵜ Alan Rosslyn

| Harry Bingham | John McLaren | Michael Ridpath |
| Robert Edric | Sara Paretsky | Robert Wilson |

Patricia Gaffney US — Aga Saga
www.patriciagaffney.com

G

Elizabeth Berg	Barbara Kingsolver	Jodi Picoult
Karen Joy Fowler	Sue Miller	Libby Purves
Ann Hood	Maggie O'Farrell	Adriana Trigiani

Neil Gaiman ⌒ ☺ 1960- — Fantasy: Contemporary
www.neilgaiman.com
🏆 British Fantasy 2006

Douglas Adams	Susanna Clarke	Tim Powers
Clive Barker	Charles de Lint	Philip Pullman
Jonathan Carroll	Christopher Moore	Martin Scott

Gillian Galbraith Sco — Crime: Police work - UK
ⵜ Alice Rice - Edinburgh

| Lin Anderson | Quintin Jardine | Denise Mina |
| Karen Campbell | Frederic Lindsay | Ian Rankin |

☺ also writes children's books

Iain Gale   Sco   War: Historical

🏃 Lt Jack Steele, Scottish Grenadiers

Roger Carpenter
Tom Connery
Bernard Cornwell

Garry Kilworth
James McGee
Allan Mallinson

William Napier
Simon Scarrow
John Wilcox

Patrick Gale   1962-
www.galewarning.org

Gilbert Adair
Guy Bellamy
Michael Frayn
Alan Hollinghurst

Marion Husband
Lloyd Jones
Katharine McMahon
Armistead Maupin

Blake Morrison
Carol Shields
Edward St Aubyn
Edmund White

Damon Galgut   1963-   SA

Sebastian Barry
Justin Cartwright
J M Coetzee

Jim Crace
Nadine Gordimer

Christopher Hope
Pamela Jooste

Stephen Gallagher   1954-   Horror
www.stephengallagher.com

Chaz Brenchley
John Farris
James Herbert

Peter James
Dean R Koontz
Graham Masterton

Mark Morris
T M Wright

Janice Galloway   1956-   Sco
www.galloway.1to1.org

Ron Butlin
Amanda Craig
Jackie Kay

A L Kennedy
Hari Kunzru
Andrew O'Hagan

Ali Smith
Alan Spence
Zoë Strachan

John Galsworthy   1867-1933

🏃 Forsyte Saga

Isabel Allende
R F Delderfield
Elizabeth Jane Howard

D H Lawrence
J B Priestley

Vikram Seth
Anthony Trollope

Joseph Garber   1943-2005   Adventure/Thriller
also wrote as Joseph R Garber

Alan Furst
James Grippando

Paul Henke
Alan Judd

Andy McNab
Chris Ryan

G

95

Gabriel Garcia Márquez ⌒ 1928- Col

Isabel Allende	Laura Esquivel	Ismail Kadare
Alessandro Baricco	Maureen Freely	Tomas Eloy Martinez
Peter Carey	Carlos Fuentes	Ben Okri
Paulo Coelho	Jostein Gaarder	Patrick Suskind

Luiz Alfredo Garcia-Roza 1936- Braz Crime: Police work - Brazil
🏃 Insp Espinosa - Rio de Janeiro

Andrea Camilleri	Michael Dibdin	Manuel Vázquez Montalbán
Raymond Chandler	José Latour	Barbara Nadel
Colin Cotterill	Donna Leon	Qiu Xiaolong

Jane Gardam ⌒ ☺ 1928-
🏆 Higham 1975   Whitbread 1991

Amanda Craig	Susan Hill	Jill Paton Walsh
Penelope Fitzgerald	Joan Lingard	Mary Wesley
James Hamilton-Paterson		

Meg Gardiner US Crime: PI
www.meggardiner.com   🏃 Evan Delaney - Santa Barbara, California

Linda Barnes	Lynn Hightower	Marcia Muller
Jan Burke	Laurie R King	Carol O'Connell
Lee Child	Theresa Monsour	Dana Stabenow

Craig Shaw Gardner 1949- US Fantasy: Humour
also writes as Peter Garrison
www.craigshawgardner.com

Robert Asprin	Tom Holt	Terry Pratchett
Mary Gentle	Christopher Moore	Martin Scott

Lisa Gardner US Adventure/Thriller
also writes as Alicia Scott
www.lisagardner.com
🏃 Pierce Quincy / Kimberly Quincy } FBI Special Agent

Max Allan Collins	Tess Gerritsen	Karin Slaughter
Linda Fairstein	Iris Johansen	Erica Spindler

Alex Garland ⌒ 1970-
🏆 Betty Trask 1997

Douglas Coupland	James Hamilton-Paterson	Timothy Mo
Esther Freud	Jack Kerouac	William Sutcliffe
William Golding	Tim Lott	

Julie Garwood   1946-   US   Historical
also writes as Emily Chase
www.juliegarwood.com

| Joy Chambers | Margaret Elphinstone | Linda Howard |
| Catherine Coulter | Diana Gabaldon | Amanda Quick |

Jonathan Gash   1933-   Crime: Amateur sleuth
also writes as Jonathan Grant   ⚘ Lovejoy, Antique dealer - London
is John Grant   Dr Clare Burtonall
⚘ CWA 1977

| Robert Barnard | Gerald Hammond | John Malcolm |
| Earlene Fowler | Alison Joseph | Catherine Sampson |

Elizabeth Gaskell   ⌂   1810-1865
www.gaskellsociety.co.uk

Elizabeth Aston	Garrison Keillor	Emma Tennant
Jane Austen	Alison Lurie	Edith Wharton
R F Delderfield		

Mark Gatiss   Crime: Amateur sleuth
⚘ Lucifer Box, Painter & secret agent - Edwardian England

Gilbert Adair	Jeremy Dyson	David Roberts
James Anderson	Jasper Fforde	Dorothy L Sayers
Jake Arnott	Malcolm Pryce	Charles Todd

Mike Gayle   1970-   Lad Lit
www.mikegayle.co.uk

| Mark Barrowcliffe | Matt Dunn | Tony Parsons |
| Matt Beaumont | Sam Holden | Matt Whyman |

Kathleen O'Neal Gear   1954-   US   Historical
also writes with Michael Gear (husband)   First North American Series

Jean M Auel	Diana Gabaldon	Edward Rutherfurd
Sara Donati	James A Michener	Judith Tarr
Thomas Eidson		

Maggie Gee   1948-

Peter Ackroyd	Anne Enright	Rachel Seiffert
Trezza Azzopardi	John Fowles	Graham Swift
Jenny Diski	Doris Lessing	Rose Tremain

Maurice Gee   1931-   NZ
🏆 Black 1978

Murray Bail	Robin Jenkins	David Malouf
Nadine Gordimer	Thomas Keneally	Rose Tremain

Sue Gee   1947-
🏆 Romantic 1997

Louise Candlish	Joan Lingard	Deborah Moggach
David Flusfeder	Penelope Lively	Salley Vickers
Margaret Forster	Charlotte Mendelson	

David Gemmell   1948-2006   Fantasy: Epic
also wrote as Ross Harding

James Barclay	Simon Green	Stan Nicholls
Terry Brooks	Paul Kearney	Brian Ruckley
Steven Erikson	Tom Lloyd	Jane Welch

Nikki Gemmell   1967-   Aus
www.nikkigemmell.com

Louise Candlish	Zoë Heller	Anita Shreve
Helen Dunmore	Sue Miller	

Mary Gentle   1956-   Fantasy: Epic
🏆 BSFA 2000

Storm Constantine	Ursula K Le Guin	Philip Pullman
Craig Shaw Gardner	China Miéville	Steph Swainston
Colin Greenland	Michael Moorcock	Sheri S Tepper
Gwyneth Jones	Tim Powers	Harry Turtledove

Elizabeth George   1949-   US   Crime: Police work - UK
www.elizabethgeorgeonline.com   DCI Thomas Lynley & DS Barbara Havers - London

Marjorie Eccles	Martha Grimes	Alison Joseph
Dick Francis	Susan Hill	Maureen O'Brien
Frances Fyfield	P D James	Camilla Way

Margaret George   1943-   US   Historical
www.margaretgeorge.com

Will Davenport	Edith Pargeter	Wilbur Smith
Christian Jacq	Jean Plaidy	Gore Vidal
Colleen McCullough		

G

Adèle Geras ⌒ ☺ 1944-   Aga Saga
www.adelegeras.com

Maeve Binchy   Audrey Howard   Rosamunde Pilcher
Amanda Brookfield   Sandra Howard   Eileen Ramsay
Patricia Fawcett   Sara MacDonald   Mary Wesley
Rebecca Gregson   Jojo Moyes   Marcia Willett

Nicci Gerrard 1958-
also writes as Nicci French when writing with Sean French

Jill Barnett   Jules Hardy   Mary Alice Monroe
Elizabeth Flock   Shirley Hazzard   Julie Myerson
Lesley Glaister   Siri Hustvedt   Marcia Preston
Tessa Hadley   Alison Jameson   Liz Rigbey

Tess Gerritsen ⌒ 1953- US   Crime: Medical
www.tessgerritsen.com   ☆ Det Jane Rizzoli & Dr Maura Isles, Detective & Pathologist
                                                              New York

Lindsay Ashford   Max Allan Collins   Jilliane Hoffman
Linwood Barclay   Joolz Denby   Jesse Kellerman
Simon Beckett   Kathryn Fox   Ken McClure
Paul Carson   Lisa Gardner   Michael Palmer

Amitav Ghosh 1956- Ind   Historical
www.amitavghosh.com

Anita Desai   Rohinton Mistry   Geoff Ryman
Kiran Desai   Arundhati Roy   Vikram Seth
Daniel Mason

G

David Gibbins 1962-   Adventure/Thriller
www.davidgibbins.com   ☆ Jack Howard, Archaeologist

Steve Berry   Douglas Preston   Paul Sussman
Dan Brown   Matthew Reilly   James Twining
Tom Harper   James Rollins

Fiona Gibson Sco   Mature Chick Lit
www.fionagibson.com

Lisa Jewell   Laura Marney   Carmen Reid
Rachel Johnson   Elizabeth Noble   Sue Townsend
Kathy Lette   John O'Farrell

⌒ may be suitable for young adults

99

William Gibson 1948- Can Science Fiction: Near future
www.williamgibsonbooks.com

Steve Aylett	John Twelve Hawks	Lucius Shepard
J G Ballard	Justina Robson	Michael Marshall Smith
Eric Brown	Nick Sagan	Kurt Vonnegut
Michael Crichton	Andrzej Sapkowski	Connie Willis

Melanie Gifford Historical

Geraldine Brooks	Victoria Holt	Robin Maxwell
Sandra Gulland	Rosalind Laker	James Runcie

Bartholomew Gill 1943-2002 US Crime: Police work - Ireland
was Mark McGarrity ⁎ Insp Peter McGarr - Dublin

Benjamin Black	John Harvey	Ian Rankin
Ruth Dudley Edwards	Brian McGilloway	

Elizabeth Gill 1950- Saga
also writes as Elizabeth Hankin

Irene Carr	Audrey Howard	Elvi Rhodes
Jean Chapman	Freda Lightfoot	Janet MacLeod Trotter
Una Horne		

John Gilstrap 1957- US Adventure/Thriller
www.johngilstrap.com

Alice Blanchard	Greg Iles	Scott Smith
Lee Child	Jefferson Parker	Stuart Woods
Brian Haig	Paullina Simons	

Mark Gimenez US Crime: Legal/financial
www.markgimenez.com

David Baldacci	David Hosp	Steve Martini
Linwood Barclay	Gregg Hurwitz	Michael Robotham
John Grisham	Patrick Lennon	Scott Turow

Lesley Glaister 1956-
🏆 S Maugham 1991

Lisa Appignanesi	Nicci Gerrard	Joanna Hines
Carol Birch	Sophie Hannah	Alice Sebold
Jenny Diski	Jules Hardy	Aline Templeton
Louise Doughty	Shirley Hazzard	Gillian White

G

Janet Gleeson

Crime: Historical - C18th
C18th England

Gwendoline Butler	David Liss	Iain Pears
John Maclachlan Gray	Edward Marston	Rosemary Stevens
Deryn Lake	Fidelis Morgan	Derek Wilson

Miranda Glover

Margaret Atwood	Valerie Martin	Maggie O'Farrell
Kim Edwards	Kate Morton	Ann Patchett

Robert Goddard 1954-

Adventure/Thriller
♀ Harry Barnett

♈ TGR 1992

Hilary Bonner	Gregory Hall	Kate Morton
Stephen Booth	Susanna Kearsley	Patrick Redmond
John Buchan	Catriona McPherson	Charles Todd
Ronald Frame	Mark Mills	Jacqueline Winspear

Gail Godwin 1937- US

www.gailgodwin.com

Margaret Atwood	Alison Lurie	Anne Tyler
Ann Hood	Joyce Carol Oates	

Leonard Goldberg 1936- US

Crime: Forensic

www.leonardgoldberg.com ♀ Joanna Blalock, Forensic pathologist, & Det Jake Sinclair
LAPD - Los Angeles

Lindsay Ashford	Patricia D Cornwell	Michael Palmer
Paul Carson	Tami Hoag	Kathy Reichs
Robin Cook		

Arthur Golden 1957- US

Alma Alexander	Catherine Lim	Su Tong
Michelle de Kretser	Anchee Min	Amy Tan
Kazuo Ishiguro	Timothy Mo	Xinran

William Golding 1911-93

www.william-golding.co.uk

♈ Black 1979   Booker 1980

Tim Binding	John Fowles	Anthony Trollope
Patricia Duncker	Alex Garland	Barry Unsworth
Umberto Eco	Thomas Hardy	Marianne Wiggins

G

Olivia Goldsmith   1949-2004   US   Glitz & Glamour

Louise Bagshawe	Judith Michael	Anne Rivers Siddons
Sandra Brown	Jane Moore	Robyn Sisman
Candace Bushnell	Katie Price	Penny Vincenzi

Philip Gooden   Crime: Historical - C16th

also writes as Philippa Morgan,   ☃ Nick Revill, Shakespearean actor
The Medieval Murderers (with Susanne Gregory,   C16th England
Michael Jecks, Bernard Knight, Ian Morson, C J Sansom)

P F Chisholm	C C Humphreys	John Pilkington
Michael Clynes	Edward Marston	C J Sansom
Patricia Finney	Fidelis Morgan	Martin Stephen
Margaret Frazer	Iain Pears	Peter Tonkin

Terry Goodkind   ☏   1948-   US   Fantasy: Epic

www.terrygoodkind.com   ☃ Richard Cypher

Carol Berg	Sara Douglass	Robert Newcomb
Trudi Canavan	David A Drake	Stan Nicholls
Mark Chadbourn	Maggie Furey	Mickey Zucker Reichert
James Clemens	Ian Irvine	Jane Welch

Carol Goodman   US   Crime: Psychological

www.carolgoodman.com

Mary Higgins Clark	Joanna Hines	Donna Tartt
Carol Anne Davis	Iris Johansen	Minette Walters
Sophie Hannah	Judith Kelman	Gillian White
John Harwood	Fiona Mountain	Laura Wilson

G

Jason Goodwin   1964-   Crime: Historical - C19th

www.jasongoodwin.net   ☃ Yashim Tagalu - Istanbul

Boris Akunin	H R F Keating	Orhan Pamuk
Michael Gregorio	R N Morris	Michael Pearce
Liz Jensen	Barbara Nadel	James Runcie

Rosie Goodwin   Saga

www.rosiegoodwin.co.uk

Aileen Armitage	Josephine Cox	Rosie Harris
Maggie Bennett	Katie Flynn	Audrey Howard
Catrin Collier	Iris Gower	Judith Lennox
Catherine Cookson	Pip Granger	Valerie Wood

Nadine Gordimer   1923-   SA

🏆 Black 1971   Booker 1974

Margaret Atwood	Damon Galgut	Pamela Jooste
André Brink	Maurice Gee	Doris Lessing
J M Coetzee	Christopher Hope	Paul Scott

Paula Gosling   1939-   US   Crime: Police work - US

also writes as Ainslie Skinner   🏃 Sheriff Matt Gabriel, Lt Jack Stryker
& Prof Kate Trevorne - 'Blackwater Bay', Michigan

🏆 CWA 1978 & 1985

Lilian Jackson Braun	Clare Francis	Laurie R King
Deborah Crombie	Martha Grimes	Archer Mayor
Jo Dereske		

Eileen Goudge   1950-   US   Glitz & Glamour

www.eileengoudge.com

Elizabeth Buchan	Elizabeth Jane Howard	Nora Roberts
Barbara Delinsky	Joan Lingard	Danielle Steel
Judith Gould	Fern Michaels	

Judith Gould   1952-   US   Glitz & Glamour

also writes as W R Gallaher; is Nicholas Bienes & Rhea Gallaher
www.judithgould.com

Elizabeth Adler	Rachel Johnson	Judith McNaught
Jilly Cooper	Jayne Ann Krentz	Judith Michael
Eileen Goudge	Susan Lewis	Madge Swindells

Steven Gould   1955-   Science Fiction: Near future

Neal Asher	Sergei Lukyanenko	Nick Sagan
Iain M Banks	Kim Stanley Robinson	Andrzej Sapkowski
Hal Duncan	Justina Robson	

Iris Gower   1939-   Wales   Saga

www.irisgower.com   Cordwainer Series - South Wales • Sweet Rosie Series
Firebird Series • Drovers Series • Palace Theatre Series - Swansea

Jessica Blair	Rosie Goodwin	Grace Thompson
Catrin Collier	Rosie Harris	Barbara Whitnell
Gloria Cook	Joan O'Neill	Barbara Wood

Posie Graeme-Evans   1952-   Aus   Historical

www.posiegraemeevans.com

Elizabeth Chadwick	Philippa Gregory	Sarah Waters
Suzannah Dunn	Jeanne Kalogridis	Alison Weir
Dorothy Dunnett		

G

103

Sue Grafton

www.suegrafton.com 1940- US Crime: PI

🏃 Kinsey Millhone - 'Santa Teresa', California

🏆 CWA 2008

Nevada Barr	Jan Burke	Denise Hamilton
Cara Black	Carol Higgins Clark	Steve Hamilton
Edna Buchanan	Liz Evans	Zoë Sharp
Alafair Burke	Earlene Fowler	Ayelet Waldman

Caroline Graham

1931- Crime: Police work - UK

🏃 DCI Tom Barnaby & DS Troy - 'Midsomer Worthy'

A C Baantjer	Margaret Duffy	Ann Purser
W J Burley	Geraldine Evans	Nicholas Rhea
Clare Curzon	J M Gregson	Roger Silverwood
Louise Doughty	Lis Howell	Sally Spencer

Heather Graham

US Crime: Hardboiled

also writes as Shannon Drake; is Heather Graham Pozzessere
www.theheathergraham.com

June Hampson	James Patterson	Martyn Waites
Tami Hoag	J D Robb	

Crime: Romantic suspense

Beverly Barton	Linda Howard	Sharon Sala
Allison Brennan	Lisa Jackson	Madge Swindells

Laurie Graham

1947-

www.lauriegraham.com

Alan Bennett	Sue Monk Kidd	Jojo Moyes
Elizabeth Berg	Lorna Landvik	Ben Richards
Amanda Craig	Sue Limb	Sue Townsend
Fannie Flagg	Elinor Lipman	Arabella Weir

Winston Graham

1909-2003

www.winstongraham.org

Pat Conroy	Sarah Harrison	Rosalind Laker
R F Delderfield	Joanna Hines	E V Thompson

Historical

🏃 Poldark Series

Rosemary Aitken	Gloria Cook	Nigel Tranter
Anita Burgh	Joanna Hines	Kate Tremayne

G

may be suitable for young adults

Almudena Grandes   1960-   Spain

Ernest Hemingway	Maggie O'Farrell
Valerio Massimo Manfredi	Arturo Pérez-Reverte

Jean-Christophe Grangé   1961-   Fr   Adventure/Thriller
🕴 Pierre Niemans & Abdouf

John Case	Alan Furst	Henry Porter
Karin Fossum	Paul Henke	Wilbur Smith

Ann Granger   1939-   Crime: Police work - UK
also writes as Ann Hulme   🕴 Div Supt Alan Markby & Meredith Mitchell - Cotswolds
Fran Varady, PI - London

Chris Collett	Hazel Holt	Sally Spencer
Geraldine Evans	Lis Howell	Ronald Tierney
Anthea Fraser	Ann Purser	Rebecca Tope
J M Gregson	Betty Rowlands	Jacqueline Winspear

Pip Granger   Saga
🕴 Zelda Fluck - Soho London, 1940s

Rosie Goodwin	Carol Rivers	Dee Williams
Connie Monk	Mary Jane Staples	Sally Worboyes
Gilda O'Neill	Elizabeth Waite	

Linda Grant   1951-
www.lindagrant.co.uk
🏆 Higham 1996   Orange 2000

Beryl Bainbridge	Margaret Forster	Anna Quindlen
Pat Barker	David Grossman	Zadie Smith
Suzanne Berne		

Rob Grant   🔗   Science Fiction: Humour
also writes as Grant Naylor (with Doug Naylor)

Douglas Adams	Harry Harrison	Terry Pratchett
David Baddiel	Tom Holt	Robert Rankin
Ben Elton		

Robert Graves   🔗   1895-1985
www.robertgraves.org

Michael Curtis Ford	Colleen McCullough	Steven Pressfield
Robert Harris	Valerio Massimo Manfredi	Erich Maria Remarque
Conn Iggulden	Allan Massie	Mary Renault

Alasdair Gray   1934-   Sco

www.alasdairgray.co.uk

🏆 Guardian 1992   Whitbread 1992

Michel Faber	A L Kennedy	Ali Smith
John Fowles	Will Self	Graham Swift
James Kelman	Iain Sinclair	Kurt Vonnegut

Alex Gray   Sco   Crime: Police work - UK

www.alex-gray.com   🏃 DCI William Lorimer & Dr Solomon Brightman, Psychologist
Glasgow

Lin Anderson	Quintin Jardine	Ian Rankin
Benjamin Black	Frederic Lindsay	Manda Scott
Karen Campbell	Stuart MacBride	Aline Templeton
Allan Guthrie	Denise Mina	Louise Welsh

John Maclachlan Gray   1946-   Can   Crime: Historical - C19th

is John Howard Gray   🏃 Edmund Whitty, Journalist - Victorian London
www.johnmaclachlangray.com

Janet Gleeson	Andrew Martin	David Pirie
Peter J Heck	Iain Pears	Rosemary Stevens
Peter Lovesey	Andrew Pepper	

Sarah Grazebrook

Diana Appleyard	Kate Long	M J Trow
Rebecca Gregson	Robin Pilcher	Jane Elizabeth Varley

Andrew M Greeley   1928-   US   Crime: Amateur sleuth

www.agreeley.com   🏃 Blackie Ryan, Bishop - Chicago

William Brodrick	Umberto Eco	Ellis Peters
Kate Charles	Alison Joseph	Peter Tremayne

Hilary Green   Saga
WW2

Anne Bennett	Pamela Evans	Margaret Mayhew
Emma Blair	Annie Groves	Annie Murray
Rita Bradshaw	Beryl Kingston	Lynda Page

Go to back for lists of
Pseudonyms • Authors by Genre • Characters and Series
Prize Winners • Crossover Authors • Further Reading • Websites

Jane Green 1968-   Chick Lit
www.janegreen.com

Tilly Bagshawe
Melissa Bank
Maria Beaumont
Mavis Cheek

Rowan Coleman
Lisa Jewell
Milly Johnson
Louise Kean

Allison Pearson
Linda Taylor
Lynne Truss
Polly Williams

Simon Green   1955-   Fantasy: Epic

Kevin J Anderson
Alan Dean Foster
David Gemmell

Holly Lisle
L E Modesitt Jr
Terry Pratchett

Martin Scott
Jane Welch

Graham Greene   1904-91

Justin Cartwright
Glen Duncan
Patricia Duncker
David Flusfeder

Maureen Freely
Alan Furst
Denis Johnson
Pauline Melville

George Orwell
Anthony Powell
Nicholas Shakespeare
Morris West

Colin Greenland   1954-   Science Fiction: Space opera
www.infinityplus.co.uk/misc/cg.htm
🏆 BSFA 1990   Arthur C Clarke 1991

Lois McMaster Bujold
C J Cherryh
Alan Dean Foster

Mary Gentle
Peter F Hamilton
Harry Harrison

Brian Herbert
Brian Stableford

G

Kerry Greenwood   1954-   Aus   Crime: PI
is Isabelle Lewis   🏃 Hon Phryne Fisher - Melbourne, 1920s
www.phrynefisher.com

Agatha Christie
Robert Edric
Janet Evanovich

Charlaine Harris
Anne Perry

J D Robb
Michelle Spring

Andrew Sean Greer   1970-   US
www.andrewgreer.com

Jeffrey Eugenides
Kazuo Ishiguro
Liz Jensen

Natsuo Kirino
Jhumpa Lahiri

Vladimir Nabokov
William Trevor

may be suitable for young adults

Michael Gregorio

is Michael G Jacob & Daniela De Gregorio
www.michaelgregorio.it

Crime: Historical - C18th

⚲ Hanno Stiffeniis, Magistrate
C19th Prussia

Boris Akunin	Andrey Kurkov	Michael Pearce
Jason Goodwin	David Liss	C J Sansom
Stuart M Kaminsky	R N Morris	Frank Tallis

Philippa Gregory ◠ 1954-

www.philippagregory.com

🏆 Romantic 2002

Historical
Wideacre Trilogy

Vanora Bennett	Suzannah Dunn	Katharine McMahon
Clare Clark	Posie Graeme-Evans	Robin Maxwell
Katharine Davies	Caroline Harvey	Kate Saunders
Christie Dickason	Joanna Hines	Alison Weir

Susanna Gregory 1958-

also writes as Simon Beaufort,
The Medieval Murderers (with Philip Gooden,
Michael Jecks, Bernard Knight, Ian Morson,
C J Sansom); is Elizabeth Cruwys
www.matthewbartholomew.co.uk

Crime: Historical - Medieval

⚲ Matthew Bartholomew - C14th England
Thomas Chaloner, Spy - C17th England

Paul Doherty	Bernard Knight	Candace Robb
Ariana Franklin	Pat McIntosh	Caroline Roe
Michael Jecks	Ellis Peters	Kate Sedley

G J M Gregson 1934-

also writes as Jim Gregson
is James Michael Gregson

Crime: Police work - UK

⚲ DCI Percy Peach & DS Lucy Blake - East Lancashire
Det John Lambert & Det Bert Hook

David Armstrong	Caroline Graham	Nicholas Rhea
Jeffrey Ashford	Ann Granger	Sally Spencer
Geraldine Evans		

Rebecca Gregson

Aga Saga

Judy Astley	Adèle Geras	Kate Long
Sarah Challis	Sarah Grazebrook	Marcia Willett
Clare Chambers	Julie Highmore	Elizabeth Wrenn

Andrew Greig 1951- Sco

Frank Barnard	Peter Ho Davies	Simon Mawer
Sebastian Barry	David Fiddimore	Jonathan Raban
F G Cottam	Marion Husband	Robert Radcliffe
Murray Davies	Robin Jenkins	Alan Spence

Kate Grenville   1950-   Aus
www.users.bigpond.com/kgrenville

🏆 Orange 2001   Commonwealth 2006

Murray Bail	Candida Crewe	Lloyd Jones
Suzanne Berne	Kiran Desai	Andrew McGahan
Carol Birch	Jessica Duchen	Imogen Parker
Peter Carey	Kim Edwards	Jane Smiley

W E B Griffin   1929-   US   Crime: Police work - US
also writes as Alex Baldwin; is William E Butterworth III   Philadelphia
www.webgriffin.com

Donald Harstad	Ed McBain	Ridley Pearson
Jack Higgins	Margaret Maron	Joseph Wambaugh

War: Modern

Corps Series • Badge of Honour Series • Brotherhood of War Series

Harold Coyle	Matthew Reilly	Terence Strong
Graham Hurley	David L Robbins	James Webb
Gordon Kent	Derek Robinson	

Niall Griffiths   🌂   1966-

Roddy Doyle	Robert Lewis	Irvine Welsh
Nick Hornby	Will Self	Jeanette Winterson

Martha Grimes   1931-   US   Crime: Police work - UK
www.marthagrimes.com   🕴 DCI Richard Jury - London

Lilian Jackson Braun	Elizabeth George	Maureen O'Brien
Barbara Cleverly	Paula Gosling	Dorothy L Sayers
Deborah Crombie	Graham Ison	Charles Todd

Jon Courtenay Grimwood   Science Fiction: Near future
www.j-cg.co.uk   🕴 Ashraf Bey

🏆 BSFA 2003 & 2006

Greg Egan	Jeff Noon	Neal Stephenson
Ian McDonald	Justina Robson	Tad Williams
John Meaney	Lucius Shepard	

James Grippando   1958-   US   Crime: Legal/financial
www.jamesgrippando.com   🕴 Jack Swyteck, Lawyer - Miami

Jeff Abbott	Steve Martini	Peter Spiegelman
William Bernhardt	Barbara Parker	Robert K Tanenbaum
Joseph Garber	Richard North Patterson	Scott Turow
John T Lescroart	Michael Ridpath	Stuart Woods

G

John Grisham 1955- US Crime: Legal/financial
www.jgrisham.com

William Bernhardt
Gianrico Carofiglio
Stephen L Carter
Linda Davies

Mark Gimenez
John Hart
Jilliane Hoffman
Craig Holden

Katherine John
Barbara Parker
Christopher Reich
Michael Ridpath

David Grossman 1954- Isr
🏆 Wingate 2004

Saul Bellow
Linda Grant
Howard Jacobson

Amos Oz
Jonathan Raban

Philip Roth
Salman Rushdie

Annie Groves Saga
is Penny Jordan 🏃 Pride Family - Preston
www.anniegroves.co.uk

Maggie Bennett
Jessica Blair
Rita Bradshaw

Glenice Crossland
Pamela Evans
Hilary Green

Margaret Mayhew
Dee Williams

Michael Gruber 1940- US Adventure/Thriller
www.michaelgruberbooks.com 🏃 Jimmy Paz - Miami

Richard Doetsch
Laura Lippman

Greg Loomis
Mark Mills

Kate Mosse
Peter Temple

G

Sandra Gulland 1944- US Historical
www.sandragulland.com 🏃 Josephine Bonaparte

Margaret Elphinstone
Melanie Gifford
Cynthia Harrod-Eagles

Anne Haverty
Rosalind Laker

Robin Maxwell
Jean Plaidy

Romesh Gunesekera 1954- Sri Lan
www.romeshgunesekera.com

J G Ballard
J M Coetzee

Michelle de Kretser
Michael Ondaatje

Roma Tearne
Paul Theroux

Xiaolu Guo 1974- China
www.guoxiaolu.com

Ha Jin
Hanif Kureishi
Anchee Min

Andy Oakes
Caryl Phillips
Qiu Xiaolong

Lisa See
Xinran

Abdulrazak Gurnah　1948-　Zan

Chimamanda Ngozi Adichie
Monica Ali
Joseph Conrad

Khaled Hosseini
Ruth Prawer Jhabvala
Rohinton Mistry

V S Naipaul
Paul Theroux

David Guterson　🌉　1956-　US

Russell Banks
Pete Dexter
Jennifer Donnelly
Charles Frazier

Peter Hoeg
Stuart M Kaminsky
Michael Kimball
William Kowalski

Alistair MacLeod
Jacquelyn Mitchard
Jane Urquhart
Daniel Woodrell

Allan Guthrie　1965-　Sco　　　　　　　　Crime: Hardboiled
www.allanguthrie.co.uk　　　　　　🚶 Pearce, ex-Con - Edinburgh
🏆 Theakston's 2007

Ken Bruen
Karen Campbell
Alex Gray

Quintin Jardine
Stuart MacBride

Denise Mina
Ian Rankin

Peter Guttridge　1951-　　　　　　　　　　Crime: Humour
www.peterguttridge.com　　　　　　　🚶 Nick Madrid, Journalist

Colin Bateman
Carl Hiaasen
Andrey Kurkov

Robert Lewis
Claire McNab
Chris Niles

Zane Radcliffe
Ian Sansom

Mark Haddon　🌉　☺　1962-
www.markhaddon.com
🏆 McKitterick 2004　　Whitbread 2003

Paulo Coelho
Neil Cross
Jostein Gaarder

Marina Lewycka
Yann Martel
Rick Moody

Alice Sebold
Miriam Toews
Jonathan Tropper

Tessa Hadley

Nicola Barker
Jill Barnett
Rachel Cusk
Therese Fowler

Nicci Gerrard
Alison Jameson
Jacquelyn Mitchard
Laura Moriarty

Maggie O'Farrell
Rachel Seiffert
Mario Vargas Llosa
Gerard Woodward

David Hagberg　1942-　US　　　　　　　　Adventure/Thriller
also writes as David Bannerman, Sean Flannery　🚶 Kirk McGarvey, ex CIA
www.david-hagberg.com

Suzanne Brockmann
Dan Brown
Stephen Coonts

Clive Cussler
Vince Flynn
Gordon Kent

Robert Ludlum
Stanley Pottinger

Brian Haig 1953- US Adventure/Thriller
www.brianhaig.com ⚐ Sean Drummond, Army lawyer

David Baldacci	John Gilstrap	Douglas Preston
Tom Clancy	Robert Ludlum	Brad Thor
Vince Flynn		

Joe Haldeman 1943- US Science Fiction: Space opera
also writes as Robert Graham
www.home.earthlink.net/~haldeman

Brian W Aldiss	Harlan Ellison	Lucius Shepard
J G Ballard	Harry Harrison	Robert Silverberg
Orson Scott Card	Robert A Heinlein	Dan Simmons

Georgie Hale Crime: Police work - UK
www.georgiehale.com ⚐ DI Ray Whitelaw & DI Dave Shenfield - 'Blackport'

Paul Charles	Lesley Horton	Stuart Pawson
Patricia Hall	Graham Hurley	Peter Robinson
Reginald Hill		

Gregory Hall 1948- Crime: Psychological

Hilary Bonner	Cynthia Harrod-Eagles	Cody McFadyen
Rhys Bowen	Frances Hegarty	John Rickards
Robert Goddard	Morag Joss	Andrew Taylor

James W Hall 1947- US Crime: PI
also writes as James Hall ⚐ Thorn • Alexandra Rafferty, Police photographer
www.jameswhall.com Florida

Edna Buchanan	Robert Ferrigno	Jonathon King
James Lee Burke	G M Ford	Elmore Leonard
Lee Child		

Patricia Hall 1940- Crime: Police work - UK
is Maureen O'Connor ⚐ DCI Michael Thackeray & Laura Ackroyd, Journalist
www.patriciahall.co.uk 'Bradfield', Yorkshire

David Armstrong	Paul Charles	Lesley Horton
Robert Barnard	John Connor	Adrian Magson
Pauline Bell	Clare Curzon	Stuart Pawson
Ken Bruen	Georgie Hale	Pauline Rowson

Sarah Hall 1974-
🏆 JLR 2006/7

Margaret Atwood	Neil Cross	D H Lawrence
Melvyn Bragg	Margaret Forster	Doris Lessing
	Thomas Hardy	Gerard Woodward

H

Barbara Hambly   1951-   US   Fantasy: Myth

www.barbarahambly.com

Marion Zimmer Bradley	Amanda Hemingway	Elizabeth Moon
C J Cherryh	Mercedes Lackey	Tim Powers
Louise Cooper	Anne McCaffrey	Melanie Rawn
Michael Jan Friedman	Julian May	Liz Williams

Denise Hamilton   US   Crime: Amateur sleuth

www.denisehamilton.com   ⚗ Eve Diamond, Journalist - Los Angeles

Edna Buchanan	Raymond Chandler	Sue Grafton
Jan Burke	G M Ford	Liza Marklund
Caroline Carver		

Jane Hamilton   1957-   US

Jennifer Donnelly	Mary Lawson	Ann Patchett
Catherine Dunne	Alice Munro	Jane Smiley
Barbara Kingsolver		

Laurell K Hamilton   ⌒   1963-   US   Paranormal

is Laurell Kaye Klein   ⚗ Anita Blake, Necromancer & crime investigator
www.laurellkhamilton.org

Kelley Armstrong	Tanya Huff	Kim Newman
Charlaine Harris	Jeanne Kalogridis	Sara Reinke
Kim Harrison	Holly Lisle	Anne Rice

Peter F Hamilton   1960-   Science Fiction: Space opera

www.peterfhamilton.co.uk

Kevin J Anderson	Greg Bear	Colin Greenland
Neal Asher	Lois McMaster Bujold	Robert Reed
Iain M Banks	C J Cherryh	Charles Stross

Ruth Hamilton   Saga

www.ruth-hamilton.co.uk   Liverpool & Lancashire

Lyn Andrews	Josephine Cox	Maureen Lee
Rita Bradshaw	Katie Flynn	Freda Lightfoot
Alexandra Connor	Meg Henderson	

Steve Hamilton   1961-   US   Crime: PI

www.authorstevehamilton.com   ⚗ Alex McKnight - 'Paradise', Michigan

C J Box	Jonathon King	Peter Spiegelman
Loren D Estleman	Elmore Leonard	Dana Stabenow
G M Ford	Michael McGarrity	Robert K Tanenbaum
Sue Grafton	Walter Mosley	Jess Walter

H

James Hamilton-Paterson 1941-

🏃 Gerald Samper - Tuscany

🏆 Whitbread 1989

John Banville	Jane Gardam	Timothy Mo
Joseph Conrad	Alex Garland	Nicholas Shakespeare
Louis de Bernières		

Dashiell Hammett 1894-1961 US Crime: PI

also wrote as Peter Collinson 🏃 The Continental Op • Sam Spade - San Francisco

Lawrence Block	Stuart M Kaminsky	Walter Mosley
James Hadley Chase	Ross Macdonald	Peter Spiegelman
Loren D Estleman	Michael Malone	Don Winslow
Kinky Friedman		

Gerald Hammond 1926- Sco Crime: Amateur sleuth

also writes as Arthur Douglas, 🏃 Keith Calder, Gunsmith }
Dalby Holden John Cunningham, Kennel owner } Scottish Borders

M C Beaton	Joyce Holms	Peter Turnbull
Dick Francis	Catriona McPherson	Margaret Yorke
Jonathan Gash		

June Hampson Crime: Hardboiled

🏃 Daisy Lane - Gosport, Hampshire

Martina Cole	Roberta Kray	Kevin Lewis
Heather Graham	Lynda La Plante	Sheila Quigley
Mandasue Heller		

Lori Handeland US Paranormal

www.lorihandeland.com 🏃 Werewolves - Wisconsin

Kelley Armstrong	Mary Janice Davidson	Sherrilyn Kenyon
Patricia Briggs	Christine Feehan	Sara Reinke
Jim Butcher	Charlaine Harris	J R Ward

Lauren Haney US Crime: Historical - Ancient

🏃 Lt Bak, Medjay police - Ancient Egypt, c1500BC

Philip Boast	Mary Reed and Eric Mayer	Steven Saylor
Margaret Doody	John Maddox Roberts	David Wishart
Michael Pearce	Lynda S Robinson	

Go to back for lists of
Pseudonyms • Authors by Genre • Characters and Series
Prize Winners • Crossover Authors • Further Reading • Websites

H

Sophie Hannah   1971-   Chick Lit
www.sophiehannah.com

Louise Candlish   Lori Lansens   Olivia Ryan
Alison Penton Harper   Laura Moriarty

Crime: Psychological

⚐ Charlie Zailer & Simon Waterhouse - CID

Mary Higgins Clark   Lesley Glaister   Jodi Picoult
Joy Fielding   Carol Goodman   Mary Stanley
Clare Francis   Frances Hegarty   Barbara Vine
Nicci French   Val McDermid   Minette Walters

Maeve Haran   1950-   Mature Chick Lit

Charlotte Bingham   Claudia Carroll   Sinead Moriarty
Claire Calman   Sarah Harrison

Duncan Harding   1926-2007   Sea: Modern
was Charles Whiting

Brian Callison   Nicholas Monsarrat   Justin Scott
James H Cobb   Dudley Pope   Terence Strong
Alexander Fullerton   Patrick Robinson   Peter Tonkin

John Harding   1951-   Lad Lit: Humour

James Delingpole   Tim Lott   Tony Parsons
Dave Eggers   John O'Farrell   Matt Whyman

Jules Hardy   1958-

Nicholas Evans   Lesley Glaister   Julie Myerson
Nicci Gerrard   Kazuo Ishiguro

Thomas Hardy   ⌒   1840-1928

Melvyn Bragg   Sarah Hall   Tim Pears
John Fowles   Jane Harris   Adam Thorpe
William Golding   D H Lawrence   Edith Wharton

Alison Penton Harper   Mature Chick Lit

Jenny Colgan   Kathy Lette   Sarah Tucker
Sophie Hannah   Chris Manby   Deborah Wright

H

Tom Harper
Adventure/Thriller

is Edwin Thomas
www.tom-harper.co.uk

Paul Christopher	A J Hartley	Paul Sussman
Richard Doetsch	Greg Loomis	Robyn Young
David Gibbins	Kate Mosse	

Historical: Medieval

🏃 Demetrios Askiates - C11th-C14th, The Crusades

Bernard Cornwell	Tim Severin	Jack Whyte
Simon Levack	Pip Vaughan-Hughes	

Charlaine Harris   1951-   US
Paranormal

is Charlaine Harris Schulz
www.charlaineharris.com

🏃 Sookie Stackhouse, Vampire

Lara Adrian	Laurell K Hamilton	Sherrilyn Kenyon
Kelley Armstrong	Lori Handeland	Robert Rankin
Patricia Briggs	Kim Harrison	Sara Reinke
Kerry Greenwood	Tanya Huff	J R Ward

Jane Harris
Historical

Vanora Bennett	Thomas Hardy	Katharine McMahon
Christie Dickason	Liz Jensen	Sarah Waters

Joanne Harris   🌉   1964-

www.joanne-harris.co.uk

Anthony Capella	Sue Monk Kidd	Michèle Roberts
Emma Donoghue	Sarah Kate Lynch	Barbara Trapido
Helen Fielding	Jojo Moyes	Salley Vickers
Lian Hearn	Lily Prior	Barbara Wood

H

Robert Harris   🌉   1957-
Adventure/Thriller

🏆 TGR 1993

Paul Adam	Brendan Dubois	Rebecca Pawel
Ronan Bennett	Joseph Kanon	Alex Scarrow
Murray Davies	Robert Littell	Guy Walters
Michael Dobbs	Glenn Meade	James Webb

Historical: Ancient

🏃 Cicero

Robert Graves	Steven Pressfield	Steven Saylor
Conn Iggulden	Mary Renault	Barry Unsworth

🌉 may be suitable for young adults

116

Rosie Harris   Wales   Saga
www.rosiebooks.co.uk   Wales and Liverpool

Anne Baker	Dilly Court	Meg Hutchinson
Anne Bennett	Katie Flynn	Kitty Neale
Benita Brown	Rosie Goodwin	Margaret Thornton
Catrin Collier	Iris Gower	Valerie Wood

Thomas Harris   1940-   US   Adventure/Thriller: Psychological
Dr Hannibal Lecter, Serial Killer • Clarice Starling, FBI

Chelsea Cain	Natsuo Kirino	Jonathan Nasaw
Thomas H Cook	Andrew Klavan	Thomas Perry
Michael Crichton	Cody McFadyen	Boston Teran
John Katzenbach	Michael Marshall	Tim Willocks

Colin Harrison   1960-   US   Adventure/Thriller

Jeffrey Archer	Phillip Margolin	Scott Turow
Michael Kimball	David Morrell	Tom Wolfe
Natsuo Kirino	John Sandford	

Cora Harrison   Crime: Historical - C16th
www.coraharrison.com   Judge Mara - Burren, Ireland

Alys Clare	Bernard Knight	Alexander McCall Smith
Ariana Franklin	Simon Levack	Peter Tremayne
Margaret Frazer	Ellis Peters	

Harry Harrison   1925-   US   Science Fiction: Humour
also writes as Felix Boyd, Frank Dempsey
www.harryharrison.com

Rob Grant	Robert A Heinlein	Robert Rankin
Colin Greenland	Tom Holt	Martin Scott
Joe Haldeman	Larry Niven	

Janis Harrison   US   Crime: Amateur sleuth
Bretta Solomon, Florist - 'River City', Missouri

M C Beaton	Patricia Harwin	Margaret Maron
Lilian Jackson Braun	Lis Howell	Keith Miles
Carolyn G Hart	Sharyn McCrumb	Gwen Moffat

Kate Harrison   Mature Chick Lit
www.kate-harrison.com

Lynne Barrett-Lee	Debby Holt	Adele Parks
Harriet Evans	Sinead Moriarty	Tina Reilly
Julia Holden	Elizabeth Noble	

H

Kim Harrison   US   Paranormal
www.kimharrison.net   ⚐ Rachel Morgan

| Patricia Briggs | Douglas Clegg | Charlaine Harris |
| Jim Butcher | Laurell K Hamilton | Kim Wilkins |

Sarah Harrison   1946-   Aga Saga
www.sarah-harrison.net

Charlotte Bingham	Maeve Haran	Wendy Perriam
Rose Boucheron	Susan Howatch	Rosie Thomas
Winston Graham	Imogen Parker	Grace Wynne-Jones

Stuart Harrison   Adventure/Thriller
www.stuartharrison.com

Alice Blanchard	Alan Judd	David Morrell
Nicholas Evans	Jonathan Kellerman	Stuart Woods
Greg Iles	Cormac McCarthy	

Cynthia Harrod-Eagles   1948-   Crime: Police work - UK
www.cynthiaharrodeagles.com   ⚐ DI Bill Slider - London

Gwendoline Butler	Gregory Hall	Barry Maitland
Deborah Crombie	Graham Ison	Andrew Taylor
Caro Fraser		

                                                                Historical
also writes as Elizabeth Bennett, Emma Woodhouse   ⚐ Morland Dynasty
🏆 Romantic 1993

Katharine Davies	Victoria Holt	Reay Tannahill
Sandra Gulland	Rosalind Laker	E V Thompson
Joanna Hines		

H Lilian Harry   1939-   Saga
also writes as Donna Baker,   Lyons Corner House Series ⎫
Nicola West   April Grove Series ⎬ Portsmouth
www.lilianharry.co.uk   'Burracombe' village, Devon

Elizabeth Daish	Beryl Matthews	Mary Jane Staples
Margaret Dickinson	Margaret Mayhew	June Tate
Audrey Howard	Victor Pemberton	

Donald Harstad   US   Crime: Police work - US
                      ⚐ Dep Sheriff Carl Houseman - Nation County, Iowa

Giles Blunt	J A Jance	Deon Meyer
C J Box	Ed McBain	Ridley Pearson
W E B Griffin	Michael McGarrity	Louise Penny
Tony Hillerman	Archer Mayor	Scott Smith

Carolyn G Hart 1936- US

Crime: Amateur sleuth

www.carolynhart.com ⚘ Annie Darling & Max Darling, Bookseller - 'Chastain', S Carolina

Lilian Jackson Braun	John Dunning	Marianne MacDonald
Simon Brett	Janis Harrison	Margaret Maron
Stephen Donaldson	Sharyn McCrumb	Barbara Vine

John Hart 1965- US

Crime: Legal/financial

www.johnhartfiction.com

William Bernhardt	John Grisham	George P Pelecanos
Edward Bunker	Matthew Klein	Patrick Quinlan
Stephen L Carter	Steve Martini	Scott Turow
James Ellroy	Brad Meltzer	Don Winslow

A J Hartley

Adventure/Thriller

www.ajhartley.net

Paul Christopher	Tom Harper	Kate Mosse
Richard Doetsch	Greg Loomis	

Caroline Harvey 1943-

Historical

is Joanna Trollope
www.joannatrollope.net

Philippa Gregory	Elizabeth Jeffrey	Robin Maxwell
Victoria Holt	Judith Lennox	Diana Norman

Jack Harvey 1960- Sco

Adventure/Thriller

is Ian Rankin
www.ianrankin.net

Christopher Brookmyre	David Martin	Terence Strong
Graham Hurley	David L Robbins	

John Harvey 1938-

Crime: Police work - UK

also writes as Terry Lennox, James Mann ⚘ DI Charlie Resnick - Nottingham
www.mellotone.co.uk DC Frank Elder, Retired policeman
🏆 Higham 1979 CWA 2004 & 2007

Robert Barnard	Clare Francis	Pauline Rowson
Glenn Chandler	Bartholomew Gill	Nicholas Royle
Chris Collett	Iain McDowall	Sally Spencer
Karin Fossum	Chris Paling	Camilla Way

Go to back for lists of
Pseudonyms • Authors by Genre • Characters and Series
Prize Winners • Crossover Authors • Further Reading • Websites

H

Patricia Harwin

Crime: Amateur sleuth

🏃 Catherine Penny - 'Far Wychwood', Cotswolds

M C Beaton
Agatha Christie
Carola Dunn

Janis Harrison
Catriona McPherson
Ann Purser

David Roberts
Jacqueline Winspear

John Harwood   1946-   Aus

Crime: Historical - C19th

Daphne Du Maurier
Carol Goodman
Susan Hill

Joan Lock
Barrie Roberts

Manda Scott
Sarah Waters

Louise Harwood

Chick Lit

Trisha Ashley
Jenny Colgan
Harriet Evans

Julia Holden
Belinda Jones
Julia Llewellyn

Kate Long
Sarah Mason

Anne Haverty   1959-   Ire

Historical

Clare Boylan
Tracy Chevalier

Emma Donoghue
Sandra Gulland

Helen Hollick
Sarah Waters

James Hawes   1960-   Wales

Humour

Christopher Brookmyre
Ben Elton
Kinky Friedman

Charles Higson
Zane Radcliffe

Tom Sharpe
Louisa Young

John Twelve Hawks

Adventure/Thriller

Sam Bourne
Paul Christopher

William Gibson
Raymond Khoury

George Orwell
Philip Pullman

Humphrey Hawksley   1964-

Adventure/Thriller

www.hhawksley.co.uk

Russell Andrews
James Clavell
Ken Follett

Greg Iles
Alan Judd

David Morrell
Tim Sebastian

Donna Hay

Chick Lit

www.donnahay.co.uk

Elizabeth Bailey
Zoë Barnes

Melissa Hill
Christina Jones
Dorothy Koomson

Sarah Mason
Jane Elizabeth Varley
Sarah Webb

H

Mo Hayder
www.mohayder.net/welcome.html

Crime: Psychological

♁ TGR 2002

☂ DI Jack Caffery - London

Ingrid Black
Robert Gregory Browne
Chelsea Cain
John Connolly

Daniel Hecht
Jilliane Hoffman
Jesse Kellerman
Natsuo Kirino

Jeff Lindsay
Richard Montanari
Steve Mosby
Michael Palmer

Elizabeth Haydon   US
www.elizabethhaydon.com

Fantasy: Epic

David Eddings
Alan Dean Foster
Lian Hearn

Anne McCaffrey
Fiona McIntosh

Juliet E McKenna
J R R Tolkien

Sparkle Hayter   1958-   Can
www.sparklehayter.com

Crime: Humour

☂ Robin Hudson, TV journalist - New York

Edna Buchanan
Stella Duffy
Liz Evans

Kinky Friedman
Lauren Henderson
Pauline McLynn

Sarah Strohmeyer
Valerie Wilson Wesley

Shirley Hazzard   1931-   US

Suzanne Berne
Jill Dawson
Nicci Gerrard

Lesley Glaister
Siri Hustvedt
Thomas Keneally

Anita Shreve
Gillian White

Lian Hearn   ⌒ ☺   1942-
is Gillian Rubenstein
www.lianhearn.com

Fantasy: Epic

Trudi Canavan
Joanne Harris
Elizabeth Haydon

Robin Hobb
William Nicholson
Garth Nix

Philip Pullman
J K Rowling

H

Daniel Hecht   US
www.danielhecht.com

Crime: Psychological

☂ Lucrezia 'Cree' Black, Parapsychologist

Carla Banks
Mo Hayder
Christiane Heggan
Alex Kava

Jonathan Kellerman
Sharyn McCrumb
Val McDermid
Jonathan Nasaw

Meg O'Brien
Erica Spindler
Stephen White
Derek Wilson

☺ also writes children's books

Peter J Heck   US   Crime: Historical - C19th
also writes jointly with Robert Asprin   ♁ Mark Twain, Amateur sleuth
www.sff.net/people/peter.heck

Arthur Conan Doyle   Peter Lovesey   Barrie Roberts
John Maclachlan Gray   Amy Myers   Norman Russell
Alanna Knight   David Pirie

Frances Hegarty   1949-   Crime: Psychological
also writes as Frances Fyfield
www.francesfyfield.co.uk

Jenny Diski   Sophie Hannah   Sally Spedding
Nicci French   Judith Kelman   Barbara Vine
Gregory Hall

Christiane Heggan   Fr   Crime: Romantic suspense

Daniel Hecht   Meg O'Brien   Sharon Sala
Tami Hoag   Karen Rose   Erica Spindler

Robert A Heinlein   1907-88   US   Science Fiction: Space and time
also wrote as Anson MacDonald
www.nitrosyncretic.com/rah

Brian W Aldiss   Philip K Dick   Jules Verne
Isaac Asimov   Joe Haldeman   John Wyndham
Ray Bradbury   Harry Harrison

Veronica Heley   1933-   Crime: Amateur sleuth
www.veronicaheley.com   ♁ Ellie Quicke • Bea Abbot - Abbot Agency

Simon Brett   Anthea Fraser   Betty Rowlands
Kate Charles   Lis Howell   Alexander McCall Smith
Clare Curzon   Marianne Macdonald   Jill Paton Walsh
Ruth Dudley Edwards   Ann Purser   Rebecca Tope

Joseph Heller   ⌒   1923-99   US

George Macdonald Fraser   Tim O'Brien   Philip Roth
John Irving   Thomas Pynchon   Leslie Thomas
Norman Mailer   Tom Robbins

Mandasue Heller   Crime: Hardboiled
                                                             Manchester

Massimo Carlotto   Roberta Kray   Val McDermid
Martina Cole   Lynda La Plante   Sheila Quigley
June Hampson   Kevin Lewis   John Rickards

H

Zoë Heller 1965-

Jill Dawson
Anne Fine
Nikki Gemmell

Joan Lingard
Valerie Martin
Clare Morrall

Julie Myerson
Ann Packer
Alice Sebold

Amanda Hemingway 1955- Fantasy

also writes as Jemma Harvey, Jan Siegel
www.amandahemingway.com

Sarah Ash
Susanna Clarke
Cecilia Dart-Thornton

Barbara Hambly
Robin Hobb
Guy Gavriel Kay

Fiona McIntosh
Patrick Rothfuss

Ernest Hemingway 1899-1961 US

www.hemingway.org

Joseph Conrad
F Scott Fitzgerald
Almudena Grandes

Norman Mailer
Nevil Shute
John Steinbeck

William Styron
Paul Theroux
Paul Watkins

Lauren Henderson 1966- Crime: Amateur sleuth

www.tartcity.com
Sam Jones, Sculptress - London

Linda Barnes
Stella Duffy
Sparkle Hayter

Pauline McLynn
Zoë Sharp

Gillian Slovo
Stella Whitelaw

Meg Henderson 1948- Sco Saga

Maggie Craig
Margaret Thomson Davis
Ruth Hamilton

Evelyn Hood
Meg Hutchinson

Gilda O'Neill
Frances Paige

Emily Hendrickson US Historical Romance

www.emilyhendrickson.net

Mary Balogh
Anne Barbour

Marion Chesney
Georgette Heyer

Stephanie Laurens
Fenella-Jane Miller

Paul Henke Wales Adventure/Thriller

www.henke.co.uk

Clive Cussler
Jon Evans
Duncan Falconer

Frederick Forsyth
Joseph Garber
Jean-Christophe Grangé

Wilbur Smith
Terence Strong

H

123

Veronica Henry
www.veronicahenry.co.uk
Mature Chick Lit

Judy Astley	Helen Fielding	Jill Mansell
Elizabeth Bailey	Rachel Johnson	Sinead Moriarty
Jilly Cooper	Marian Keyes	Tasmina Perry

Philip Hensher   1965-
🏆 S Maugham 1997

Jeffrey Archer	John Lanchester	Muriel Spark
William Boyd	James Robertson	Evelyn Waugh
Michael Dobbs	Tom Sharpe	

Brian Herbert   1947-   US
also writes jointly with Kevin J Anderson
www.dunenovels.com
Science Fiction: Space opera
Dune Saga

Brian W Aldiss	Colin Greenland	Terry Pratchett
Kevin J Anderson	Frank Herbert	Kristine Kathryn Rusch
David Brin	Christopher Paolini	Charles Stross

Frank Herbert   1920-86   US
www.frankherbert.net
Science Fiction: Space opera

Brian W Aldiss	Brian Herbert	Christopher Paolini
Kevin J Anderson	Ursula K Le Guin	Adam Roberts
David Brin	Larry Niven	Sheri S Tepper

James Herbert   1943-
Horror

Richard Bachman	Stephen King	Bentley Little
Stephen Gallagher	Dean R Koontz	Phil Rickman
Peter James	Stephen Laws	

Richard Herman   1939-   US
Adventure/Thriller

Dale Brown	Graham Hurley	David Morrell
James H Cobb	Greg Iles	Bill Napier
Stephen Coonts	Michael Kimball	Justin Scott

Anne Herries
is Linda Sole
www.lindasole.co.uk
Historical

Elizabeth Bailey	Jean Plaidy	E V Thompson
Elizabeth Chadwick	Reay Tannahill	Alison Weir
Diana Norman		

H

David Hewson 1953-
www.davidhewson.com

Crime: Police work - Italy
🯅 Det Nic Costa & Gianni Peroni - Rome

Andrea Camilleri	Magdalen Nabb	James Rollins
Michael Dibdin	Barbara Nadel	Daniel Silva
Donna Leon	Martin O'Brien	Fred Vargas

Georgette Heyer ⌒ 1902-74

Historical Romance: C19th

Elizabeth Aston	Anne Barbour	Fenella-Jane Miller
Jane Austen	Elizabeth Chadwick	Diana Norman
Elizabeth Bailey	Emily Hendrickson	Amanda Quick
Mary Balogh	Stephanie Laurens	Julia Quinn

Carl Hiaasen ⌒ ☺ 1953- US

Crime: Humour
Florida

www.carlhiaasen.com
🏆 CWA 1992

Robert G Barrett	Tim Dorsey	Shane Maloney
Christopher Brookmyre	Peter Guttridge	Zane Radcliffe
Peter Corris	Douglas Lindsay	Donald Westlake

Jack Higgins ⌒ ☺ 1929-

Adventure/Thriller
🯅 Sean Dillon

also writes as Martin Fallon, James Graham, Hugh Marlowe
is Harry Patterson

Harold Coyle	W E B Griffin	Jim Thompson
Daniel Easterman	Graham Hurley	Brad Thor
Colin Forbes	Stephen Leather	Eric Van Lustbader
Tom Gabbay	Craig Thomas	James Webb

Julie Highmore

Aga Saga

www.juliehighmore.com

Raffaella Barker	Rebecca Gregson	Robin Pilcher
Susannah Bates	Rachel Johnson	Bernadette Strachan
Susie Boyt	Chris Manby	Marcia Willett
Sarah Challis	Elizabeth Noble	Isabel Wolff

H

Patricia Highsmith ⌒ 1921-95 US

Crime: Psychological
🯅 Tom Ripley - London

also wrote as Clare Morgan
www.kirjasto.sci.fi/highsm.htm

Karin Alvtegen	Jeff Lindsay	Robert Louis Stevenson
Gianrico Carofiglio	Gabrielle Lord	Neil White
Douglas Kennedy	Patrick Quinlan	Stuart Woods

☺ also writes children's books

125

Lynn Hightower　1956-　US

also writes as Lynn S Hightower
www.lynnhightower.com

Crime: Police work - US
⚘ Det Sonora Blair - Cincinnati

Patricia D Cornwell	Thomas Laird	Kathy Reichs
Meg Gardiner	Michael Malone	Jess Walter
Tami Hoag	Theresa Monsour	

Charles Higson　⌒ ☺　1958-

Humour

Joseph Connolly	Colin Forbes	James Hawes
Ben Elton	Stephen Fry	Alexei Sayle
James Follett		

Dave Hill

Susan Hill	William Trevor
Sam Holden	Matt Whyman

Elizabeth Ann Hill

Saga

Rosemary Aitken	Connie Monk	E V Thompson
Gloria Cook	Sheila Newberry	Nicola Thorne
Elizabeth Jeffrey		

Jane Hill　US

www.janehill.co.uk

Crime: Psychological

Nicci French	Danuta Reah	Gillian White
Val McDermid	Minette Walters	Laura Wilson
Sarah Rayne	Camilla Way	

Melissa Hill　Ire

www.melissahill.info

Chick Lit

Clare Dowling	Alison Jameson	Anita Notaro
Imogen Edwards-Jones	Cathy Kelly	Geraldine O'Neill
Donna Hay	Monica McInerney	Morag Prunty

Reginald Hill　⌒　1936-

also writes as Dick Morland, Patrick Ruell,
Charles Underhill
www.randomhouse.com/features/reghill
🏆 CWA 1990

Crime: Police work - UK
⚘ DS Pascoe & DI Dalziel - Yorkshire
Joe Sixsmith, PI - Luton

Glenn Chandler	Lesley Horton	Iain McDowall
Geraldine Evans	Graham Hurley	Brian McGilloway
Georgie Hale	Bill James	Louise Penny
Susan Hill	Ken McCoy	Charles Todd

Susan Hill 1942-

www.susan-hill.com

🏆 JLR 1972   Whitbread 1972

Virginia Andrews	John Harwood	Kate Morton
Sara Donati	Dave Hill	Ann Patchett
Daphne Du Maurier	Jennifer Johnston	Peter Temple
Jane Gardam	Penelope Lively	William Trevor

Crime: Police work - UK

🚶 DCI Simon Serrailler - 'Lafferton'

Kate Charles	Elizabeth George	P D James
Deborah Crombie	Reginald Hill	Sarah Rayne
Judith Cutler		

Tobias Hill   1970-   Adventure/Thriller

Martin Amis	Paul Christopher	Ian Rankin
J G Ballard	Tim Lott	Will Self
Peter Carey		

Tony Hillerman   1925- US   Crime: Police work - US

🚶 Jim Chee & Joe Leaphorn - Navajo Reservation, Arizona

Nevada Barr	Donald Harstad	Michael Malone
C J Box	J A Jance	Deon Meyer
James Lee Burke	Sharyn McCrumb	Eliot Pattison
Robert Ferrigno	Michael McGarrity	Alexander McCall Smith

Joanna Hines   1949-   Adventure/Thriller: Psychological

www.joannahines.co.uk

Nicci French	Lesley Glaister	Minette Walters
Frances Fyfield	Carol Goodman	Gillian White

Historical

Daphne Du Maurier	Philippa Gregory	Susanna Kearsley
Winston Graham	Cynthia Harrod-Eagles	

Victoria Hislop

www.victoriahislop.com

Louis de Bernières	Lori Lansens	Ann Patchett
Kim Edwards	Mary Lawson	Alice Sebold
John Fowles	Valerie Martin	Gail Tsukiyama

may be suitable for young adults

Tami Hoag
1959- US

Crime: Psychological

www.tamihoag.com

🚶 Elena Estes, ex-Cop, now horse trainer
Det Sam Kovac & Tinks Liska, Minneapolis Police Dept

Carla Banks	Christiane Heggan	Meg O'Brien
Chelsea Cain	Lynn Hightower	Karen Rose
Leonard Goldberg	Iris Johansen	Jenny Siler
Heather Graham	Maile Meloy	Stephen White

Robin Hobb
1952- US

Fantasy: Epic

is Megan Lindholm
www.robinhobb.com

Joe Abercrombie	Cecilia Dart-Thornton	Tom Lloyd
Sarah Ash	Jude Fisher	Scott Lynch
Carol Berg	Lian Hearn	Fiona McIntosh
James Clemens	Amanda Hemingway	Karen Miller

Peter Hoeg
1957- Den

🏆 CWA 1994

Jostein Gaarder	Henning Mankell	Jane Smiley
David Guterson	Haruki Murakami	Jane Urquhart
Stuart M Kaminsky	Annie Proulx	

Alice Hoffman
1952- US

www.alicehoffman.com

Michael Collins	Janette Turner Hospital	Jacquelyn Mitchard
Candida Crewe	Sue Monk Kidd	Bella Pollen
Katharine Davies	William Kowalski	Anna Quindlen
A M Homes	Alice McDermott	Lisa Tucker

H

Jilliane Hoffman
US

Crime: Legal/financial

www.jillianehoffman.com

🚶 C J Townsend, State Attorney - Miami

Robert Gregory Browne	Mo Hayder	Richard Montanari
Chelsea Cain	Alex Kava	Karin Slaughter
Tess Gerritsen	Jesse Kellerman	P J Tracy
John Grisham	J A Kerley	Scott Turow

Craig Holden
US

Crime: Legal/financial

www.craigholden.com

David Baldacci	E L Doctorow	Lisa Scottoline
Stephen L Carter	F Scott Fitzgerald	Scott Turow
Linda Davies	John Grisham	

Julia Holden
Mature Chick Lit

Kate Harrison	Rachel Johnson	Tina Reilly
Louise Harwood	Sophie Kinsella	Robyn Sisman
Debby Holt	Carmen Reid	Sarah Tucker

Sam Holden
Lad Lit

Mark Barrowcliffe	Sophie King	Tony Parsons
Mike Gayle	David Nicholls	Matt Whyman
Dave Hill		

Wendy Holden 1965-
Chick Lit

also writes as Taylor Holden
www.taylorholden.co.uk

Melissa Bank	Carmen Reid	Cathy Woodman
Lucy Diamond	Daisy Waugh	Deborah Wright
Bella Pollen	Isabel Wolff	Liz Young

Robert Holdstock 1948-
Fantasy: Literary

also writes as Robert Black, Ken Blake, Chris Carlsen, Robert Faulcon, Richard Kirk
www.robertholdstock.com
🏆 BSFA 1984 & 1988

Marion Zimmer Bradley	Graham Joyce	Tim Powers
Charles de Lint	Guy Gavriel Kay	Gene Wolfe

Linda Holeman 1949- Can
Historical

www.lindaholeman.com

Kim Edwards	Cormac McCarthy	Jojo Moyes
Ken Follett	Mark Mills	Lisa See
Khaled Hosseini		

James Holland
War: Modern

🏃 Sgt Jack Tanner - WW2

Frank Barnard	James Delingpole	Robert Radcliffe
Elizabeth Darrell	David Fiddimore	

Helen Hollick 1953-
Historical

www.helenhollick.net

🏃 Arthurian Trilogy

Marion Zimmer Bradley	Stephen Hunt	Sharon Penman
Barbara Erskine	Stephen R Lawhead	Mary Stewart
Anne Haverty		

Alan Hollinghurst 1954-

🏆 S Maugham 1989   Black 1994   Man Booker 2004

Gilbert Adair	Patrick Gale	Edward St Aubyn
Michael Cunningham	Armistead Maupin	Edmund White

Andrew Holmes   Humour

David Baddiel	Magnus Mills	Nigel Williams
David Nobbs	Keith Waterhouse	R D Wingfield

Joyce Holms   Sco   Crime: Amateur sleuth

www.joyceholms.com   🏃 Fizz Fitzgerald & Tam Buchanan, Legal student & lawyer
Edinburgh

David Ashton	Gerald Hammond	Betty Rowlands
M C Beaton	Hazel Holt	Rebecca Tope
Natasha Cooper	Quintin Jardine	Jill Paton Walsh
Liz Evans	M R D Meek	Stella Whitelaw

Anne Holt   1958-   Nor   Crime: Police work - Norway

🏃 Supt Yngvar Stubo & Johanna Vik - Oslo

Karin Alvtegen	Kjell Eriksson	Henning Mankell
K O Dahl	Mari Jungstedt	Jo Nesbo
Ake Edwardson		

Debby Holt   Mature Chick Lit

www.debbyholt.co.uk

Katie Fforde	Sophie King	Jill Mansell
Kate Harrison	Debbie Macomber	Robyn Sisman
Julia Holden		

H

Hazel Holt   1928-   Crime: Amateur sleuth

www.hazelholt.co.uk   🏃 Sheila Malory - 'Taviscombe'

Caroline Carver	Lis Howell	Catherine Sampson
Jo Dereske	Alison Joseph	Dorothy L Sayers
Ann Granger	Marianne Macdonald	Dorothy Simpson
Joyce Holms	Ann Purser	Rebecca Tope

Tom Holt   📞   1961-   Fantasy: Humour

www.tom-holt.com

Douglas Adams	Craig Shaw Gardner	Christopher Moore
Robert Asprin	Rob Grant	Robert Rankin
George Macdonald Fraser	Harry Harrison	Martin Scott

(continues on next page)

Tom Holt (continued)   Humour

Jasper Fforde   Tom Sharpe   Nigel Williams
Garrison Keillor   Sue Townsend   P G Wodehouse
David Nobbs

Victoria Holt 1906-93   Historical: Romantic suspense
also wrote as Philippa Carr, Jean Plaidy; was Eleanor Alice Burford Hibbert

Catherine Coulter   Cynthia Harrod-Eagles   Sara Hylton
Sara Donati   Caroline Harvey   Claire Lorrimer
Melanie Gifford   Harriet Hudson

A M Homes 1961- US
www.amhomesbooks.com

Ron Butlin   Catherine Ryan Hyde   Hilary Mantel
Kim Edwards   Lori Lansens   Henry Sutton
Jonathan Franzen   Mary Lawson   Jonathan Trigell
Alice Hoffman   Cormac McCarthy   Jonathan Tropper

Ann Hood US   Aga Saga
www.annhood.us

Elizabeth Berg   Catherine Ryan Hyde   Sue Miller
Patricia Gaffney   Kate Jacobs   Elizabeth Noble
Gail Godwin

Evelyn Hood 1936- Sco   Saga
www.evelynhood.co.uk   Scotland

Maggie Bennett   Gwen Kirkwood   Mary Withall
Maggie Craig   Linda Sole   Valerie Wood
Meg Henderson

H

Christopher Hope 1944- SA
♈ Higham 1981   Whitbread 1984

William Boyd   J M Coetzee   Pamela Jooste
André Brink   Damon Galgut   Amos Oz
Justin Cartwright   Nadine Gordimer   Richard Powers

Billy Hopkins 1928-   Saga
www.billysbooks.info

Philip Boast   Freda Lightfoot   Lynda Page
Harry Bowling   Annie Murray   Victor Pemberton
Melvyn Bragg

Rachel Hore
www.rachelhore.co.uk

Aga Saga

Annabel Dilke	Sara MacDonald	Robin Pilcher
Elizabeth Edmondson	Chris Manby	Daisy Waugh
Kate Long		

Shifra Horn   Isr
www.shifra-horn.com/index2.php

Isabel Allende	Doris Lessing	Salman Rushdie
Laura Esquivel	Rohinton Mistry	Célestine Hitiura Vaite

Nick Hornby   ☎ ☺ 1957-

Lad Lit

www.nickhornby.net

Guy Bellamy	Matt Dunn	David Nicholls
Paul Burke	Niall Griffiths	John O'Farrell
James Delingpole	Andrey Kurkov	Ben Richards
Glen Duncan	Mil Millington	Matt Whyman

Una Horne

Saga
NE England

Rita Bradshaw	Catherine Cookson	Wendy Robertson
Irene Carr	Elizabeth Gill	Janet MacLeod Trotter
Jean Chapman		

Babs Horton   1953-

Crime: Psychological

www.babshorton.co.uk

Sarah Diamond	Margaret Murphy	Liz Rigbey
Mark Mills	Sarah Rayne	Carol Smith

Lesley Horton

Crime: Police work - UK
🏃 DI Handford & DS Khalid Ali - Bradford, Yorkshire

www.lesleyhorton.co.uk

Ann Cleeves	Patricia Hall	David Lawrence
John Connor	Reginald Hill	Iain McDowall
Georgie Hale	Graham Hurley	Nick Oldham

David Hosp   1970- US

Adventure/Thriller
🏃 Scott Finn, Attorney - Boston

www.davidhosp.com

Alex Barclay	John T Lescroart	Peter Spiegelman
Mark Gimenez	Cody McFadyen	P J Tracy
J A Kerley	Richard North Patterson	

H

Janette Turner Hospital 1942- Aus
www.janetteturnerhospital.com

Robert Drewe
Alice Hoffman
Thomas Keneally

David Malouf
Toni Morrison

Michèle Roberts
Salman Rushdie

Khaled Hosseini 1965- Afg
www.khaledhosseini.com

Chinua Achebe
Chimamanda Ngozi Adichie
Thalassa Ali
Niccolo Ammaniti

Nadeem Aslam
Abdulrazak Gurnah
Linda Holeman
Ruth Prawer Jhabvala

Yasmina Khadra
Daniel Mason
Rohinton Mistry
Carlos Ruiz Zafón

Audrey Howard 1929- Saga
Liverpool & Lancashire

🏆 Romantic 1988
Anne Baker
Katie Flynn
Adèle Geras

Elizabeth Gill
Rosie Goodwin
Lilian Harry

Sue Sully
Valerie Wood

Elizabeth Jane Howard 1923-

Rachel Billington
Rose Boucheron
Victoria Clayton
Annabel Dilke

John Galsworthy
Eileen Goudge
Sandra Howard
Angela Huth

Charlotte Moore
Rosamunde Pilcher
Anna Quindlen
Anthony Trollope

Linda Howard 1950- US Crime: Romantic suspense
is Linda S Howington

Beverly Barton
Allison Brennan
Julie Garwood

Heather Graham
Lisa Jackson
Judith McNaught

J D Robb
Nora Roberts
Sharon Sala

Richard Howard War: Historical
🏃 Sgt Alain Lausard - C18th French Dragoon • Bonaparte Series

Bernard Cornwell
Philip McCutchan
Allan Mallinson

Patrick O'Brian
Patrick Rambaud
Simon Scarrow

John Wilcox
Robyn Young

Sandra Howard 1941- Aga Saga

Diana Appleyard
Michael Dobbs
Adèle Geras

Elizabeth Jane Howard
Eve Makis
Elizabeth Noble

Rosy Thornton
Joanna Trollope

133

Susan Howatch 1940-   Saga
Church of England Series • St Benet's Trilogy

Daphne Du Maurier	Susanna Kearsley	Kate Tremayne
Sarah Harrison	Sue Sully	Anthony Trollope

Lis Howell   Crime: Amateur sleuth
☂ Suzy Spencer & Robert Clark, Norbridge Chronicles

M C Beaton	Ann Granger	Katherine John
Kate Charles	Janis Harrison	Louise Penny
Ruth Dudley Edwards	Veronica Heley	Ann Purser
Caroline Graham	Hazel Holt	Patricia Wentworth

Harriet Hudson 1938-   Saga
is Amy Myers
www.amymyers.net

Elizabeth Daish	Lesley Pearse	Audrey Willsher
Victoria Holt	Margaret Pemberton	T R Wilson
Sara Hylton	Marcia Willett	Sally Worboyes

Tanya Huff 1957- Can   Horror
☂ Henry Fitzroy & Vicki Nelson, PI

Kelley Armstrong	Christine Feehan	Holly Lisle
Keri Arthur	Laurell K Hamilton	Richard Matheson
Poppy Z Brite	Charlaine Harris	Sara Reinke
Mary Janice Davidson	Jeanne Kalogridis	J R Ward

C C Humphreys   Can   Historical
www.cchumphreys.com   ☂ Jack Absolute - C18th
Jean Rombaud, Executioner - C16th England

Bernard Cornwell	John Pilkington	Peter Tonkin
Patricia Finney	C J Sansom	John Wilcox
Philip Gooden	Martin Stephen	

Stephen Hunt   Fantasy: Myth

Alma Alexander	Helen Hollick	Scarlett Thomas
Susanna Clarke	Stephen R Lawhead	Gene Wolfe
G W Dahlquist		

Gwen Hunter 1956- US   Adventure/Thriller
also writes as Gary Hunter   ☂ Dr Rhea Lynch - South Carolina
www.gwenhunter.com

Virginia Andrews	Stephen Hunter	Paullina Simons
Beverly Barton	Sharon Sala	Lisa Tucker

H

Stephen Hunter
1946- US · Adventure/Thriller

| Tom Gabbay | Chris Ryan | Paullina Simons |
| Gwen Hunter | John Sandford | James Webb |

Graham Hurley
1946- · Adventure/Thriller

www.grahamhurley.co.uk

Geoffrey Archer	W E B Griffin	Jack Higgins
Dale Brown	Jack Harvey	Christopher Nicole
Lee Child	Richard Herman	Chris Ryan

Crime: Police work - UK
🏃 DI Joe Faraday - Portsmouth

Paul Charles	Lesley Horton	Peter Robinson
Robert Edric	Peter James	Pauline Rowson
Georgie Hale	Quintin Jardine	Michelle Spring
Reginald Hill	Iain McDowall	Peter Temple

Gregg Hurwitz
1973- US · Adventure/Thriller

www.gregghurwitz.net

David Baldacci	Brian Freeman	Patrick Lennon
Linwood Barclay	Scott Frost	Michael Robotham
Harlan Coben	Mark Gimenez	

Marion Husband

www.marionhusband.com

| Patrick Gale | Robin Jenkins |
| Andrew Greig | Robert Radcliffe |

Siri Hustvedt
1955- US

Jeffrey Eugenides	Jhumpa Lahiri	Zadie Smith
Nicci Gerrard	Salman Rushdie	Tim Winton
Shirley Hazzard	Anita Shreve	

Meg Hutchinson
1933- · Saga

also writes as Margaret Astbury · Birmingham

Maggie Bennett	Meg Henderson	Annie Murray
Rita Bradshaw	Gwen Kirkwood	Jessica Stirling
Sara Fraser	Elisabeth McNeill	Rowena Summers
Rosie Harris	Gwen Madoc	Audrey Willsher

H

Go to back for lists of
Pseudonyms • Authors by Genre • Characters and Series
Prize Winners • Crossover Authors • Further Reading • Websites

Angela Huth 1938-

Elizabeth Buchan	Shena Mackay	Alan Titchmarsh
Katharine Davies	Margaret Mayhew	Louise Tondeur
Elizabeth Jane Howard	Deborah Moggach	Mary Wesley

Shaun Hutson 1958- Horror
www.shaunhutson.com

Simon Clark	Mark Morris	John Saul
Richard Laymon	Christopher Pike	Whitley Strieber
Bentley Little	Phil Rickman	Koji Suzuki

Aldous Huxley 1894-1963

Margaret Atwood	D H Lawrence	Anthony Powell
Ray Bradbury	George Orwell	Kurt Vonnegut
Liz Jensen		

Catherine Ryan Hyde US
www.cryanhyde.com

Mitch Albom	Elisabeth Hyde	Jodi Picoult
A M Homes	Lori Lansens	Anita Shreve
Ann Hood	Kate Morton	

Elisabeth Hyde US Crime: Psychological
www.elisabethhyde.com

Jeff Abbott	Catherine Ryan Hyde	Jodi Picoult
Anita Diamant	Kazuo Ishiguro	Lionel Shriver
Jessica Duchen		

Sara Hylton Saga

Victoria Holt	Claire Lorrimer	Mary Jane Staples
Harriet Hudson	Margaret Pemberton	Danielle Steel
Elizabeth Lord	Judith Saxton	

Conn Iggulden 1971- Historical: Ancient
www.connigguiden.com
Julius Caesar • Genghis Khan

Stephen Baxter	Robert Harris	Manda Scott
Lindsey Davis	Christian Jacq	Tim Severin
Michael Curtis Ford	William Napier	Jack Whyte
Robert Graves	Scott Oden	Robyn Young

Greg Iles
1960- US — Adventure/Thriller
www.gregiles.com

Linwood Barclay	Richard Herman	Kyle Mills
John Gilstrap	Alan Judd	Christopher Nicole
Stuart Harrison	Robert Ludlum	Matthew Reilly
Humphrey Hawksley	Glenn Meade	Robert Ryan

Arnaldur Indridason
1961- Ice — Crime: Police work - Iceland
ぇ Insp Erlendur Sveinsson & Sigurdur Oli - Reykjavik
♛ CWA 2005

Karin Alvtegen	Kjell Eriksson	Deon Meyer
David Ashton	Karin Fossum	Jo Nesbo
Kate Atkinson	Matti Joensuu	Yrsa Sigurdardottir
Ake Edwardson	Mari Jungstedt	Maj Sjöwall & Per Wahlöö

Hammond Innes
1913-1998 — Adventure/Thriller
was Ralph Hammond-Innes

Jon Cleary	Nicholas Monsarrat	Nevil Shute
Alexander Fullerton	James Pattinson	Peter Tonkin
Alistair MacLean	Douglas Reeman	

Michael Innes
1906-94 Sco — Crime: Police work - UK
was John Innes Mackintosh Stewart
ぇ DI John Appleby - London

Malcolm Bradbury	Jill Paton Walsh	Neil White
Dorothy L Sayers	Patricia Wentworth	Jacqueline Winspear

Ian Irvine
1950- Aus — Fantasy: Epic
www.ian-irvine.com

Stephen Donaldson	Jude Fisher	Juliet E McKenna
David A Drake	Terry Goodkind	Freda Warrington
David Eddings	Robert Jordan	

John Irving
1942- US

Jonathan Coe	Larry McMurtry	Tom Robbins
Joseph Heller	Rick Moody	John Updike
William Kowalski	Tim O'Brien	Tom Wolfe
Terry McMillan	Thomas Pynchon	Tobias Wolff

Kazuo Ishiguro
1954- Ja
♛ Holtby 1982   Whitbread 1986   Booker 1989

Michelle de Kretser	Jules Hardy	Michael Ondaatje
Ronald Frame	Elisabeth Hyde	Adam Thorpe
Arthur Golden	Patrick McGrath	Gail Tsukiyama
Andrew Sean Greer	Timothy Mo	

Graham Ison

www.grahamison.co.uk

Crime: Police work - UK

⚷ DI Brock & DS Poole
DI Hardcastle & DS Charles Marriott - WWI } London

Paul Charles	Cynthia Harrod-Eagles	Michael Pearce
Barbara Cleverly	Maureen O'Brien	Anne Perry
Martha Grimes	Robin Paige	Charles Todd

Lee Jackson

www.victorianlondon.org

Crime: Historical - C19th

⚷ Insp Decimus Webb - London

James McGee	Andrew Martin	Iain Pears
Edward Marston	Fidelis Morgan	Anne Perry

Lisa Jackson   US

is Susan Lynn Crose
www.lisajackson.com

Crime: Romantic suspense

Beverly Barton	Heather Graham	Sharon Sala
Allison Brennan	Linda Howard	Karin Slaughter
Sandra Brown	J D Robb	

Anna Jacobs   Aus

also writes as Sherry-Anne Jacobs, Shannah Jay
www.annajacobs.com

Saga

⚷ Annie Gibson - Lancashire
Kershaw Sisters

Julia Bryant	Dilly Court	Penny Jordan
Irene Carr	Katharine Davies	Maureen Lee
Catrin Collier	Elizabeth Elgin	Elizabeth Murphy
Alexandra Connor	Katie Flynn	Annie Murray

Kate Jacobs   Can

www.katejacobsbooks.com

Aga Saga

Rowan Coleman	Gil McNeil	Jennifer Weiner
Ann Hood	Sue Miller	Jane Yardley

I
J

Howard Jacobson   1942-

⚟ Wingate 2000 & 2007

Malcolm Bradbury	Michael Frayn	Frederic Raphael
Michael Chabon	David Grossman	Tom Sharpe
Edward Docx	Amos Oz	Adam Thirlwell

Christian Jacq   1947-   Fr

also writes as J B Livingstone

Historical: Ancient
Egypt

Jean M Auel	Colleen McCullough	Manda Scott
Margaret George	Valerio Massimo Manfredi	Wilbur Smith
Conn Iggulden	Steven Pressfield	Robyn Young

138

Bill James   1929-   Wales   Crime: Hardboiled

also writes as David Craig,   DCI Colin Harpur & ACC Desmond Iles - Wales
Judith James; is James Tucker   Simon Abelard, Intelligence Officer

Jeffrey Ashford	Reginald Hill	David Peace
Ken Bruen	Simon Kernick	Mark Timlin
Martin Edwards		

Erica James   1960-

Romantic 2006

Amanda Brookfield	Cathy Kelly	Ann Purser
Lucy Clare	Jojo Moyes	Rebecca Shaw
Jan Karon	Melissa Nathan	Rosy Thornton

Henry James   1843-1916   US

Joseph Conrad	W Somerset Maugham	Muriel Spark
E M Forster	Iris Murdoch	Edith Wharton

P D James   1920-   Crime: Police work - UK

Supt Adam Dalgleish, DI Kate Miskin
& Sgt Francis Benton-Smith • Cordelia Gray, PI } London

CWA 1971, 1975 & 1986

Jane Adams	Brian Cooper	Susan Hill
Vivien Armstrong	Ake Edwardson	Morag Joss
Kate Charles	Kate Ellis	Guillermo Martinez
Jodi Compton	Elizabeth George	M R D Meek

Peter James   1948-   Crime: Police work - UK

www.peterjames.com   DS Roy Grace - Brighton

Simon Beckett	Graham Hurley	Martin O'Brien
Mark Billingham	David Lawrence	Peter Robinson
Benjamin Black	Stuart MacBride	Pauline Rowson
W J Burley	Iain McDowall	Neil White

Horror

Richard Bachman	Stephen Gallagher	Stephen King
Jeremy Dyson	James Herbert	Paul Magrs

Alison Jameson   Ire

Melissa Bank	Nicci Gerrard	Jacquelyn Mitchard
Jill Barnett	Tessa Hadley	Laura Moriarty
Therese Fowler	Melissa Hill	Freya North

may be suitable for young adults

J

J A Jance 1944- US

is Judith Ann Jance
www.jajance.com

Crime: Police work - US

🚶 Det J P Beaumont - Seattle
Sheriff Joanna Brady - Bisbee ⎫
Alison Reynolds, ex-TV Journalist ⎭ Arizona

Mary Higgins Clark	J A Kerley	Richard Montanari
G M Ford	Ed McBain	Robert B Parker
Donald Harstad	Michael McGarrity	Dana Stabenow
Tony Hillerman	Claire McNab	Ayelet Waldman

Quintin Jardine 1945- Sco

also writes as Matthew Reid
www.quintinjardine.com

Crime: Police work - UK

🚶 DCC Bob Skinner - Edinburgh
Oz Blackstone & Primavera Phillips

Glenn Chandler	Allan Guthrie	Frederic Lindsay
Michael Dobbs	Joyce Holms	Stuart MacBride
Gillian Galbraith	Graham Hurley	Brian McGilloway
Alex Gray	Paul Johnston	Craig Russell

Michael Jecks 1960-

also writes as The Medieval Murderers
(with Philip Gooden, Susanne Gregory,
Bernard Knight, Ian Morson, C J Sansom)
www.michaeljecks.co.uk

Crime: Historical - Medieval

🚶 Sir Baldwin Furnshill & Simon Puttock, Bailiff
C14th Devon

Simon Beaufort	Susanna Gregory	Caroline Roe
Paul Doherty	Bernard Knight	Kate Sedley
Ariana Franklin	Pat McIntosh	Peter Tonkin
Margaret Frazer	Ellis Peters	Pip Vaughan-Hughes

Elizabeth Jeffrey

is Olive Whaley

Saga

Margaret Dickinson	Jeannie Johnson	Beryl Kingston
Caroline Harvey	Penny Jordan	Mary Mackie
Elizabeth Ann Hill	Margaret Kaine	Robin Maxwell

Roderic Jeffries 1926-

also writes as Peter Alding, Jeffrey Ashford,
Roderic Graeme, Graham Hastings

Crime: Police work - Spain

🚶 DI Enrique Alvarez - Mallorca

Catherine Aird	Manuel Vázquez Montalbán	Rebecca Pawel
José Latour	Magdalen Nabb	Michael Pearce
Donna Leon		

J

Robin Jenkins 1912-2005 Sco

Ronald Frame	Andrew Greig	Andrew O'Hagan
Maurice Gee	Marion Husband	James Robertson
		Alan Spence

Liz Jensen 1959-

www.lizjensen.com

Kate Atkinson	Jason Goodwin	Aldous Huxley
Joseph Connolly	Andrew Sean Greer	Graham Joyce
Jill Dawson	Jane Harris	George Orwell

Lisa Jewell 1968- Chick Lit

www.lisa-jewell.co.uk
🏆 Nathan 2008

Susannah Bates	Belinda Jones	Paige Toon
Rebecca Campbell	Julia Llewellyn	Daisy Waugh
Fiona Gibson	Josie Lloyd & Emlyn Rees	Liz Young
Jane Green	Clare Naylor	Laura Zigman

Ruth Prawer Jhabvala 1927- Ger

🏆 Booker 1975

Anita Desai	Khaled Hosseini	Paul Scott
E M Forster	V S Naipaul	Carolyn Slaughter
Abdulrazak Gurnah		

Ha Jin 1956- China

Alma Alexander	Anchee Min	Lisa See
Roopa Farooki	Qiu Xiaolong	Amy Tan
Xiaolu Guo	Richard Russo	Mario Vargas Llosa

Matti Joensuu 1948- Fin Crime: Police work - Finland

🏃 Sgt Timo Harjunpaa - Helsinki

Ann Cleeves	Arnaldur Indridason	Jo Nesbo
Ake Edwardson	Mari Jungstedt	Yrsa Sigurdardottir
Kjell Eriksson	Henning Mankell	

Iris Johansen 1938- US Crime: Forensic

www.irisjohansen.com
🏃 Eve Duncan, Forensic sculptor
Sarah Patrick & Monty, Search & rescue worker & dog

Max Allan Collins	Carol Goodman	Keith McCarthy
Patricia D Cornwell	Tami Hoag	Erica Spindler
Lisa Gardner	Judith Kelman	

Katherine John 1948- Wales Crime: Police work - UK

is Catrin Collier
🏃 Sgt Trevor Joseph
www.katherinejohn.com

Catherine Aird	Lis Howell	Leslie Thomas
Steve Berry	Adrian Magson	Peter Turnbull
John Grisham	Nicholas Rhea	R D Wingfield

J

Denis Johnson   1949-   US

Trezza Azzopardi	Don DeLillo	Christopher Koch
Ron Butlin	Glen Duncan	Thomas Pynchon
Michael Chabon	Nathan Englander	Philip Roth
Joseph Conrad	Graham Greene	Jonathan Trigell

Jeannie Johnson   Saga

www.jeanniejohnson.net

Elizabeth Bailey	Elizabeth Jeffrey	Freda Lightfoot
Margaret Dickinson	Joan Jonker	Carol Rivers
June Francis	Maureen Lee	Mary Jane Staples

Milly Johnson   Chick Lit

www.millyjohnson.co.uk

Sherry Ashworth	Jenny Colgan	Jill Mansell
Maria Beaumont	Jane Green	Carole Matthews
Rowan Coleman	Marian Keyes	Sheila O'Flanagan

Rachel Johnson   Mature Chick Lit

www.racheljohnson.co.uk

Maggie Alderson	Judith Gould	Marian Keyes
Nicholas Coleridge	Veronica Henry	Sophie King
Jilly Cooper	Julie Highmore	Julia Llewellyn
Fiona Gibson	Julia Holden	Maile Meloy

Jennifer Johnston   1930-   Ire

♀ Authors 1973   Whitbread 1979

Rose Doyle	Joan Lingard	Edna O'Brien
Anne Enright	Shena Mackay	Colm Toibin
Susan Hill	Eoin McNamee	William Wall
Nell Leyshon	Valerie Martin	Niall Williams

Paul Johnston   1957-   Sco   Crime: PI

www.paul-johnston.co.uk   ⚐ Quintilian Dalrymple - C21st Edinburgh
Alex Mavros, PI - Greece • Matt Wells, Author - London

♀ CWA 1997

Eric Brown	Jonathan Kellerman	Paul J McAuley
Chelsea Cain	Douglas Lindsay	J D Robb
Quintin Jardine		

J

Go to back for lists of
Pseudonyms • Authors by Genre • Characters and Series
Prize Winners • Crossover Authors • Further Reading • Websites

Belinda Jones 1967- Chick Lit

http://web.mac.com/divabelinda

Louise Harwood
Lisa Jewell
Carole Matthews

Melissa Nathan
Morag Prunty
Victoria Routledge

Paige Toon
Daisy Waugh
Lauren Weisberger

Christina Jones 1948- Chick Lit

www.christinajones.co.uk

Louise Bagshawe
Claire Calman
Jilly Cooper

Anne Dunlop
Donna Hay
Kathy Lette

Sheila Norton
Anita Notaro
Plum Sykes

Gwyneth Jones 1952- Science Fiction: Near future

also writes as Ann Halam

http://homepage.ntlworld.com/gwynethann

🏆 Arthur C Clarke 2002

Steve Aylett
Sara Douglass
Mary Gentle

Ian McDonald
Geoff Ryman
Neal Stephenson

Sheri S Tepper
Liz Williams

J V Jones 1963- Fantasy: Epic

www.jvj.com

Kate Elliott
David Farland
Maggie Furey

Katherine Kurtz
Christopher Paolini
Kristine Kathryn Rusch

Steph Swainston
Freda Warrington

Lloyd Jones 1955- NZ

🏆 McKitterick 2005   Commonwealth 2007

Murray Bail
Nicola Barker
Peter Carey

Patrick Gale
Kate Grenville
Barbara Kingsolver

Matthew Kneale
Christopher Koch
Gerard Woodward

Joan Jonker 1923-2007 Saga

Liverpool

Lyn Andrews
Benita Brown
Alexandra Connor

Elizabeth Daish
Margaret Dickinson
Jeannie Johnson

Penny Jordan
Maureen Lee
Sharon Owens

Pamela Jooste 1946- SA

Justin Cartwright
J M Coetzee
Giles Foden

Damon Galgut
Nadine Gordimer
Christopher Hope

Doris Lessing
Paul Scott

J

143

Penny Jordan 1946-   Saga

also writes as Caroline Courtney, Annie Groves, Lydia Hitchcock, Melinda Wright
is Penelope Jones Halsall

Barbara Delinsky	Joan Jonker	Judith McNaught
Anna Jacobs	Margaret Kaine	Una-Mary Parker
Elizabeth Jeffrey	Jayne Ann Krentz	

Robert Jordan 1948-2007 US   Fantasy: Epic

also wrote as Chang Lung, Regan O'Neal, Jackson O'Reilly, Regan O'Reilly
was James Oliver Rigney, Jr

Ashok K Banker	Andrew McGahan	Sean Russell
Louise Cooper	John Marco	J R R Tolkien
David Farland	Robert Newcomb	Jane Welch
Ian Irvine	Stan Nicholls	Janny Wurts

Alison Joseph 1958-   Crime: Amateur sleuth

⚥ Sister Agnes Bourdillon, Nun

Marian Babson	Jonathan Gash	Hazel Holt
William Brodrick	Elizabeth George	Morag Joss
Elizabeth Ferrars	Andrew M Greeley	Marianne Macdonald

Morag Joss   Crime: Psychological

⚥ Sara Selkirk, Cellist - Bath

🏆 CWA 2003

Hilary Bonner	Alison Joseph	Fiona Mountain
Gregory Hall	Marianne Macdonald	Sarah Rayne
P D James	Guillermo Martinez	Ruth Rendell

Graham Joyce 1954-   Fantasy: Dark

www.grahamjoyce.net

🏆 British Fantasy 1993, 1996, 1997 & 2000

Jonathan Carroll	Liz Jensen	Scott Nicholson
Christopher Fowler	David Martin	Phil Rickman
Robert Holdstock	Mark Morris	

James Joyce 1882-1941 Ire

Martin Amis	D H Lawrence	Vladimir Nabokov
Dermot Bolger	John McGahern	Virginia Woolf
William Faulkner	Iris Murdoch	

Alan Judd
1946-   Adventure/Thriller

     🚶 Charles Thoroughgood

🏆 Guardian 1991   Holtby 1992

John Fullerton	Humphrey Hawksley	Andy McNab
Joseph Garber	Greg Iles	Daniel Silva
Stuart Harrison	John Le Carré	

Mari Jungstedt
1962-   Swe   Crime: Police work - Sweden

🚶 CI Anders Knutas - Gotland, Sweden • Det Karin Jacobsson

Karin Alvtegen	Anne Holt	Jo Nesbo
Ake Edwardson	Arnaldur Indridason	Hakan Nesser
Kjell Eriksson	Matti Joensuu	Yrsa Sigurdardottir
Karin Fossum	Åsa Larsson	Maj Sjöwall & Per Wahlöö

Ismail Kadare
1936-   Alb

🏆 Man Booker Int 2005

John Banville	George Orwell	Bernhard Schlink
Gabriel Garcia Márquez	Orhan Pamuk	Rachel Seiffert
James Meek		

Margaret Kaine
Saga

www.margaretkaine.com   1950s Staffordshire potteries

🏆 Sagittarius 2003

Benita Brown	Freda Lightfoot	Elizabeth Murphy
Elizabeth Jeffrey	Claire Lorrimer	Sharon Owens
Penny Jordan	Gwen Madoc	Lesley Pearse

Jeanne Kalogridis
1954-   US   Historical

also writes as J M Dillard
www.jeannekalogridis.com

Suzannah Dunn	Tanya Huff	Anne Rice
Posie Graeme-Evans	Katharine McMahon	Dan Simmons
Laurell K Hamilton		

Stuart M Kaminsky
1934-   US   Crime: Historical - C20th

www.stuartkaminsky.com

🚶 Toby Peters - 1940s Hollywood
Insp Porfiry Rostnikov, Police - Moscow
Abe Lieberman, Police - Chicago

J
K

Raymond Chandler	Michael Gregorio	Peter Hoeg
James Hadley Chase	David Guterson	Philip Kerr
James Ellroy	Dashiell Hammett	Rosemary Martin

Susan Kandel   US   Crime: Amateur sleuth
www.susankandel.com   ⚑ Cece Caruso, Writer - Los Angeles

Gilbert Adair	M C Beaton	Carola Dunn
James Anderson	Agatha Christie	Jacqueline Winspear

Joseph Kanon   1946-   US   Adventure/Thriller
www.josephkanon.com

Ronan Bennett	John Lawton	Robert Ryan
Dan Fesperman	John Le Carré	Alex Scarrow
Robert Harris	Henry Porter	Robert Wilson

Manju Kapur   Ind

Kavita Daswani	Amulya Malladi	Preethi Nair
Patricia Duncker	Nisha Minhas	Carolyn Slaughter
Sharon Maas	Anita Nair	

Jan Karon   1937-   US
is Janice Meredith Wilson   Mitford Series - USA
www.mitfordbooks.com

Maeve Binchy	Garrison Keillor	Miss Read
Fannie Flagg	Joan Medlicott	Rebecca Shaw
Erica James	Ann Purser	Adriana Trigiani

John Katzenbach   1950-   US   Adventure/Thriller
www.johnkatzenbach.com

Russell Andrews	Jeffery Deaver	Dean R Koontz
Michael Connelly	Thomas Harris	Stephen White

Alex Kava   US   Crime: Psychological
www.alexkava.com   ⚑ Maggie O'Dell, FBI Agent

Robert Gregory Browne	J A Kerley	Susan R Sloan
Daniel Hecht	Jonathan Nasaw	Erica Spindler
Jilliane Hoffman	Meg O'Brien	Lisa Tucker
Jonathan Kellerman	Jenny Siler	Stephen White

Guy Gavriel Kay   1954-   Can   Fantasy: Epic
www.brightweavings.com

R Scott Bakker	Amanda Hemingway	Greg Keyes
Mark Chadbourn	Robert Holdstock	J R R Tolkien
Charles de Lint	Katharine Kerr	Jane Welch

Jackie Kay 1961- Sco

🏆 Guardian 1998

Janice Galloway	Marge Piercy	Virginia Woolf
A L Kennedy	Ali Smith	Alan Warner
Andrew O'Hagan	Alan Spence	

Louise Kean 1974- Chick Lit

Jane Green	Serena Mackesy	Kathleen Tessaro
Marian Keyes	Anna Maxted	Kate Thompson
Julia Llewellyn	Tasmina Perry	Cathy Woodman

Paul Kearney 1967- Ire Fantasy: Epic

www.paulkearneyonline.com

Stephen Donaldson	Maggie Furey	Stephen R Lawhead
Kate Elliott	David Gemmell	Harry Turtledove
Raymond E Feist		

Susanna Kearsley 1966- Can

also writes as Emma Cole
www.susannakearsley.com

Daphne Du Maurier	Susan Howatch	Nora Roberts
Robert Goddard	James Long	Mary Stewart
Joanna Hines		

H R F Keating 1926- Crime: Police work - UK

also writes as Evelyn Hervey

🚶 Insp Ghote - Bombay
DS Harriet Martens - 'Greater Birchester'

🏆 CWA 1980

Jason Goodwin	Magdalen Nabb	Georges Simenon
Lynda La Plante	Michael Pearce	Janwillem van de Wetering
Priscilla Masters		

Garrison Keillor 1942- US Humour

is Gary Edward Keillor

Richard Ford	Jan Karon	Richard Russo
Elizabeth Gaskell	Lorna Landvik	Miriam Toews
Tom Holt	Armistead Maupin	

Faye Kellerman 1952- US Crime: Police work - US

www.fayekellerman.net

🚶 Lt Pete Decker, Officer Cindy Decker & Rina Lazarus -
Los Angeles • DS Romulus Poe - Las Vegas

Jan Burke	Ed McBain	Jefferson Parker
Joy Fielding	Carol O'Connell	Ridley Pearson

Jesse Kellerman   1978-   US   Crime: Police work - US
www.jessekellerman.com

Karin Alvtegen	Mo Hayder	Jeff Lindsay
Tess Gerritsen	Jilliane Hoffman	Phillip Margolin

Jonathan Kellerman   1949-   US   Crime: Police work - US
www.jonathankellerman.com   ☆ Det Milo Sturgis & Alex Delaware, Psychologist - Los Angeles • Det Petra O'Connor - Hollywood

John Connolly	Paul Johnston	James Patterson
Robert Ellis	Alex Kava	Ridley Pearson
Stuart Harrison	Jonathan Nasaw	Erica Spindler
Daniel Hecht	Jefferson Parker	Stephen White

Cathy Kelly   ⌒   Ire   Chick Lit
www.cathy-kelly.com
🏆 Romantic 2001

Catherine Alliott	Melissa Hill	Kate O'Riordan
Judy Astley	Erica James	Patricia Scanlan
Zoë Barnes	Josie Lloyd & Emlyn Rees	Linda Taylor
Clare Dowling	Geraldine O'Neill	Kate Thompson

Jim Kelly   Crime: Amateur sleuth
☆ Philip Dryden, Journalist - Ely, Cambridgeshire
🏆 CWA 2006

Jo Dereske	G M Ford	Peter Robinson
Martin Edwards	Ed O'Connor	Chris Simms
R J Ellory	Ruth Rendell	Michelle Spring

Sheelagh Kelly   Saga
☆ Feeney Family - Yorkshire • Prince Family

Helen Cannam	Maureen Lee	Liz Ryan
Beryl Kingston	D M Purcell	Patricia Shaw
Mary A Larkin	Elvi Rhodes	

Susan B Kelly   1955-   Crime: Police work - UK
also writes as Susan Kelly   ☆ DCI Nick Trevellyan & Alison Hope
Supt Gregory Summers - Thames Valley

Vivien Armstrong	Natasha Cooper	Veronica Stallwood
Paul Charles	Colin Dexter	Charles Todd

Go to back for lists of
Pseudonyms • Authors by Genre • Characters and Series
Prize Winners • Crossover Authors • Further Reading • Websites

James Kelman   1946-   Sco

🏆 Black 1989   Booker 1994

Des Dillon	A L Kennedy	Alan Warner
Michel Faber	Caryl Phillips	Irvine Welsh
Alasdair Gray		

Judith Kelman   1945-   US   Adventure/Thriller

www.jkelman.com

Virginia Andrews	Frances Hegarty	Fiona Mountain
Joy Fielding	Iris Johansen	Hilary Norman
Carol Goodman		

Thomas Keneally   1935-   Aus

also writes as William Coyle

🏆 Booker 1982

Peter Carey	Maurice Gee	Brian Moore
E L Doctorow	Shirley Hazzard	Julian Rathbone
Robert Drewe	Janette Turner Hospital	Adam Thorpe
Charles Frazier	Andrew McGahan	Tim Winton

A L Kennedy   1965-   Sco

is Alison Louise Kennedy
www.alkennedy.co.uk

🏆 S Maugham 1994   Encore 1996   Costa 2007

Ron Butlin	Michel Faber	Alasdair Gray
Amanda Craig	Ronald Frame	Jackie Kay
Glen Duncan	Janice Galloway	James Kelman

Douglas Kennedy   1955-   US   Adventure/Thriller

🏆 TGR 1998

Nicholas Coleridge	Andrew Klavan	Michael Taylor
F G Cottam	Richard North Patterson	Paul Watkins
Patricia Highsmith	Lionel Shriver	Stuart Woods

Alexander Kent   ☺   1924-   Sea: Historical

is Douglas Reeman   🚶 Richard Bolitho • Adam Bolitho
www.douglasreeman.com

Tom Connery	Alexander Fullerton	Patrick Rambaud
David Donachie	Jonathan Lunn	Peter Smalley
C S Forester	Philip McCutchan	Julian Stockwin

☺ also writes children's books

149

Gordon Kent   US   Adventure/Thriller

is Ken & Christian Cameron   ⚔ Alan Craik - US Naval Intelligence • Mike Dukas

James Barrington	W E B Griffin	John J Nance
Dale Brown	David Hagberg	Brad Thor
Tom Clancy	Charles McCarry	

Sherrilyn Kenyon   ⌒   1965-   US   Paranormal

also writes as Kinley MacGregor
www.sherrilynkenyon.com

Kelley Armstrong	Lori Handeland	Sara Reinke
Mary Janice Davidson	Charlaine Harris	J R Ward
Christine Feehan	Holly Lisle	

J A Kerley   US   Crime: Police work - US

also writes as Jack Kerley; is John Albert Kerley   ⚔ Det Carson Ryder - Southern States
www.jackkerley.com

Alex Barclay	David Hosp	Richard Montanari
Robert Gregory Browne	J A Jance	Chris Mooney
James Lee Burke	Alex Kava	Steve Mosby
Jilliane Hoffman	Cody McFadyen	Craig Russell

Simon Kernick   1966-   Crime: Hardboiled

www.simonkernick.com   ⚔ DI John Gallan & DS Tina Boyd - London

Jeff Abbott	Robert Edric	Barry Maitland
Anna Blundy	Joseph Finder	David Peace
Ken Bruen	Bill James	Mark Timlin

Jack Kerouac   ⌒   1922-69   US

Michel Faber	Larry McMurtry	Thomas Pynchon
Alex Garland	Ben Okri	John Steinbeck
Jay McInerney		

Katharine Kerr   ⌒   1944-   US   Fantasy: Myth

is Nancy Brahtin
www.deverry.com

Mark Chadbourn	Guy Gavriel Kay	Anne McCaffrey
Cecilia Dart-Thornton	Greg Keyes	Gregory Maguire
Kate Elliott	Stephen R Lawhead	Judith Tarr

⌒ may be suitable for young adults

Philip Kerr   1956-   Sco   Adventure/Thriller

www.pbkerr.com

Geoffrey Archer
Ronan Bennett
Michael Cordy
Michael Crichton

Robert Edric
Alan Furst
Stuart M Kaminsky
John Lawton

Carlo Lucarelli
Rebecca Pawel
Frank Tallis
Nigel West

Greg Keyes   1963-   US   Fantasy: Epic

www.gregkeyes.com

R Scott Bakker
James Barclay
Guy Gavriel Kay
Katharine Kerr

Stephen R Lawhead
Tim Lebbon
George R R Martin
Patrick Rothfuss

Brian Ruckley
Sean Russell
H G Wells
Tad Williams

Marian Keyes   1963-   Ire   Chick Lit

www.mariankeyes.com

🏆 Nathan 2007

Melissa Bank
Maria Beaumont
Hester Browne
Claudia Carroll

Rowan Coleman
Clare Dowling
Veronica Henry
Milly Johnson

Rachel Johnson
Louise Kean
Kate O'Riordan
Grace Wynne-Jones

Yasmina Khadra   1956-   Alg

is Mohammed Moulessehoul

Chinua Achebe
Thalassa Ali

Nadeem Aslam
Khaled Hosseini

Carlos Ruiz Zafón
Markus Zusak

Raymond Khoury   1960-   Leb   Adventure/Thriller: Historical

www.raymondkhoury.com

Sam Bourne
Dan Brown
John Case
Michael Cordy

John Twelve Hawks
Chris Kuzneski
Kate Mosse
Audrey Niffenegger

Arturo Pérez-Reverte
Matthew Reilly
James Robertson
Paul Sussman

Sue Monk Kidd   1948-   US

www.suemonkkidd.com

Connie May Fowler
Laurie Graham
Joanne Harris
Alice Hoffman

Barbara Kingsolver
Lorna Landvik
Jacquelyn Mitchard
Joyce Carol Oates

Ann Packer
Nicholas Sparks
Mary Stanley
Miriam Toews

151

Garry Kilworth ☎ ☺

War: Historical - C19th

also writes as Garry Douglas
www.garry-kilworth.com

🏃 Sgt 'Fancy' Jack Crossman - Crimea War

Roger Carpenter	Iain Gale	Simon Scarrow
Bernard Cornwell	Allan Mallinson	John Wilcox
George Macdonald Fraser		

Michael Kimball   1949-   US

Adventure/Thriller

www.michaelkimball.com/about.htm

David Guterson	Stephen King	Robert Ryan
Colin Harrison	David Morrell	John Sandford
Richard Herman	Christopher Nicole	Alex Scarrow

Haven Kimmel   US

www.havenkimmel.com

Jennifer Donnelly	Fannie Flagg	Adriana Trigiani
Leif Enger	Mary Lawson	Anne Tyler

Danny King   1969-

Crime: Humour

www.dannykingbooks.com

Mark Barrowcliffe	Joe R Lansdale	Malcolm Pryce
Colin Bateman	Douglas Lindsay	Mike Ripley

Jonathon King   US

Crime: Amateur sleuth

www.jonathonking.com

🏃 Max Freeman, Retired policeman - Florida

James Lee Burke	James W Hall	Michael Malone
Robert Ferrigno	Steve Hamilton	John Rickards

Laurie R King   1952-   US

Crime: Historical - C20th

also writes as Laurie King
www.laurieking.com

🏃 Sherlock Holmes & Mary Russell - C20th London
Det Kate Martinelli & Det A Hawkin - San Fransisco
Anne Waverley

Jan Burke	John Dunning	Claire McNab
Barbara Cleverly	Meg Gardiner	Robin Paige
Arthur Conan Doyle	Paula Gosling	Charles Todd

Sophie King

Mature Chick Lit

is Jane Bidder
www.sophieking.info

Louise Candlish	Rachel Johnson	Sarah Tucker
Sam Holden	Sophie Kinsella	Jane Wenham-Jones
Debby Holt	Adele Parks	Polly Williams

K

Stephen King 1947- US Horror

also writes as Richard Bachman
www.stephenking.com

The Dark Tower Series

🏆 British Fantasy 1999 & 2005

Douglas Clegg	Michael Kimball	Andrew Pyper
John Farris	Stephen Laws	John Saul
James Herbert	Tim Lebbon	Dan Simmons
Peter James	Gregory Maguire	T M Wright

Barbara Kingsolver 1955- US

www.kingsolver.com

Gail Anderson-Dargatz	Patricia Gaffney	Nicole Krauss
Kim Edwards	Jane Hamilton	Jacquelyn Mitchard
Louise Erdrich	Lloyd Jones	Kate Morton
Janet Fitch	Sue Monk Kidd	Amy Tan

Beryl Kingston 1931- Saga

www.berylkingston.co.uk

🏃 Easter Empire - London

Philip Boast	Elizabeth Jeffrey	Gilda O'Neill
Rose Boucheron	Sheelagh Kelly	Carol Rivers
Hilary Green	Sheila Newberry	June Tate

Sophie Kinsella 1969- Chick Lit

is Madeleine Wickham
www.sophiekinsella.co.uk

Melissa Bank	Meg Cabot	Eve Makis
Susannah Bates	Claudia Carroll	Sara Shepard
Maria Beaumont	Julia Holden	Kathleen Tessaro
Hester Browne	Sophie King	Laura Zigman

Natsuo Kirino 1951- Ja Adventure/Thriller

Andrew Sean Greer	Mo Hayder	Boris Starling
Thomas Harris	Stuart MacBride	P J Tracy
Colin Harrison	Haruki Murakami	Banana Yoshimoto

Gwen Kirkwood Saga

www.gwenkirkwood.co.uk

'Fiarlyden' Series - Scotland

Doris Davidson	Meg Hutchinson	Eileen Ramsay
Christine Marion Fraser	Elisabeth McNeill	Mary Withall
Evelyn Hood		

🏠 may be suitable for young adults

153

Andrew Klavan   1954-   US   Adventure/Thriller: Psychological

also writes as Keith Peterson   ⚐ Scott Weiss & Jim Bishop, PI - San Francisco
www.andrewklavan.com
♗ TGR 1996

Chaz Brenchley	Sharyn McCrumb	Tim Willocks
Thomas Harris	Scott Smith	Stuart Woods
Douglas Kennedy		

Matthew Klein   US   Crime: Hardboiled

www.matthewklein.org

Benjamin Black	Joseph Finder	Patrick Quinlan
Edward Bunker	John Hart	Peter Temple
James Ellroy	George P Pelecanos	Don Winslow

Matthew Kneale   1960-   Historical

♗ JLR 1992   Whitbread 2000

William Boyd	Margaret Elphinstone	James Robertson
Will Davenport	Lloyd Jones	Jane Stevenson
Robert Drewe	Julian Rathbone	Evelyn Waugh

Alanna Knight   1923-   Sco   Crime: Historical - C19th

www.alannaknight.com   ⚐ DI Jeremy Faro • Rose McQuinn - C19th Edinburgh
Tam Eildor - Jacobean Scotland

David Ashton	Joan Lock	David Pirie
Arthur Conan Doyle	Peter Lovesey	Norman Russell
Sara Fraser	Catriona McPherson	Catherine Shaw
Peter J Heck	Amy Myers	Martin Stephen

Bernard Knight   1931-   Wales   Crime: Historical - Medieval

also writes as The Medieval Murderers   ⚐ Sir John de Wolfe, 'Crowner John'
(with Philip Gooden, Susanne Gregory, Michael Jecks,   C12th Devon
Ian Morson, C J Sansom)
www.bernardknight.homestead.com

Alys Clare	Cora Harrison	Ian Morson
Paul Doherty	Michael Jecks	Sharan Newman
Susanna Gregory	Pat McIntosh	Kate Sedley

India Knight   1965-   Mature Chick Lit

Raffaella Barker	Gil McNeil	Adele Parks
Emily Barr	Anna Maxted	Daisy Waugh
Lucy Dawson	Clare Naylor	Isabel Wolff

Christopher Koch   1932-   Aus

Geraldine Brooks	Denis Johnson	Timothy Mo
Helen Dunmore	Lloyd Jones	Geoff Ryman

Dorothy Koomson   Chick Lit

www.dorothykoomson.co.uk

Trisha Ashley	Gil McNeil	Carmen Reid
Louise Candlish	Melissa Nathan	Kate Thompson
Donna Hay	Alexandra Potter	Grace Wynne-Jones

Dean R Koontz   1945-   US   Adventure/Thriller

also writes as Brian Coffey, Deanne Dwyer, K R Dwyer,
Leigh Nicols, Owen West, Aaron Wolfe
www.deankoontz.com

Richard Bachman	John Katzenbach	Richard Matheson
Robert Gregory Browne	Richard Laymon	John Saul
Stephen Gallagher	Robert McCammon	Koji Suzuki
James Herbert	Gregory Maguire	Tim Willocks

Gunnar Kopperud   1946-   Nor

J G Ballard	J M Coetzee	Paul Theroux
Pat Barker	Sebastian Faulks	

William Kowalski   1973-   US

www.williamkowalski.com

Karen Joy Fowler	Alice Hoffman	Jonathan Tropper
David Guterson	John Irving	Anne Tyler

Nicole Krauss   1974-   US

William Brodrick	Nathan Englander	Eva Rice
Hester Browne	Jonathan Safran Foer	Muriel Spark
Michael Chabon	Jonathan Franzen	Emma Tennant
Kim Edwards	Barbara Kingsolver	Barbara Trapido

Roberta Kray   Crime: Hardboiled

Massimo Carlotto	June Hampson	Kevin Lewis
Martina Cole	Mandasue Heller	Sheila Quigley

Go to back for lists of
Pseudonyms • Authors by Genre • Characters and Series
Prize Winners • Crossover Authors • Further Reading • Websites

155

Jayne Ann Krentz   1948-   US   Glitz & Glamour

also writes as Jayne Castle, Stephanie James, Amanda Quick
www.jayneannkrentz.com

Sandra Brown	Judith Gould	Judith McNaught
Candace Bushnell	Penny Jordan	Madge Swindells
Janet Dailey		

Hari Kunzru   1969-

www.harikunzru.com

🏆 Betty Trask 2002   S Maugham 2003

Peter Carey	Loren D Estleman	Zadie Smith
E L Doctorow	Janice Galloway	Meera Syal

Hanif Kureishi   🔗   1954-

www.hanifkureishi.com

🏆 Whitbread 1990

Monica Ali	Caryl Phillips	Meera Syal
Xiaolu Guo	Zadie Smith	Louisa Young
Armistead Maupin		

Andrey Kurkov   1961-   Rus   Crime: Humour

🏃 Lieut Viktor Slutsky - Russia & Ukraine

Boris Akunin	Michael Gregorio	Marina Lewycka
Tom Bradby	Peter Guttridge	Douglas Lindsay
Christopher Fowler	Nick Hornby	R N Morris

Katherine Kurtz   1944-   US   Fantasy: Epic

www.deryni.net

David Bilsborough	Michael Moorcock	Brian Ruckley
J V Jones	Melanie Rawn	Janny Wurts
Mercedes Lackey	Mickey Zucker Reichert	

Chris Kuzneski   1969-   US   Adventure/Thriller

🏃 Jonathon Payne & D J Jones, MANIAC Special Forces

Steve Berry	John Case	Kate Mosse
Sam Bourne	Michael Cordy	James Rollins
Dan Brown	Raymond Khoury	Paul Sussman

Lynda La Plante   🔗   1946-   Crime: Police work - US

🏃 DCI Jane Tennison • Supt Mike Walker • Lorraine Page, PI - Los Angeles
Det Anna Travis & DCI James Langton - London

Martina Cole	June Hampson	Sara Paretsky
John Connor	Mandasue Heller	Sheila Quigley
	H R F Keating	Medora Sale

Mercedes Lackey   1950-   US   Fantasy: Epic
www.mercedeslackey.com

Carol Berg	Tanith Lee	Elizabeth Moon
David Farland	Holly Lisle	Melanie Rawn
Barbara Hambly	Anne McCaffrey	Mickey Zucker Reichert
Katherine Kurtz	L E Modesitt Jr	R A Salvatore

Jhumpa Lahiri   1967-

Kavita Daswani	Roopa Farooki	Preethi Nair
Chitra Banerjee Divakaruni	Andrew Sean Greer	Thirty Umrigar
Edward Docx	Siri Hustvedt	
Leif Enger	Anita Nair	

Nick Laird   1975-   Ire
♛ Betty Trask 2006

Kingsley Amis	William Boyd	Zadie Smith
Kate Atkinson	David Lodge	

Thomas Laird   Crime: Police work - US
🏃 Det Jimmy Parisi - Chicago

Michael Connelly	Dennis Lehane	George P Pelecanos
Lynn Hightower	Carol O'Connell	Jess Walter

Deryn Lake   1937-   Crime: Historical - C18th
is Dinah Lampitt   🏃 John Rawlings, Apothecary - C18th London
www.derynlake.com

Gwendoline Butler	James McGee	Catherine Shaw
Janet Gleeson	Matthew Pearl	Rosemary Stevens
David Liss	Andrew Pepper	

Rosalind Laker   1925-   Historical
also writes as Barbara Paul; is Barbara Ovstedal
www.rosalindlaker.com

Elizabeth Chadwick	Winston Graham	Judith Lennox
Jean Chapman	Sandra Gulland	Edith Pargeter
Melanie Gifford	Cynthia Harrod-Eagles	Maureen Peters

John Lanchester   1962-
♛ Betty Trask 1996   Hawthornden 1997

Alan Bennett	Philip Hensher	Henry Sutton
Jonathan Coe	David Nicholls	Nigel Williams

Lorna Landvik 1954-

Elizabeth Berg	Garrison Keillor	Jojo Moyes
Fannie Flagg	Sue Monk Kidd	Richard Russo
Laurie Graham	Maile Meloy	Adriana Trigiani

L Joe R Lansdale 1951- US   Crime: Humour

www.joerlansdale.com

⚐ Hap Collins & Leonard Pine
Constable Sunset Jones - 1930s } Texas

Poppy Z Brite	Tim Dorsey	Danny King
Robert Crais	Loren D Estleman	Zane Radcliffe

Lori Lansens Can

Kim Edwards	A M Homes	Toni Morrison
Sophie Hannah	Catherine Ryan Hyde	Kate Morton
Victoria Hislop	Mary Lawson	John Steinbeck

Mary A Larkin 1935- Ire   Saga

is Mary A McNulty   Northern Ireland
www.marylarkin.co.uk

Lyn Andrews	Sheelagh Kelly	Victor Pemberton
Frank Delaney	Geraldine O'Neill	Miss Read
Rose Doyle	Sharon Owens	Denise Robertson

Åsa Larsson 1966- Swe   Crime: Police work - Sweden

⚐ Rebecka Martinsson, Lawyer

K O Dahl	Mari Jungstedt	Maj Sjöwall & Per Wahlöö
Ake Edwardson	Jo Nesbo	Minette Walters
Kjell Eriksson		

José Latour 1940- Cuba   Crime: Police work - Cuba

www.joselatourauthor.com   ⚐ Capt Trujillo - Havana

Luiz Alfredo Garcia-Roza	Elmore Leonard	Donald Westlake
Roderic Jeffries	Martin Cruz Smith	Don Winslow

Stephanie Laurens Aus   Historical Romance: C19th

www.stephanielaurens.com   ⚐ The Hon Barnaby Adair

Mary Balogh	Elizabeth Darrell	Fenella-Jane Miller
Anne Barbour	Emily Hendrickson	Julia Quinn
Marion Chesney	Georgette Heyer	

Stephen R Lawhead 1950- US Fantasy: Myth
www.stephenlawhead.com

C J Cherryh	Paul Kearney	Morgan Llywelyn
Helen Hollick	Katharine Kerr	Caiseal Mor
Stephen Hunt	Greg Keyes	Jane Welch

D H Lawrence 1885-1930
also wrote as Jessie Chambers, Lawrence H Davison

John Galsworthy	Thomas Hardy	James Joyce
Sarah Hall	Aldous Huxley	Alan Sillitoe

David Lawrence Crime: Psychological
is David Harsent ⚑ DS Stella Mooney - London

Vivien Armstrong	John Connor	Peter James
Lindsay Ashford	Lesley Horton	Stuart MacBride
Mark Billingham		

Stephen Laws 1952- Horror
www.stephenlaws.com

Ramsey Campbell	Richard Matheson	Phil Rickman
James Herbert	Christopher Pike	Peter Straub
Stephen King		

Mary Lawson Can
🏆 McKitterick 2003

Raffaella Barker	Victoria Hislop	Alice McDermott
William Brodrick	A M Homes	David Park
Joy Chambers	Haven Kimmel	Carol Shields
Jane Hamilton	Lori Lansens	Mary Stanley

John Lawton 1949- Crime: Police work - UK
⚑ CDS Frederick Troy - London

Ted Allbeury	Len Deighton	Joseph Kanon
Stephen J Cannell	Ken Follett	Philip Kerr
Jon Cleary	Alan Furst	Alex Scarrow

Richard Laymon 1947-2001 US Horror
also wrote as Richard Kelly, Carol Laymon

Clive Barker	Dean R Koontz	Christopher Pike
John Farris	Bentley Little	Koji Suzuki
Shaun Hutson	Scott Nicholson	T M Wright

John Le Carré 1931- Adventure/Thriller

is David John Moore Cornwell George Smiley, Spy
www.johnlecarre.com
CWA 1977 & 2005

Ronan Bennett	Charles Cumming	Joseph Kanon
William Bernhardt	Brian Freemantle	Charles McCarry
William Brodrick	Tom Gabbay	Kyle Mills
John Burdett	Alan Judd	Robin White

Ursula K Le Guin ☺ 1929- US Fantasy: Epic

www.ursulakleguin.com

Trudi Canavan	Christopher Paolini	Sheri S Tepper
Mary Gentle	Geoff Ryman	Sean Williams
Frank Herbert	Steph Swainston	Gene Wolfe
C S Lewis	Judith Tarr	Sarah Zettel

Stephen Leather Adventure/Thriller

www.stephenleather.com Dan 'Spider' Shepherd, Undercover cop

Geoffrey Archer	Jack Higgins	Tim Sebastian
Tom Bradby	James Long	Gerald Seymour
Harold Coyle		

Tim Lebbon 1969- Fantasy: Dark

www.timlebbon.net
British Fantasy 2007

Storm Constantine	Stephen King	Scott Lynch
Greg Keyes	Brian Lumley	Patrick Rothfuss

Harper Lee 1926- US

is Nelle Harper Lee
Pulitzer 1961

Suzanne Berne	Carson McCullers	J D Salinger
Pat Conroy	Toni Morrison	John Steinbeck
Jennifer Donnelly	Stewart O'Nan	Alice Walker

Maureen Lee Saga

www.maureenlee.co.uk Pearl Street - Liverpool
Romantic 2000

Lyn Andrews	Anna Jacobs	Sheelagh Kelly
Anne Baker	Jeannie Johnson	Margaret Mayhew
Ruth Hamilton	Joan Jonker	Elizabeth Murphy

may be suitable for young adults

Tanith Lee ⌒ ☺ 1947-

also writes as Esther Garber; is Tanith Lee Kaiine
www.tanithlee.com

Fantasy: Dark
Venus (Venice)

Dan Abnett	Ben Counter	Holly Lisle
Marion Zimmer Bradley	Cecilia Dart-Thornton	Freda Warrington
C J Cherryh	Mercedes Lackey	Liz Williams

Dennis Lehane 1965- US

www.dennislehane.com

Crime: Police work - US
🏃 Patrick Kenzie & Angie Gennaro - Boston, Mass

Michael Connelly	Magdalen Nabb	Andrew Pyper
John Connolly	Reggie Nadelson	John Sandford
G M Ford	James Patterson	John Shannon
Thomas Laird	Thomas Perry	Boston Teran

Patrick Lennon

www.patrick-lennon.com

Adventure/Thriller
🏃 PI Tom Fletcher - Cambridgeshire

David Baldacci	Brian Freeman	Gregg Hurwitz
Linwood Barclay	Brian Freemantle	Michael Robotham
R J Ellory	Mark Gimenez	

Judith Lennox 1953-

Saga

Diana Gabaldon	Rosalind Laker	Mary Stewart
Rosie Goodwin	Imogen Parker	Margaret Thornton
Caroline Harvey	Rosamunde Pilcher	

Donna Leon 1942- US

www.donnaleon.co.uk
🏆 CWA 2000

Crime: Police work - Italy
🏃 Commissario Guido Brunetti - Venice

Andrea Camilleri	David Hewson	Eliot Pattison
Gianrico Carofiglio	Roderic Jeffries	Qiu Xiaolong
Michael Dibdin	Carlo Lucarelli	Ronald Tierney
Luiz Alfredo Garcia-Roza	Magdalen Nabb	Fred Vargas

Elmore Leonard ⌒ 1925- US

www.elmoreleonard.com
🏆 CWA 2006

Crime: Hardboiled

Lawrence Block	Steve Hamilton	Mario Puzo
Tim Dorsey	José Latour	Patrick Quinlan
Kinky Friedman	Shane Maloney	Jason Starr
James W Hall	Thomas Perry	Donald Westlake

☺ also writes children's books

John T Lescroart   1948-   US   Crime: Legal/financial
www.johnlescroart.com   ☂ Dismas Hardy, Attorney - San Francisco
                                              Abe Glitsky, Policeman

William Bernhardt	Linda Fairstein	Steve Martini
Harry Bingham	James Grippando	Nancy Taylor Rosenberg
Stephen L Carter	David Hosp	Lisa Scottoline

Doris Lessing   ⌒   1919-
also writes as Jane Somers; is Doris Tayler
www.lessing.redmood.com

J M Coetzee	Shifra Horn	Iris Murdoch
Maggie Gee	Pamela Jooste	Gillian Slovo
Nadine Gordimer	Anne Michaels	Muriel Spark
Sarah Hall		

Kathy Lette   1958-   Aus   Chick Lit
www.kathylette.com

Sherry Ashworth	Alison Penton Harper	Alexandra Potter
Meg Cabot	Christina Jones	Sara Shepard
Fiona Gibson	Josie Lloyd & Emlyn Rees	Laura Zigman

Simon Levack   Crime: Historical - C16th
www.simonlevack.com   ☂ Yaotl, Slave youth - Mexico

Michael Clynes	Cora Harrison	Peter Tonkin
Paul Doherty	William Napier	Paul Watkins
Tom Harper		

Andrea Levy   ⌒   1956-
www.andrealevy.co.uk
🏆 Orange 2004   Whitbread 2004   Commonwealth 2005

Monica Ali	Pauline Melville	Meera Syal
Marina Lewycka	Caryl Phillips	Alex Wheatle
Ian McEwan	Zadie Smith	

C S Lewis   ⌒   ☺   1898-1963   Fantasy: Literary
was Clive Staples Lewis

Ursula K Le Guin	Dan Simmons	Jules Verne
Philip Pullman	J R R Tolkien	Sarah Zettel

Go to back for lists of
Pseudonyms • Authors by Genre • Characters and Series
Prize Winners • Crossover Authors • Further Reading • Websites

L

Kevin Lewis　1970-　　　Crime: Hardboiled
www.kevinlewisonline.com

Martina Cole	June Hampson	Roberta Kray
G M Ford	Mandasue Heller	Patrick Quinlan

Robert Lewis　　　Crime: Humour　L
♣ Robin Llewellyn, PI

Colin Bateman	Niall Griffiths	Malcolm Pryce
Christopher Brookmyre	Peter Guttridge	Ian Sansom
Jasper Fforde		

Roy Lewis　1933-　Wales　　　Crime: Amateur sleuth
also writes as J R Lewis, David Springfield　　♣ Arnold Landon, Archaeologist - Newcastle
Eric Ward, Solicitor - Tyneside
DI John Crow, Northumberland police

Paul Adam	John Malcolm	Catherine Sampson
Jeffrey Ashford	M R D Meek	Derek Wilson
Kate Ellis		

Susan Lewis　　　Glitz & Glamour
www.susanlewis.com

Louise Bagshawe	Judith Gould	Imogen Parker
Sally Beauman	Freya North	Danielle Steel

Marina Lewycka　1946-　　　Humour
🏆 Saga for Wit 2005

Mavis Cheek	Laura Marney	Eva Rice
Mark Haddon	Armistead Maupin	Alexei Sayle
Andrey Kurkov	Magnus Mills	Paul Torday
Andrea Levy	D B C Pierre	Carlos Ruiz Zafón

Nell Leyshon
www.nellleyshon.co.uk

Helen Dunmore	Penelope Lively
Jennifer Johnston	William Trevor

Freda Lightfoot　　　Saga
also writes as Marion Carr　　　Manchester
www.fredalightfoot.co.uk

Rita Bradshaw	Elizabeth Gill	Jeannie Johnson
Alexandra Connor	Ruth Hamilton	Margaret Kaine
Glenice Crossland	Billy Hopkins	Claire Lorrimer

163

Catherine Lim 1942- Sing
www.catherinelim.sg

Colin Cotterill	Anchee Min	Lisa See
Arthur Golden	Timothy Mo	Amy Tan

L Sue Limb ⌒ ☺ 1946- Humour
www.suelimb.com

Mavis Cheek	Allison Pearson	Arabella Weir
Kate Fenton	Sue Townsend	Louise Wener
Laurie Graham		

Douglas Lindsay 1964- Sco Crime: Humour
www.barney-thomson.com ⚐ Barney Thomson, Barber - Scotland

Colin Bateman	Carl Hiaasen	Danny King
Christopher Brookmyre	Paul Johnston	Andrey Kurkov
Tim Dorsey		

Frederic Lindsay 1933- Sco Crime: Police work - UK
⚐ DI Jim Meldrum - Scotland

Karen Campbell	Quintin Jardine	Peter Turnbull
Gillian Galbraith	Denise Mina	Louise Welsh
Alex Gray	Ian Rankin	

Jeff Lindsay 1952- US Crime: Psychological
⚐ Dexter Morgan, Policeman & serial killer

Karin Alvtegen	Patricia Highsmith	Chris Mooney
R J Ellory	Jesse Kellerman	P J Tracy
Mo Hayder	Cody McFadyen	Laura Wilson

Johanna Lindsey 1952- US Glitz & Glamour

Jude Deveraux	Una-Mary Parker	Jean Saunders
Lesley Lokko	Tasmina Perry	Madge Swindells
Fern Michaels	Katie Price	

Joan Lingard ⌒ ☺ 1932- Sco
www.joanlingard.co.uk

Anne Fine	Eileen Goudge	Bernard MacLaverty
Jane Gardam	Zoë Heller	Deborah Moggach
Sue Gee	Jennifer Johnston	Meg Rosoff

Elinor Lipman 1950- US
www.elinorlipman.com

Karen Joy Fowler	Curtis Sittenfeld	Rebecca Wells
Laurie Graham	Adriana Trigiani	Mary Wesley
Carol Shields		

Laura Lippman 1959- US Crime: PI
www.lauralippman.com
⚉ Tess Monaghan - Baltimore

Suzanne Berne	Carol Higgins Clark	Michael Gruber
Benjamin Black	Michael Collins	Theresa Monsour
Edna Buchanan	Jodi Compton	Susan R Sloan
Jan Burke	Richard Flanagan	Valerie Wilson Wesley

Holly Lisle 1960- US Fantasy: Epic
www.hollylisle.com

Marion Zimmer Bradley	Laurell K Hamilton	Mercedes Lackey
Kate Elliott	Tanya Huff	Tanith Lee
Simon Green	Sherrilyn Kenyon	

David Liss 1966- US Crime: Historical - C18th
www.davidliss.com
⚉ Benjamin Weaver, ex Pugilist

Gwendoline Butler	Michael Gregorio	Fidelis Morgan
Janet Gleeson	Deryn Lake	Derek Wilson

Toby Litt 🌥 1968-
www.tobylitt.com

Jake Arnott	Ian McEwan	Haruki Murakami
Colin Bateman	Alistair MacLeod	Tim Parks
David Flusfeder	Hilary Mantel	

Robert Littell 1935- US Adventure/Thriller
🏆 CWA 1973

Stephen J Cannell	Alan Furst	Charles McCarry
Nelson DeMille	Robert Harris	Glenn Meade
Ken Follett		

Bentley Little 1960- US Horror
also writes as Phillip Emmons

Clive Barker	Shaun Hutson	Scott Nicholson
Simon Clark	Richard Laymon	Dan Simmons
James Herbert	Mark Morris	

Penelope Lively ☎ ☺ 1933-

www.penelopelively.co.uk

🏆 Booker 1987

Rachel Billington	Sue Gee	Charlotte Mendelson
A S Byatt	Susan Hill	Louise Voss
Penelope Fitzgerald	Nell Leyshon	Meg Wolitzer

Julia Llewellyn   Mature Chick Lit

Cecelia Ahern	Lisa Jewell	Melissa Nathan
Lucy Dawson	Rachel Johnson	Carmen Reid
Louise Harwood	Louise Kean	Olivia Ryan

Sam Llewellyn ☎ ☺ 1948-   Adventure/Thriller

www.samllewellyn.com

Eoin Colfer	Philip McCutchan	Justin Scott
Bernard Cornwell	Dudley Pope	Peter Tonkin

Tom Lloyd 1979-   Fantasy: Epic

www.tomlloyd.co.uk

Joe Abercrombie	David Gemmell	Scott Lynch
Stephen Donaldson	Robin Hobb	Karen Miller
Raymond E Feist		

Josie Lloyd & Emlyn Rees   Chick Lit

Rebecca Campbell	Kathy Lette	Sue Margolis
Lisa Jewell	Serena Mackesy	Isabel Wolff
Cathy Kelly	Chris Manby	Cathy Woodman

Morgan Llywelyn 1937- Ire   Historical

also writes as Shannon Lewis

Marion Zimmer Bradley	Diana Norman	Sharon Penman
Charles de Lint	Edith Pargeter	Judith Tarr
Stephen R Lawhead		

Joan Lock   Crime: Historical - C19th

www.joanlock.co.uk   🚶 DI Ernest Best - Victorian London

John Harwood	Peter Lovesey	Norman Russell
Alanna Knight	Anne Perry	M J Trow

☎ may be suitable for young adults

David Lodge 1935-

Hawthornden 1975   Whitbread 1980

Kingsley Amis	Nick Laird	Leslie Thomas
Tim Binding	Stanley Middleton	Paul Torday
Malcolm Bradbury	John Mortimer	Keith Waterhouse
Michael Frayn	Alan Sillitoe	Evelyn Waugh

L

Lesley Lokko 1964-   Sco   Glitz & Glamour

www.lesleylokko.com

Louise Bagshawe	Jackie Collins	Tasmina Perry
Tilly Bagshawe	Johanna Lindsey	Penny Vincenzi
Sally Beauman	Fern Michaels	

James Long   Adventure/Thriller

also writes as Will Davenport

Stephen J Cannell	Frederick Forsyth	Susanna Kearsley
Will Davenport	Diana Gabaldon	Stephen Leather

Kate Long   Aga Saga

www.katelong.co.uk

Amanda Brookfield	Sarah Grazebrook	Anna Maxted
Marika Cobbold	Rebecca Gregson	Robin Pilcher
Anne Doughty	Louise Harwood	Joanna Trollope
Anne Fine	Rachel Hore	Marcia Willett

Greg Loomis   US   Adventure/Thriller

www.greggloomis.com

Dan Brown	Michael Gruber	A J Hartley
Paul Christopher	Tom Harper	Kate Mosse
Richard Doetsch		

Elizabeth Lord   Saga
London

Harry Bowling	Sara Hylton	Elizabeth Waite
Pamela Evans	Mary Jane Staples	Jeanne Whitmee

Gabrielle Lord 1946-   Aus   Crime: PI
PI Gemma Lincoln - Sydney

www.gabriellelord.com

Peter Corris	Karin Slaughter	Peter Temple
Patricia Highsmith	Carol Smith	Minette Walters
S J Rozan	Michelle Spring	

Claire Lorrimer   1921-   Saga
also writes as Beatrice Coogan, Patricia Robins   ⚲ Rochford Family
www.clairelorrimer.com

Victoria Holt	Freda Lightfoot	Miss Read
Sara Hylton	Connie Monk	Barbara Whitnell
Margaret Kaine	Victor Pemberton	Janet Woods

Tim Lott   1956-
www.timlott.co.uk
🏆 Whitbread 1999

Matt Beaumont	Alex Garland	Kevin Sampson
Neil Cross	John Harding	William Sutcliffe
Stephen Fry	Tobias Hill	

James Lovegrove   1965-   Science Fiction: Near future
www.jameslovegrove.com

J G Ballard	Eric Brown	Michael Marshall Smith
John Birmingham	John Meaney	Neal Stephenson

Peter Lovesey   1936-   Crime: Historical - C19th & Police - UK
also writes as Peter Lear   ⚲ Sgt Cribb & PC Thackeray - C19th England
www.peterlovesey.com   Peter Diamond, Police - C20th Bath
🏆 CWA 1978, 1982, 1995, 1996 & 2000

Rhys Bowen	Peter J Heck	Amy Myers
Gyles Brandreth	Alanna Knight	Andrew Pepper
Sara Fraser	Joan Lock	Norman Russell
John Maclachlan Gray	Andrew Martin	Catherine Shaw

Shari Low   1968-   Chick Lit
www.sharilow.com

Rebecca Campbell	Kate O'Riordan	Paige Toon
Clare Dowling	Andrea Semple	Sarah Webb
Sabine Durrant	Linda Taylor	

Carlo Lucarelli   1960-   It   Crime: Police work - Italy
⚲ Insp Grazia Negro, Fascist period - Bologna • Comm De Luca, Milan

Andrea Camilleri	Philip Kerr	Magdalen Nabb
Michael Dibdin	Donna Leon	

Go to back for lists of
Pseudonyms • Authors by Genre • Characters and Series
Prize Winners • Crossover Authors • Further Reading • Websites

Robert Ludlum

🔖 1927-2001　US　　　　Adventure/Thriller

also wrote as Jonathan Ryder, Michael Shepherd

Covert-One Series

www.ludlumbooks.com

🏃 Jason Bourne

Tom Bradby	Frederick Forsyth	Gayle Lynds
John Burdett	David Hagberg	Kyle Mills
Brendan Dubois	Brian Haig	Douglas Preston
Joseph Finder	Greg Iles	Eric Van Lustbader

L

Sergei Lukyanenko

🔖 1968-　Rus　　　Fantasy: Contemporary

www.rusf.ru/lukian/english

Neal Asher	Steven Gould	J K Rowling
Iain M Banks	Philip Pullman	Andrzej Sapkowski
Hal Duncan	Justina Robson	

Brian Lumley

1937-　　　　　　　　　　　　　　Horror

www.brianlumley.com

🏃 Harry Keogh

Poppy Z Brite	Mark Morris	Whitley Strieber
Tim Lebbon	Kim Newman	T M Wright
Gregory Maguire	Anne Rice	

Jonathan Lunn

Sea: Historical

is Daniel Hall

🏃 Kit Killigrew - C19th

G S Beard	Philip McCutchan	Dudley Pope
C S Forester	James L Nelson	Peter Smalley
Alexander Kent	Patrick O'Brian	Julian Stockwin

Alison Lurie

🔖 1926-　US

www.people.cornell.edu/pages/al28

🏆 Pulitzer 1985

Jane Austen	Elizabeth Gaskell	Edith Wharton
Rachel Billington	Gail Godwin	Meg Wolitzer
Louise Erdrich		

Sarah Kate Lynch

1962-　NZ

www.sarah-katelynch.com

Anthony Capella	Nicky Pellegrino	Barbara Trapido
Emma Donoghue	Lily Prior	Barbara Wood
Joanne Harris	Michèle Roberts	

🔖 may be suitable for young adults

169

Scott Lynch 1978- US

www.scottlynch.us

Fantasy: Epic

🏃 Locke Lamora

Joe Abercrombie	Raymond E Feist	George R R Martin
Chaz Brenchley	Robin Hobb	Karen Miller
Stephen Donaldson	Tim Lebbon	Steph Swainston
Hal Duncan	Tom Lloyd	Liz Williams

Gayle Lynds US

www.gaylelynds.com

Adventure/Thriller

Alex Berenson	Robert Ludlum	Henry Porter
Jon Evans	Chris Petit	Stella Rimington
Dan Fesperman		

Amin Maalouf 1949- Leb

www.aminmaalouf.org/english

Adventure/Thriller

James Clavell	Umberto Eco	Julian Rathbone
Bryce Courtenay	Orhan Pamuk	Alan Savage
Daniel Easterman	Arturo Pérez-Reverte	Colin Thubron

Sharon Maas 1951- Guy

www.sharonmaas.com

Kavita Daswani	Manju Kapur	Preethi Nair
Chitra Banerjee Divakaruni	Pauline Melville	Carolyn Slaughter
Roopa Farooki	Nisha Minhas	

Paul J McAuley 1955-

www.omegacom.demon.co.uk

Science Fiction: Technical

🏆 Arthur C Clarke 1996

Gregory Benford	Ian McDonald	Linda Nagata
Paul Johnston	John Meaney	Richard Powers
Jack McDevitt		

Ed McBain 1926-2005 US

also wrote as Curt Cannon, Hunt Collins, Evan Hunter, Richard Marsten; was Salvatore Lombino
www.edmcbain.com

Crime: Police work - US

🏃 Det Steve Carella - 87th Precinct, 'Isola' Police Department

Robert Ellis	J A Jance	Carol O'Connell
Kjell Eriksson	Faye Kellerman	Robert B Parker
W E B Griffin	Michael Malone	J D Robb
Donald Harstad	Deon Meyer	Joseph Wambaugh

Stuart MacBride   Sco

www.stuartmacbride.com

Crime: Police work - UK

🏃 DS Logan MacRae - Aberdeen

🏆 CWA 2007

Campbell Armstrong
Mark Billingham
Karen Campbell
Margaret Duffy

Alex Gray
Allan Guthrie
Peter James
Quintin Jardine

Natsuo Kirino
David Lawrence
Denise Mina
Steve Mosby

Patrick McCabe   1955-   Ire

Dermot Bolger
Roddy Doyle
Colum McCann

John McGahern
Patrick McGrath
Eoin McNamee

Joseph O'Connor
Andrew O'Hagan
Glenn Patterson

Anne McCaffrey   1926-   US   Science Fiction: Space and time

also writes jointly with Eizabeth Ann Scarborough
www.annemccaffrey.net

Sarah Ash
Lois McMaster Bujold
Susanna Clarke
James Clemens

G W Dahlquist
Barbara Hambly
Elizabeth Haydon
Katharine Kerr

Mercedes Lackey
Julian May
Robert Newcomb
Christopher Paolini

Robert McCammon   1952-   US   Horror

www.robertmccammon.com

John Farris
Dean R Koontz
Graham Masterton

Anne Rice
John Saul
Peter Straub

Whitley Strieber
T M Wright

Colum McCann   1965-   Ire

www.colummccann.com

Dermot Bolger
Patrick McCabe

Brian Moore
Joseph O'Connor

Michael Ondaatje
Colm Toibin

Charles McCarry   1930-   US   Adventure/Thriller

🏃 Paul Christopher, FBI agent

Tom Gabbay
Gordon Kent
John Le Carré

Robert Littell
John J Nance
Gerald Seymour

Daniel Silva
Martin Cruz Smith
Nigel West

Go to back for lists of
Pseudonyms • Authors by Genre • Characters and Series
Prize Winners • Crossover Authors • Further Reading • Websites

Cormac McCarthy   1933-   US

www.cormacmccarthy.com   South-west USA

🏆 Black 2006   Pulitzer 2007

Russell Banks	Charles Frazier	Stewart O'Nan
Pete Dexter	Stuart Harrison	J D Salinger
William Faulkner	Linda Holeman	William Wall
Richard Flanagan	A M Homes	Daniel Woodrell

Keith McCarthy   Crime: Forensic

🏃 Helena Flemming, Solicitor & John Eisenmenger, Pathologist

Simon Beckett	Iris Johansen	Kathy Reichs
Max Allan Collins	Nigel McCrery	Karin Slaughter
Patricia D Cornwell		

Wil McCarthy   1966-   US   Science Fiction: Technical

www.wilmccarthy.com

Stephen Baxter	Gregory Benford	Linda Nagata
Greg Bear	Michael Moorcock	Robert Charles Wilson

Ken McClure   1942-   Sco   Crime: Medical

also writes as Ken Begg   🏃 Steven Dunbar
www.kenmcclure.com

Paul Adam	Robin Cook	Tess Gerritsen
Paul Carson	Michael Crichton	Michael Palmer

Ken McCoy   1940-   Crime: PI

www.kenmccoy.co.uk   🏃 Sam 'Mad' Carew, ex-Policeman

Jake Arnott	Martin Edwards	Sheila Quigley
Stephen Booth	Reginald Hill	Cath Staincliffe
Martina Cole	Iain McDowall	Martyn Waites
Alan Dunn	Stuart Pawson	R D Wingfield

Saga
North-east England

Catherine Cookson	Denise Robertson	Michael Taylor
Kitty Neale	Wendy Robertson	Janet MacLeod Trotter
Elvi Rhodes	Jean Saunders	Annie Wilkinson

Nigel McCrery   1953-   Crime: Forensic

🏃 Sam Ryan, Pathologist - Cambridge

Lin Anderson	Patricia D Cornwell	Val McDermid
Simon Beckett	Aaron Elkins	Kathy Reichs
Benjamin Black	Kathryn Fox	Karin Slaughter
Max Allan Collins	Keith McCarthy	Aline Templeton

Sharyn McCrumb 1948- US

Crime: Psychological

www.sharynmccrumb.com

🏃 Sheriff Spenser Arrowood

Elizabeth McPherson, Anthropologist - Appalachians, East Tennessee

Douglas Adams	Carolyn G Hart	Andrew Klavan
Nevada Barr	Daniel Hecht	Margaret Maron
Janis Harrison	Tony Hillerman	Carol O'Connell

Carson McCullers 1917-1967 US

www.carson-mccullers.com

Southern USA

William Faulkner	Harper Lee	Curtis Sittenfeld
F Scott Fitzgerald	J D Salinger	Alice Walker
Connie May Fowler	Anne Rivers Siddons	

Colleen McCullough 1937- Aus

Historical

is Colleen McCullough-Robinson

Margaret George	Mary Renault	Simon Scarrow
Robert Graves	Rosemary Rowe	Patricia Shaw
Christian Jacq	Edward Rutherfurd	Wilbur Smith

Philip McCutchan 1920-1996

Sea: Historical & Modern

also wrote as Duncan MacNeil

🏃 Donald Cameron

St Vincent Halfhyde ⎱ Royal Navy

Commodore Kemp, Merchant Marine • Tom Chatto, Merchant Navy

Capt James Ogilvie, Queens Own Royal Strathspeys

Brian Callison	Alexander Kent	Dudley Pope
Alexander Fullerton	Sam Llewellyn	Patrick Robinson
Richard Howard	Jonathan Lunn	Peter Tonkin

Val McDermid 1955- Sco

Crime: Psychological

www.valmcdermid.com

🏃 DCI Carol Jordan & Dr Tony Hill, Psychologist

Kate Brannigan, PI - Manchester • Lindsay Gordon, Journalist - Glasgow

Fiona Cameron, Academic psychologist

🏆 CWA 1995   Theakston's 2006

Lindsay Ashford	Daniel Hecht	Patrick Redmond
Elizabeth Corley	Mandasue Heller	Manda Scott
Garry Disher	Jane Hill	Zoë Sharp
Sophie Hannah	Nigel McCrery	Sue Walker

Alice McDermott 1953- US

Alice Hoffman	Anne Michaels	Anita Shreve
Mary Lawson	Carol Shields	Adriana Trigiani

173

Andy McDermott

Adventure/Thriller

www.andy-mcdermott.com   ⚘ Nina Wilde & Eddie Chase, Archaeologist, ex-SAS

Lincoln Child	Clive Cussler	Matthew Reilly
Harold Coyle	Douglas Preston	James Rollins

Jack McDevitt   1935-   US

Science Fiction: Space and time

www.sfwa.org/members/mcdevitt

⚘ Alex Benedict

Poul Anderson	Paul J McAuley	Alastair Reynolds
Stephen Baxter	Ken MacLeod	Kurt Vonnegut
Arthur C Clarke	Larry Niven	

M

Ian McDonald   1960-

Science Fiction: Space and time

🏆 BSFA 2004 & 2007

Stephen Baxter	Gwyneth Jones	Brian Stableford
Greg Egan	Paul J McAuley	Connie Willis
Jon Courtenay Grimwood	Linda Nagata	

Marianne MacDonald   1934-   Can

Crime: Amateur sleuth

www.marianne-macdonald.com   ⚘ Dido Hoare, Antiquarian bookseller - London

John Dunning	Hazel Holt	Fiona Mountain
Carolyn G Hart	Alison Joseph	Ann Purser
Veronica Heley	Morag Joss	Veronica Stallwood

Ross Macdonald   1915-83   US

Crime: PI

also wrote as John Macdonald, John Ross Macdonald   ⚘ Lew Archer - California
was Kenneth Millar

Lawrence Block	James Crumley	James Sallis
Raymond Chandler	Dashiell Hammett	Peter Spiegelman
James Hadley Chase	George P Pelecanos	

Sara MacDonald

Aga Saga

Sally Beauman	Elizabeth Edmondson	Robin Pilcher
Sarah Challis	Adèle Geras	Rosamunde Pilcher
Lucy Clare	Rachel Hore	Marcia Willett
Annabel Dilke	Charlotte Moore	Elizabeth Wrenn

Sophia McDougall   1981-

Historical

Stephen Baxter	Simon Scarrow	Harry Turtledove
Allan Massie	Robert Silverberg	David Wishart
Steven Saylor		

Iain McDowall   Sco   Crime: Police work - UK
www.crowby.co.uk   🕺 DCI Jacobson & DS Kerr - 'Crowby', Midlands

Hilary Bonner	John Harvey	Peter James
Stephen Booth	Reginald Hill	Ken McCoy
Joseph Connolly	Lesley Horton	Pauline Rowson
Colin Dexter	Graham Hurley	Aline Templeton

Ian McEwan   1948-
www.ianmcewan.com
🏆 Whitbread 1987   Booker 1998   WHSmith 2002   Black 2005

Gilbert Adair	William Boyd	Toby Litt
Niccolo Ammaniti	Anita Brookner	Patrick McGrath
Trezza Azzopardi	Peter Ho Davies	Blake Morrison
Iain Banks	Andrea Levy	Gerard Woodward

Cody McFadyen   1968-   US   Crime: Psychological
www.codymcfadyen.com   🕺 Smokey Barrett

Gregory Hall	J A Kerley	Chris Mooney
Thomas Harris	Jeff Lindsay	Boris Starling
David Hosp	Richard Montanari	P J Tracy

Andrew McGahan   1966-   Aus   Adventure/Thriller

Murray Bail	Robert Jordan	Graham Masterton
Kate Grenville	Thomas Keneally	Tim Winton

John McGahern   1934-2006   Ire
www.johnmcgahern.com

John Banville	Patrick McCabe	Edna O'Brien
Sebastian Barry	Eoin McNamee	David Park
James Joyce	Brian Moore	William Wall

Michael McGarrity   US   Crime: Police work - US
www.michaelmcgarrity.net   🕺 Kevin Kerney - New Mexico

Nevada Barr	Steve Hamilton	J A Jance
C J Box	Donald Harstad	Archer Mayor
Robert Ferrigno	Tony Hillerman	

James McGee   1950-   Crime: Historical - C19th
is Glen Moy   🕺 Matthew Hawkwood, Bow Street runner

David Ashton	Deryn Lake	Anne Perry
Iain Gale	Edward Marston	C J Sansom
Lee Jackson	Andrew Pepper	Martin Stephen

Brian McGilloway   1974-   Ire

www.brianmcgilloway.com

Crime: Police work

✲ Insp Benedict Devlin - Londonderry

Mark Billingham	Reginald Hill	Eoin McNamee
Benjamin Black	Quintin Jardine	Ian Rankin
Bartholomew Gill		

Patrick McGrath   1950-

Michel Faber	Patrick McCabe	Graham Swift
Kazuo Ishiguro	Ian McEwan	Tobias Wolff

Elizabeth McGregor

also writes as Holly Fox

Crime: Psychological

Kate Atkinson	Meg O'Brien	Barbara Vine
Nicci French	Louis Sanders	Sue Walker
J Wallis Martin	Carol Smith	Gillian White

Jay McInerney   1955-   US

Bret Easton Ellis	Jack Kerouac	J D Salinger
F Scott Fitzgerald	Armistead Maupin	Matt Thorne
Michael Jan Friedman		

Monica McInerney   Aus

www.monicamcinerney.com

Mature Chick Lit

Liz Byrski	Anne Dunlop	Morag Prunty
Colette Caddle	Melissa Hill	Tina Reilly
Clare Dowling	Jojo Moyes	Jane Wenham-Jones

Fiona McIntosh   Aus

www.fionamcintosh.com

Fantasy: Epic

David Eddings	Robin Hobb	Melanie Rawn
Elizabeth Haydon	Karen Miller	Margaret Weis
Amanda Hemingway	Elizabeth Moon	

Pat McIntosh   Sco

Crime: Historical - Medieval

✲ Gil Cunningham, Notary in training - Glasgow

Simon Beaufort	Michael Jecks	Kate Sedley
Alys Clare	Bernard Knight	Peter Tremayne
Susanna Gregory	Candace Robb	

M

Hope McIntyre 1946-

is Caroline Upcher
www.carolineupcher.com

Crime: Amateur sleuth
♁ Lee Bartholomew, Ghost writer - London

Judith Cutler
Anthea Fraser

Shane Maloney
Gwen Moffat

Veronica Stallwood
Rebecca Tope

Shena Mackay 1944- Sco

Anita Burgh
Mavis Cheek
Angela Huth

Jennifer Johnston
Valerie Martin
Marge Piercy

Gwendoline Riley
Muriel Spark

Juliet E McKenna 1965-

www.julietemckenna.com

Fantasy: Epic

James Barclay
David Farland
Jude Fisher

Elizabeth Haydon
Ian Irvine
George R R Martin

K J Parker
Freda Warrington

Serena Mackesy

www.serenamackesy.com

Chick Lit

Jessica Adams
Zoë Barnes
Helen Fielding

Louise Kean
Josie Lloyd & Emlyn Rees
Chris Manby

Sue Margolis
Kate O'Riordan

Mary Mackie

also writes as Alex Andrews, Caroline Charles, Cathy Christopher,
Mary Christopher, Susan Stevens

Saga
Lincolnshire
Norfolk

Margaret Dickinson
Elizabeth Jeffrey
Connie Monk

Elizabeth Murphy
Judith Saxton

Sue Sully
T R Wilson

Tamara McKinley Aus

www.tamaramckinley.co.uk

Saga

Domenica de Rosa
Santa Montefiore
Di Morrissey

Judy Nunn
Katherine Scholes

Patricia Shaw
Peter Watt

John McLaren 1951- Sco

Crime: Legal/financial

Harry Bingham
Caro Fraser
Reg Gadney

Brad Meltzer
Barbara Parker
Nancy Taylor Rosenberg

Lisa Scottoline
Peter Spiegelman
Scott Turow

Bernard MacLaverty 1942- Ire

www.bernardmaclaverty.com

Ronald Frame
Joan Lingard
Allan Massie

Joseph O'Connor
David Park
Julian Rathbone

Adam Thorpe
Niall Williams

Alistair MacLean 1922-87 Sco Adventure/Thriller

also wrote as Ian Stuart

James Follett
Hammond Innes
Andy McNab

Nicholas Monsarrat
Alan Savage
Nevil Shute

Terence Strong
Peter Tonkin

Alistair MacLeod 1936- Can

🏆 IMPAC 2001

William Boyd
Jim Crace
David Guterson

Toby Litt
Yann Martel
Anne Michaels

Alice Munro
Michael Ondaatje
David Park

Ken MacLeod 1954- Sco Science Fiction: Space and time

🏆 BSFA 1999

Steve Aylett
Iain M Banks
Ray Bradbury

Greg Egan
Jack McDevitt
John Meaney

China Miéville
Richard Morgan
Adam Roberts

Pauline McLynn Ire Crime: Humour

www.paulinemclynn.com

🏃 Leo Street, PI - Dublin

Janet Evanovich
Liz Evans

Sparkle Hayter
Lauren Henderson

Zane Radcliffe
Sarah Strohmeyer

Katharine McMahon Historical

www.katharinemcmahon.com

Suzannah Dunn
Patrick Gale
Philippa Gregory

Jane Harris
Jeanne Kalogridis
Robin Maxwell

Edith Pargeter
Patricia Shaw

Terry McMillan 1951- US

www.terrymcmillan.com

Esther Freud
John Irving
Toni Morrison

Alice Walker
Rebecca Wells

Valerie Wilson Wesley
Meg Wolitzer

🌈 may be suitable for young adults

Larry McMurtry 1936- US

🏆 Pulitzer 1986

Pat Conroy
Thomas Eidson
Nicholas Evans

Charles Frazier
John Irving
Jack Kerouac

James A Michener
Richard Russo

Andy McNab ☺ 1960- War: Modern

www.andymcnab.co.uk

🏃 Nick Stone - SIS

Michael Asher
Murray Davies
Barry Eisler

Duncan Falconer
John Fullerton
Joseph Garber

Alan Judd
Alistair MacLean

M

Claire McNab 1940- Aus Crime: Police work - Australia

also writes as Claire Carmichael
www.clairemcnab.com

🏃 DI Carol Ashton - Sydney
Denise Cleever, Intelligence agent - Australia
Kylie Kendall, PI - Los Angeles

Jan Burke
Jon Cleary
Stella Duffy

Peter Guttridge
J A Jance
Laurie R King

Chris Niles
Carol O'Connell
Medora Sale

Eoin McNamee 1961- Ire Adventure/Thriller

also writes as John Creed

Jennifer Johnston
Patrick McCabe
John McGahern

Brian McGilloway
Edna O'Brien

Colm Toibin
William Trevor

Judith McNaught 1944- US

www.judithmcnaught.com

Catherine Coulter
Barbara Delinsky
Judith Gould

Linda Howard
Penny Jordan
Jayne Ann Krentz

Amanda Quick
LaVyrle Spencer
Danielle Steel

Gil McNeil Mature Chick Lit

Trisha Ashley
Kate Jacobs
India Knight

Dorothy Koomson
Jill Mansell
Sheila Norton

Adele Parks
Daisy Waugh

Elisabeth McNeill 1931- Sco Saga

Scotland

Emma Blair
Doris Davidson
Meg Hutchinson

Gwen Kirkwood
Elvi Rhodes
Sally Stewart

Jessica Stirling
Mary Withall

Debbie Macomber   1948-   US   Mature Chick Lit

www.debbiemacomber.com

Lucy Dawson	Debby Holt	Patricia Scanlan
Katie Fforde	Tina Reilly	Sarah Tucker

Catriona McPherson   1965-   Sco   Crime: Amateur sleuth

also writes as Catriona McCloud   🕴 Dandy Gilver - 1920s Scotland
www.dandygilver.co.uk

Agatha Christie	Robert Goddard	David Roberts
Barbara Cleverly	Gerald Hammond	Alexander McCall Smith
Arthur Conan Doyle	Patricia Harwin	Andrew Taylor
Carola Dunn	Alanna Knight	Jacqueline Winspear

Gwen Madoc   Wales   Saga

Swansea

June Francis	Beryl Matthews	Mary Jane Staples
Meg Hutchinson	Gilda O'Neill	Janet Tanner
Margaret Kaine	Sharon Owens	Dee Williams

Paul Magrs   1969-   Horror

Jeremy Dyson	Eve Makis	Magnus Mills
Jasper Fforde	Hilary Mantel	Haruki Murakami
Peter James		

Adrian Magson   Crime: Police work - UK

www.adrianmagson.com   Riley Gavin, Journalist, & Frank Palmer, ex- Military investigator

Jo Bannister	Margaret Duffy	Katherine John
Christopher Brookmyre	Patricia Hall	Denise Mina
Caroline Carver		

Gregory Maguire   1954-   US   Fantasy: Myth

www.gregorymaguire.com

Simon Clark	Dean R Koontz	Tim Powers
Katharine Kerr	Brian Lumley	Philip Pullman
Stephen King		

Norman Mailer   1923-2007   US

🏆 Pulitzer 1980

Don Delillo	Thomas Pynchon	John Updike
Joseph Heller	John Steinbeck	Gore Vidal
Ernest Hemingway	William Styron	Tom Wolfe

Barry Maitland
1941-   Sco   **Crime:** Police work - UK

www.barrymaitland.com   ☂ DCI David Brock & DS Kathy Kolla - London

Jo Bannister	Stephen Booth	Simon Kernick
Mark Billingham	Anthea Fraser	Ed O'Connor
Victoria Blake	Cynthia Harrod-Eagles	Peter Temple

Eve Makis

Jessica Adams	Sophie Kinsella	Alan Titchmarsh
Paulo Coelho	Paul Magrs	Louise Tondeur
Sandra Howard	Deborah Moggach	Louise Voss

M

John Malcolm
1936-   **Crime:** Amateur sleuth

☂ Tim Simpson, Art investment advisor

Aaron Elkins	Roy Lewis	Iain Pears
Earlene Fowler	Keith Miles	Derek Wilson
Jonathan Gash		

Amulya Malladi
1974-   Ind

www.amulyamalladi.com

Anita Desai	Manju Kapur	Preethi Nair
Chitra Banerjee Divakaruni	Rohinton Mistry	Thirty Umrigar
Roopa Farooki	Anita Nair	

Allan Mallinson
                                       War: Historical

☂ Matthew Hervey, Captain - C19th Light Dragoons

G S Beard	Alexander Fullerton	Christopher Nicole
Roger Carpenter	Iain Gale	Patrick O'Brian
Tom Connery	Richard Howard	Patrick Rambaud
Bernard Cornwell	Garry Kilworth	John Wilcox

Michael Malone
1942-   US   **Crime:** Police work - US

☂ Chief Cuddy Mangum & Det Justin Savile - 'Hillston', North Carolina

James Lee Burke	Lynn Hightower	Ed McBain
Thomas H Cook	Tony Hillerman	Jefferson Parker
Dashiell Hammett	Jonathon King	Stuart Woods

Shane Maloney
1953-   Aus   **Crime:** Amateur sleuth

www.shanemaloney.com   ☂ Murray Whelan, Political adviser - Melbourne

Robert G Barrett	Carl Hiaasen	Hope McIntyre
Jon Cleary	Elmore Leonard	Don Winslow
Garry Disher		

David Malouf   1934-   Aus

🏆 Commonwealth 1991   IMPAC 1996

Murray Bail	Robert Drewe	Janette Turner Hospital
Peter Carey	Richard Flanagan	Ben Okri
James Clavell	Maurice Gee	Morris West

Chris Manby   1972-   Chick Lit

also writes as Stephanie Ash

Jessica Adams	Rachel Hore	Sinead Moriarty
Meg Cabot	Josie Lloyd & Emlyn Rees	Sara Shepard
Alison Penton Harper	Serena Mackesy	Linda Taylor
Julie Highmore	Sue Margolis	Kate Thompson

Valerio Massimo Manfredi   1943-   It   Historical

🏃 Alexander the Great

Almudena Grandes	Allan Massie	Manda Scott
Robert Graves	Steven Pressfield	Wilbur Smith
Christian Jacq	Mary Renault	Robyn Young

Henning Mankell   ◠ ☺   1948-   Swe   Crime: Police work - Sweden

www.henningmankell.com

🏃 Insp Kurt Wallander - Ystad

🏆 CWA 2001

Ake Edwardson	Matti Joensuu	Hakan Nesser
Kjell Eriksson	Liza Marklund	Yrsa Sigurdardottir
Peter Hoeg	Archer Mayor	Janwillem van de Wetering
Anne Holt	Jo Nesbo	Fred Vargas

Jill Mansell   ◠   Mature Chick Lit

www.jillmansell.co.uk

Trisha Ashley	Debby Holt	Bernadette Strachan
Tilly Bagshawe	Milly Johnson	Polly Williams
Meg Cabot	Gil McNeil	Cathy Woodman
Veronica Henry	Sara Shepard	Liz Young

Hilary Mantel   1952-

🏆 Holtby 1990   Hawthornden 1996

Candida Crewe	Toby Litt	Alice Sebold
Rachel Cusk	Paul Magrs	Henry Sutton
A M Homes	Julie Myerson	

John Marco   US   Fantasy: Epic

www.johnmarco.com

James Barclay	Steven Erikson	Raymond E Feist
Terry Brooks	David Farland	Robert Jordan

M

Phillip Margolin
1944- US **Crime:** Legal/financial

also writes as Phillip M Margolin
www.phillipmargolin.com

William Bernhardt
Colin Harrison
Jesse Kellerman

Steve Martini
Barbara Parker
Richard North Patterson

Nancy Taylor Rosenberg
John Sandford
Lisa Scottoline

Sue Margolis
Chick Lit

Cecelia Ahern
Catherine Alliott
Josie Lloyd & Emlyn Rees

Serena Mackesy
Chris Manby
Jane Moore

Sheila O'Flanagan
Isabel Wolff

M

Juliet Marillier
1948- NZ **Fantasy:** Myth

www.julietmarillier.com

Sarah Ash
Jean M Auel
Ashok K Banker

Trudi Canavan
Storm Constantine
Cecilia Dart-Thornton

Charles de Lint
Caiseal Mor

Liza Marklund
1962- Swe **Crime:** Amateur sleuth

♔ Annika Bengtzon, Journalist - Stockholm

Edna Buchanan
Jan Burke
G M Ford

Karin Fossum
Denise Hamilton

Henning Mankell
Maj Sjöwall & Per Wahlöö

Laura Marney
Sco **Humour**

Des Dillon
Anne Donovan

Fiona Gibson
Marina Lewycka

Zoë Strachan
Lynne Truss

Margaret Maron
1959- US **Crime:** Amateur sleuth

www.margaretmaron.com

♔ Deborah Knott, Judge - North Carolina
Sigrid Harald - New York Police

Nevada Barr
Lilian Jackson Braun
Jan Burke

Carol Higgins Clark
W E B Griffin
Janis Harrison

Carolyn G Hart
Sharyn McCrumb

Ngaio Marsh
1895-1982 NZ **Crime:** Police work - UK

♔ DI Roderick Alleyn

Barbara Cleverly
Elizabeth Ferrars

David Roberts
Dorothy L Sayers

Dorothy Simpson
Patricia Wentworth

Michael Marshall   1965-   Adventure/Thriller

is Michael Marshall-Smith
www.michaelmarshallsmith.com

♁ Ward Hopkins, ex-CIA

Alex Barclay	Thomas Harris	James Patterson
Chelsea Cain	Richard Morgan	John Rickards
Jeffery Deaver	Steve Mosby	Nick Stone
Joseph Finder	Jeff Noon	James Twining

Edward Marston   1940-   Wales   Crime: Historical - Medieval

also writes as A E Marston,
Christopher Mountjoy; is Keith Miles
www.edwardmarston.com

♁ Nicholas Bracewell, Theatre - C16th
Ralph Delchard & Gervase Bret - C11th } England
Christopher Redmayne & Jonathan Bale - C17th
Insp Robert Colbeck - C19th   London

Conrad Allen	Patricia Finney	Andrew Martin
David Ashton	Janet Gleeson	James McGee
Simon Beaufort	Philip Gooden	Andrew Pepper
Christie Dickason	Lee Jackson	Martin Stephen

Yann Martel   1963-   Spain

🏆 Man Booker 2002

Murray Bail	Louis de Bernières	V S Naipaul
Iain Banks	Mark Haddon	D B C Pierre
Susanna Clarke	Alistair MacLeod	Arundhati Roy
Jim Crace	David Mitchell	Paul Theroux

Andrew Martin   1952-   Crime: Historical - C19th

Jim Stringer, Railwayman

John Maclachlan Gray	Peter Lovesey	Anne Perry
Lee Jackson	Edward Marston	Frank Tallis

David Martin   1946-   US   Horror

Chaz Brenchley	Graham Masterton	Whitley Strieber
Jack Harvey	Richard Matheson	Koji Suzuki
Graham Joyce	Kim Newman	

George R R Martin   1948-   US   Fantasy: Epic

www.georgerrmartin.com

R Scott Bakker	David A Drake	Juliet E McKenna
Ashok K Banker	Maggie Furey	Stan Nicholls
James Barclay	Greg Keyes	Patrick Rothfuss
C J Cherryh	Scott Lynch	Harry Turtledove

J Wallis Martin

Adventure/Thriller: Psychological

is Julia Wallis Martin
www.wallis-martin.co.uk

Nicci French	Maureen O'Brien	Sue Walker
Elizabeth McGregor	Ruth Rendell	Minette Walters
Margaret Murphy	Manda Scott	Robert Wilson

Rosemary Martin

US

Crime: Amateur sleuth

is Rosemary Stevens

☜ Bebe Bennett, Secretary - New York

www.rosemarymartin.com

Kinky Friedman	Rosemary Stevens
Stuart M Kaminsky	Sarah Strohmeyer

Valerie Martin

1948- US

☘ Orange 2003

Margaret Atwood	Zoë Heller	Clare Morrall
Pat Barker	Victoria Hislop	Toni Morrison
Kim Edwards	Jennifer Johnston	Julie Myerson
Miranda Glover	Shena Mackay	Ann Patchett

Guillermo Martinez

1962- Arg

Crime: Psychological

Colin Dexter	Morag Joss	Fred Vargas
P D James	Matthew Pearl	

Tomas Eloy Martinez

1934- Arg

Isabel Allende	Gabriel Garcia Márquez	Manuel Vázquez Montalbán
Carlos Fuentes	Armistead Maupin	Mario Vargas Llosa

Steve Martini

1946- US

Crime: Legal/financial

www.stevemartini.com

☜ Paul Madriani, Lawyer - San Diego

Harry Bingham	James Grippando	Brad Meltzer
Alafair Burke	John Hart	Barbara Parker
Linda Fairstein	John T Lescroart	Susan R Sloan
Mark Gimenez	Phillip Margolin	Robert K Tanenbaum

Daniel Mason

1976- US

F G Cottam	Amitav Ghosh	Lionel Shriver
Michelle de Kretser	Khaled Hosseini	Alan Spence
Sebastian Faulks	George Orwell	Colin Thubron

Sarah Mason · Chick Lit

🏆 Romantic 2003

Trisha Ashley	Louise Harwood	Olivia Ryan
Claire Calman	Donna Hay	Jennifer Weiner
Anne Dunlop	Melissa Nathan	Arabella Weir

Allan Massie · 1938- Sco

Michael Dobbs	Bernard MacLaverty
Ronald Frame	Frederic Raphael

Historical: Ancient

Robert Graves	Robert Nye	Simon Scarrow
Sophia McDougall	Rosemary Rowe	Marilyn Todd
Valerio Massimo Manfredi	Steven Saylor	David Wishart

Priscilla Masters · 1952- Crime: Police work - UK

www.joannapiercy.com

🚶 Martha Gunn, Coroner - Shrewsbury
DI Joanna Piercy & DS Mike Korpanski - 'Moorlands', Staffordshire

Jo Bannister	John Connor	Margaret Duffy
Stephen Booth	Deborah Crombie	Marjorie Eccles
Glenn Chandler	Judith Cutler	H R F Keating

Graham Masterton · 1946- Sco · Horror

also writes as Alan Blackwood, Thomas Luke
www.grahammasterton.co.uk

Bret Easton Ellis	Stephen Gallagher	David Martin
John Farris	Robert McCammon	Kim Newman
Christopher Fowler	Andrew McGahan	Whitley Strieber

Richard Matheson · 1926- US · Horror

also writes as Logan Swanson

Tanya Huff	David Martin	Peter Straub
Dean R Koontz	Brian Stableford	Koji Suzuki
Stephen Laws		

Beryl Matthews · Saga

 Webster Family

Benita Brown	Gwen Madoc	Mary Jane Staples
Elizabeth Elgin	Judith Saxton	June Tate
Lilian Harry		

Go to back for lists of
Pseudonyms • Authors by Genre • Characters and Series
Prize Winners • Crossover Authors • Further Reading • Websites

Carole Matthews

Chick Lit

www.carolematthews.com

Jessica Adams	Zoë Barnes	Milly Johnson
Catherine Alliott	Claudia Carroll	Belinda Jones
Tilly Bagshawe	Isla Dewar	Olivia Ryan

W Somerset Maugham 1874-1965

| Joseph Conrad | Michel Faber | J B Priestley |
| Charles Dickens | Henry James | Morris West |

Armistead Maupin 1944- US

www.armisteadmaupin.com

Robert G Barrett	Garrison Keillor	Jay McInerney
Patrick Gale	Hanif Kureishi	Tomas Eloy Martinez
Alan Hollinghurst	Marina Lewycka	Edmund White

Simon Mawer 1948-

www.simonmawer.com

Beryl Bainbridge	Michael Frayn	Andrew O'Hagan
William Boyd	Andrew Greig	Niall Williams
Sebastian Faulks	Iris Murdoch	

Anna Maxted 1969-

Chick Lit

Elizabeth Buchan	Sabine Durrant	Kate Long
Martina Devlin	Louise Kean	Jane Moore
Isla Dewar	India Knight	Adele Parks

Robin Maxwell US

Historical

www.robinmaxwell.com

Suzannah Dunn	Sandra Gulland	Katharine McMahon
Melanie Gifford	Caroline Harvey	Edith Pargeter
Philippa Gregory	Elizabeth Jeffrey	Maureen Peters

Julian May 1931- US

Fantasy: Epic

also writes as Lee N Falconer, Ian Thorne

David Bilsborough	Anne McCaffrey	Robert Silverberg
Marion Zimmer Bradley	Michael Moorcock	Gene Wolfe
Barbara Hambly		

may be suitable for young adults

M

187

Peter May

1951- Sco

www.petermay.co.uk

Crime: Police work - China

🏃 Det Li Yan & Margaret Campbell, Pathologist

Martina Cole	Andy Oakes	Lisa See
Patricia D Cornwell	Qiu Xiaolong	Martin Cruz Smith
Colin Cotterill	Kathy Reichs	

Eric Mayer   see **Mary Reed**

Eric Mayer   see **Mary Reed**

Margaret Mayhew

Saga

Anne Baker	Hilary Green	Angela Huth
Anne Bennett	Annie Groves	Maureen Lee
Elizabeth Elgin	Lilian Harry	Victor Pemberton

Archer Mayor

US

www.archermayor.com

Crime: Police work - US

🏃 Lt Joe Gunther - Brattleboro, Vermont

Giles Blunt	Michael McGarrity	Theresa Monsour
Paula Gosling	Henning Mankell	Robert B Parker
Donald Harstad		

Glenn Meade

1957- Ire

Adventure/Thriller

Campbell Armstrong	Tom Clancy	Greg Iles
Michael Asher	Frederick Forsyth	Robert Littell
Alex Barclay	Robert Harris	

John Meaney

Science Fiction: Technical

www.johnmeaney.com

Iain M Banks	James Lovegrove	Robert Reed
Greg Bear	Paul J McAuley	Alastair Reynolds
Jon Courtenay Grimwood	Ken MacLeod	Adam Roberts

Joan Medlicott

1932- US

www.joanmedlicott.com

Saga

🏃 Ladies of Covington Series

Janet Dailey	Rebecca Shaw	Marcia Willett
Jan Karon	Anne Rivers Siddons	Audrey Willsher
Belva Plain	LaVyrle Spencer	T R Wilson

James Meek

1962- Sco

🏆 Ondaatje 2006

Peter Ackroyd	Will Ferguson	Orhan Pamuk
Louis de Bernières	Ismail Kadare	Edward St Aubyn
Helen Dunmore	Michael Moorcock	Barry Unsworth

M

M R D Meek
1918- Sco **Crime:** Amateur sleuth
also writes as Alison Cairns ⚓ Lennox Kemp, Solicitor - London
is Margaret Reid Duncan Meek

Kate Charles	Frances Fyfield	Roy Lewis
Martin Edwards	Joyce Holms	R D Wingfield
Ruth Dudley Edwards	P D James	

Maile Meloy
US

www.mailemeloy.com

Tami Hoag	Melissa Nathan	Bella Pollen
Rachel Johnson	Ann Packer	Anita Shreve
Lorna Landvik	Lesley Pearse	

Brad Meltzer
1970- US **Adventure/Thriller:** Legal/financial

www.bradmeltzer.com

David Baldacci	John Hart	Christopher Reich
Stephen L Carter	John McLaren	Michael Ridpath
Linda Davies	Steve Martini	

Pauline Melville
1948- Guy

🏆 Guardian 1990 Whitbread 1997

Patricia Duncker	Andrea Levy	Bernice Rubens
Graham Greene	Sharon Maas	Evelyn Waugh

Charlotte Mendelson
1972-

www.charlottemendelson.com

🏆 JLR 2003 S Maugham 2004

Kate Atkinson	Susan Fletcher	Penelope Lively
Anita Brookner	Margaret Forster	Maggie O'Farrell
Stevie Davies	Sue Gee	

Deon Meyer
1958- SA **Adventure/Thriller**

www.deonmeyer.com ⚓ Zatopek "Zed" van Heerden, Retired policeman
South Africa

Donald Harstad	Arnaldur Indridason	Joseph Wambaugh
Tony Hillerman	Ed McBain	

Judith Michael
1934- US **Glitz & Glamour**
is Judith Barnard and Michael Fain

Sally Beauman	Jackie Collins	Judith Gould
Celia Brayfield	Olivia Goldsmith	Tasmina Perry

Anne Michaels
1958-   Can

🏆 Guardian 1997   Orange 1997   Wingate 1997

Doris Lessing	Caryl Phillips	Rachel Seiffert
Alice McDermott	Michèle Roberts	Miriam Toews
Alistair MacLeod	Bernhard Schlink	Jane Urquhart

Fern Michaels
1933-   US   Glitz & Glamour

is Mary Ruth Kuczkir
www.fernmichaels.com

Jackie Collins	Eileen Goudge	Lesley Lokko
Jude Deveraux	Johanna Lindsey	LaVyrle Spencer

James A Michener
1907-1997   US

Stephen Baxter	Larry McMurtry	Leon Uris
Kathleen O'Neal Gear	Edward Rutherfurd	Gore Vidal

Stanley Middleton
1919-

🏆 Booker 1974

Kingsley Amis	David Lodge	Alan Sillitoe
Melvyn Bragg	J B Priestley	

China Miéville
1972-   Science Fiction: Space and time

🏆 Arthur C Clarke 2001 & 2005   British Fantasy 2001 & 2003

Stephen Baxter	Philip Pullman	Michael Marshall Smith
Mary Gentle	Alastair Reynolds	Steph Swainston
Ken MacLeod	Adam Roberts	Sean Williams
Richard Morgan	Kim Stanley Robinson	David Zindell

Keith Miles
1940-   Wales   Crime: Amateur sleuth

also writes as Conrad Allen, Martin Inigo,   🏃 Alan Saxton, Professional golfer
Edward Marston   Merlin Richards, Architect - USA
www.edwardmarston.com

Conrad Allen	John Dunning	Iain Pears
Simon Brett	Janis Harrison	Medora Sale
Kate Charles	John Malcolm	

Andrew Miller
1960-

🏆 Black 1997   IMPAC 1999

Tracy Chevalier	Colin Thubron	Barry Unsworth
Julian Rathbone	Rose Tremain	Peter Watt
Jane Stevenson		

Fenella-Jane Miller
Historical Romance
www.fenellajanemiller.co.uk

Mary Balogh
Anne Barbour
Marion Chesney
Emily Hendrickson
Georgette Heyer
Stephanie Laurens
Amanda Quick

Karen Miller
Aus
Fantasy: Epic
www.karenmiller.net

Joe Abercrombie
David Bilsborough
Stephen Donaldson
Raymond E Feist
Robin Hobb
Tom Lloyd
Scott Lynch
Fiona McIntosh

Sue Miller
1943- US

Russell Banks
Elizabeth Berg
Connie May Fowler
Patricia Gaffney
Nikki Gemmell
Ann Hood
Kate Jacobs
Maggie O'Farrell
Marge Piercy
Christina Schwarz
Lisa Tucker
Sarah Willis

Mil Millington
Lad Lit: Humour

Mark Barrowcliffe
Paul Burke
James Delingpole
Matt Dunn
Nick Hornby
Alexei Sayle
Jonathan Tropper

Kyle Mills
1966- US
Adventure/Thriller
www.kylemills.com
🏃 Mark Beamon - FBI

Dale Brown
Tom Clancy
Brendan Dubois
Frederick Forsyth
Greg Iles
John Le Carré
Robert Ludlum

Magnus Mills
1954-
Humour
🏆 McKitterick 1999

Alan Bennett
Jonathan Coe
Roddy Doyle
Andrew Holmes
Marina Lewycka
Paul Magrs
James Robertson
Graham Swift
Keith Waterhouse

Mark Mills
US
🏆 CWA 2004

Paul Adam
Joy Chambers
Linda Davies
Daphne Du Maurier
Thomas Eidson
Robert Goddard
Michael Gruber
Linda Holeman
Babs Horton
Bella Pollen
Catherine Shaw
Paul Torday

Anchee Min   1957-   China   Historical

Alma Alexander	Ha Jin	Su Tong
Arthur Golden	Catherine Lim	Amy Tan
Xiaolu Guo	Lisa See	Xinran

Denise Mina   1966-   Sco   Crime: Amateur sleuth
www.denisemina.co.uk   🏃 Maureen O'Donnell - Glasgow and London
Paddy Meehan, Journalist - Glasgow

🏆 CWA 1998

Gillian Galbraith	Stuart MacBride	Aline Templeton
Alex Gray	Adrian Magson	Sue Walker
Allan Guthrie	Manda Scott	Camilla Way
Frederic Lindsay	Chris Simms	Louise Welsh

Nisha Minhas   Malay   Chick Lit

Manju Kapur	Preethi Nair	Paige Toon
Sharon Maas	Linda Taylor	Grace Wynne-Jones

Rohinton Mistry   1952-   Can
🏆 Commonwealth 1992 & 1996   Holtby 1996

Chimamanda Ngozi Adichie	Charles Dickens	Khaled Hosseini
Thalassa Ali	Amitav Ghosh	Amulya Malladi
Vikram Chandra	Abdulrazak Gurnah	R K Narayan
Amit Chaudhuri	Shifra Horn	Paul Scott

Jacquelyn Mitchard   1955-   US
www.jacquelynmitchard.com

Jill Barnett	Tessa Hadley	Barbara Kingsolver
Elizabeth Berg	Alice Hoffman	Mary Alice Monroe
Elizabeth Flock	Alison Jameson	Marcia Preston
David Guterson	Sue Monk Kidd	Lisa Tucker

David Mitchell   1969-
🏆 JLR 1999   Faber 2005

Susanna Clarke	Joolz Denby	Andrew Taylor
Jonathan Coe	Yann Martel	Gail Tsukiyama
Jim Crace	Haruki Murakami	Jane Urquhart
Louis de Bernières	Lionel Shriver	Banana Yoshimoto

> *Go to back for lists of*
> Pseudonyms • Authors by Genre • Characters and Series
> Prize Winners • Crossover Authors • Further Reading • Websites

Timothy Mo 1953-
www.timothymo.com

☙ Faber 1979   Hawthornden 1982   Black 1999

Michelle de Kretser	James Hamilton-Paterson	Catherine Lim
Alex Garland	Kazuo Ishiguro	Caryl Phillips
Arthur Golden	Christopher Koch	Amy Tan

L E Modesitt Jr 1943- US   Fantasy: Epic
www.lemodesittjr.com   Erde

C J Cherryh	Simon Green	R A Salvatore
Louise Cooper	Mercedes Lackey	Janny Wurts
David A Drake	Mickey Zucker Reichert	

Gwen Moffat 1924-   Crime: Amateur sleuth
☈ Melinda Pink, Travel writer

Ruth Dudley Edwards	Hope McIntyre	Betty Rowlands
Janis Harrison	Fiona Mountain	Patricia Wentworth

Deborah Moggach 1948-
www.deborahmoggach.com

Carol Birch	Esther Freud	Eve Makis
Candida Crewe	Sue Gee	Rose Tremain
Jill Dawson	Angela Huth	Susan Vreeland
Barbara Ewing	Joan Lingard	Gillian White

Connie Monk   Saga
West Country

Pip Granger	Mary Mackie	Dee Williams
Elizabeth Ann Hill	Janet Tanner	Janet Woods
Claire Lorrimer	Margaret Thornton	

Grace Monroe   Adventure/Thriller
is Linda Watson-Brown & Maria Thomson   ☈ Brodie MacLennan, Lawyer - Edinburgh
www.gracemonroe.net

Victoria Blake	Steve Mosby	Claire Seeber
Alice Blanchard	Karen Rose	Paullina Simons
Elizabeth Corley		

Mary Alice Monroe US
www.maryalicemonroe.com

Jill Barnett	Nicci Gerrard	Marcia Preston
Elizabeth Flock	Jacquelyn Mitchard	Anne Rivers Siddons
Therese Fowler		

193

Nicholas Monsarrat 1910-79 — Sea: Modern

Duncan Harding	Alistair MacLean	Nevil Shute
Hammond Innes	Justin Scott	Peter Tonkin

Theresa Monsour US — Crime: Police work - US

♂ Det Paris Murphy - Minneapolis

Ingrid Black	Lynn Hightower	J D Robb
Giles Blunt	Laura Lippman	Dana Stabenow
Allison Brennan	Archer Mayor	Jess Walter
Meg Gardiner	Carol O'Connell	Joseph Wambaugh

M

Manuel Vázquez Montalbán 1939-2003 Spain — Crime: PI

♂ Pepe Carvalho - Barcelona

Michael Dibdin	Tomas Eloy Martinez	Arturo Pérez-Reverte
Luiz Alfredo Garcia-Roza	Barbara Nadel	Fred Vargas
Roderic Jeffries	Rebecca Pawel	Carlos Ruiz Zafón

Richard Montanari US — Adventure/Thriller

www.richardmontanari.com
♂ Jessica Balzano & Kevin Byrne
Jack Paris } Cleveland USA

Harlan Coben	J A Jance	James Patterson
Kathryn Fox	J A Kerley	John Rickards
Mo Hayder	Cody McFadyen	Craig Russell
Jilliane Hoffman	Steve Mosby	P J Tracy

Santa Montefiore 1970- — Aga Saga

www.santamontefiore.co.uk

Judy Astley	Marika Cobbold	Tamara McKinley
Amanda Brookfield	Domenica de Rosa	Susan Sallis
Sarah Challis	Jessica Duchen	Marcia Willett

Rick Moody 1961- US

Jeffrey Eugenides	John Irving	John Updike
Mark Haddon	Philip Roth	

Elizabeth Moon 1945- US — Fantasy: Epic

www.elizabethmoon.com

Terry Brooks	Barbara Hambly	R A Salvatore
Lois McMaster Bujold	Mercedes Lackey	Freda Warrington
Kate Elliott	Fiona McIntosh	Margaret Weis
Alan Dean Foster	Mickey Zucker Reichert	Janny Wurts

Chris Mooney   US   Adventure/Thriller
www.chrismooneybooks.com   ⚐ CSI Darby McCormick

Alex Barclay	Kathryn Fox	Cody McFadyen
Chelsea Cain	Brian Freeman	James Patterson
Thomas H Cook	J A Kerley	Karen Rose
Stephen Coonts	Jeff Lindsay	Craig Russell

Michael Moorcock   1939-   Fantasy: Epic
also writes as Edward P Bradbury, James Colvin
www.multiverse.org
🏆 Guardian 1977

M

Jonathan Carroll	Mary Gentle	James Meek
Storm Constantine	Katherine Kurtz	Linda Nagata
Louise Cooper	Wil McCarthy	Christopher Priest
Philip K Dick	Julian May	Kristine Kathryn Rusch

Brian Moore   1921-1999   Can

Dermot Bolger	John McGahern	Morris West
Thomas Keneally	Joseph O'Connor	Tim Winton
Colum McCann	Colm Toibin	

Charlotte Moore   1959-   Aga Saga
also writes as Charlotte McKay

Judy Astley	Sara MacDonald	Kate Saunders
Patricia Fawcett	Robin Pilcher	Mary Wesley
Elizabeth Jane Howard		

Christopher Moore   1946-   US   Fantasy: Humour
www.chrismoore.com

Robert Asprin	Craig Shaw Gardner	Terry Pratchett
Neil Gaiman	Tom Holt	Robert Rankin

Jane Moore   1962-   Chick Lit
www.janemoore.com

Lucy Diamond	Anna Maxted	Patricia Scanlan
Olivia Goldsmith	Sheila O'Flanagan	Plum Sykes
Sue Margolis	Adele Parks	

Caiseal Mor   Aus   Fantasy: Myth
www.mahjee.com

Ashok K Banker	Cecilia Dart-Thornton	Juliet Marillier
James Barclay	Charles de Lint	Judith Tarr
Marion Zimmer Bradley	Stephen R Lawhead	Sarah Zettel

Fidelis Morgan 1952-   Crime: Historical - C17th

also writes as Morgan Benedict   ⚐ Countess Ashby-de-la-Zouche & Alpiew, Maid
www.fidelismorgan.com   C17th London

Gwendoline Butler	Janet Gleeson	David Liss
P F Chisholm	Philip Gooden	Iain Pears
Christie Dickason	Lee Jackson	Laura Joh Rowland

Richard Morgan 1966-   Science Fiction: Near future

www.richardkmorgan.com   ⚐ Takeshi Kovacs
🏆 Arthur C Clarke 2008

Neal Asher	Michael Marshall	J D Robb
Michael Crichton	China Miéville	Justina Robson
Ken MacLeod	Alastair Reynolds	Nick Sagan

Laura Moriarty

www.lauramoriarty.net

Jill Barnett	Sophie Hannah	Ann Packer
Therese Fowler	Alison Jameson	Sarah Willis
Tessa Hadley		

Sinead Moriarty   Ire   Mature Chick Lit

www.sineadmoriarty.com

Cecelia Ahern	Maeve Haran	Chris Manby
Judy Astley	Kate Harrison	Allison Pearson
Colette Caddle	Veronica Henry	

Clare Morrall 1952-

Margaret Atwood	Julie Myerson	Salley Vickers
Zoë Heller	Alice Sebold	Amanda Eyre Ward
Valerie Martin		

David Morrell 1943-   Can   Adventure/Thriller

www.davidmorrell.net   ⚐ Rambo

Campbell Armstrong	Stuart Harrison	Michael Kimball
David Baldacci	Humphrey Hawksley	Alan Savage
Colin Harrison	Richard Herman	Eric Van Lustbader

Mark Morris 1963-   Horror

also writes as J M Morris
www.markmorriswriter.com

Richard Bachman	Shaun Hutson	Brian Lumley
Simon Clark	Graham Joyce	Kim Newman
Stephen Gallagher	Bentley Little	Scott Nicholson

R N Morris
is Roger N Morris

Crime: Police work - Russia
🏃 Det Porfiry Petrovich - C19th St Petersburg

Boris Akunin	Michael Gregorio	Frank Tallis
John Burdett	Andrey Kurkov	Laura Wilson
Jason Goodwin	Michael Pearce	

Blake Morrison   1950-
www.blakemorrison.com

Martin Amis	Margaret Drabble	Ian McEwan
Julian Barnes	Patrick Gale	

Toni Morrison   1931-   US
is Chloe Anthony Wofford
🏆 Pulitzer 1988

William Faulkner	Harper Lee	Amy Tan
Janette Turner Hospital	Terry McMillan	Alice Walker
Lori Lansens	Valerie Martin	

Di Morrissey   1948-   Aus   Saga
www.dimorrissey.com

Joy Chambers	Tamara McKinley	Katherine Scholes
Frank Coates	Judy Nunn	

Ian Morson   1947-
also writes as The Medieval Murderers
(with Philip Gooden, Susanna Gregory, Michael Jecks,
Bernard Knight, C J Sansom)
http://mysite.wanadoo-members.co.uk/Ian_Morson

Crime: Historical - C13th
🏃 William Falconer, Regent Master
Oxford University
Nick Zuliani, Adventurer
Mongolia

Alys Clare	Candace Robb	Kate Sedley
Bernard Knight	Caroline Roe	Peter Tremayne
Ellis Peters		

John Mortimer   1923-   Humour
🏃 Horace Rumpole, Barrister - London • Leslie Titmus - 'Rapstone Valley'

Malcolm Bradbury	David Lodge	Keith Waterhouse
Caro Fraser	Frederic Raphael	P G Wodehouse

Kate Morton   Aus
www.katemorton.com

Joy Chambers	Robert Goddard	Lori Lansens
Jennifer Donnelly	Susan Hill	Ann Patchett
Kim Edwards	Catherine Ryan Hyde	Bella Pollen
Miranda Glover	Barbara Kingsolver	Eva Rice

M

197

Steve Mosby

Crime: Psychological

Mo Hayder
J A Kerley
Stuart MacBride

Michael Marshall
Grace Monroe
Richard Montanari

Meg O'Brien
Thomas Perry

Walter Mosley 1952- US

Crime: Hardboiled

www.waltermosley.com

🚶 Easy Rawlins • Socrates Fortlow
Fearless Jones & Paris Minton } Los Angeles

🏆 CWA 1991

Stephen Donaldson
Steve Hamilton
Dashiell Hammett

Chuck Palahniuk
Patrick Quinlan
James Sallis

Cath Staincliffe
Jason Starr

Kate Mosse 🌉 1961-

Historical

www.mosselabyrinth.co.uk

Paul Christopher
Richard Doetsch
Sara Donati
Barbara Erskine

Michael Gruber
Tom Harper
A J Hartley
Raymond Khoury

Chris Kuzneski
Greg Loomis
Arturo Pérez-Reverte
Manda Scott

Fiona Mountain

Crime: Amateur sleuth

www.fionamountain.com

🚶 Natasha Blake, Genealogist

Mary Higgins Clark
Carol Goodman
Morag Joss

Judith Kelman
Marianne MacDonald

Gwen Moffat
Betty Rowlands

Jojo Moyes 1969-

www.jojomoyes.com

🏆 Romantic 2004

Maeve Binchy
Sarah Challis
Nicholas Coleridge
Jennifer Donnelly

Fannie Flagg
Adèle Geras
Laurie Graham
Joanne Harris

Linda Holeman
Erica James
Lorna Landvik
Monica McInerney

Marcia Muller 1944- US

Crime: PI

www.marciamuller.com

🚶 Sharon McCone - San Francisco

Nicola Barker
Linda Barnes
Cara Black

Carol Higgins Clark
Stella Duffy
Meg Gardiner

Rick Riordan
John Shannon

🌉 may be suitable for young adults

Alice Munro   1931-   Can

🏆 WHSmith 1995

Gail Anderson-Dargatz	Jane Hamilton	Curtis Sittenfeld
William Faulkner	Alistair MacLeod	Amy Tan
Richard Ford	Edna O'Brien	Miriam Toews

Haruki Murakami   1949-   Ja

www.murakami.ch

James Clavell	Bret Easton Ellis	Toby Litt
Michelle de Kretser	Peter Hoeg	Paul Magrs
Jeremy Dyson	Natsuo Kirino	David Mitchell

Iris Murdoch   �́   1919-1999

🏆 Whitbread 1974   Booker 1978

Jostein Gaarder	Doris Lessing	Emma Tennant
Henry James	Simon Mawer	A N Wilson
James Joyce	Muriel Spark	Virginia Woolf

Elizabeth Murphy   Saga

🕴 Ward Family

Anne Baker	Anna Jacobs	Mary Mackie
Benita Brown	Margaret Kaine	Margaret Thornton
Katie Flynn	Maureen Lee	

Margaret Murphy   1959-   Crime: Psychological

www.margaretmurphy.co.uk

Ingrid Black	Babs Horton	Sarah Rayne
Joy Fielding	J Wallis Martin	Chris Simms
Frances Fyfield	Ridley Pearson	Laura Wilson

Annie Murray   1960-   Saga

www.anniemurray.co.uk   Birmingham

Rita Bradshaw	Sara Fraser	Anna Jacobs
Jean Chapman	Hilary Green	Sheila Newberry
Alexandra Connor	Billy Hopkins	Rowena Summers
Dilly Court	Meg Hutchinson	June Tate

Amy Myers   1938-   Crime: Historical - C19th

also writes as Laura Daniels, Harriet Hudson   🕴 Auguste Didier, Chef - C19th Europe
www.amymyers.net   Peter & Georgia Marsh,
Marsh & Daughter Series - C20th England

David Ashton	Alanna Knight	Catherine Shaw
Sara Fraser	Peter Lovesey	M J Trow
Peter J Heck	Elizabeth Peters	

Julie Myerson   1960-

Susan Fletcher	Zoë Heller	Clare Morrall
Nicci Gerrard	Hilary Mantel	Muriel Spark
Jules Hardy	Valerie Martin	

Magdalen Nabb   1947-2007   Crime: Police work - Italy
www.magdalennabb.com   🏃 Marshal Guarnaccia - Florence

Michael Dibdin	H R F Keating	Carlo Lucarelli
David Hewson	Dennis Lehane	Georges Simenon
Roderic Jeffries	Donna Leon	

Vladimir Nabokov   1899-1977   Rus

Martin Amis	James Joyce	Jonathan Trigell
John Banville	Cynthia Ozick	John Updike
Andrew Sean Greer	Thomas Pynchon	

Barbara Nadel   Crime: Police work - Turkey
🏃 Cetin Ikmen - Istanbul
Francis Hancock, Undertaker - London, East End

🏆 CWA 2005

Michael Dibdin	David Hewson	Eliot Pattison
Luiz Alfredo Garcia-Roza	Manuel Vázquez Montalbán	Michael Pearce
Jason Goodwin	Orhan Pamuk	Qiu Xiaolong

Reggie Nadelson   US   Crime: PI
www.reggienadelson.com   🏃 Artie Cohen - New York

Lawrence Block	Robert Crais	Dennis Lehane
Raymond Chandler	Loren D Estleman	S J Rozan
Michael Connelly		

Linda Nagata   1960-   US   Science Fiction: Technical
is Linda Webb
www.maui.net/~nagata

Paul J McAuley	Michael Moorcock	Brian Stableford
Wil McCarthy	Kim Stanley Robinson	Robert Charles Wilson
Ian McDonald		

V S Naipaul   1932-   Carib
🏆 Booker 1971

Chimamanda Ngozi Adichie	Kiran Desai	Ruth Prawer Jhabvala
Vikram Chandra	Chitra Banerjee Divakaruni	Yann Martel
Joseph Conrad	Abdulrazak Gurnah	

Anita Nair Ind
www.anitanair.net

Kavita Daswani	Jhumpa Lahiri	Arundhati Roy
Roopa Farooki	Amulya Malladi	Thirty Umrigar
Manju Kapur		

Preethi Nair 1971- Ind
www.preethinair.com

Kavita Daswani	Jhumpa Lahiri	Nisha Minhas
Roopa Farooki	Sharon Maas	Thirty Umrigar
Manju Kapur	Amulya Malladi	Jane Yardley

Nora Naish Aga Saga

Elizabeth Palmer	Jean Saunders	Mary Wesley
Ann Purser	Kate Saunders	Jane Yardley

John J Nance 1946- US Adventure/Thriller
www.johnjnance.com 🦑 Kat Bronsky - Aviation

Dale Brown	Gordon Kent	Craig Thomas
Tom Clancy	Charles McCarry	Lisa Tucker
Vince Flynn		

Bill Napier 1940- Sco Adventure/Thriller

John Case	Michael Crichton	Douglas Preston
Michael Cordy	Richard Herman	James Rollins

William Napier 1965- Historical: Ancient
is Christopher Hart 🦑 Attila the Hun - C5th

Stephen Baxter	Iain Gale	Scott Oden
Bernard Cornwell	Conn Iggulden	Steven Pressfield
Michael Curtis Ford	Simon Levack	

R K Narayan 1906-2001 Ind
was Rasipuram Krishnaswamy Narayan

Vikram Chandra	Anita Desai	Arundhati Roy
Amit Chaudhuri	Rohinton Mistry	Vikram Seth

Go to back for lists of
Pseudonyms • Authors by Genre • Characters and Series
Prize Winners • Crossover Authors • Further Reading • Websites

Jonathan Nasaw 1947- US

Crime: Psychological

🏃 Agent E L Pender - FBI

Giles Blunt	Daniel Hecht	James Patterson
Patricia D Cornwell	Alex Kava	Christopher Reich
Jeffery Deaver	Jonathan Kellerman	Michael Robotham
Thomas Harris	Meg O'Brien	Stephen White

Melissa Nathan 1968-2006

Chick Lit

www.melissanathan.com

Jessica Adams	Belinda Jones	Maile Meloy
Maggie Alderson	Dorothy Koomson	Freya North
Hester Browne	Julia Llewellyn	Victoria Routledge
Erica James	Sarah Mason	Grace Wynne-Jones

Clare Naylor

Chick Lit

Lucy Dawson	India Knight	Robyn Sisman
Martina Devlin	Sheila Norton	Plum Sykes
Lisa Jewell	Anita Notaro	Lauren Weisberger

Kitty Neale

Saga

is Brenda Warren

South London

www.kittyneale.co.uk

Harry Bowling	Katie Flynn	Mary Jane Staples
Dilly Court	Rosie Harris	Sally Worboyes
Josephine Cox	Ken McCoy	

James L Nelson 1962- US

Sea: Historical

www.jameslnelson.com 🏃 Thomas Marlowe, ex Pirate - USA • Brethren of the Coast Trilogy
Revolution at Sea Saga • Samuel Bowater, American Civil War

David Donachie	Jonathan Lunn	Julian Stockwin
C S Forester	Patrick O'Brian	

Irene Nemirovsky 1903-1942 Ukr

Kate Atkinson	Elliot Perlman	Rachel Seiffert
Pat Barker	Bernhard Schlink	Markus Zusak
Sebastian Faulks		

Jo Nesbo 1959- Nor

Crime: Police work - Norway

www.jonesbo.com 🏃 DI Harry Hole, Oslo

Karin Alvtegen	Arnaldur Indridason	Henning Mankell
Ake Edwardson	Matti Joensuu	Hakan Nesser
Karin Fossum	Mari Jungstedt	Yrsa Sigurdardottir
Anne Holt	Åsa Larsson	Frank Tallis

Hakan Nesser 1950- Swe Crime: Police work - Sweden
🚶 Insp Van Veeteren

Karin Alvtegen
Kate Atkinson
Colin Dexter

Ake Edwardson
Kjell Eriksson
Karin Fossum

Mari Jungstedt
Henning Mankell
Jo Nesbo

Sheila Newberry Saga
WW2

Catherine Cookson
June Francis
Elizabeth Ann Hill

Beryl Kingston
Annie Murray
Gilda O'Neill

June Tate
Dee Williams

Robert Newcomb US Fantasy: Epic
www.robertnewcomb.com

Sarah Ash
James Barclay
Carol Berg

James Clemens
Stephen Donaldson
Terry Goodkind

Robert Jordan
Anne McCaffrey

Kim Newman 1959- Paranormal
also writes as Jack Yeovil
www.johnnyalucard.com
Anno Dracula Series

Poppy Z Brite
Christopher Fowler
Laurell K Hamilton

Brian Lumley
David Martin

Graham Masterton
Mark Morris

Sharan Newman 1949- US Crime: Historical - C12th
www.sharannewman.com
🚶 Catherine LeVendeur - France

Alys Clare
Ariana Franklin
Margaret Frazer

Bernard Knight
Ellis Peters
Caroline Roe

Peter Tremayne
Robyn Young

David Nicholls Lad Lit

Guy Bellamy
Jonathan Coe
Nicholas Coleridge

Sam Holden
Nick Hornby
John Lanchester

Geoff Nicholson
Matt Thorne

Stan Nicholls Fantasy: Epic
www.stannicholls.com

James Barclay
Terry Brooks
David Eddings

David Gemmell
Terry Goodkind
Robert Jordan

George R R Martin
Tad Williams

Geoff Nicholson   1953-   Humour

http://geoff-nicholson.tripod.com

Jonathan Coe	David Nicholls	Leslie Thomas
Joseph Connolly	Tom Sharpe	Nigel Williams
Stephen Fry	Iain Sinclair	

Scott Nicholson   1963-   US   Horror

www.hauntedcomputer.com

Douglas Clegg	Bentley Little	Christopher Pike
Graham Joyce	Mark Morris	Phil Rickman
Richard Laymon		

N

William Nicholson   ☎ ☺   1948-   Fantasy: Epic

www.williamnicholson.co.uk

Trudi Canavan	Lian Hearn	Harry Turtledove
Justin Cartwright	Garth Nix	Margaret Weis
Eoin Colfer	J K Rowling	

Christopher Nicole   1930-   Adventure/Thriller

also writes as Caroline Gray, Mac Marlow, Alan Savage, Andrew York

James Clavell	Greg Iles	Allan Mallinson
James H Cobb	Michael Kimball	Eric Van Lustbader
Graham Hurley		

Audrey Niffenegger   1963-   US   Science Fiction: Space and time

www.audreyniffenegger.com

Paulo Coelho	Barbara Erskine	Eva Rice
Harlan Ellison	Diana Gabaldon	Alice Sebold
Margaret Elphinstone	Raymond Khoury	Carlos Ruiz Zafón

Chris Niles   NZ   Crime: Amateur sleuth

♀ Sam Ridley, Radio journalist - Sydney

Jan Burke	Claire McNab	Rebecca Tope
Peter Guttridge	Mike Ripley	Jill Paton Walsh

Larry Niven   1938-   US   Science Fiction: Space and time

also writes jointly with Jerry Pournelle
www.larryniven.org

Kevin J Anderson	Ben Bova	Jack McDevitt
Neal Asher	Harry Harrison	Kim Stanley Robinson
Isaac Asimov	Frank Herbert	

Garth Nix ☺ 1963- Aus   Fantasy: Myth

www.garthnix.com

Trudi Canavan	Tim Powers	J K Rowling
Lian Hearn	Philip Pullman	Judith Tarr
William Nicholson		

David Nobbs 1935-   Humour

www.davidnobbs.com

🏃 Reginald Perrin

Roddy Doyle	Leslie Thomas	Nigel Williams
Andrew Holmes	Alan Titchmarsh	P G Wodehouse
Tom Holt	Paul Torday	

Elizabeth Noble 1968-   Aga Saga

N

www.elizabethnoblebooks.com

Zoë Barnes	Julie Highmore	Bernadette Strachan
Marika Cobbold	Ann Hood	Amanda Eyre Ward
Fiona Gibson	Sandra Howard	Madeleine Wickham
Kate Harrison	Kate Saunders	Jane Yardley

Jeff Noon 1957-   Science Fiction: Near future

🏆 Arthur C Clarke 1994

Steve Aylett	Geoff Ryman	Neal Stephenson
Jon Courtenay Grimwood	Michael Marshall Smith	Kurt Vonnegut
Michael Marshall		

Diana Norman 1935-   Historical

also writes as Arianna Franklin

Barbara Ewing	Georgette Heyer	Jean Plaidy
Caroline Harvey	Morgan Llywelyn	Connie Willis
Anne Herries	Maureen Peters	

Hilary Norman

also writes as Alexandra Henry
www.hilarynorman.co.uk

Sally Beauman	Lesley Pearse
Celia Brayfield	Karen Rose

     Adventure/Thriller

Mary Higgins Clark	Clare Francis
Martina Cole	Judith Kelman

Freya North
1968-   Chick Lit

www.freyanorth.co.uk

🏆 Romantic 2008

Maggie Alderson	Melissa Nathan	Daisy Waugh
Alison Jameson	Sheila Norton	Deborah Wright
Susan Lewis	Bella Pollen	Laura Zigman

Sheila Norton
Chick Lit

Lynne Barrett-Lee	Gil McNeil	Freya North
Claire Calman	Clare Naylor	Liz Young
Christina Jones		

Anita Notaro
Ire   Chick Lit

Colette Caddle	Christina Jones	Alexandra Potter
Anne Dunlop	Clare Naylor	Victoria Routledge
Melissa Hill	Bella Pollen	Patricia Scanlan

Judy Nunn
1945- Aus   Saga

www.judynunn.com

Frank Coates	Di Morrissey	Alexandra Raife
Tamara McKinley	Imogen Parker	Wilbur Smith

Robert Nye
1939-

🏆 Guardian 1976   Hawthornden 1976

Peter Ackroyd	Julian Rathbone	Rose Tremain
John Fowles	Iain Sinclair	Barry Unsworth
Allan Massie	Jane Stevenson	

Patrick O'Brian
1914-2000   Sea: Historical

was Richard Patrick Russ   🏃 Jack Aubrey & Stephen Maturin - C18th/19th

G S Beard	C S Forester	Allan Mallinson
Tom Connery	Richard Howard	James L Nelson
David Donachie	Jonathan Lunn	Peter Smalley

Edna O'Brien
1932- Ire

Ronan Bennett	Jennifer Johnston	Joyce Carol Oates
Dermot Bolger	John McGahern	J D Salinger
Clare Boylan	Eoin McNamee	Fay Weldon
Anne Enright	Alice Munro	Niall Williams

⌒ may be suitable for young adults

Martin O'Brien
also writes as Jack Drummond

Crime: Police work - France

🏃 CI Daniel Jacquot - Marseilles

Andrea Camilleri	David Hewson	Georges Simenon
Agatha Christie	Peter James	Fred Vargas

Maureen O'Brien   1943-
www.maureenobrien.co.uk

Crime: Police work - UK

🏃 Insp John Bright - London

Paul Charles	Martha Grimes	J Wallis Martin
Elizabeth Ferrars	Graham Ison	Ruth Rendell
Elizabeth George		

Meg O'Brien   US
www.megobrien.com

Crime: Psychological

🏃 Jesse James, Newspaper Reporter - Up State New York

Daniel Hecht	Alex Kava	Jonathan Nasaw
Christiane Heggan	Elizabeth McGregor	Erica Spindler
Tami Hoag	Steve Mosby	Stephen White

O

Tim O'Brien   1946-   US
www.authortimobrien.com

Michael Collins	Richard Ford	Joseph Heller
Michael Cunningham	Charles Frazier	John Irving

Gareth O'Callaghan   Ire

Adventure/Thriller

John Case	Alex Scarrow	Nick Stone
Lee Child	Katherine Scholes	James Twining
Joseph Finder	Boris Starling	Paul Watkins

Carol O'Connell   1947-   US

Crime: Police work - US

🏃 Sgt Kathleen Mallory - New York

Linda Davies	Thomas Laird	Claire McNab
Meg Gardiner	Ed McBain	Theresa Monsour
Faye Kellerman	Sharyn McCrumb	Kathy Reichs

Ed O'Connor

Crime: Psychological

🏃 DI Alison Dexter & DI John Underwood - 'New Bolden', Cambridgeshire

Jane Adams	Jim Kelly	Danuta Reah
Stephen Booth	Barry Maitland	Chris Simms
John Connor		

Joseph O'Connor 1963- Ire

Sebastian Barry	Patrick McCabe	Glenn Patterson
Dermot Bolger	Colum McCann	William Trevor
Roddy Doyle	Bernard MacLaverty	William Wall
Charles Frazier	Brian Moore	Niall Williams

John O'Farrell 1962- Lad Lit: Humour

Guy Bellamy	Fiona Gibson	Nick Hornby
James Delingpole	John Harding	Tony Parsons

Maggie O'Farrell 1972- Ire
www.maggieofarrell.com

♥ S Maugham 2005

Louise Candlish	Miranda Glover	Sue Miller
Helen Dunmore	Almudena Grandes	Elliot Perlman
Susan Fletcher	Tessa Hadley	Roma Tearne
Patricia Gaffney	Charlotte Mendelson	Sarah Willis

O

Sheila O'Flanagan 1962- Ire Chick Lit
www.sheilaoflanagan.net

Rowan Coleman	Milly Johnson	Geraldine O'Neill
Martina Devlin	Sue Margolis	Lesley Pearse
Clare Dowling	Jane Moore	Plum Sykes

Andrew O'Hagan 1968- Sco
♥ Holtby 1999 Black 2003

Ronan Bennett	Janice Galloway	Simon Mawer
Melvyn Bragg	Robin Jenkins	Tim Pears
Glen Duncan	Jackie Kay	Alan Spence
Giles Foden	Patrick McCabe	Edward St Aubyn

Stewart O'Nan 1961- US
www.stewart-onan.com

Thomas Eidson	Charles Frazier	Cormac McCarthy
Louise Erdrich	Harper Lee	Richard Russo

Geraldine O'Neill Ire Saga
www.geraldineoneill.com

Maeve Binchy	Mary A Larkin	D M Purcell
Melissa Hill	Sheila O'Flanagan	Liz Ryan
Cathy Kelly	Joan O'Neill	

Gilda O'Neill — Saga
East End of London

Pip Granger
Meg Henderson
Beryl Kingston

Gwen Madoc
Sheila Newberry
Pamela Oldfield

Carol Rivers
June Tate
Jeanne Whitmee

Joan O'Neill — Ire — Saga
Ireland

Josephine Cox
Frank Delaney
Rose Doyle

Catherine Dunne
Iris Gower
Geraldine O'Neill

Liz Ryan
Nicola Thorne

Kate O'Riordan — Ire — Aga Saga

Sherry Ashworth
Colette Caddle
Martina Devlin

Cathy Kelly
Marian Keyes

Shari Low
Serena Mackesy

Perri O'Shaughnessy — US — Crime: Legal/financial
is Pamela & Mary O'Shaughnessy
www.perrio.com
Nina Reilly, Attorney
Lake Tahoe, California

Alafair Burke
Linda Davies
Linda Fairstein

Nancy Taylor Rosenberg
Lisa Scottoline

Susan R Sloan
Robert K Tanenbaum

Andy Oakes — 1952- — Crime: Police work - China
Sun Piao - Shangai

Gianrico Carofiglio
R J Ellory

Xiaolu Guo
Peter May

Qiu Xiaolong
Lisa See

Joyce Carol Oates — 1938- — US
also writes as Lauren Kelly, Rosamond Smith

Katharine Davies
Jenny Diski
William Faulkner

Connie May Fowler
Gail Godwin
Sue Monk Kidd

Edna O'Brien
Cynthia Ozick
Edith Wharton

Scott Oden — 1967- — US — Historical: Ancient
www.menofbronze.com

Bernard Cornwell
Michael Curtis Ford

Conn Iggulden
William Napier

Steven Pressfield
Wilbur Smith

☺ also writes children's books

Ben Okri 1959- Nigeria

🏆 Booker 1991

Chinua Achebe	Jack Kerouac	Helen Oyeyemi
Roopa Farooki	David Malouf	Caryl Phillips
Gabriel Garcia Márquez		

Pamela Oldfield 1931- Saga

Heron Saga - Kent • Foxearth Trilogy

Tessa Barclay	Victor Pemberton	Jeanne Whitmee
Christine Marion Fraser	Carol Rivers	Janet Woods
Gilda O'Neill		

Nick Oldham 1956- Crime: Police work - UK

www.nickoldham.net 🚶 DCI Henry Christie - Blackpool

Judith Cutler	Nicholas Rhea	Mark Timlin
Lesley Horton	Sally Spencer	R D Wingfield
Stuart Pawson	Leslie Thomas	

Michael Ondaatje 1943- Sri Lan

🏆 Irish Times 1991 Booker 1992

Anthony Capella	Romesh Gunesekera	David Park
Stevie Davies	Kazuo Ishiguro	Colin Thubron
Michelle de Kretser	Colum McCann	Miriam Toews
Kiran Desai	Alistair MacLeod	Marianne Wiggins

George Orwell 1903-50

was Eric Blair

Margaret Atwood	Graham Greene	Liz Jensen
Ray Bradbury	John Twelve Hawks	Ismail Kadare
Ben Elton	Aldous Huxley	Daniel Mason

Sharon Owens 1968- Ire Saga

www.sharonowens.co.uk

Margaret Dickinson	Margaret Kaine	Kate Thompson
Katie Fforde	Mary A Larkin	Paige Toon
Joan Jonker	Gwen Madoc	

Helen Oyeyemi 1984-

Chimamanda Ngozi Adichie	Sebastian Faulks	Ali Smith
Kiran Desai	Ben Okri	

Amos Oz 1939- Isr

Saul Bellow
Michael Chabon

William Faulkner
David Grossman

Christopher Hope
Howard Jacobson

Cynthia Ozick 1928- US

Lisa Appignanesi
Vladimir Nabokov

Joyce Carol Oates
Philip Roth

John Updike

Ann Packer 1959- US
www.annpacker.com

Zoë Heller
Sue Monk Kidd
Maile Meloy
Laura Moriarty

Nicky Pellegrino
Jodi Picoult
Ann Purser
Alice Sebold

Anita Shreve
Lionel Shriver
Anne Tyler

Lynda Page 1950- Saga
www.lyndapage.co.uk Leicester

Lyn Andrews
Rita Bradshaw
Katie Flynn

Sara Fraser
Hilary Green
Billy Hopkins

Margaret Thornton
Audrey Willsher

Frances Paige Sco Saga
⚐ MacKintosh Sisters • McGrath Family
Scotland

Tessa Barclay
Maggie Bennett
Doris Davidson

Meg Henderson
Nicky Pellegrino

Jessica Stirling
Mary Withall

Robin Paige US Crime: Historical - C19th
is Susan Wittig Albert and Bill Albert ⚐ Sir Charles Sheridan, Peer & Kate Ardleigh, Writer
www.mysterypartners.com 1900 England

Catherine Aird
David Dickinson
Carola Dunn

Graham Ison
Laurie R King
David Roberts

Charles Todd
Jacqueline Winspear

Chuck Palahniuk 1961- US Crime: Hardboiled
www.chuckpalahniuk.net

Lorenzo Carcaterra
Douglas Coupland
Don DeLillo

Stephen Donaldson
Bret Easton Ellis

James Ellroy
Walter Mosley

Chris Paling 1956-   Adventure/Thriller

| Robert Edric | John Harvey | Nicholas Royle |
| Sebastian Faulks | Ian Rankin | Martyn Waites |

Elizabeth Palmer 1942-   Aga Saga

| Diana Appleyard | Victoria Clayton | Nora Naish |
| Amanda Brookfield | Katie Fforde | Libby Purves |

Michael Palmer 1942- US   Adventure/Thriller: Medical
www.michaelpalmerbooks.com

Paul Carson	Tess Gerritsen	Mo Hayder
Robin Cook	Leonard Goldberg	Ken McClure
Michael Crichton		

Orhan Pamuk 1952- Tur   Crime: Historical
www.orhanpamuk.com   Istanbul
🏆 IMPAC 2003

Louis de Bernières	Jason Goodwin	Barbara Nadel
Umberto Eco	Ismail Kadare	Vikram Seth
Maureen Freely	Amin Maalouf	Carlos Ruiz Zafón
Jostein Gaarder	James Meek	Markus Zusak

Christopher Paolini ⌒ ☺ 1983- US   Fantasy: Epic
www.alagaesia.com

Trudi Canavan	Frank Herbert	Matthew Pearl
David Eddings	J V Jones	Philip Pullman
Raymond E Feist	Ursula K Le Guin	J R R Tolkien
Brian Herbert	Anne McCaffrey	J K Rowling

Sara Paretsky 1947- US   Crime: PI
www.saraparetsky.com   ⚐ V I Warshawski - Chicago
🏆 CWA 1988, 2002 & 2004

Cara Black	Reg Gadney	Zoë Sharp
Anna Blundy	Lynda La Plante	Gillian Slovo
Edna Buchanan	Rick Riordan	Dana Stabenow
Carol Higgins Clark	John Shannon	Stella Whitelaw

Edith Pargeter 1913-95   Historical
also wrote as Ellis Peters

Margaret George	Katharine McMahon	Jean Plaidy
Rosalind Laker	Robin Maxwell	Nigel Tranter
Morgan Llywelyn	Sharon Penman	

212

David Park 1954- Ire

Dermot Bolger
Mary Lawson
John McGahern

Bernard MacLaverty
Alistair MacLeod
Michael Ondaatje

Glenn Patterson
Colm Toibin
William Trevor

Barbara Parker US   Crime: Legal/financial
www.barbaraparker.com   ⚐ Gail Connor & Anthony Quintana, Lawyers - Miami

Stephen L Carter
James Grippando
John Grisham

John McLaren
Phillip Margolin

Steve Martini
Scott Turow

Imogen Parker 1958-   Mature Chick Lit

Maeve Binchy
Victoria Clayton
Kate Grenville

Sarah Harrison
Judith Lennox

Susan Lewis
Judy Nunn

Jefferson Parker 1953- US   Crime: Police work - US
also writes as T Jefferson Parker   California
www.tjeffersonparker.com

John Connolly
Barry Eisler
John Gilstrap

Faye Kellerman
Jonathan Kellerman
Michael Malone

Ridley Pearson
John Shannon
Joseph Wambaugh

P

K J Parker   Fantasy: Epic
www.kjparker.com

Chaz Brenchley
Juliet E McKenna

Tim Powers
Steph Swainston

Freda Warrington
Jane Welch

Robert B Parker 1932- US   Crime: PI
www.robertbparker.net   ⚐ Spenser, PI
                                 Sunny Randall, PI } Boston, Mass
                                 Chief Jesse Stone - 'Paradise', Mass

Lawrence Block
Raymond Chandler
James Hadley Chase
Harlan Coben

Robert Crais
Dick Francis
Kinky Friedman
J A Jance

Ed McBain
Thomas Perry
John Shannon
Donald Westlake

Una-Mary Parker 1930-   Glitz & Glamour

Sally Beauman
Barbara Taylor Bradford
Anita Burgh

Barbara Delinsky
Penny Jordan
Johanna Lindsey

LaVyrle Spencer
Danielle Steel

Adele Parks   1969-   Mature Chick Lit
www.adeleparks.com

Trisha Ashley   Kate Harrison   Anna Maxted
Emily Barr   Sophie King   Jane Moore
Lucy Dawson   India Knight   Paige Toon
Martina Devlin   Gil McNeil   Jennifer Weiner

Tim Parks   1954-
www.timparks.co.uk
🏆 S Maugham 1986   Betty Trask 1986
Julian Barnes   Bret Easton Ellis   Amanda Prantera
William Boyd   Toby Litt   Barbara Trapido
Domenica de Rosa

Julie Parsons   1951-   Ire   Adventure/Thriller: Psychological

Mary Higgins Clark   Ruth Rendell   Barbara Vine
Neil Cross   Liz Rigbey   Margaret Yorke
Sarah Diamond   Louis Sanders

Tony Parsons   🌉   1955-   Lad Lit

Paul Burke   Mike Gayle   John O'Farrell
Neil Cross   John Harding   Ben Richards
Matt Dunn   Sam Holden   Matt Whyman

Ann Patchett   1963-   US
www.annpatchett.com
🏆 Orange 2002
Gail Anderson-Dargatz   Jane Hamilton   Kate Morton
Trezza Azzopardi   Susan Hill   Nicholas Shakespeare
Margaret Drabble   Victoria Hislop   Jane Urquhart
Miranda Glover   Valerie Martin   Susan Vreeland

Glenn Patterson   1961-   Ire

Dermot Bolger   Patrick McCabe   David Park
David Flusfeder   Joseph O'Connor   Colm Toibin

James Patterson   🌉 ☺   1947-   US   Crime: Psychological
also writes jointly with Peter De Jonge, Andrew Gross,   🏃 Det Alex Cross - Washington DC
Michael Ledwidge, Maxine Paetro, Howard Roughan   'Women's Murder Club' - San Francisco
www.jamespatterson.com   Hugh de Lac - Medieval France

Chelsea Cain   Heather Graham   Richard Montanari
Jeffery Deaver   Jonathan Kellerman   Chris Mooney
Robert Ellis   Dennis Lehane   Jonathan Nasaw
Brian Freemantle   Michael Marshall   James Siegel

Richard North Patterson 1947- US Crime: Legal/financial
♁ Christopher Paget, Attorney - San Francisco

Janet Fitch	Douglas Kennedy	Michael Ridpath
James Grippando	Phillip Margolin	Nancy Taylor Rosenberg
David Hosp		

James Pattinson 1915- Adventure/Thriller

Brian Callison	Clive Cussler	Hammond Innes
James H Cobb	Alexander Fullerton	Douglas Reeman

Eliot Pattison 1971- Sco Crime: PI
www.eliotpattison.com ♁ Insp Shan Tao Yun, Former policeman - China

Paul Adam	Donna Leon	Lisa See
Michael Dibdin	Barbara Nadel	Martin Cruz Smith
Tony Hillerman	Qiu Xiaolong	

Rebecca Pawel US Crime: Historical - C20th
www.rebeccapawel.com ♁ Carlos Tejada - Civil War Spain

Robert Harris	Manuel Vázquez Montalbán	David Roberts
Roderic Jeffries	Arturo Perez-Reverte	Guy Walters
Philip Kerr		

Stuart Pawson 1940- Crime: Police work - UK
www.meanstreets.co.uk ♁ DI Charlie Priest - Yorkshire

Robert Barnard	Georgie Hale	Nick Oldham
Pauline Bell	Patricia Hall	Nicholas Rhea
Chris Collett	Ken McCoy	Peter Turnbull

David Peace 1967- Crime: Hardboiled
Red Riding Quartet - Yorkshire • Det Minami - Tokyo

🏆 Black 2004

Jake Arnott	Bill James	Ian Rankin
Ken Bruen	Simon Kernick	Danuta Reah
Lorenzo Carcaterra		

Michael Pearce 1933- Crime: Historical - C20th
♁ The Mamur Zapt (Gareth Owen), Secret police - early C20th Egypt
Dmitri Kameron, Lawyer - Tsarist Russia • Seymour, Special Branch

🏆 CWA 1993

Boris Akunin	Lauren Haney	R N Morris
Barbara Cleverly	Graham Ison	Barbara Nadel
Jason Goodwin	Roderic Jeffries	Elizabeth Peters
Michael Gregorio	H R F Keating	Laura Joh Rowland

P

Matthew Pearl   1975-   US   Crime: Historical
www.matthewpearl.com

Lee Child	Guillermo Martinez	Frank Tallis
Jonathan Franzen	Christopher Paolini	Donna Tartt
Deryn Lake	Richard Powers	

Iain Pears   1955-   Crime: Amateur sleuth
⚘ Jonathan Argyll, Art historian

Gwendoline Butler	Philip Gooden	Keith Miles
John Dunning	John Maclachlan Gray	Fidelis Morgan
Earlene Fowler	Lee Jackson	Arturo Pérez-Reverte
Janet Gleeson	John Malcolm	Derek Wilson

Tim Pears   1956-
www.timpears.com
🏆 Hawthornden 1994

Kate Atkinson	Glen Duncan	Thomas Hardy
Tim Binding	Robert Edric	Andrew O'Hagan
Jonathan Coe	William Faulkner	J B Priestley

Lesley Pearse   1945-
www.lesleypearse.co.uk

Zoë Barnes	Harriet Hudson	Sheila O'Flanagan
Emma Blair	Margaret Kaine	Michael Taylor
Susie Boyt	Maile Meloy	Polly Williams
Jilly Cooper	Hilary Norman	Elizabeth Wrenn

Allison Pearson   Humour

Anna Blundy	Sue Limb	Libby Purves
Amanda Craig	Sinead Moriarty	Louise Wener
Jane Green		

Ridley Pearson   1953-   US   Crime: Police work - US
also writes as Wendell McCall,   ⚘ Sgt Lou Boldt & Daphne Matthews, Forensic psychologist
Joyce Reardon   Seattle
www.ridleypearson.com

Giles Blunt	Faye Kellerman	Medora Sale
Jeffery Deaver	Jonathan Kellerman	John Sandford
W E B Griffin	Margaret Murphy	P J Tracy
Donald Harstad	Jefferson Parker	Jess Walter

George P Pelecanos 1957- US

Crime: Hardboiled

🏃 Nick Stefanos • Derek Strange & Terry Quinn
Washington DC

Jeff Abbott	R J Ellory	Ross Macdonald
Edward Bunker	John Hart	Patrick Quinlan
James Lee Burke	Matthew Klein	Jim Thompson
James Crumley	Thomas Laird	Louise Welsh

Nicky Pellegrino 1964- It

Trisha Ashley	Domenica de Rosa	Ann Packer
Amanda Craig	Sarah Kate Lynch	Frances Paige

Margaret Pemberton 1943-

Historical
London Sequence

also writes as Maggie Hudson

Harry Bowling	Harriet Hudson	Patricia Shaw
Dorothy Dunnett	Sara Hylton	Nicola Thorne
Margaret Elphinstone	Judith Saxton	

Victor Pemberton

Saga
London

www.victorpemberton.com

Philip Boast	Billy Hopkins	Pamela Oldfield
Harry Bowling	Mary A Larkin	Carol Rivers
Pamela Evans	Claire Lorrimer	Mary Jane Staples
Lilian Harry	Margaret Mayhew	Sally Worboyes

P

Sharon Penman 1945- US

Historical
🏃 Justin de Quincey - C12th France

www.sharonkaypenman.com

Elizabeth Chadwick	Helen Hollick	Mary Stewart
Will Davenport	Morgan Llywelyn	Nigel Tranter
Dorothy Dunnett	Edith Pargeter	

Louise Penny 1958- Can

Crime: Police work - Canada
🏃 CI Armand Gamache, Quebec

www.louisepenny.com

🏆 CWA 2006

David Armstrong	Stephen Booth	Donald Harstad
Simon Beckett	Ann Cleeves	Reginald Hill
Victoria Blake	Barbara Cleverly	Lis Howell
Giles Blunt	Christopher Fowler	Medora Sale

Go to back for lists of
Pseudonyms • Authors by Genre • Characters and Series
Prize Winners • Crossover Authors • Further Reading • Websites

Andrew Pepper

Crime: Historical - C19th
🏃 Pyke, Bow Street Runners

John Maclachlan Gray	James McGee	Barrie Roberts
Deryn Lake	Edward Marston	Rosemary Stevens
Peter Lovesey	Anne Perry	

Arturo Pérez-Reverte 1951- Spain

Adventure/Thriller: Historical
www.perez-reverte.com
🏃 Captain Alatriste - C17th Spain

Andrea Camilleri	Raymond Khoury	Kate Mosse
Umberto Eco	Amin Maalouf	Rebecca Pawel
Almudena Grandes	Manuel Vázquez Montalbán	Iain Pears

Elliot Perlman 1964- Aus

Peter Corris	Irene Nemirovsky	Peter Temple
Robert Drewe	Maggie O'Farrell	Markus Zusak
Jonathan Franzen	Philip Roth	

Wendy Perriam 1940-

www.wendyperriam.com

Kingsley Amis	Gwendoline Riley	Emma Tennant
Clare Boylan	Muriel Spark	Fay Weldon
Sarah Harrison		

Anne Perry 1938- NZ

Crime: Historical - C19th/C20th
www.anneperry.net
🏃 Insp Thomas Pitt & Charlotte Pitt
Insp William Monk & Hester Monk } C19th England
World War 1 Series - C20th England

Conrad Allen	Sara Fraser	Joan Lock
David Ashton	Kerry Greenwood	James McGee
David Dickinson	Graham Ison	Andrew Martin
Arthur Conan Doyle	Lee Jackson	Andrew Pepper

Tasmina Perry

Glitz & Glamour

Catherine Alliott	Katie Fforde	Johanna Lindsey
Louise Bagshawe	Veronica Henry	Lesley Lokko
Jackie Collins	Louise Kean	Judith Michael

Thomas Perry 1947- US

Adventure/Thriller: Psychological
🏃 Jane Whitefield, Native American

Lawrence Block	Robert Ellis	Elmore Leonard
James Lee Burke	Thomas Harris	Steve Mosby
Michael Connelly	Dennis Lehane	Robert B Parker

Elizabeth Peters 1927- US Crime: Historical - C19th

also writes as Barbara Michaels; is Barbara Mertz
www.ameliapeabody.com

Amelia Peabody, Egyptologist

Barbara Cleverly	Sara Fraser	Michael Pearce
Clare Curzon	Amy Myers	Lynda S Robinson
David Dickinson		

Ellis Peters 1913-95 Crime: Historical - Medieval

was Edith Pargeter
🏆 CWA 1980

Brother Cadfael - C13th Shropshire • CI George Felse, Police - UK

Simon Beaufort	Andrew M Greeley	Ian Morson
Paul Doherty	Susanna Gregory	Sharan Newman
Ariana Franklin	Cora Harrison	Mary Reed and Eric Mayer
Margaret Frazer	Michael Jecks	Pip Vaughan-Hughes

Maureen Peters 1935- Wales Historical

also writes as Veronica Black, Catherine Darby, Elizabeth Law

Tracy Chevalier	Diana Norman	Kate Tremayne
Rosalind Laker	Jean Plaidy	Barbara Wood
Robin Maxwell	Reay Tannahill	

Chris Petit 1949- Adventure/Thriller

Alex Berenson	Gayle Lynds	Nicholas Royle
Jon Evans	Henry Porter	Iain Sinclair
Dan Fesperman	Stella Rimington	

Caryl Phillips 1958- Carib

www.carylphillips.com
🏆 Sunday Times 1992   Black 1993   Commonwealth 2004

Nadeem Aslam	Hanif Kureishi	Timothy Mo
Xiaolu Guo	Andrea Levy	Ben Okri
James Kelman	Anne Michaels	

Jodi Picoult 1967- US

www.jodipicoult.com

Mitch Albom	Karen Joy Fowler	Elisabeth Hyde
Barbara Delinsky	Patricia Gaffney	Ann Packer
Susan Fletcher	Sophie Hannah	Curtis Sittenfeld
Connie May Fowler	Catherine Ryan Hyde	Lisa Tucker

P

may be suitable for young adults

Marge Piercy   1936-   US

www.margepiercy.com

🏆 Arthur C Clarke 1993

Louise Doughty	Sue Miller	Robert James Waller
Jackie Kay	Jane Smiley	Louisa Young
Shena Mackay		

D B C Pierre   1961-   US

is Peter Findlay

🏆 Man Booker 2003   Whitbread 2003

Martin Amis	Yann Martel	Lionel Shriver
Paul Auster	J D Salinger	Jonathan Trigell
Marina Lewycka		

Christopher Pike   ⌒ ☺   1954-   US   Horror

is Kevin Christopher McFadden

Shaun Hutson	Scott Nicholson	John Saul
Stephen Laws	Phil Rickman	Peter Straub
Richard Laymon		

Robin Pilcher   1950-   Sco   Aga Saga

www.robinpilcher.co.uk

Amanda Brookfield	Julie Highmore	Charlotte Moore
Marika Cobbold	Rachel Hore	Rosamunde Pilcher
Elizabeth Edmondson	Kate Long	Alexandra Raife
Sarah Grazebrook	Sara MacDonald	Jean Saunders

Rosamunde Pilcher   1924-   Aga Saga

also writes as Jane Fraser

🏆 Romantic 1996

Sarah Challis	Adèle Geras	Robin Pilcher
Lucy Clare	Elizabeth Jane Howard	Jean Saunders
Victoria Clayton	Judith Lennox	Sally Stewart
Annabel Dilke	Sara MacDonald	Marcia Willett

John Pilkington   Crime: Historical - C16th

🏃 Thomas the Falconer - Elizabethan London

P F Chisholm	Philip Gooden	Martin Stephen
Michael Clynes	C C Humphreys	Peter Tonkin
Patricia Finney	C J Sansom	

☺ also writes children's books

David Pirie 1946- Sco Crime: Historical - C19th

🏃 Arthur Conan Doyle & Dr Joseph Bell - Edinburgh

Gwendoline Butler	John Maclachlan Gray	Barrie Roberts
David Dickinson	Peter J Heck	M J Trow
Arthur Conan Doyle	Alanna Knight	

Jenny Pitman 1946- Crime: Amateur sleuth

🏃 Jan Hardy, Race horse trainer

Dick Francis	Richard Pitman	Lyndon Stacey
John Francome	Graeme Roe	

Richard Pitman Crime: Amateur sleuth

also writes jointly with Joe McNally Horse racing

Dick Francis	Jenny Pitman	Lyndon Stacey
John Francome	Graeme Roe	

Jean Plaidy 1906-93 Historical

also wrote as Philippa Carr, Victoria Holt; was Eleanor Alice Burford Hibbert

Christie Dickason	Sandra Gulland	Edith Pargeter
Dorothy Dunnett	Anne Herries	Maureen Peters
Margaret George	Diana Norman	Alison Weir

Belva Plain 1919- US Saga

www.belvaplain.com 🏃 Werner Family - USA

Janet Dailey	Joan Medlicott	Sue Sully
Barbara Delinsky	Anne Rivers Siddons	Rosie Thomas
Jude Deveraux	LaVyrle Spencer	

Bella Pollen

Melissa Bank	Maile Meloy	Freya North
Alice Hoffman	Mark Mills	Anita Notaro
Wendy Holden	Kate Morton	

Dudley Pope 1925-1997 Sea: Historical & Modern

G S Beard	C S Forester	Jonathan Lunn
Tom Connery	Duncan Harding	Philip McCutchan
David Donachie	Sam Llewellyn	

P

Henry Porter 1953- Adventure/Thriller
ⵝ Robert Harland

ⵣ CWA 2005

Ronan Bennett	David Fiddimore	Gayle Lynds
Alex Berenson	John Fullerton	Chris Petit
Charles Cumming	Jean-Christophe Grangé	Stella Rimington
Jon Evans	Joseph Kanon	Robert Wilson

Alexandra Potter 1970- Chick Lit

Jessica Adams	Dorothy Koomson	Paige Toon
Maria Beaumont	Kathy Lette	Sarah Tucker
Harriet Evans	Anita Notaro	Fiona Walker
Helen Fielding	Bernadette Strachan	Sara Shepard

Stanley Pottinger US Adventure/Thriller

www.stanleypottinger.com

Russell Andrews	Nelson DeMille	Nigel West
Suzanne Brockmann	David Hagberg	Gillian White

Anthony Powell 1905-2000

E M Forster	Aldous Huxley	Evelyn Waugh
Graham Greene	J B Priestley	A N Wilson

Richard Powers 1957- US

ⵣ WHSmith 2004

William Boyd	Richard Ford	Matthew Pearl
Don DeLillo	Christopher Hope	Thomas Pynchon
Jonathan Safran Foer		

Science Fiction: Near future

Neal Asher	Paul J McAuley	Neal Stephenson
John Birmingham	Lucius Shepard	Tobias Wolff
Jeffrey Eugenides		

Tim Powers 1952- US Fantasy: Contemporary
also writes as William Ashbless (with James P Blaylock)

Charles de Lint	Barbara Hambly	K J Parker
Philip K Dick	Robert Holdstock	H G Wells
Neil Gaiman	Gregory Maguire	Connie Willis
Mary Gentle	Garth Nix	Gene Wolfe

Amanda Prantera 1942-

J M Coetzee	Tim Parks	
Amanda Craig	Rupert Thomson	Barry Unsworth
	Barbara Trapido	Peter Watt

P

Terry Pratchett ⌒ ☺ 1948-   Fantasy: Humour
Discworld
www.terrypratchettbooks.com

♛ BSFA 1989

Robert Asprin	Craig Shaw Gardner	Christopher Moore
Susanna Clarke	Rob Grant	Robert Rankin
Eoin Colfer	Simon Green	Martin Scott
Jasper Fforde	Brian Herbert	Kim Wilkins

Steven Pressfield 1943- US   Historical
Ancient Greece
www.stevenpressfield.com

Stephen Baxter	Robert Harris	Scott Oden
Bernard Cornwell	Christian Jacq	Mary Renault
Michael Curtis Ford	Valerio Massimo Manfredi	Tim Severin
Robert Graves	William Napier	Jack Whyte

Douglas Preston 1956- US   Adventure/Thriller
also writes jointly with Lincoln Child
www.prestonchild.com

Dan Brown	Michael Crichton	Robert Ludlum
Lincoln Child	Richard Doetsch	Andy McDermott
Michael Cordy	David Gibbins	Bill Napier
Harold Coyle	Brian Haig	James Rollins

Marcia Preston US
www.marciapreston.com

Jill Barnett	Elizabeth Flock	Jacquelyn Mitchard
Barbara Delinsky	Nicci Gerrard	Mary Alice Monroe

Katie Price 1978-   Glitz & Glamour
is Katrina Alexandra Infield (Jordan)
www.katieprice.co.uk

Celia Brayfield	Jackie Collins	Johanna Lindsey
Candace Bushnell	Olivia Goldsmith	Harold Robbins

Christopher Priest 1943-   Science Fiction: Space and time
www.christopher-priest.co.uk

♛ BSFA 1998 & 2002   Arthur C Clarke 2003

J G Ballard	Robert Silverberg	Robert Charles Wilson
Philip K Dick	H G Wells	David Zindell
Michael Moorcock	Connie Willis	

☺ also writes children's books

223

J B Priestley · 1894-1984
www.jbpriestley.co.uk

R F Delderfield	Stanley Middleton	Anthony Powell
John Galsworthy	Tim Pears	H G Wells
W Somerset Maugham		

Lily Prior · Humour
www.lilyprior.com

Anthony Capella	Laura Esquivel	Sarah Kate Lynch
Mavis Cheek	Joanne Harris	Ian Sansom
Chitra Banerjee Divakaruni		

Annie Proulx · 1935- · US
also wrote previously as E Annie Proulx
🏆 Irish Times 1993 · Pulitzer 1994

Suzanne Berne	Thomas Eidson	Jonathan Franzen
Kiran Desai	Louise Erdrich	Peter Hoeg
Robb Forman Dew	Fannie Flagg	Donna Tartt

Morag Prunty · 1964- · Ire · Chick Lit
www.recipes.ie/home.html

Cecelia Ahern	Claudia Carroll	Monica McInerney
Hester Browne	Melissa Hill	Jennifer Weiner
Colette Caddle	Belinda Jones	Laura Zigman

Malcolm Pryce · 1960- · Crime: Humour
www.malcolmpryce.com · 🚶 Louie Knight, PI - Aberystwyth

Colin Bateman	Jasper Fforde	Danny King
Christopher Brookmyre	Christopher Fowler	Robert Lewis
Tim Dorsey	Mark Gatiss	Ian Sansom

Philip Pullman 🌙 ☺ · 1946- · Fantasy
www.philip-pullman.com
🏆 Whitbread 2001

Eoin Colfer	John Twelve Hawks	Gregory Maguire
G W Dahlquist	Lian Hearn	China Miéville
Neil Gaiman	C S Lewis	Garth Nix
Mary Gentle	Sergei Lukyanenko	Christopher Paolini

Go to back for lists of
Pseudonyms • Authors by Genre • Characters and Series
Prize Winners • Crossover Authors • Further Reading • Websites

P

D M Purcell

Saga

also wrote previously as Deirdre Purcell

Ireland

Frank Delaney
Rose Doyle
Sheelagh Kelly
Geraldine O'Neill
Liz Ryan
Susan Sallis
Patricia Scanlan
Kate Thompson
Sally Worboyes

Ann Purser

www.annpurser.com

'Round Ringford'

Marika Cobbold
Erica James
Jan Karon
Nora Naish
Ann Packer
Miss Read
Jean Saunders
Rebecca Shaw
Célestine Hitiura Vaite

Crime: Amateur sleuth

Lois Meade, Cleaner - 'Long Farnden'

Caroline Graham
Ann Granger
Patricia Harwin
Veronica Heley
Hazel Holt
Lis Howell
Marianne MacDonald
Betty Rowlands

Libby Purves 1950-

Candida Clark
Anne Fine
Patricia Gaffney
Elizabeth Palmer
Allison Pearson
Joanna Trollope
Louise Voss
Louise Wener
Ann Widdecombe

P

Mario Puzo 1920-1999 US

www.mariopuzo.com

The Godfather

Lorenzo Carcaterra
Elmore Leonard
Harold Robbins
Joseph Wambaugh

Thomas Pynchon 1937- US

Paul Auster
Ron Butlin
Don Delillo
Nathan Englander
Joseph Heller
John Irving
Denis Johnson
Jack Kerouac
Norman Mailer
Vladimir Nabokov
Richard Powers
Tom Robbins

Andrew Pyper 1968- Can

Crime: Psychological

www.andrewpyper.com

Stephen Booth
Nicci French
Stephen King
Dennis Lehane
John Saul
Chris Simms
Erica Spindler
Stephen White

Qiu Xiaolong   1953-   China

www.qiuxiaolong.com

Crime: Police work - China
🏃 Insp Chen - Shanghai

Andrea Camilleri	Donna Leon	Eliot Pattison
Luiz Alfredo Garcia-Roza	Peter May	Lisa See
Xiaolu Guo	Barbara Nadel	Frank Tallis
Ha Jin	Andy Oakes	Xinran

Amanda Quick   1948-   US

also writes as Jayne Castle; is Jayne Ann Krentz
www.amandaquick.com

Historical Romance

Elizabeth Bailey	Julie Garwood	Fenella-Jane Miller
Catherine Coulter	Georgette Heyer	Julia Quinn
Elizabeth Darrell	Judith McNaught	Patricia Shaw

Sheila Quigley

Crime: Hardboiled
🏃 DI Lorraine Hunt - Sunderland

Lindsay Ashford	Mandasue Heller	Lynda La Plante
Martina Cole	Roberta Kray	Ken McCoy
June Hampson		

Anna Quindlen   1953-   US

Elizabeth Berg	Linda Grant	Jane Smiley
Robb Forman Dew	Alice Hoffman	Miriam Toews
Margaret Forster	Elizabeth Jane Howard	

Patrick Quinlan

www.patrickquinlan.com

Crime: Hardboiled

Edward Bunker	Matthew Klein	Walter Mosley
John Hart	Elmore Leonard	George P Pelecanos
Patricia Highsmith	Kevin Lewis	Don Winslow

Julia Quinn   1970-   US

is Julie Cotler Pottinger
www.juliaquinn.com

Historical Romance

Elizabeth Bailey	Marion Chesney	Stephanie Laurens
Mary Balogh	Georgette Heyer	Amanda Quick
Anne Barbour		

Jonathan Raban   1942-   US

www.jonathanraban.com

Sebastian Faulks	Richard Ford	David Grossman
	Andrew Greig	Alan Spence

Robert Radcliffe

War: Modern

Frank Barnard
David Fiddimore
Andrew Greig

James Holland
Marion Husband

Derek Robinson
Paul Watkins

Zane Radcliffe   1969-   Ire

Crime: Humour

Colin Bateman
Christopher Brookmyre
Peter Guttridge

James Hawes
Carl Hiaasen

Joe R Lansdale
Pauline McLynn

Alexandra Raife

Saga
Scotland

Margaret Thomson Davis
Judy Nunn
Robin Pilcher
Miss Read

Elvi Rhodes
Denise Robertson
Liz Ryan
Linda Sole

Mary Stewart
Janet Tanner
Adriana Trigiani
T R Wilson

Patrick Rambaud   1946-   Fr

War: Historical
Napoleonic wars

Bernard Cornwell
Richard Howard

Alexander Kent
Allan Mallinson

Simon Scarrow
John Wilcox

Eileen Ramsay   Sco

Saga
Scotland

www.eileenramsay.co.uk

Emma Blair
Jessica Blair
Maggie Craig

Doris Davidson
Adèle Geras
Gwen Kirkwood

Miss Read
Denise Robertson
Mary Withall

R

Ian Rankin   1960-   Sco

Crime: Police work - UK

also writes as Jack Harvey
www.ianrankin.net

DI John Rebus & DC Siobhan Clarke - Edinburgh

CWA 1997 & 2005

Lin Anderson
Robert G Barrett
Gillian Galbraith
Bartholomew Gill

Alex Gray
Allan Guthrie
Tobias Hill
Frederic Lindsay

Brian McGilloway
Chris Paling
David Peace
Nicholas Royle

Robert Rankin   1949-

Science Fiction: Humour

Douglas Adams
Jasper Fforde
Rob Grant

Charlaine Harris
Harry Harrison
Tom Holt

Christopher Moore
Terry Pratchett
Martin Scott

227

Frederic Raphael 1931- US

Saul Bellow
Howard Jacobson

Allan Massie
John Mortimer

Julian Rathbone 1935-2008 Adventure/Thriller
🏃 Comm Jan Argand

Suzanne Berne
Amin Maalouf

Bernard MacLaverty
Craig Thomas

Historical

Melvyn Bragg
Dorothy Dunnett
Thomas Keneally

Matthew Kneale
Andrew Miller
Robert Nye

James Robertson
Nigel Tranter
Barry Unsworth

Melanie Rawn 1954- US Fantasy: Epic
also writes as Ellen Randolph
www.melanierawn.com

Sarah Ash
Carol Berg
Marion Zimmer Bradley

Louise Cooper
Barbara Hambly
Katherine Kurtz

Mercedes Lackey
Fiona McIntosh
Margaret Weis

Sarah Rayne Crime: Psychological
also writes as Frances Gordon, Bridget Wood; is Bridget Wood
www.sarahrayne.co.uk

Carla Banks
Hilary Bonner
Caroline Carver
Sarah Diamond

Jane Hill
Susan Hill
Babs Horton
Morag Joss

Margaret Murphy
Patrick Redmond
Louis Sanders
Sally Spedding

Miss Read 1913- Saga
is Mrs Dora Saint
Fairacre • Thrush Green

Jan Karon
Mary A Larkin
Claire Lorrimer

Ann Purser
Alexandra Raife

Eileen Ramsay
Rebecca Shaw

Danuta Reah Crime: Psychological
also writes as Carla Banks
www.danutareah.co.uk

Jane Adams
Carla Banks
Stephen Booth

John Connor
Jane Hill
Ed O'Connor

David Peace
Sally Spedding
Margaret Yorke

Patrick Redmond
1966-   Crime: Psychological
www.patrickredmond.co.uk

Nicci French	Sarah Rayne	Tony Strong
Robert Goddard	Boris Starling	Barbara Vine
Val McDermid		

Robert Reed
1956- US   Science Fiction: Space opera
www.robertreedwriter.com

Stephen Baxter	Greg Egan	Alastair Reynolds
David Brin	Peter F Hamilton	Sean Williams
Arthur C Clarke	John Meaney	

Mary Reed and Eric Mayer
US   Crime: Historical - Ancient
http://home.epix.net/~maywrite   ⚗John the Eunuch, Lord Chamberlain - C6th Constantinople

Alys Clare	Lauren Haney	Lynda S Robinson
Margaret Frazer	Ellis Peters	Peter Tremayne

Douglas Reeman
1924-   Sea: Modern
also writes as Alexander Kent   ⚗Mike Blackwood
www.douglasreeman.com

Brian Callison	Alexander Fullerton	James Pattinson
Roger Carpenter	Hammond Innes	Patrick Robinson
James H Cobb		

Emlyn Rees   see Josie Lloyd

Christopher Reich
1961- US   Crime: Legal/financial
www.christopherreich.com

Harry Bingham	Brad Meltzer	Robert K Tanenbaum
John Burdett	Jonathan Nasaw	Scott Turow
John Grisham	Michael Ridpath	

Mickey Zucker Reichert
1962- US   Fantasy: Epic
www.mickeyzuckerreichert.com

Terry Brooks	Katherine Kurtz	Elizabeth Moon
David Eddings	Mercedes Lackey	R A Salvatore
Terry Goodkind	L E Modesitt Jr	Janny Wurts

Kathy Reichs
1950- US   Crime: Forensic
www.kathyreichs.com   ⚗Dr Temperance Brennan, Pathologist - Montreal, North Carolina

Simon Beckett	Linda Fairstein	Keith McCarthy
Max Allan Collins	Kathryn Fox	Nigel McCrery
Jeffery Deaver	Leonard Goldberg	Peter May
Aaron Elkins	Lynn Hightower	Carol O'Connell

R

Carmen Reid
Sco   Chick Lit
www.carmenreid.com

Lucy Diamond	Julia Holden	Julia Llewellyn
Anne Dunlop	Wendy Holden	Olivia Ryan
Fiona Gibson	Dorothy Koomson	Jennifer Weiner

Matthew Reilly
1974- Aus   Adventure/Thriller
www.matthewreilly.com   ⚐ Capt Shane Schofield - US Marine Corps

James Barrington	Harold Coyle	Greg Iles
Steve Berry	James Follett	Raymond Khoury
Lincoln Child	David Gibbins	Andy McDermott
Stephen Coonts	W E B Griffin	David L Robbins

Tina Reilly
Ire   Mature Chick Lit
www.tinareilly.info

Jenny Colgan	Kate Harrison	Debbie Macomber
Sabine Durrant	Julia Holden	Daisy Waugh
Imogen Edwards-Jones	Monica McInerney	Laura Zigman

Sara Reinke
US   Paranormal
www.sarareinke.com

Mary Janice Davidson	Lori Handeland	Tanya Huff
Christine Feehan	Charlaine Harris	Sherrilyn Kenyon
Laurell K Hamilton		

R

Erich Maria Remarque
⌒ 1898-1970 Ger

Pat Barker	Robert Graves
Sebastian Faulks	Paul Watkins

Mary Renault
1905-83   Historical
was Eileen Mary Challans

Michael Curtis Ford	Valerio Massimo Manfredi	Wilbur Smith
Robert Graves	Steven Pressfield	Su Tong
Robert Harris	Simon Scarrow	Gore Vidal
Colleen McCullough	Manda Scott	Jack Whyte

Ruth Rendell
⌒ 1930-   Crime: Police work - UK
also writes as Barbara Vine   ⚐ CI George Wexford - 'Kingsmarkham'
♛ CWA 1976, 1984 & 1986

W J Burley	J Wallis Martin	Michael Robotham
Ake Edwardson	Maureen O'Brien	Dorothy Simpson
Morag Joss	Julie Parsons	June Thomson
Jim Kelly	Nicholas Rhea	Laura Wilson

Alastair Reynolds   1966-   Wales   Science Fiction: Space opera
www.alastairreynolds.com

🏆 BSFA 2001

Kevin J Anderson	John Meaney	Robert Reed
Neal Asher	China Miéville	Adam Roberts
Jack McDevitt	Richard Morgan	Kim Stanley Robinson

Nicholas Rhea   1936-   Crime: Police work - UK
also writes as Andrew Arncliffe,   🚶 PC Nick Parish - 'Adensfield', Yorkshire
Christopher Coram, James Ferguson,   DS Mark Pemberton
Tom Ferris; is Peter Norman Walker   DI Montague Pluke
www.nicholasrhea.co.uk

Robert Barnard	Katherine John	Ruth Rendell
Caroline Graham	Nick Oldham	Leslie Thomas
J M Gregson	Stuart Pawson	M J Trow

Elvi Rhodes   c 1930-   Saga
www.elvirhodes.com   Yorkshire

Helen Cannam	Ken McCoy	Susan Sallis
Elizabeth Gill	Elisabeth McNeill	Linda Sole
Sheelagh Kelly	Alexandra Raife	

Anne Rice   1941-   US   Paranormal
also writes as Anne Rampling   Vampire Chronicles
www.annerice.com

R Scott Bakker	Laurell K Hamilton	Robert McCammon
Poppy Z Brite	Jeanne Kalogridis	Kim Wilkins
Storm Constantine	Brian Lumley	

R

Eva Rice

Kim Edwards	Kate Morton	Emma Tennant
Nicole Krauss	Audrey Niffenegger	Barbara Trapido
Marina Lewycka	Lionel Shriver	Elizabeth Wrenn

Ben Richards   1964-

Mavis Cheek	Laurie Graham	Tony Parsons
Douglas Coupland	Nick Hornby	Will Self
Jennifer Donnelly		

John Rickards   1978-   Crime: Psychological
www.johnrickards.com   🚶 PI Alex Rourke - Boston, USA

Brian Freeman	Jonathon King	Richard Montanari
Gregory Hall	Michael Marshall	Craig Russell
Mandasue Heller		

Phil Rickman

Horror

also writes as Will Kingdom
www.philrickman.co.uk

🏃 Merrily Watkins, Exorcist

Carla Banks	Graham Joyce	Christopher Pike
James Herbert	Stephen Laws	Sally Spedding
Shaun Hutson	Scott Nicholson	Kim Wilkins

Michael Ridpath   1961-

Adventure/Thriller: Legal/financial

www.michaelridpath.com

🏃 Alex Calder, Bond trader

Harry Bingham	James Grippando	Richard North Patterson
Linda Davies	John Grisham	Christopher Reich
Reg Gadney	Brad Meltzer	

Liz Rigbey

Crime: Psychological

Mary Higgins Clark	Nicci Gerrard	Julie Parsons
Carol Anne Davis	Babs Horton	Jenny Siler
Anne Fine		

Gwendoline Riley   1979-

🏆 S Maugham 2008

Anita Brookner	Wendy Perriam	Muriel Spark
Esther Freud	Ali Smith	Emma Tennant
Shena Mackay		

Stella Rimington   1935-

Adventure/Thriller

🏃 Liz Carlyle, MI5

Alex Berenson	Dan Fesperman	Gayle Lynds
Linda Davies	Ian Fleming	Chris Petit
Len Deighton	Alan Furst	Henry Porter

Rick Riordan   US

Crime: PI

www.rickriordan.com

🏃 Tres Navarre - San Antonio, Texas

Linda Barnes	Marcia Muller	John Shannon
Carol Higgins Clark	Sara Paretsky	Ronald Tierney
Loren D Estleman	S J Rozan	

Mike Ripley   1952-

Crime: Amateur sleuth

🏃 Fitzroy Maclean Angel, Taxi driver - London

🏆 CWA 1989 & 1991

Gilbert Adair	Danny King	Mark Timlin
Colin Bateman	Chris Niles	Patricia Wentworth
Alan Dunn	Leslie Thomas	R D Wingfield

Carol Rivers 1947- Saga
www.carolrivers.com

Isle of Dogs, London

Elizabeth Adler	Pip Granger	Gilda O'Neill
Harry Bowling	Jeannie Johnson	Victor Pemberton
Anita Burgh	Beryl Kingston	Mary Jane Staples
Pamela Evans	Pamela Oldfield	Elizabeth Waite

Candace Robb 1950- Crime: Historical - Medieval
www.candacerobb.com

🕇 Owen Archer - C14th York • Margaret Kerr - C13th Scotland

Simon Beaufort	Susanna Gregory	Caroline Roe
Alys Clare	Pat McIntosh	Kate Sedley
Ariana Franklin	Ian Morson	

J D Robb 1950- US Crime: Police work - US
also writes as Nora Roberts; is Elly Wilder
www.jdrobb.com

🕇 Eve Dallas - Future New York

Beverly Barton	Kerry Greenwood	Ed McBain
Allison Brennan	Linda Howard	Theresa Monsour
Robert Ellis	Lisa Jackson	Richard Morgan
Heather Graham	Paul Johnston	Sharon Sala

David L Robbins 1954- US War: Modern
www.davidlrobbins.com

F G Cottam	Jack Harvey	Terence Strong
Elizabeth Darrell	Matthew Reilly	James Webb
W E B Griffin		

Harold Robbins 1912-1997 US Glitz & Glamour
also wrote as Frank Lane

Sandra Brown	Jackie Collins	Mario Puzo
Nicholas Coleridge	Katie Price	Sidney Sheldon

Tom Robbins 1936- US

Joseph Heller	Thomas Pynchon
John Irving	Tobias Wolff

Adam Roberts 1965- Science Fiction: Space opera
www.adamroberts.com

Eric Brown	Ken MacLeod	Alastair Reynolds
Lois McMaster Bujold	John Meaney	Nick Sagan
Frank Herbert	China Miéville	Gene Wolfe

R

Barrie Roberts   1939-2007

www.barrieroberts.com

Crime: Historical - C19th
🏃 Sherlock Holmes - C19th England
Chris Tyroll, Lawyer - West Midlands

Boris Akunin	Arthur Conan Doyle	Peter J Heck
Judith Cutler	Martin Edwards	Andrew Pepper
David Dickinson	John Harwood	David Pirie

David Roberts

Crime: Historical - C20th
🏃 Lord Edward Corinth & Verity Browne, Journalist - 1930s England

James Anderson	Catriona McPherson	Dorothy L Sayers
Carola Dunn	Ngaio Marsh	Charles Todd
Mark Gatiss	Robin Paige	Stella Whitelaw
Patricia Harwin	Rebecca Pawel	Jacqueline Winspear

John Maddox Roberts   1947-   US

also writes as Mark Ramsay

Crime: Historical - Ancient
🏃 Decius Caecelius Metellus the Younger
Politics - Ancient Rome

Lindsey Davis	Rosemary Rowe	Marilyn Todd
Lauren Haney	Steven Saylor	David Wishart
Lynda S Robinson		

Michèle Roberts   1949-   Fr

www.micheleroberts.co.uk
🏆 WHSmith 1993

Emma Donoghue	Sarah Kate Lynch	Jeanette Winterson
Joanne Harris	Anne Michaels	Virginia Woolf
Janette Turner Hospital		

R

Nora Roberts   1950-   US

also writes as J D Robb; is Elly Wilder
www.noraroberts.com

Crime: Romantic suspense
🏃 Quinn Family
Three Sisters Island Trilogy

Virginia Andrews	Catherine Coulter	Linda Howard
Beverly Barton	Janet Dailey	Susanna Kearsley
Sandra Brown	Jude Deveraux	Sharon Sala
Candace Bushnell	Eileen Goudge	Célestine Hitiura Vaite

Denise Robertson

Saga
🏃 Beloved People Trilogy - NE England

Irene Carr	Mary A Larkin	Eileen Ramsay
Jean Chapman	Ken McCoy	Janet Tanner
Catherine Cookson	Alexandra Raife	Janet MacLeod Trotter

James Robertson   1958-   Sco   Historical

William Boyd	Robin Jenkins	Julian Rathbone
William Brodrick	Raymond Khoury	Robert Louis Stevenson
Margaret Elphinstone	Matthew Kneale	Jonathan Tropper
Philip Hensher	Magnus Mills	Markus Zusak

Wendy Robertson   Saga
www.wendyrobertson.com   'Priorton', NE England

Irene Carr	Elizabeth Elgin	Janet MacLeod Trotter
Jean Chapman	Una Horne	Valerie Wood
Josephine Cox	Ken McCoy	

Derek Robinson   1932-   War: Modern
www.derekrobinson.info

Frank Barnard	David Fiddimore	Paul Watkins
F G Cottam	W E B Griffin	Guy Walters
Murray Davies	Robert Radcliffe	

Kim Stanley Robinson   1952-   US   Science Fiction: Near future
🏆 BSFA 1992

Greg Bear	Steven Gould	Larry Niven
Ben Bova	China Miéville	Alastair Reynolds
Michael Crichton	Linda Nagata	Brian Stableford

Lynda S Robinson   1951-   US   Crime: Historical - Ancient
also writes as Suzanne Robinson   🏃 Lord Meren, Chief adviser to Tutankhamun
www.meren.com   Ancient Egypt

Philip Boast	Elizabeth Peters	John Maddox Roberts
Paul Doherty	Mary Reed and Eric Mayer	Steven Saylor
Lauren Haney		

Patrick Robinson   1940-   Ire   Sea: Modern
🏃 Admiral Arnold Morgan, US National Security Advisor

Dale Brown	Philip McCutchan	Peter Tonkin
James H Cobb	Douglas Reeman	Robin White
Duncan Harding		

Peter Robinson   1950-   Crime: Police work - UK
www.inspectorbanks.com   🏃 CI Alan Banks - Yorkshire

Kate Atkinson	Georgie Hale	Pauline Rowson
Glenn Chandler	Graham Hurley	Dorothy Simpson
Chris Collett	Peter James	Aline Templeton
Colin Dexter	Jim Kelly	Camilla Way

R

Michael Robotham
1960-   Crime: Psychological

www.michaelrobotham.com   ⚐ Joseph O'Loughlin

David Baldacci	Gregg Hurwitz	Jonathan Nasaw
Linwood Barclay	Patrick Lennon	Ruth Rendell
Mark Gimenez		

Justina Robson
Science Fiction: Near future

www.justinarobson.co.uk

Eric Brown	Steven Gould	Richard Morgan
Hal Duncan	Jon Courtenay Grimwood	Andrzej Sapkowski
William Gibson	Sergei Lukyanenko	

Caroline Roe
Can   Crime: Historical - C14th

also writes as Medora Sale   ⚐ Isaac of Girona, Jewish physician - Spain
is Caroline Medora Sale Roe

Susanna Gregory	Sharan Newman	Pip Vaughan-Hughes
Michael Jecks	Candace Robb	Robyn Young
Ian Morson	Tim Severin	

Graeme Roe
Crime: Amateur sleuth

⚐ Jay Jessup, National Hunt trainer

Dick Francis	Jenny Pitman	Lyndon Stacey
John Francome	Richard Pitman	

James Rollins
1961-   US   Adventure/Thriller

also writes as James Clemens   ⚐ Sigma Force
www.jamesrollins.com

Steve Berry	Michael Cordy	Andy McDermott
Sam Bourne	David Gibbins	Bill Napier
Michael Byrnes	David Hewson	Douglas Preston
Paul Christopher	Chris Kuzneski	Paul Sussman

Karen Rose
US   Crime: Romantic suspense

www.karenrosebooks.com   ⚐ Daniel Vartanian

Victoria Blake	Tami Hoag	Sharon Sala
Allison Brennan	Grace Monroe	Claire Seeber
Elizabeth Corley	Chris Mooney	Karin Slaughter
Christiane Heggan	Hilary Norman	P J Tracy

Nancy Taylor Rosenberg
1946-   US   Crime: Legal/financial

www.nancytrosenberg.com   ⚐ Lily Forrester, DA - California

Alafair Burke	John T Lescroart	Perri O'Shaughnessy
Carol Higgins Clark	John McLaren	Richard North Patterson
Linda Fairstein	Phillip Margolin	Susan R Sloan

R

Meg Rosoff US
www.megrosoff.co.uk

Jennifer Donnelly	Joan Lingard	Jeanette Winterson
Anne Fine	Mary Stanley	Markus Zusak

Philip Roth 1933- US
🏆 Pulitzer 1998   WHSmith 2001 & 2005

Lisa Appignanesi	Dave Eggers	Rick Moody
Saul Bellow	David Grossman	Cynthia Ozick
Michael Chabon	Joseph Heller	Elliot Perlman
Edward Docx	Denis Johnson	Adam Thirlwell

Patrick Rothfuss 1973- US   Fantasy: Epic
www.patrickrothfuss.com

R Scott Bakker	Amanda Hemingway	George R R Martin
Chaz Brenchley	Greg Keyes	J K Rowling
Steven Erikson	Tim Lebbon	Brian Ruckley

Victoria Routledge 1975-   Mature Chick Lit

Trisha Ashley	Melissa Nathan	Linda Taylor
Celia Brayfield	Anita Notaro	Lauren Weisberger
Belinda Jones	Robyn Sisman	Deborah Wright

Rosemary Rowe 1942-   Crime: Historical - Ancient
is Rosemary Aitken   ⚥ Libertus, Mosaicist - Roman Britain
www.raitken.wyenet.co.uk

R

Philip Boast	Colleen McCullough	Steven Saylor
Lindsey Davis	Allan Massie	Marilyn Todd
Margaret Doody	John Maddox Roberts	David Wishart

Laura Joh Rowland 1954- US   Crime: Historical - C17th
www.laurajohrowland.com   ⚥ Sano Ichiro, Samurai - C17th Japan

James Clavell	Fidelis Morgan	Martin Stephen
Lindsey Davis	Michael Pearce	

Betty Rowlands 1923-   Crime: Amateur sleuth
www.bettyrowlands.com   ⚥ Melissa Craig, Writer - Cotswolds
                    Sukey Reynolds, Scene of Crime Officer

Natasha Cooper	Veronica Heley	Fiona Mountain
Marjorie Eccles	Joyce Holms	Ann Purser
Ann Granger	Gwen Moffat	

237

J K Rowling ☎ ☺ 1965-   Fantasy: Epic

is Joanne Kathleen Rowling   ⚲ Harry Potter
www.jkrowling.com
🏆 WHSmith 2006

Jim Butcher	Sergei Lukyanenko	Christopher Paolini
Eoin Colfer	William Nicholson	Patrick Rothfuss
Lian Hearn	Garth Nix	

Pauline Rowson   Crime: Police work - UK

www.rowmark.co.uk   ⚲ DI Andy Horton - Hayling Island

Robert Barnard	Patricia Hall	Iain McDowall
Pauline Bell	John Harvey	Peter Robinson
Ann Cleeves	Graham Hurley	Dorothy Simpson
Colin Dexter	Peter James	Neil White

Arundhati Roy   1961-   Ind

🏆 Booker 1997

Monica Ali	Kiran Desai	Anita Nair
Vikram Chandra	Roopa Farooki	R K Narayan
Amit Chaudhuri	Amitav Ghosh	Vikram Seth
Stevie Davies	Yann Martel	Thirty Umrigar

Nicholas Royle   1963-   Adventure/Thriller

⚲ Frank Warner, Journalist

John Harvey	Ian Rankin	Matt Thorne
Chris Paling	Iain Sinclair	Martyn Waites
Chris Petit		

R

S J Rozan   US   Crime: PI

www.sjrozan.com   ⚲ Lydia Chin & Bill Smith - New York

Linda Barnes	Reggie Nadelson	Dana Stabenow
Gabrielle Lord	Rick Riordan	Valerie Wilson Wesley

Bernice Rubens   1928-2004

🏆 Booker 1970

Beryl Bainbridge	Pauline Melville	A N Wilson
Anita Brookner	Carolyn Slaughter	Jeanette Winterson
Margaret Drabble		

Brian Ruckley   Sco   Fantasy: Epic

www.brianruckley.com

R Scott Bakker	David Gemmell	Katherine Kurtz
Steven Erikson	Greg Keyes	Patrick Rothfuss
		Sean Russell

James Runcie
Historical

www.jamesruncie.com

Tracy Chevalier	Melanie Gifford	Salley Vickers
Barbara Ewing	Jason Goodwin	Susan Vreeland

Kristine Kathryn Rusch   1960- US   Science Fiction: Space and time

also writes as Kristine Grayson, Kris Nelscott, Sandy Schofield
writes jointly with Dean Wesley Smith
www.kristinekathrynrusch.com

Kevin J Anderson	Michael Moorcock	Robert Charles Wilson
Brian Herbert	R A Salvatore	David Zindell
J V Jones	Robert Silverberg	

Salman Rushdie   1947-

🏆 Black 1981   Booker 1981   Whitbread 1988 & 1995   Best of the Booker 2008

Monica Ali	Richard Flanagan	Siri Hustvedt
Amit Chaudhuri	David Grossman	Vikram Seth
Michelle de Kretser	Shifra Horn	Emma Tennant
Anita Desai	Janette Turner Hospital	Marianne Wiggins

Craig Russell   1956-   Sco

Crime: Police work - Germany
🚶 Det Jan Fabel - Hamburg

www.craigrussell.com
🏆 CWA 2008

Quintin Jardine	Chris Mooney	C J Sansom
J A Kerley	John Rickards	Boris Starling
Richard Montanari		

Norman Russell

Crime: Historical - C19th
🚶 DI Saul Jackson & Sgt Bottomley - Warwickshire

Arthur Conan Doyle	Joan Lock	Rosemary Stevens
Peter J Heck	Peter Lovesey	M J Trow
Alanna Knight		

Sean Russell   1952-   Can

Fantasy: Epic

www.sfsite.com/seanrussell/index.htm

Stephen Donaldson	Robert Jordan	Sheri S Tepper
Steven Erikson	Greg Keyes	Tad Williams
Jude Fisher	Brian Ruckley	

Richard Russo   1949-   US

🏆 Pulitzer 2002

Ron Butlin	Garrison Keillor	Stewart O'Nan
Richard Ford	Lorna Landvik	Anne Tyler
Ha Jin	Larry McMurtry	

Edward Rutherfurd   1948-   Historical
is Francis E Wintle
www.edwardrutherfurd.com

Jean M Auel	Frank Delaney	Colleen McCullough
Stephen Baxter	Christie Dickason	James A Michener
Clare Clark	Dorothy Dunnett	Manda Scott
Bernard Cornwell	Kathleen O'Neal Gear	Leon Uris

Chris Ryan   ☎ ☺   1961-   Adventure/Thriller
www.oliviaryan.com

Geoffrey Archer	Duncan Falconer	Stephen Hunter
Michael Asher	Joseph Garber	Graham Hurley
Murray Davies		

Liz Ryan   Saga
Ireland

Maeve Binchy	Geraldine O'Neill	Alexandra Raife
Frank Delaney	Joan O'Neill	Olivia Ryan
Sheelagh Kelly	D M Purcell	

Olivia Ryan   Chick Lit

Hester Browne	Julia Llewellyn	Carmen Reid
Lucy Diamond	Sarah Mason	Liz Ryan
Sophie Hannah	Carole Matthews	

R

Robert Ryan   Adventure/Thriller
www.robert-ryan.net

F G Cottam	Greg Iles	Michael Kimball
Barry Eisler	Joseph Kanon	Guy Walters
Alan Furst		

Geoff Ryman   1951-   Can

Paul Auster	Christopher Koch
Jim Crace	Adam Thorpe

Science Fiction: Near future

🏆 Arthur C Clarke 1990   BSFA 2005   Arthur C Clarke 2006

Louise Erdrich	Ursula K Le Guin	Gene Wolfe
Amitav Ghosh	Jeff Noon	John Wyndham
Gwyneth Jones		

☺ also writes children's books

240

Nick Sagan
1970- US   **Science Fiction:** Near future

www.nicksagan.com

Greg Egan	Richard Morgan	Neal Stephenson
William Gibson	Adam Roberts	Tad Williams
Steven Gould		

Sharon Sala
US   **Crime:** Romantic suspense

also writes as Dinah McCall

Allison Brennan	Linda Howard	J D Robb
Heather Graham	Gwen Hunter	Nora Roberts
Christiane Heggan	Lisa Jackson	Karen Rose

Medora Sale
Can   **Crime:** Police work - Canada

also writes as Caroline Roe   🏃 DI John Sanders & Harriet Jeffries, Architectural photographer
is Caroline Medora Sale Roe   Toronto

Giles Blunt	Keith Miles	Louise Penny
Lynda La Plante	Ridley Pearson	
Claire McNab		

J D Salinger
🕮 1919- US

is Jerome David Salinger

Nicola Barker	Carson McCullers	D B C Pierre
Harper Lee	Jay McInerney	Curtis Sittenfeld
Cormac McCarthy	Edna O'Brien	Miriam Toews

James Sallis
1944- US   **Crime:** Hardboiled

www.jamessallis.com   🏃 Lew Griffin, Academic - New Orleans

James Lee Burke	Walter Mosley	Boston Teran
Raymond Chandler	Cath Staincliffe	John Williams
Ross Macdonald	Jason Starr	

Susan Sallis
1929-   Saga

also writes as Susan Meadmore   🏃 Rising Family - West Country

Rosemary Aitken	Santa Montefiore	Sally Stewart
Gloria Cook	D M Purcell	Rowena Summers
Elizabeth Elgin	Elvi Rhodes	

R A Salvatore
1959- US   **Fantasy:** Epic

www.rasalvatore.com

Sara Douglass	L E Modesitt Jr	Kristine Kathryn Rusch
David A Drake	Elizabeth Moon	Margaret Weis
Mercedes Lackey	Mickey Zucker Reichert	

S

241

Catherine Sampson

Crime: Amateur sleuth

www.catherinesampson.com

🏃 Robin Ballantyne, TV Journalist

Simon Brett	Alan Dunn	Hazel Holt
Natasha Cooper	Anthea Fraser	Roy Lewis
Judith Cutler	Jonathan Gash	

Kevin Sampson

Lad Lit

Liverpool

Christopher Brookmyre	William Sutcliffe	Irvine Welsh
Paul Burke	Matt Thorne	Louise Wener
Tim Lott		

Louis Sanders   1964-   Fr

Crime: Psychological

Dordogne, France

Elizabeth McGregor	Sarah Rayne	Laura Wilson
Julie Parsons	Sally Spedding	Margaret Yorke

John Sandford   1944-   US

Crime: Police work - US

is John Roswell Camp

www.johnsandford.org

🏃 Lucas Davenport • Prey Series

Kidd & LuEllen, Con artist & computer hacker } Mississippi

Ingrid Black	Scott Frost	Dennis Lehane
Alafair Burke	Colin Harrison	Phillip Margolin
Jodi Compton	Stephen Hunter	Ridley Pearson
Thomas H Cook	Michael Kimball	James Siegel

C J Sansom

Crime: Historical - C16th

also writes as The Medieval Murderers (with Philip Gooden, Susanne Gregory, Michael Jecks, Bernard Knight, Ian Morson)

🏃 Dr Matthew Shardlake

Henrician London

🏆 CWA 2005

P F Chisholm	Michael Gregorio	Craig Russell
Michael Clynes	C C Humphreys	Martin Stephen
Patricia Finney	James McGee	Frank Tallis
Philip Gooden	John Pilkington	Peter Tonkin

Ian Sansom

Crime: Amateur sleuth

www.iansansom.net

🏃 Israel Armstrong, Mobile librarian

Colin Bateman	Robert Lewis	Alexander McCall Smith
Christopher Brookmyre	Lily Prior	Sue Townsend
Peter Guttridge	Malcolm Pryce	

Go to back for lists of
Pseudonyms • Authors by Genre • Characters and Series
Prize Winners • Crossover Authors • Further Reading • Websites

Andrzej Sapkowski 1948- Pol — Science Fiction: Near future

Neal Asher
Iain M Banks
Hal Duncan
William Gibson
Steven Gould
Sergei Lukyanenko
Justina Robson

John Saul 1942- US — Horror

www.johnsaul.com

Ramsey Campbell
Douglas Clegg
Shaun Hutson
Stephen King
Dean R Koontz
Robert McCammon
Christopher Pike
Andrew Pyper

Jean Saunders 1932- — Aga Saga

also writes as Sally Blake, Jean Innes, Rachel Moore, Jodie Nicol, Rowena Summers
www.hometown.aol.co.uk/jeanrowena

Johanna Lindsey
Ken McCoy
Nora Naish
Robin Pilcher
Rosamunde Pilcher
Ann Purser
Madge Swindells
Mary Wesley
Madeleine Wickham

Kate Saunders — Aga Saga

Claire Calman
Lucy Clare
Philippa Gregory
Charlotte Moore
Nora Naish
Elizabeth Noble
Robyn Sisman
Mary Wesley

Alan Savage 1930- — War: Modern

is Christopher Nicole

Frank Barnard
James Clavell
Elizabeth Darrell
David Fiddimore
Amin Maalouf
Alistair MacLean
David Morrell
Eric Van Lustbader
Guy Walters

Julian Jay Savarin — Adventure/Thriller

Geoffrey Archer
Campbell Armstrong
Dale Brown
Stephen Coonts
Clive Cussler
Wilbur Smith
Craig Thomas

Judith Saxton 1936- — Saga

also writes as Katie Flynn, Judy Turner
Neyler Family

Janet Dailey
Sara Hylton
Mary Mackie
Beryl Matthews
Margaret Pemberton
Linda Sole
Janet Tanner
Nicola Thorne
Jeanne Whitmee

Dorothy L Sayers 1893-1957   Crime: Amateur sleuth
www.sayers.org.uk   🚶 Lord Peter Wimsey

James Anderson	Martha Grimes	Ngaio Marsh
Agatha Christie	Hazel Holt	David Roberts
Mark Gatiss	Michael Innes	Patricia Wentworth

Alexei Sayle 1952-   Humour

Anna Blundy	Charles Higson	Will Self
Paul Burke	Marina Lewycka	Matt Thorne
Will Ferguson	Mil Millington	

Steven Saylor 1956- US   Crime: Historical - Ancient
www.stevensaylor.com   🚶 Gordianus the Finder - Ancient Rome

Lindsey Davis	Robert Harris	Lynda S Robinson
Margaret Doody	Sophia McDougall	Rosemary Rowe
Michael Curtis Ford	Allan Massie	Marilyn Todd
Lauren Haney	John Maddox Roberts	David Wishart

Patricia Scanlan Ire   Chick Lit

Catherine Alliott	Martina Devlin	Anita Notaro
Maria Beaumont	Cathy Kelly	D M Purcell
Clare Boylan	Debbie Macomber	Robyn Sisman
Claudia Carroll	Jane Moore	Jane Elizabeth Varley

Alex Scarrow   Adventure/Thriller
www.scarrow.co.uk

John Case	Joseph Kanon	Gareth O'Callaghan
Frederick Forsyth	Michael Kimball	Tim Sebastian
Robert Harris	John Lawton	Robin White

Simon Scarrow 1962-   Historical
www.scarrow.co.uk   🚶 Lucius Cornelius Macro & Quintus Licinus Cato
Centurions - C1st AD, Roman Europe
Duke of Wellington & Napoleon Bonaparte - C18th & C19th Europe

Roger Carpenter	Iain Gale	Sophia McDougall
Bernard Cornwell	Richard Howard	Allan Massie
Lindsey Davis	Garry Kilworth	Patrick Rambaud
Michael Curtis Ford	Colleen McCullough	Mary Renault

Bernhard Schlink 1944- Ger

Pat Barker	Anne Michaels	Rachel Seiffert
Ismail Kadare	Irene Nemirovsky	William Styron

Katherine Scholes 1959- Aus
www.katherinescholes.com

Joseph Finder	Di Morrissey	Peter Watt
Tamara McKinley	Gareth O'Callaghan	

Christina Schwarz US Adventure/Thriller: Psychological

Mary Higgins Clark	Janet Fitch	Sue Miller
Joy Fielding	Clare Francis	Susan R Sloan

Justin Scott 1944- US Adventure/Thriller
also writes as Paul Garrison   🚶 Ben Abbott, Real Estate Agent - Connecticut

Brian Callison	James Follett	Sam Llewellyn
James H Cobb	Duncan Harding	Nicholas Monsarrat
Clive Cussler	Richard Herman	Eric Van Lustbader

Manda Scott Sco Crime: Psychological
www.mandascott.co.uk   🚶 Kellen Stewart - Glasgow

Lin Anderson	Val McDermid	Sally Spedding
Alex Gray	J Wallis Martin	Barbara Vine
John Harwood	Denise Mina	Louise Welsh

Historical
🚶 Boudica, Roman Britain

Jean M Auel	Valerio Massimo Manfredi	Edward Rutherfurd
Conn Iggulden	Kate Mosse	Leon Uris
Christian Jacq	Mary Renault	

Martin Scott Fantasy: Humour
is Martin Millar
www.martinmillar.com

Robert Asprin	Simon Green	Terry Pratchett
Neil Gaiman	Harry Harrison	Robert Rankin
Craig Shaw Gardner	Tom Holt	

Paul Scott 1920-78
🏆 Booker 1977

Thalassa Ali	Ruth Prawer Jhabvala	Rohinton Mistry
E M Forster	Pamela Jooste	Vikram Seth
Nadine Gordimer		

S

⌂ may be suitable for young adults

Lisa Scottoline   1955-   US   Crime: Legal/financial
www.scottoline.com   ⚑ Rosato & Associates - Philadelphia

William Bernhardt	John T Lescroart	Perri O'Shaughnessy
Linda Fairstein	John McLaren	Susan R Sloan
Craig Holden	Phillip Margolin	Erica Spindler

Tim Sebastian   1952-   Adventure/Thriller

Geoffrey Archer	Jon Evans	Alex Scarrow
Campbell Armstrong	Humphrey Hawksley	Nick Stone
Tom Bradby	Stephen Leather	Nigel West

Alice Sebold ⌒   1963-   US

Mitch Albom	Mark Haddon	Clare Morrall
Kate Atkinson	Zoë Heller	Audrey Niffenegger
Anita Diamant	Victoria Hislop	Ann Packer
Lesley Glaister	Hilary Mantel	Lionel Shriver

Kate Sedley   1926-   Crime: Historical - Medieval
is Brenda Clarke   ⚑ Roger the Chapman - C15th England

P F Chisholm	Susanna Gregory	Pat McIntosh
Alys Clare	Michael Jecks	Ian Morson
Ariana Franklin	Bernard Knight	Candace Robb

Lisa See   1955-   US   Crime: Police work - China
www.lisasee.com   ⚑ David Stark, Attorney & Insp Liu Hulan

Alma Alexander	Linda Holeman	Andy Oakes
Anita Diamant	Catherine Lim	Eliot Pattison
Xiaolu Guo	Peter May	Qiu Xiaolong
Ha Jin	Anchee Min	Xinran

Claire Seeber   Adventure/Thriller: Psychological
www.claireseeber.com

Victoria Blake	Grace Monroe	Paullina Simons
Alice Blanchard	Karen Rose	Gillian White
Elizabeth Corley		

Rachel Seiffert   1971-

Margaret Atwood	Maggie Gee	Anne Michaels
Trezza Azzopardi	Tessa Hadley	Irene Nemirovsky
Julian Barnes	Ismail Kadare	Bernhard Schlink

S

Will Self 1961-

www.will-self.com

Faber 1993

J G Ballard	Bret Easton Ellis	Tobias Hill
Iain Banks	Alasdair Gray	Ben Richards
Glen Duncan	Niall Griffiths	Alexei Sayle

Andrea Semple 1975-   Chick Lit

www.andreasemple.com

Lynne Barrett-Lee	Shari Low	Sarah Webb
Meg Cabot	Sara Shepard	Laura Zigman
Sabine Durrant	Kathleen Tessaro	

Vikram Seth 1952- Ind

Commonwealth 1994   WHSmith 1994

Amit Chaudhuri	Amitav Ghosh	Arundhati Roy
Kiran Desai	R K Narayan	Salman Rushdie
John Galsworthy	Orhan Pamuk	Paul Scott

Tim Severin 1940-   Historical

www.timseverin.net

Thorgils Leiffson, Viking - C11th
Hector Lynch, Seafarer - C17th

Stephen Baxter	Conn Iggulden	Wilbur Smith
Bernard Cornwell	Steven Pressfield	Robyn Young
Tom Harper	Caroline Roe	

Gerald Seymour 1941-   Adventure/Thriller

Campbell Armstrong	Clive Egleton	Stephen Leather
James Barrington	Jon Evans	Charles McCarry
Tom Bradby	Frederick Forsyth	James Siegel
John Burdett	John Fullerton	Nigel West

Nicholas Shakespeare 1957-

S Maugham 1990

Malcolm Bradbury	James Hamilton-Paterson	Rose Tremain
Louis de Bernières	Ann Patchett	Mario Vargas Llosa
Graham Greene		

John Shannon 1943- US   Crime: PI

www.jackliffey.com

Jack Liffey - Los Angeles

Raymond Chandler	Dennis Lehane	Jefferson Parker
Michael Connelly	Marcia Muller	Robert B Parker
Robert Crais	Sara Paretsky	Rick Riordan

247

Zoë Sharp

www.zoesharp.com

Crime: Amateur sleuth

🏃 Charlie Fox, Self-defence expert

Cara Black	Sue Grafton	Sara Paretsky
Janet Evanovich	Lauren Henderson	Cath Staincliffe
Liz Evans	Val McDermid	

Tom Sharpe 🕾 1928-

Humour

Anna Blundy	George Macdonald Fraser	Tom Holt
Joseph Connolly	James Hawes	Howard Jacobson
Ruth Dudley Edwards	Philip Hensher	Geoff Nicholson

Catherine Shaw

Crime: Amateur sleuth

🏃 Vanessa Duncan - C19th Cambridge

Alanna Knight	Mark Mills	Jill Paton Walsh
Deryn Lake	Amy Myers	Patricia Wentworth
Peter Lovesey	Rebecca Tope	

Patricia Shaw 1928- Aus

Historical

Sheelagh Kelly	Katharine McMahon	Amanda Quick
Colleen McCullough	Margaret Pemberton	E V Thompson
Tamara McKinley		

Rebecca Shaw

www.rebeccashaw.com

Saga

Barleybridge Series • Turnham Malpas Series

Patricia Fawcett	Joan Medlicott	Célestine Hitiura Vaite
Erica James	Ann Purser	Ann Widdecombe
Jan Karon	Miss Read	Annie Wilkinson

Sidney Sheldon 1917-2007 US

Adventure/Thriller

www.sidneysheldon.com

Jeffrey Archer	Nicholas Coleridge	Wilbur Smith
Barbara Taylor Bradford	Harold Robbins	Danielle Steel
Lorenzo Carcaterra		

Lucius Shepard 1947- US

Science Fiction: Near future

www.lucius-shepard.com

William Gibson	Richard Powers	Tad Williams
Jon Courtenay Grimwood	Dan Simmons	David Zindell
Joe Haldeman		

Sara Shepard   US   Chick Lit

Meg Cabot   Chris Manby   Andrea Semple
Sophie Kinsella   Jill Mansell   Kathleen Tessaro
Kathy Lette   Alexandra Potter   Lauren Weisberger

Carol Shields   1935-2003   Can

🏆 Pulitzer 1995   Orange 1998

Trezza Azzopardi   Mary Lawson   Nicholas Sparks
Joan Barfoot   Elinor Lipman   Donna Tartt
Robb Forman Dew   Alice McDermott   Miriam Toews
Patrick Gale   Lionel Shriver   Marianne Wiggins

Anita Shreve   1946-   US

Elizabeth Berg   Shirley Hazzard   Maile Meloy
Suzanne Berne   Siri Hustvedt   Ann Packer
Louise Candlish   Catherine Ryan Hyde Curtis Sittenfeld
Nikki Gemmell   Alice McDermott   Robert James Waller

Lionel Shriver   1957-   US

🏆 Orange 2005

Neil Cross   Douglas Kennedy   D B C Pierre
Peter Ho Davies   Daniel Mason   Eva Rice
Susan Fletcher   David Mitchell   Alice Sebold
Elisabeth Hyde   Ann Packer   Carol Shields

Nevil Shute   1899-1960   Adventure/Thriller

was Nevil Shute Norway
www.nevilshute.org

Jon Cleary   Hammond Innes   Nicholas Monsarrat
Ernest Hemingway   Alistair MacLean   Morris West

Anne Rivers Siddons   1936-   US   Saga

www.anneriverssiddons.com

Pat Conroy   Carson McCullers   Rosie Thomas
Janet Dailey   Joan Medlicott   Adriana Trigiani
Karen Joy Fowler   Mary Alice Monroe   Joanna Trollope
Olivia Goldsmith   Belva Plain   Rebecca Wells

James Siegel   US   Adventure/Thriller

www.jamessiegel.co.uk

Dale Brown   John Sandford   Daniel Silva
Brendan Dubois   Gerald Seymour   Tony Strong
James Patterson

249

Yrsa Sigurdardottir
1963- Ice **Crime:** Amateur sleuth

♈ Thora Gudmundsdottir, Lawyer

Ake Edwardson	Matti Joensuu	Henning Mankell
Karin Fossum	Mari Jungstedt	Jo Nesbo
Arnaldur Indridason		

Jenny Siler
1971- US **Crime:** Psychological

also writes as Alex Carr
www.jennysiler.com

Carol Anne Davis	Liz Rigbey	Jess Walter
Tami Hoag	Karin Slaughter	Stephen White
Alex Kava	Barbara Vine	

Alan Sillitoe
1928-

Kingsley Amis	D H Lawrence	Stanley Middleton
Melvyn Bragg	David Lodge	Graham Swift

Daniel Silva
1960- US Adventure/Thriller

www.danielsilvabooks.com

♈ Michael Osbourne - CIA
Gabriel Allon - Israeli Secret Service

Charles Cumming	Frederick Forsyth	James Siegel
Brendan Dubois	David Hewson	Boris Starling
Richard Flanagan	Alan Judd	Nick Stone
Ian Fleming	Charles McCarry	Brad Thor

Robert Silverberg
1935- US Science Fiction: Space and time

also writes as Calvin M Knox, David Osborne, Robert Randall
www.majipoor.com

Arthur C Clarke	Sophia McDougall	Kristine Kathryn Rusch
David Eddings	Julian May	Freda Warrington
Joe Haldeman	Christopher Priest	

Roger Silverwood
Crime: Police work - UK

www.rogersilverwood.uwclub.net ♈ DI Michael Angel - Bromersley, South Yorkshire

Caroline Graham	Sally Spencer	Camilla Way
Dorothy Simpson	June Thomson	Neil White

Georges Simenon
1903-89 Belg **Crime:** Police work - France

♈ Commissaire Jules Maigret - Paris

A C Baantjer	H R F Keating	Janwillem van de Wetering
Andrea Camilleri	Magdalen Nabb	Fred Vargas
K O Dahl	Martin O'Brien	

S

Dan Simmons 1948- US · Horror

www.dansimmons.com

Richard Bachman	Stephen King	Whitley Strieber
Clive Barker	Bentley Little	T M Wright
Jeanne Kalogridis	Scott Smith	

Science Fiction: Space opera

♦ British Fantasy 1990 · BSFA 1991

Kevin J Anderson	David Brin	Joe Haldeman
Poul Anderson	Orson Scott Card	C S Lewis
Neal Asher	Arthur C Clarke	Lucius Shepard

Chris Simms · Crime: Psychological

www.chrissimms.info · ☆ DI Jon Spicer - Manchester

Mark Billingham	Margaret Murphy	Carol Smith
Jim Kelly	Ed O'Connor	Barbara Vine
Denise Mina	Andrew Pyper	Laura Wilson

Paullina Simons 1963- US · Adventure/Thriller

is Paullina Handler
www.paullinasimons.com

Victoria Blake	Jeffery Deaver	Stephen Hunter
Alice Blanchard	Nicholas Evans	Grace Monroe
Pat Conroy	John Gilstrap	Claire Seeber
Elizabeth Corley	Gwen Hunter	Scott Smith

Dorothy Simpson 1933- · Crime: Police work - UK

☆ DI Luke Thanet & DS Lineham - 'Sturrenden', Kent

♦ CWA 1985

David Armstrong	Ngaio Marsh	Pauline Rowson
Clare Curzon	Ruth Rendell	Roger Silverwood
Hazel Holt	Peter Robinson	

Iain Sinclair 1943-

♦ Black 1991 · Encore 1992

Peter Ackroyd	Alasdair Gray	Chris Petit
Charles Dickens	Geoff Nicholson	Nicholas Royle
Christopher Fowler	Robert Nye	

Robyn Sisman US · Mature Chick Lit

Louise Bagshawe	Debby Holt	Kate Saunders
Olivia Goldsmith	Clare Naylor	Patricia Scanlan
Julia Holden	Victoria Routledge	Sarah Tucker

S

Curtis Sittenfeld   US

www.curtissittenfeld.com

Melissa Bank	Alice Munro	Anita Shreve
Elinor Lipman	Jodi Picoult	Tom Wolfe
Carson McCullers	J D Salinger	

Maj Sjöwall & Per Wahlöö   1935-   Swe   Crime: Police work - Sweden

🏃 Martin Beck - Stockholm

Karin Alvtegen	Arnaldur Indridason	Åsa Larsson
K O Dahl	Mari Jungstedt	Liza Marklund
Karin Fossum		

Carolyn Slaughter

🏆 Faber 1977

Thalassa Ali	Ruth Prawer Jhabvala	Sharon Maas
E M Forster	Manju Kapur	Bernice Rubens

Karin Slaughter   1971-   US   Crime: Forensic

www.karinslaughter.com   🏃 Sara Linton, Medical examiner, & Jeffrey Tolliver, Police chief 'Heartsdale', Georgia

Beverly Barton	Lisa Gardner	Nigel McCrery
Max Allan Collins	Lisa Jackson	Karen Rose
Joolz Denby	Gabrielle Lord	Jenny Siler
Kathryn Fox	Keith McCarthy	Erica Spindler

Susan R Sloan   US   Crime: Legal/financial

Linda Fairstein	Steve Martini	Christina Schwarz
Alex Kava	Perri O'Shaughnessy	Lisa Scottoline
Laura Lippman	Nancy Taylor Rosenberg	

Gillian Slovo   1952-   SA

J M Coetzee	Lauren Henderson	Sara Paretsky
Martin Edwards	Doris Lessing	Michelle Spring

Peter Smalley   Sea: Historical - C18th

🏃 Capt William Rennie

G S Beard	Alexander Kent	Patrick O'Brian
David Donachie	Jonathan Lunn	Julian Stockwin
C S Forester		

Jane Smiley
1949- US

🏆 Pulitzer 1992

Thomas Eidson	Peter Hoeg	Robert James Waller
Kate Grenville	Marge Piercy	Meg Wolitzer
Jane Hamilton	Anna Quindlen	Banana Yoshimoto

Alexander McCall Smith
1948- Sco Crime: PI

www.alexandermccallsmith.co.uk

🏃 Precious Ramotswe - Botswana
Isabel Dalhousie ⎫
44 Scotland Street Series ⎬ Edinburgh
Prof Dr Moritz-Maria von Igelfeld - Regensburg, Germany

🏆 Saga for Wit 2003

Kate Atkinson	Veronica Heley	Ian Sansom
Colin Cotterill	Tony Hillerman	Célestine Hitiura Vaite
Cora Harrison	Catriona McPherson	Valerie Wilson Wesley

Ali Smith
1962- Sco

🏆 Encore 2002   Whitbread 2005

Kate Atkinson	Alasdair Gray	Gwendoline Riley
Ron Butlin	Jackie Kay	Zoë Strachan
Janice Galloway	Helen Oyeyemi	

Carol Smith
Crime: Psychological

www.carolsmithbooks.com

Anna Blundy	Gabrielle Lord	Tony Strong
Sarah Diamond	Elizabeth McGregor	Laura Wilson
Babs Horton	Chris Simms	

Martin Cruz Smith
1942- US Crime: Police work - Russia

also writes as Martin Quinn, Simon Quinn

🏃 Insp Arkady Renko - USSR

🏆 CWA 1981

Ronan Bennett	Charles Cumming	Peter May
John Burdett	Garry Disher	Eliot Pattison
Stephen J Cannell	José Latour	Peter Spiegelman
Thomas H Cook	Charles McCarry	Joseph Wambaugh

Michael Marshall Smith
1965- Science Fiction: Near future

also writes as Michael Marshall
www.michaelmarshallsmith.com

🏆 British Fantasy 1995

Christopher Fowler	China Miéville	Tad Williams
William Gibson	Jeff Noon	John Wyndham
James Lovegrove	Neal Stephenson	

S

Scott Smith   1965-   US   Adventure/Thriller

| Alice Blanchard | Donald Harstad | Dan Simmons |
| John Gilstrap | Andrew Klavan | Paullina Simons |

Wilbur Smith   1933-   Zam   Adventure/Thriller
www.wilbursmithbooks.com

Michael Asher	Nelson DeMille	Judy Nunn
Frank Coates	Jean-Christophe Grangé	Julian Jay Savarin
Bryce Courtenay	Paul Henke	Sidney Sheldon

Historical: Ancient Egypt

Joy Chambers	Colleen McCullough	Mary Renault
Margaret George	Valerio Massimo Manfredi	Tim Severin
Christian Jacq	Scott Oden	Paul Sussman

Zadie Smith   1975-

🏆 Black 2000   Guardian 2000   Whitbread 2000   Betty Trask 2001   Sunday Times 2001   Wingate 2003   Orange 2006   S Maugham 2006

Monica Ali	Siri Hustvedt	Andrea Levy
Trezza Azzopardi	Hari Kunzru	Meera Syal
Amit Chaudhuri	Hanif Kureishi	Alex Wheatle
Linda Grant	Nick Laird	Louisa Young

Linda Sole   Saga
also writes as Lynn Granville, Anne Herries, Emma Quincey   Rose Saga
www.lindasole.co.uk

Margaret Dickinson	Elvi Rhodes	Grace Thompson
Evelyn Hood	Judith Saxton	Kate Tremayne
Alexandra Raife	E V Thompson	Jeanne Whitmee

S

Muriel Spark   1918-2006   Sco
www.nls.uk/murielspark

Anne Donovan	Nicole Krauss	Julie Myerson
Philip Hensher	Shena Mackay	Wendy Perriam
Henry James	Iris Murdoch	Gwendoline Riley

Nicholas Sparks   1965-   US
www.nicholassparks.com

Mitch Albom	Sue Monk Kidd	Jane Urquhart
Nicholas Evans	Carol Shields	Robert James Waller
Janet Fitch	Rosie Thomas	Sarah Willis

Sally Spedding
www.sallyspedding.com

Crime: Psychological

Nicci French	Danuta Reah	Manda Scott
Frances Hegarty	Phil Rickman	Barbara Vine
Sarah Rayne	Louis Sanders	Sue Walker

Alan Spence 1947- Sco
www.alanspence.co.uk

Des Dillon	Andrew Greig	Daniel Mason
Anne Donovan	Robin Jenkins	Andrew O'Hagan
Janice Galloway	Jackie Kay	Jonathan Raban

LaVyrle Spencer 1943- US
Saga

also writes as Elizabeth Gage

Janet Dailey	Joan Medlicott	Belva Plain
Barbara Delinsky	Fern Michaels	Danielle Steel
Judith McNaught	Una-Mary Parker	

Sally Spencer

Crime: Police work - UK

also writes as James Garcia Woods
is Alan Rustage
www.sallyspencer.com

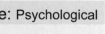 DCI Charlie Woodend - Lancashire
Insp Sam Blackstone - C19th London

David Armstrong	J M Gregson	Roger Silverwood
Caroline Graham	John Harvey	Aline Templeton
Ann Granger	Nick Oldham	June Thomson

Peter Spiegelman US

Crime: Legal/financial

www.peterspiegelman.com

 PI John March - New York

Lawrence Block	Steve Hamilton	John McLaren
Jeffery Deaver	Dashiell Hammett	Martin Cruz Smith
Richard Flanagan	David Hosp	Robert K Tanenbaum
James Grippando	Ross Macdonald	Scott Turow

S

Erica Spindler 1957- US

Crime: Psychological

www.ericaspindler.com

Ingrid Black	Iris Johansen	Andrew Pyper
Lisa Gardner	Alex Kava	Lisa Scottoline
Daniel Hecht	Jonathan Kellerman	Karin Slaughter
Christiane Heggan	Meg O'Brien	Stephen White

Go to back for lists of
Pseudonyms • Authors by Genre • Characters and Series
Prize Winners • Crossover Authors • Further Reading • Websites

Michelle Spring   Can   Crime: PI

☥ Laura Principal - Cambridge

Judith Cutler
Liz Evans
Kerry Greenwood
Graham Hurley
Jim Kelly
Gabrielle Lord
Gillian Slovo
Veronica Stallwood

Edward St Aubyn   1960-

☥ Patrick Melrose

J G Ballard
Patrick Gale
Alan Hollinghurst
James Meek
Andrew O'Hagan
John Updike
Evelyn Waugh
Edmund White
Gerard Woodward

Dana Stabenow   1952-   US   Crime: PI

www.stabenow.com

☥ Kate Shugak • Sgt Liam Campbell
Alaska

Linda Barnes
Nevada Barr
Giles Blunt
C J Box
Meg Gardiner
Steve Hamilton
J A Jance
Theresa Monsour
Sara Paretsky
S J Rozan
Ayelet Waldman
Stephen White

Brian Stableford   1948-   Science Fiction: Technical

also writes as Francis Amery, Brian Craig
http://freespace.virgin.net/diri.gini/brian.htm

Gregory Benford
Colin Greenland
Ian McDonald
Richard Matheson
Linda Nagata
Kim Stanley Robinson
David Zindell

Lyndon Stacey   Crime: Amateur sleuth

www.lyndon-stacey.com

Horse racing

S

Dick Francis
John Francome
Jenny Pitman
Richard Pitman
Graeme Roe

Cath Staincliffe   1956-   Crime: PI

☥ Sal Kilkenny - Manchester

Cara Black
John Connor
Judith Cutler
Ken McCoy
Walter Mosley
James Sallis
Zoë Sharp
Valerie Wilson Wesley
Stella Whitelaw

Veronica Stallwood   Crime: Amateur sleuth

www.veronicastallwood.com

☥ Kate Ivory, Writer - Oxford

Natasha Cooper
Susan B Kelly
Marianne Macdonald
Hope McIntyre
Michelle Spring
M J Trow
Jill Paton Walsh

Mary Stanley 1952- Ire

www.marystanley.com

Elizabeth Buchan	Sophie Hannah	Mary Lawson
Anne Fine	Sue Monk Kidd	Meg Rosoff

Mary Jane Staples 1911-2007 Saga

also writes as James Sinclair, Reginald Staples 🏃 Staples Family - London • Adams Family

Benita Brown	Jeannie Johnson	Kitty Neale
Pip Granger	Elizabeth Lord	Victor Pemberton
Lilian Harry	Gwen Madoc	Carol Rivers
Sara Hylton	Beryl Matthews	Audrey Willsher

Boris Starling 1969- Crime: Psychological

www.borisstarling.com

🏆 TGR 2000

John Connolly	Gareth O'Callaghan	Daniel Silva
Natsuo Kirino	Patrick Redmond	Tony Strong
Cody McFadyen	Craig Russell	P J Tracy

Jason Starr 1966- US Crime: Hardboiled

www.jasonstarr.com

James Crumley	Walter Mosley	Jim Thompson
James Ellroy	James Sallis	John Williams
Elmore Leonard	Boston Teran	

Danielle Steel 1947- US Saga

www.daniellesteel.com

Barbara Taylor Bradford	Sara Hylton	Una-Mary Parker
Jude Deveraux	Susan Lewis	Sidney Sheldon
Eileen Goudge	Judith McNaught	LaVyrle Spencer

John Steinbeck ⌒ 1902-68 US

www.steinbeck.org

Gail Anderson-Dargatz	Jack Kerouac	Robert Louis Stevenson
Will Ferguson	Lori Lansens	William Styron
F Scott Fitzgerald	Harper Lee	Paul Theroux
Ernest Hemingway	Norman Mailer	Leon Uris

Martin Stephen Crime: Historical - C17th

🏃 Henry Gresham, Royal agent - C17th England

Patricia Finney	Alanna Knight	John Pilkington
Philip Gooden	James McGee	Laura Joh Rowland
C C Humphreys	Edward Marston	C J Sansom

Kay Stephens

Saga

Stonemoor Series - Yorkshire

Aileen Armitage
Anne Bennett
Helen Cannam

Alexandra Connor
Elizabeth Elgin

Kate Tremayne
Valerie Wood

Neal Stephenson   1959-   US   Science Fiction: Near future

also writes as Stephen Bury
www.nealstephenson.com
♈ Arthur C Clarke 2004

Steve Aylett
John Birmingham
Eric Brown
Greg Egan

Jon Courtenay Grimwood
Gwyneth Jones
James Lovegrove
Jeff Noon

Richard Powers
Nick Sagan
Michael Marshall Smith
John Wyndham

Rosemary Stevens   US   Crime: Historical - C19th

also writes as Rosemary Martin
www.rosemarystevens.com

🏃 Beau Brummell, Regency fop

Janet Gleeson
John Maclachlan Gray

Deryn Lake
Rosemary Martin

Andrew Pepper
Norman Russell

Jane Stevenson   1959-   Sco   Historical

Tracy Chevalier
Clare Clark
Dorothy Dunnett

Matthew Kneale
Andrew Miller
Robert Nye

Rose Tremain
Sarah Waters

Robert Louis Stevenson   ⌒   1850-1894   Sco

www.nls.uk/rlstevenson

John Buchan
Joseph Conrad

Frank Delaney
Patricia Highsmith

James Robertson
John Steinbeck

Mary Stewart   ⌒   1916-   Sco

Helen Hollick
Susanna Kearsley
Judith Lennox

Sharon Penman
Alexandra Raife
Sally Stewart

Sue Sully
Janet Tanner
Mary Withall

Sally Stewart   Saga

Elizabeth Daish
Christine Marion Fraser
Elisabeth McNeill

Rosamunde Pilcher
Susan Sallis

Mary Stewart
Mary Withall

S

Jessica Stirling 1935- Sco Saga

also writes as Caroline Crosby
is Hugh C Rae
(formerly with Margaret M Coghlan)
www.jessicastirling.com

⚇ Clare Kelso • Nicholson Family • Patterson Family
Holly Beckman - Glasgow • Conway Family
Scotland

Emma Blair
Maggie Craig
Doris Davidson

Margaret Thomson Davis
Christine Marion Fraser
Meg Hutchinson

Elisabeth McNeill
Frances Paige

Julian Stockwin 1944- Sea: Historical

www.julianstockwin.com

⚇ Thomas Paine Kydd - C18th/19th England

G S Beard
David Donachie
C S Forester

Alexander Kent
Jonathan Lunn

James L Nelson
Peter Smalley

Nick Stone 1961- Adventure/Thriller

www.nickstone.co.uk

⚇ PI Max Mingus

🏆 CWA 2006

Simon Beckett
Mark Billingham
John Connolly

Robert Ellis
Michael Marshall
Gareth O'Callaghan

Tim Sebastian
Daniel Silva

Bernadette Strachan 1962- Chick Lit

www.bernadettestrachan.co.uk

Lynne Barrett-Lee
Harriet Evans
Julie Highmore

Jill Mansell
Elizabeth Noble

Alexandra Potter
Plum Sykes

Zoë Strachan 1975- Sco

www.zoestrachan.com

Isla Dewar
Anne Donovan

Janice Galloway
Laura Marney

Ali Smith

S

Peter Straub 1943- US Horror

www.peterstraub.net

Richard Bachman
Jonathan Carroll
Bret Easton Ellis

John Farris
Stephen Laws
Robert McCammon

Richard Matheson
Christopher Pike
T M Wright

Whitley Strieber 1945- US Horror

Ramsey Campbell
John Farris
Shaun Hutson

Brian Lumley
Robert McCammon
David Martin

Graham Masterton
Dan Simmons

Sarah Strohmeyer

US   Crime: Humour

www.sarahstrohmeyer.com   ♟ Bubbles Yablonsky, Journalist - Lehigh, Pennsylvania

Linda Barnes	Sparkle Hayter	Ayelet Waldman
Janet Evanovich	Pauline McLynn	Donald Westlake
Liz Evans	Rosemary Martin	

Terence Strong

1946-   War: Modern

Brian Callison	W E B Griffin	Paul Henke
Duncan Falconer	Duncan Harding	Alistair MacLean
David Fiddimore	Jack Harvey	David L Robbins

Tony Strong

1962-   Crime: Psychological

www.tonystrong.com   ♟ Terry Williams

Mark Billingham	Carol Smith	Scott Turow
Patrick Redmond	Boris Starling	Barbara Vine
James Siegel		

Charles Stross

1964-   Science Fiction: Space opera

Poul Anderson	Lois McMaster Bujold	Brian Herbert
Iain M Banks	Orson Scott Card	Liz Williams
Stephen Baxter	Peter F Hamilton	Sean Williams

William Styron

1925-2006   US

Pat Conroy	Norman Mailer	John Steinbeck
William Faulkner	Bernhard Schlink	Alice Walker
Ernest Hemingway		

S | Su Tong

China

Alma Alexander	Anchee Min	Amy Tan
Arthur Golden	Mary Renault	Xinran

Sue Sully

Saga

West Country

Anita Burgh	Susan Howatch	Mary Stewart
Daphne Du Maurier	Mary Mackie	Rowena Summers
Audrey Howard	Belva Plain	Michael Taylor

Go to back for lists of
Pseudonyms • Authors by Genre • Characters and Series
Prize Winners • Crossover Authors • Further Reading • Websites

Rowena Summers 1932- Saga

is Jean Saunders
West country
www.hometown.aol.co.uk/jeanrowena

Lyn Andrews	Meg Hutchinson	Sue Sully
Anne Baker	Annie Murray	E V Thompson
Anita Burgh	Susan Sallis	

Patrick Suskind 🕿 1949- Ger

Isabel Allende	Paulo Coelho	Carlos Fuentes
Alessandro Baricco	Laura Esquivel	Gabriel Garcia Márquez

Paul Sussman 1968- Adventure/Thriller

🏃 Insp Khalifa - Luxor, Egypt

Steve Berry	Tom Harper	James Rollins
Dan Brown	Raymond Khoury	Wilbur Smith
David Gibbins	Chris Kuzneski	

William Sutcliffe 1971- Humour

Matt Beaumont	Tim Lott	Matt Thorne
Alex Garland	Kevin Sampson	Evelyn Waugh

Henry Sutton 1963-

Jonathan Coe	John Lanchester	Nigel Williams
A M Homes	Hilary Mantel	

Koji Suzuki Ja Horror

Simon Clark	Dean R Koontz	David Martin
Shaun Hutson	Richard Laymon	T M Wright

Steph Swainston Fantasy: Epic

www.stephswainston.co.uk

Mary Gentle	Scott Lynch	Jane Welch
J V Jones	China Miéville	Janny Wurts
Ursula K Le Guin	K J Parker	

Graham Swift 1949-

🏆 Faber 1983   Guardian 1983   Holtby 1983   Black 1996   Booker 1996

Julian Barnes	Maggie Gee	Alan Sillitoe
Margaret Drabble	Alasdair Gray	Gillian White
Anne Enright	Patrick McGrath	T R Wilson
John Fowles	Magnus Mills	Gerard Woodward

Madge Swindells
www.madgeswindells.com

Crime: Romantic suspense

Jackie Collins
Judith Gould

Heather Graham
Jayne Ann Krentz

Johanna Lindsey
Jean Saunders

Meera Syal 🎭 1963-

Monica Ali
Chitra Banerjee Divakaruni
Roopa Farooki
Esther Freud

Hari Kunzru
Hanif Kureishi
Andrea Levy
Zadie Smith

Thirty Umrigar
Lou Wakefield
Alex Wheatle
Louisa Young

Plum Sykes 1969-

Chick Lit

Candace Bushnell
Christina Jones
Jane Moore

Clare Naylor
Sheila O'Flanagan

Bernadette Strachan
Lauren Weisberger

Frank Tallis
www.franktallis.com

Crime: Historical - C20th

🏃 Dr Max Liebermann, Psychoanalyst, & DI Oscar Rheinhardt
early 1900s, Vienna

Boris Akunin
Michael Gregorio
Philip Kerr

Andrew Martin
R N Morris
Jo Nesbo

Matthew Pearl
Qiu Xiaolong
C J Sansom

Amy Tan 1952- US
www.amytan.net

Alma Alexander
Anita Desai
Arthur Golden
Ha Jin

Barbara Kingsolver
Catherine Lim
Anchee Min
Timothy Mo

Toni Morrison
Alice Munro
Su Tong
Gail Tsukiyama

Robert K Tanenbaum US

Crime: Legal/financial

🏃 Roger 'Butch' Karp, Asst Chief DA - New York

Linda Fairstein
Frances Fyfield
James Grippando

Steve Hamilton
Steve Martini
Perri O'Shaughnessy

Christopher Reich
Peter Spiegelman

Reay Tannahill 1929-2007 Sco

Historical

🏆 Romantic 1990

Maggie Craig
Dorothy Dunnett
Barbara Erskine

Diana Gabaldon
Cynthia Harrod-Eagles

Anne Herries
Maureen Peters

Janet Tanner

Saga

www.janettanner.co.uk

🏃 Hillsbridge Family - Somerset

Dilly Court	Connie Monk	Judith Saxton
Sara Fraser	Alexandra Raife	Mary Stewart
Gwen Madoc	Denise Robertson	Grace Thompson

Judith Tarr   US

Fantasy: Myth

www.sff.net/people/judith-tarr/library.html

Storm Constantine	Ursula K Le Guin	Garth Nix
Kathleen O'Neal Gear	Morgan Llywelyn	Sarah Zettel
Katharine Kerr	Caiseal Mor	

Donna Tartt   1963-   US

🏆 WHSmith 2003

Suzanne Berne	Jeffrey Eugenides	Matthew Pearl
Edward Docx	Jonathan Franzen	Annie Proulx
Robert Edric	Carol Goodman	Carol Shields

June Tate   1930s

Saga

WW2

Julia Bryant	Lilian Harry	Annie Murray
Elizabeth Elgin	Beryl Kingston	Sheila Newberry
June Francis	Beryl Matthews	Gilda O'Neill

Andrew Taylor   1951-

Crime: Police work - UK

also writes as Andrew Saville, John Robert Taylor
www.andrew-taylor.net

🏃 Jill Francis & DI Richard Thornhill
'Lydmouth', 1950s Welsh Borders
Roth Trilogy - North London

🏆 CWA 1982, 2001 & 2003

James Anderson	Gregory Hall	Sue Walker
Benjamin Black	Cynthia Harrod-Eagles	Camilla Way
William Brodrick	Catriona McPherson	Laura Wilson
Ann Cleeves	David Mitchell	R D Wingfield

Linda Taylor

Humour

Trisha Ashley	Cathy Kelly	Nisha Minhas
Victoria Clayton	Shari Low	Victoria Routledge
Jane Green	Chris Manby	Keith Waterhouse

Michael Taylor

Saga

www.michaeltaylorauthor.com

R F Delderfield	Lesley Pearse	Kate Tremayne
Douglas Kennedy	Sue Sully	Dee Williams
Ken McCoy	E V Thompson	

T

Roma Tearne · Sri Lan

www.romatearne.com

Chimamanda Ngozi Adichie	Candida Clark	Maggie O'Farrell
Kate Atkinson	Romesh Gunesekera	Rose Tremain

Peter Temple · 1946- · Aus · Crime: PI

Jack Irish - Melbourne

🏆 CWA 2007

Benjamin Black	Garry Disher	Matthew Klein
Giles Blunt	Michael Gruber	Gabrielle Lord
Caroline Carver	Susan Hill	Barry Maitland
Peter Corris	Graham Hurley	Elliot Perlman

Aline Templeton · Sco · Crime: Police work - UK

DI Marjory Fleming - Scotland

Hilary Bonner	Alex Gray	Denise Mina
Natasha Cooper	Nigel McCrery	Peter Robinson
Lesley Glaister	Iain McDowall	Sally Spencer

Emma Tennant · 1937- · Sco

also writes as Catherine Aydy

Elizabeth Aston	Elizabeth Gaskell	Eva Rice
Jane Austen	Nicole Krauss	Gwendoline Riley
Penelope Fitzgerald	Iris Murdoch	Salman Rushdie
Esther Freud	Wendy Perriam	Fay Weldon

Sheri S Tepper · 1929- · US · Fantasy: Epic

also writes as B J Oliphant, A J Orde

Marion Zimmer Bradley	Frank Herbert	Ursula K Le Guin
C J Cherryh	Gwyneth Jones	Sean Russell
Mary Gentle		

Boston Teran · US · Crime: Hardboiled

www.bostonteran.com · *Sheriff John Victor Sully - California*

🏆 CWA 2000

Alice Blanchard	James Crumley	Dennis Lehane
Lorenzo Carcaterra	Robert Ferrigno	James Sallis
Massimo Carlotto	Thomas Harris	Jason Starr

Kathleen Tessaro · US · Chick Lit

Susannah Bates	Louise Kean	Sara Shepard
Anne Dunlop	Sophie Kinsella	Rosy Thornton
Sabine Durrant	Andrea Semple	Lauren Weisberger

T

Paul Theroux 1941- US

🏆 Whitbread 1978   Black 1981

Candida Clark	Romesh Gunesekera	Yann Martel
Pat Conroy	Abdulrazak Gurnah	John Steinbeck
Giles Foden	Ernest Hemingway	Adam Thorpe
Maureen Freely	Gunnar Kopperud	Colin Thubron

Adam Thirlwell 1978-

Martin Amis	Howard Jacobson
Edward Docx	Philip Roth

Craig Thomas 1942-   Adventure/Thriller

also writes as David Grant

Geoffrey Archer	Tom Gabbay	Julian Rathbone
Harold Coyle	Jack Higgins	Julian Jay Savarin
James Follett	John J Nance	

Leslie Thomas 1931-   Wales

www.lesliethomas.co.uk

Wales

George Macdonald Fraser	Geoff Nicholson	Alan Titchmarsh
Joseph Heller	David Nobbs	Keith Waterhouse
David Lodge		

Crime: Police work - UK

🏃 'Dangerous' Davies

Natasha Cooper	Nicholas Rhea	June Thomson
Katherine John	Mike Ripley	Neil White
Nick Oldham		

Rosie Thomas 1947-   Wales   Saga

also writes as Jancy King

🏆 Romantic 1985 & 2007

Barbara Taylor Bradford	Rowan Coleman	Anne Rivers Siddons
Liz Byrski	Sarah Harrison	Nicholas Sparks
Candida Clark	Belva Plain	Jane Elizabeth Varley

T

Scarlett Thomas 1972-   Fantasy

Susanna Clarke	G W Dahlquist
Douglas Coupland	Stephen Hunt

Go to back for lists of
Pseudonyms • Authors by Genre • Characters and Series
Prize Winners • Crossover Authors • Further Reading • Websites

E V Thompson
1926-   Historical
also writes as James Munro   ☆ Retallick Family

Gloria Cook	Anne Herries	Rowena Summers
R F Delderfield	Elizabeth Ann Hill	Michael Taylor
Winston Graham	Patricia Shaw	Kate Tremayne
Cynthia Harrod-Eagles	Linda Sole	Barbara Wood

Grace Thompson
Wales   Saga
also writes as Kay Christopher   Valley Series - Wales • Pendragon Island Series

Catrin Collier	Linda Sole	Elizabeth Waite
Catherine Cookson	Janet Tanner	Annie Wilkinson
Iris Gower	Margaret Thornton	Dee Williams

Jim Thompson
1906-1977   US   Crime: Psychological

Edward Bunker	Jack Higgins	John Williams
James Crumley	George P Pelecanos	Don Winslow
James Ellroy	Jason Starr	

Kate Thompson
☏ ☺   1956-   Mature Chick Lit
www.kate-thompson.com   Ireland

Colette Caddle	Cathy Kelly	Sharon Owens
Martina Devlin	Dorothy Koomson	D M Purcell
Louise Kean	Chris Manby	

June Thomson
1930-   Crime: Police work - UK
                                    ☆ DCI Jack Finch - Essex

W J Burley	Anthea Fraser	Sally Spencer
Arthur Conan Doyle	Ruth Rendell	Leslie Thomas
Elizabeth Ferrars	Roger Silverwood	

Rupert Thomson
1955-

Douglas Clegg	Jim Crace	John Fowles
Douglas Coupland	Suzannah Dunn	Amanda Prantera

Brad Thor
1970-   US   Adventure/Thriller
www.bradthor.com   ☆ Scot Harvath, Secret Service agent

David Baldacci	Vince Flynn	Gordon Kent
Tom Clancy	Brian Haig	Daniel Silva
Clive Cussler	Jack Higgins	

T

Matt Thorne   1974-   Lad Lit

🏆 Encore 2000

David Baddiel
Neil Cross
Jay McInerney

David Nicholls
Nicholas Royle
Kevin Sampson

Alexei Sayle
William Sutcliffe

Nicola Thorne   SA   Saga

also writes as Katherine Yorke; is Rosemary Ellerbeck
www.nicolathorne.com

Champagne Series
🕴 Askham Family

Tessa Barclay
Barbara Taylor Bradford
Annabel Dilke

Elizabeth Ann Hill
Joan O'Neill
Margaret Pemberton

Judith Saxton
Barbara Whitnell
Barbara Wood

Margaret Thornton   1934-   Saga

Blackpool

Jessica Blair
Julia Bryant
Alexandra Connor
Glenice Crossland

June Francis
Rosie Harris
Judith Lennox
Connie Monk

Elizabeth Murphy
Lynda Page
Grace Thompson
Barbara Whitnell

Rosy Thornton   Chick Lit

www.rosythornton.com

Susannah Bates
Charlotte Bingham
Hester Browne

Sandra Howard
Erica James
Kathleen Tessaro

Alan Titchmarsh
Barbara Trapido
Deborah Wright

Adam Thorpe   1956-

🏆 Holtby 1993

Paul Auster
Thomas Hardy
Kazuo Ishiguro

Thomas Keneally
Bernard MacLaverty

Geoff Ryman
Paul Theroux

Colin Thubron   1939-

Amin Maalouf
Daniel Mason

Andrew Miller
Michael Ondaatje

Paul Theroux
Jeanette Winterson

T

Ronald Tierney   1944-   US   Crime: PI

www.ronaldtierney.com

🕴 Deets Shanahan - Indianapolis

Andrea Camilleri
Michael Dibdin

Loren D Estleman
Ann Granger

Donna Leon
Rick Riordan

Mark Timlin 1950- Crime: PI

also writes as Johnny Angelo, Jim Ballantyne, Tony Williams   🏃 Nick Sharman
www.nicksharman.co.uk   London

Jake Arnott	Simon Kernick	Mike Ripley
Ken Bruen	Nick Oldham	Louise Welsh
Bill James		

Alan Titchmarsh 1950- Humour

www.alantitchmarsh.com

Melvyn Bragg	Eve Makis	Rosy Thornton
Katie Fforde	David Nobbs	Keith Waterhouse
Angela Huth	Leslie Thomas	

Charles Todd Crime: Historical - C20th

is Charles & Caroline Todd   🏃 Insp Ian Rutledge - 1920s England
www.charlestodd.com

David Armstrong	Robert Goddard	Susan B Kelly
Pat Barker	Martha Grimes	Laurie R King
Rhys Bowen	Reginald Hill	Robin Paige
Mark Gatiss	Graham Ison	David Roberts

Marilyn Todd 1958- Crime: Historical - Ancient

🏃 Claudia Seferius - Ancient Rome

Philip Boast	Allan Massie	Steven Saylor
Lindsey Davis	John Maddox Roberts	Peter Tremayne
Margaret Doody	Rosemary Rowe	

Miriam Toews Can

Mark Haddon	Anne Michaels	Anna Quindlen
Garrison Keillor	Alice Munro	J D Salinger
Sue Monk Kidd	Michael Ondaatje	Carol Shields

Colm Toibin 1955- Ire

www.colmtoibin.com
🏆 Encore 1993   IMPAC 2006

Peter Ackroyd	Eoin McNamee	Glenn Patterson
Jennifer Johnston	Brian Moore	William Wall
Colum McCann	David Park	Niall Williams

☺ also writes children's books

J R R Tolkien ☎ ☺ 1892-1973 Fantasy: Epic

was John Ronald Reuel Tolkien
www.tolkiensociety.org

R Scott Bakker	Cecilia Dart-Thornton	Guy Gavriel Kay
David Bilsborough	Jude Fisher	Christopher Paolini
Terry Brooks	Elizabeth Haydon	Tad Williams
Susanna Clarke	Robert Jordan	Sarah Zettel

Louise Tondeur 1972-

Kate Atkinson	Margaret Forster	Joanna Trollope
Joolz Denby	Angela Huth	Jonathan Tropper
Anne Fine	Eve Makis	Louise Voss

Peter Tonkin 1950- Crime: Historical - C16th

🏃 Tom Musgrave, Master of Defence - C16th England

P F Chisholm	Philip Gooden	John Pilkington
Michael Clynes	Michael Jecks	C J Sansom
Patricia Finney	Simon Levack	

Sea: Modern
Mariner Series

Duncan Harding	Sam Llewellyn	Nicholas Monsarrat
C C Humphreys	Philip McCutchan	Patrick Robinson
Hammond Innes	Alistair MacLean	

Paige Toon 1975- Chick Lit

www.paigetoon.com

Meg Cabot	Belinda Jones	Sharon Owens
Lucy Dawson	Shari Low	Adele Parks
Lisa Jewell	Nisha Minhas	Alexandra Potter

Rebecca Tope 1948- Crime: Amateur sleuth

www.rebeccatope.com
🏃 Drew Slocombe, Undertaker • PC Den Cooper
Devon

Liz Evans	Joyce Holms	Chris Niles
Ann Granger	Hazel Holt	Catherine Shaw
Veronica Heley	Hope McIntyre	Stella Whitelaw

Paul Torday 1946-

Malcolm Bradbury	Marina Lewycka	David Nobbs
Kim Edwards	David Lodge	Sue Townsend
Michael Frayn	Mark Mills	Evelyn Waugh

T

Sue Townsend ☺ 1946- Humour

Alan Bennett	Laurie Graham	Ian Sansom
Clare Boylan	Tom Holt	Paul Torday
Fiona Gibson	Sue Limb	Lou Wakefield

P J Tracy US Crime: Psychological
is P J & Traci Lambrecht
www.pjtracy.net

Russell Andrews	David Hosp	Richard Montanari
John Connolly	Natsuo Kirino	Ridley Pearson
Brian Freeman	Jeff Lindsay	Karen Rose
Jilliane Hoffman	Cody McFadyen	Boris Starling

Nigel Tranter 1909-2000 Sco Historical
also wrote as Nye Tredgold
www.nigeltranter.co.uk

R F Delderfield	Winston Graham	Sharon Penman
Dorothy Dunnett	Edith Pargeter	Julian Rathbone

Barbara Trapido 1941- SA

Jane Austen	Nicole Krauss	Amanda Prantera
Amanda Craig	Sarah Kate Lynch	Eva Rice
Joanne Harris	Tim Parks	Rosy Thornton

Rose Tremain 1943-
🏆 Black 1992   Whitbread 1999   Orange 2008

Geraldine Brooks	Andrew Miller	Nicholas Shakespeare
Maggie Gee	Deborah Moggach	Jane Stevenson
Maurice Gee	Robert Nye	Roma Tearne

Kate Tremayne Historical Romance
is Pauline Bentley 🕴 Loveday Series - Cornwall
www.katetremayne.com

Winston Graham	Linda Sole	Michael Taylor
Susan Howatch	Kay Stephens	E V Thompson
Maureen Peters		

Peter Tremayne 1943- Ire Crime: Historical - Medieval
also writes as Peter MacAlan; is Peter Beresford Ellis 🕴 Sister Fidelma - C7th Ireland

Margaret Frazer	Cora Harrison	Sharan Newman
Andrew M Greeley	Pat McIntosh	Mary Reed and Eric Mayer
	Ian Morson	Marilyn Todd

T

William Trevor   1928-   Ire

🏆 Whitbread 1976, 1983 & 1994

John Banville	Andrew Sean Greer	Eoin McNamee
Sebastian Barry	Dave Hill	Joseph O'Connor
Frank Delaney	Susan Hill	David Park
Ronald Frame	Nell Leyshon	William Wall

Jonathan Trigell   1974-

🏆 JLR 2004

Ron Butlin	Denis Johnson	D B C Pierre
Nathan Englander	Vladimir Nabokov	Alan Warner
A M Homes		

Adriana Trigiani   US   Saga

www.adrianatrigiani.com   Big Stone Gap Series - Virginia

Elizabeth Berg	Patricia Gaffney	Elinor Lipman
Suzanne Berne	Jan Karon	Alice McDermott
Leif Enger	Haven Kimmel	Alexandra Raife
Fannie Flagg	Lorna Landvik	Anne Rivers Siddons

Anthony Trollope   1815-82

www.anthonytrollope.com

Charles Dickens	William Golding	Susan Howatch
John Galsworthy	Elizabeth Jane Howard	Tom Wolfe

Joanna Trollope   1943-   Aga Saga

also writes as Caroline Harvey
www.joannatrollope.net

🏆 Romantic 1980

Diana Appleyard	Catherine Dunne	Libby Purves
Claire Calman	Caro Fraser	Anne Rivers Siddons
Anne Doughty	Sandra Howard	Louise Tondeur
Jessica Duchen	Kate Long	Jane Elizabeth Varley

T

Jonathan Tropper   1970-   US

www.jonathantropper.com

Matt Beaumont	Mark Haddon	James Robertson
Michael Cunningham	A M Homes	Louise Tondeur
Frank Delaney	William Kowalski	Lisa Tucker
Richard Ford	Mil Millington	Anne Tyler

may be suitable for young adults

271

Janet MacLeod Trotter   1958-   Saga

www.janetmacleodtrotter.com   NE England

Irene Carr	Una Horne	Wendy Robertson
Catherine Cookson	Ken McCoy	Barbara Whitnell
Elizabeth Gill	Denise Robertson	Annie Wilkinson

M J Trow   1949-   Wales   Crime: Amateur sleuth

is Meirion James Trow   ⚲ Peter Maxwell, Teacher
                              Det Supt Sholto Lestrade - C19th England

Arthur Conan Doyle	Amy Myers	Norman Russell
Sarah Grazebrook	David Pirie	Veronica Stallwood
Joan Lock	Nicholas Rhea	

Lynne Truss   Humour

www.lynnetruss.com

Susie Boyt	Helen Fielding	Arabella Weir
Mavis Cheek	Jane Green	Louise Wener
Isla Dewar	Laura Marney	

Gail Tsukiyama   US

| Victoria Hislop | David Mitchell | Banana Yoshimoto |
| Kazuo Ishiguro | Amy Tan | Carlos Ruiz Zafón |

Lisa Tucker   US

www.lisatucker.com

Emily Barr	Alex Kava	Jodi Picoult
Barbara Delinsky	Sue Miller	Jonathan Tropper
Alice Hoffman	Jacquelyn Mitchard	Jennifer Weiner
Gwen Hunter	John J Nance	Sarah Willis

Sarah Tucker   Mature Chick Lit

www.sarahtucker.info

Alison Penton Harper	Debbie Macomber	Polly Williams
Julia Holden	Alexandra Potter	Grace Wynne-Jones
Sophie King	Robyn Sisman	Liz Young

Peter Turnbull   1950-   Crime: Police work - UK

 P Division - Glasgow • DCI Hennessy & DS Yellich - York

Jo Bannister	Geraldine Evans	Frederic Lindsay
Robert Barnard	Gerald Hammond	Stuart Pawson
Pauline Bell	Katherine John	

Scott Turow 1949- US Crime: Legal/financial
www.scottturow.com

🏆 CWA 1987

Stephen L Carter	John Hart	Barbara Parker
Mark Gimenez	Jilliane Hoffman	Christopher Reich
James Grippando	Craig Holden	Peter Spiegelman
Colin Harrison	John McLaren	Tony Strong

Harry Turtledove 1949- US Fantasy: Epic
also writes as Eric G Iverson, N H Turtletaub
www.sfsite.com/~silverag/turtledove.html

Carol Berg	Mary Gentle	George R R Martin
Sara Douglass	Paul Kearney	William Nicholson
David Farland	Sophia McDougall	Guy Walters

James Twining 1972- Adventure/Thriller
www.jamestwining.com

🚶 Tom Kirk, Art thief

Steve Berry	David Gibbins	Paul Watkins
Sam Bourne	Michael Marshall	Nigel West
Clive Cussler	Gareth O'Callaghan	Tim Willocks

Anne Tyler 1941- US

🏆 Pulitzer 1989

Joan Barfoot	Catherine Dunne	William Kowalski
Candida Crewe	Karen Joy Fowler	Ann Packer
Jill Dawson	Gail Godwin	Richard Russo
Suzannah Dunn	Haven Kimmel	Jonathan Tropper

Thirty Umrigar 1961- Ind
www.umrigar.com

Chitra Banerjee Divakaruni	Amulya Malladi	Arundhati Roy
Roopa Farooki	Anita Nair	Meera Syal
Jhumpa Lahiri	Preethi Nair	

Barry Unsworth 🎧 1930- Historical

🏆 Booker 1992

John Banville	Robert Harris	Amanda Prantera
Jim Crace	James Meek	Julian Rathbone
Robert Edric	Andrew Miller	Peter Watt
William Golding	Robert Nye	Marianne Wiggins

T U

Go to back for lists of
Pseudonyms • Authors by Genre • Characters and Series
Prize Winners • Crossover Authors • Further Reading • Websites

John Updike   1932-   US

🏆 Pulitzer 1982 & 1991

Saul Bellow	Jonathan Franzen	Vladimir Nabokov
E L Doctorow	John Irving	Cynthia Ozick
Jeffrey Eugenides	Norman Mailer	Edward St Aubyn
Ben Faccini	Rick Moody	Tobias Wolff

Leon Uris   1924-2003   US

James A Michener	Manda Scott	Morris West
Edward Rutherfurd	John Steinbeck	

Jane Urquhart   1949-   Can

Thomas Eidson	Anne Michaels	Nicholas Sparks
David Guterson	David Mitchell	Robert James Waller
Peter Hoeg	Ann Patchett	Ann Widdecombe

Célestine Hitiura Vaite   1966-   Tah

www.celestinevaite.com

Cecelia Ahern	Shifra Horn	Rebecca Shaw
Sally Beauman	Ann Purser	Alexander McCall Smith
Laura Esquivel	Nora Roberts	Louise Voss

Janwillem van de Wetering   1931-2008   Neth   Crime: Police work
- Netherlands

🏃 Adjutant Grijpstra & Sgt de Gier - Amsterdam

A C Baantjer	Henning Mankell
H R F Keating	Georges Simenon

Eric Van Lustbader   Crime: PI

also writes as Eric Lustbader
www.ericvanlustbader.com

🏃 Nicholas Linnear - Japan

Bryce Courtenay	David Morrell	Alan Savage
Jack Higgins	Christopher Nicole	Justin Scott
Robert Ludlum		

U V

Fred Vargas   1957-   Fr   Crime: Police work - France

🏃 Commissaire Adamsberg - Paris

🏆 CWA 2006 & 2007

K O Dahl	Donna Leon	Manuel Vázquez Montalbán
Colin Dexter	Henning Mankell	Martin O'Brien
David Hewson	Guillermo Martinez	Georges Simenon

Mario Vargas Llosa   1936-   Peru

Isabel Allende	Carlos Fuentes	Tomas Eloy Martinez
Louis de Bernières	Tessa Hadley	Nicholas Shakespeare
Maureen Freely	Ha Jin	

Jane Elizabeth Varley   Aga Saga
www.janevarley.com

Diana Appleyard	Donna Hay	Joanna Trollope
Louise Bagshawe	Patricia Scanlan	Salley Vickers
Sarah Grazebrook	Rosie Thomas	Penny Vincenzi

Pip Vaughan-Hughes   1964-   Crime: Historical - C13th
🏃 Brother Petroc - Europe

Alys Clare	Tom Harper	Caroline Roe
Bernard Cornwell	Michael Jecks	Robyn Young
Ariana Franklin	Ellis Peters	

Jules Verne   1828-1905   Fr   Science Fiction: Space and time

Robert A Heinlein	Kurt Vonnegut	Connie Willis
C S Lewis	H G Wells	David Zindell

Salley Vickers   1948-
www.salleyvickers.com

Anita Brookner	Patricia Duncker	Clare Morrall
Stevie Davies	Ken Follett	James Runcie
Jill Dawson	Sue Gee	Jane Elizabeth Varley
Anita Diamant	Joanne Harris	Susan Vreeland

Gore Vidal   1925-   US
also writes as Edgar Box

Kingsley Amis	Norman Mailer	Mary Renault
Margaret George	James A Michener	Tom Wolfe

Penny Vincenzi   1939-   Glitz & Glamour
🏃 Lytton Trilogy
www.pennyvincenzi.com

Elizabeth Adler	Sandra Brown	Lesley Lokko
Susannah Bates	Jackie Collins	Jane Elizabeth Varley
Sally Beauman	Annabel Dilke	Grace Wynne-Jones
Barbara Taylor Bradford	Olivia Goldsmith	Laura Zigman

V

Barbara Vine 1930- Crime: Psychological

is Ruth Rendell

🏆 CWA 1987 & 1991

Carol Anne Davis	Elizabeth McGregor	Jenny Siler
Sophie Hannah	Julie Parsons	Chris Simms
Carolyn G Hart	Patrick Redmond	Sally Spedding
Frances Hegarty	Manda Scott	Tony Strong

Kurt Vonnegut 1922-2007 US Science Fiction: Space and time

www.vonnegut.com

Brian W Aldiss	William Gibson	Jack McDevitt
J G Ballard	Alasdair Gray	Jeff Noon
Philip K Dick	Aldous Huxley	Jules Verne

Louise Voss

Candida Clark	Eve Makis	Louise Tondeur
Penelope Lively	Libby Purves	Célestine Hitiura Vaite

Susan Vreeland 1946- US Historical

www.svreeland.com

Tracy Chevalier	Deborah Moggach	James Runcie
Will Davenport	Ann Patchett	Salley Vickers
Anita Diamant		

Per Wahlöö 1926-1975 see Maj Sjöwall

Elizabeth Waite Saga

London

Philip Boast	Pip Granger	Grace Thompson
Harry Bowling	Elizabeth Lord	Jeanne Whitmee
Pamela Evans	Carol Rivers	Audrey Willsher

Martyn Waites 1963- Crime: Hardboiled

www.martynwaites.com

🏃 Stephen Larkin
Joe Donovan } Journalist - NE England

Ken Bruen	Robert Edric	Chris Paling
Paul Charles	Heather Graham	Nicholas Royle
Alan Dunn	Ken McCoy	

V
W

Go to back for lists of
Pseudonyms • Authors by Genre • Characters and Series
Prize Winners • Crossover Authors • Further Reading • Websites

Lou Wakefield · Aga Saga

Elizabeth Buchan	Meera Syal	Madeleine Wickham
Marika Cobbold	Sue Townsend	Isabel Wolff
Katie Fforde	Mary Wesley	Jane Yardley

Ayelet Waldman · 1964- US · Crime: PI

www.ayeletwaldman.com

Jo Dereske	John Dunning	Dana Stabenow
Stephen Donaldson	Sue Grafton	Sarah Strohmeyer
Stella Duffy	J A Jance	

Alice Walker ⌒ 1944- US

🏆 Pulitzer 1983

Emma Donoghue	Carson McCullers	Toni Morrison
William Faulkner	Terry McMillan	William Styron
Harper Lee		

Fiona Walker ⌒ 1969- · Chick Lit

www.fionawalker.com

Jessica Adams	Emily Barr	Alexandra Potter
Catherine Alliott	Susie Boyt	Cathy Woodman
Louise Bagshawe	Jilly Cooper	

Sue Walker Sco · Crime: Psychological

www.sue-walker.com

Simon Beckett	Elizabeth McGregor	Sally Spedding
Nicci French	J Wallis Martin	Andrew Taylor
Val McDermid	Denise Mina	

William Wall 1955- Ire

http://homepage.eircom.net/~williamwall/williamwall

Sebastian Barry	John McGahern	Colm Toibin
Jennifer Johnston	Joseph O'Connor	William Trevor
Cormac McCarthy		

Robert James Waller 1939- US

Nicholas Evans	Anita Shreve	Nicholas Sparks
Richard Ford	Jane Smiley	Jane Urquhart
Marge Piercy		

⌒ may be suitable for young adults

Jill Paton Walsh   1937-
www.greenbay.co.uk/jpw.html

Peter Ackroyd	Jane Gardam
Umberto Eco	Catherine Shaw

Crime: Amateur sleuth
🏃 Imogen Quy, Nurse - St Agatha's College, Cambridge

Simon Brett	Veronica Heley	Chris Niles
Colin Dexter	Joyce Holms	Veronica Stallwood
Ruth Dudley Edwards	Michael Innes	

Jess Walter   US
www.jesswalter.com

Crime: Police work - US
🏃 Caroline Maybry - Spokane, Washington State

Giles Blunt	Thomas Laird	Ridley Pearson
Steve Hamilton	Theresa Monsour	Jenny Siler
Lynn Hightower		

Guy Walters
http://web.mac.com/guywalters

War

Elizabeth Darrell	Rebecca Pawel	Alan Savage
David Fiddimore	Derek Robinson	Harry Turtledove
Robert Harris	Robert Ryan	

Minette Walters   1949-
www.minettewalters.co.uk

Crime: Psychological

🏆 CWA 1992, 1994 & 2003

Lindsay Ashford	Carol Anne Davis	Joanna Hines
Suzanne Berne	Carol Goodman	Åsa Larsson
Ingrid Black	Sophie Hannah	Gabrielle Lord
Candida Clark	Jane Hill	J Wallis Martin

Joseph Wambaugh   1937-   US
www.josephwambaugh.net

Crime: Police work - US
California

James Ellroy	Deon Meyer	Mario Puzo
W E B Griffin	Theresa Monsour	Martin Cruz Smith
Ed McBain	Jefferson Parker	Stuart Woods

Amanda Eyre Ward   1972-   US
www.amandaward.com

Aga Saga

Clare Chambers	Clare Morrall	Madeleine Wickham
Marika Cobbold	Elizabeth Noble	Ann Widdecombe
Elizabeth Flock	Mary Wesley	Jane Yardley

J R Ward   US   Paranormal
is Jessica Bird
www.jrward.com

Lara Adrian
Kelley Armstrong
Keri Arthur

Mary Janice Davidson
Christine Feehan
Lori Handeland

Charlaine Harris
Tanya Huff
Sherrilyn Kenyon

Alan Warner   1964-   Sco
🏆 S Maugham 1996   Encore 1998

Iain Banks
Ron Butlin

Jackie Kay
James Kelman

Jonathan Trigell
Irvine Welsh

Freda Warrington   1956-   Fantasy: Epic
www.members.aol.com/fredamike

Robert Asprin
James Barclay
Storm Constantine
Ben Counter

Sara Douglass
Ian Irvine
J V Jones
Tanith Lee

Juliet E McKenna
Elizabeth Moon
K J Parker
Robert Silverberg

Keith Waterhouse   1929-   Humour

Malcolm Bradbury
Ben Elton
Andrew Holmes

David Lodge
Magnus Mills
John Mortimer

Linda Taylor
Leslie Thomas
Alan Titchmarsh

Sarah Waters   1966-   Wales
www.sarahwaters.com
🏆 Sunday Times 2000   S Maugham 2000   CWA 2002

Clare Clark
Stevie Davies
Emma Donoghue

Posie Graeme-Evans
Jane Harris
John Harwood

Anne Haverty
Jane Stevenson
Markus Zusak

Paul Watkins   1964-   Wales   Adventure/Thriller
www.paulwatkins.com
🏆 Encore 1990   Holtby 1995

Ernest Hemingway
Douglas Kennedy
Simon Levack

Gareth O'Callaghan
Robert Radcliffe
Erich Maria Remarque

Derek Robinson
James Twining
Nigel West

Peter Watt   Aus   Historical
www.peterwatt.com

Bryce Courtenay
Robert Drewe
Tamara McKinley

Andrew Miller
Amanda Prantera

Katherine Scholes
Barry Unsworth

Daisy Waugh 1967- Chick Lit

Wendy Holden	Belinda Jones	Freya North
Rachel Hore	India Knight	Tina Reilly
Lisa Jewell	Gil McNeil	Sarah Webb

Evelyn Waugh 1903-66

Malcolm Bradbury	Philip Hensher	Anthony Powell
Justin Cartwright	Matthew Kneale	Edward St Aubyn
Joseph Connolly	David Lodge	William Sutcliffe
Glen Duncan	Pauline Melville	Paul Torday

Camilla Way 1973- Crime: Police work - UK

Elizabeth George	Denise Mina	Andrew Taylor
John Harvey	Peter Robinson	Neil White
Jane Hill	Roger Silverwood	

James Webb 1946- US War
www.jameswebb.com

Nelson DeMille	Robert Harris	Stephen Hunter
W E B Griffin	Jack Higgins	David L Robbins

Sarah Webb 1969- Ire Chick Lit
www.sarahwebb.info

Susannah Bates	Anne Dunlop	Andrea Semple
Maria Beaumont	Donna Hay	Daisy Waugh
Clare Dowling	Shari Low	

Jennifer Weiner 1970- US Chick Lit
www.jenniferweiner.com

Maggie Alderson	Helen Fielding	Adele Parks
Melissa Bank	Janet Fitch	Morag Prunty
Emily Barr	Kate Jacobs	Carmen Reid
Lucy Dawson	Sarah Mason	Lisa Tucker

Alison Weir 1951- Historical: C16th
www.alisonweir.org.uk

Vanora Bennett	Posie Graeme-Evans	Jean Plaidy
Christie Dickason	Philippa Gregory	Deborah Wright
Suzannah Dunn	Anne Herries	Robyn Young

Arabella Weir — Chick Lit

Sherry Ashworth
Mavis Cheek
Lucy Diamond

Imogen Edwards-Jones
Laurie Graham
Sue Limb

Sarah Mason
Lynne Truss

Margaret Weis — 1948- US — Fantasy: Epic
www.margaretweis.com

Terry Brooks
David A Drake
Fiona McIntosh

Elizabeth Moon
William Nicholson

Melanie Rawn
R A Salvatore

Lauren Weisberger — 1977 US — Chick Lit
www.laurenweisberger.com

Claudia Carroll
Belinda Jones
Clare Naylor

Victoria Routledge
Sara Shepard

Plum Sykes
Kathleen Tessaro

Jane Welch — 1964- — Fantasy: Epic
www.janewelch.com

David Farland
David Gemmell
Terry Goodkind

Simon Green
Robert Jordan
Guy Gavriel Kay

Stephen R Lawhead
K J Parker
Steph Swainston

Fay Weldon — 1933-

Beryl Bainbridge
Elizabeth Buchan
Margaret Forster

Edna O'Brien
Wendy Perriam

Emma Tennant
Jeanette Winterson

H G Wells — 1866-1946 — Science Fiction: Space and time
also wrote as Reginald Bliss

Stephen Baxter
E M Forster
Greg Keyes

Tim Powers
Christopher Priest
J B Priestley

Jules Verne
John Wyndham

Rebecca Wells — 1963- US
www.ya-ya.com — Louisiana

Louise Erdrich
Fannie Flagg
Karen Joy Fowler

Elinor Lipman
Terry McMillan

Anne Rivers Siddons
Sarah Willis

Irvine Welsh  1958- Sco

www.irvinewelsh.net

| Des Dillon | Niall Griffiths | Kevin Sampson |
| Roddy Doyle | James Kelman | Alan Warner |

Louise Welsh 1968- Sco Crime: Hardboiled

♛ CWA 2002

Lin Anderson	Frederic Lindsay	Manda Scott
Jake Arnott	Denise Mina	Mark Timlin
Alex Gray	George P Pelecanos	

Louise Wener

| Sue Limb | Libby Purves | Lynne Truss |
| Allison Pearson | Kevin Sampson | |

Jane Wenham-Jones Chick Lit

www.janewenham-jones.com

Rebecca Campbell	Anne Dunlop	Sophie King
Jenny Colgan	Imogen Edwards-Jones	Monica McInerney
Louise Doughty		

Patricia Wentworth 1878-1961 Crime: Amateur sleuth

was Dora Amy Elles ⚲ Miss Maud Silver

Ruth Dudley Edwards	Michael Innes	Mike Ripley
Elizabeth Ferrars	Ngaio Marsh	Dorothy L Sayers
Lis Howell	Gwen Moffat	Catherine Shaw

Mary Wesley 1912-2002 Aga Saga

Clare Chambers	Angela Huth	Jean Saunders
Victoria Clayton	Elinor Lipman	Kate Saunders
Jane Gardam	Charlotte Moore	Lou Wakefield
Adèle Geras	Nora Naish	Amanda Eyre Ward

Valerie Wilson Wesley 1947- US Crime: PI

www.tamarahayle.com ⚲ Tamara Hayle - Newark, New Jersey

Janet Evanovich	Terry McMillan	Alexander McCall Smith
Sparkle Hayter	S J Rozan	Cath Staincliffe
Laura Lippman		

Go to back for lists of
Pseudonyms • Authors by Genre • Characters and Series
Prize Winners • Crossover Authors • Further Reading • Websites

282

Morris West 1916-1999 Aus

Graham Greene
David Malouf

W Somerset Maugham
Brian Moore

Nevil Shute
Leon Uris

Nigel West 1951- Adventure/Thriller
is Rupert Allason
www.nigelwest.com

Len Deighton
Philip Kerr
Charles McCarry

Stanley Pottinger
Tim Sebastian
Gerald Seymour

James Twining
Paul Watkins
Robin White

Donald Westlake 1933- US Crime: Humour
also writes as Tucker Coe, Allan Marshall,
Richard Stark, Donald E Westlake
www.donaldwestlake.com

🏃 John Dortmunder, Burglar

Tim Dorsey
Carl Hiaasen

José Latour
Elmore Leonard

Robert B Parker
Sarah Strohmeyer

Edith Wharton 1862-1937 US

Jane Austen
Robb Forman Dew
Penelope Fitzgerald

E M Forster
Elizabeth Gaskell
Thomas Hardy

Henry James
Alison Lurie
Joyce Carol Oates

Alex Wheatle 1963-

Monica Ali
Vikram Chandra

Andrea Levy
Zadie Smith

Meera Syal

Edmund White 1940- US
www.edmundwhite.com

Patrick Gale
Alan Hollinghurst

Armistead Maupin
Edward St Aubyn

Gillian White
also writes as Georgina Fleming

Helen Dunmore
Lesley Glaister

Shirley Hazzard
Deborah Moggach

Graham Swift

Adventure/Thriller: Psychological

Sarah Diamond
Carol Goodman
Jane Hill

Joanna Hines
Elizabeth McGregor

Stanley Pottinger
Claire Seeber

Neil White

Crime: Police work - UK

DC Laura McGanity & Jack Garrett - Lancashire

Mark Billingham	Peter James	Leslie Thomas
Patricia Highsmith	Pauline Rowson	Camilla Way
Michael Innes	Roger Silverwood	

Robin White   US

Adventure/Thriller

Ted Allbeury	John Le Carré	Alex Scarrow
James Barrington	Patrick Robinson	Nigel West
Dale Brown		

Stephen White   US

Crime: Psychological

Alan Gregory, Psychologist - Boulder, Colorado

Jeffery Deaver	Alex Kava	Andrew Pyper
Daniel Hecht	Jonathan Kellerman	Jenny Siler
Tami Hoag	Jonathan Nasaw	Erica Spindler
John Katzenbach	Meg O'Brien	Dana Stabenow

Stella Whitelaw   1941-

Crime: PI

Jordan Lacey - Sussex

Simon Brett	Lauren Henderson	David Roberts
Judith Cutler	Joyce Holms	Cath Staincliffe
Liz Evans	Sara Paretsky	Rebecca Tope

Jeanne Whitmee

Saga

London

Pamela Evans	Gilda O'Neill	Elizabeth Waite
Elizabeth Lord	Judith Saxton	Barbara Whitnell
Pamela Oldfield	Linda Sole	Dee Williams

Barbara Whitnell

Saga

Cornwall

Rosemary Aitken	Nicola Thorne	Jeanne Whitmee
Iris Gower	Margaret Thornton	Barbara Wood
Claire Lorrimer	Janet MacLeod Trotter	

Matt Whyman

Lad Lit

Matt Beaumont	Dave Hill	Nick Hornby
Mike Gayle	Sam Holden	Tony Parsons
John Harding		

Jack Whyte   1940-   Sco

www.camulod.com

Historical: C12th
Europe & Near East

Bernard Cornwell
Tom Harper

Conn Iggulden
Steven Pressfield

Mary Renault
Robyn Young

Madeleine Wickham   1969-

also writes as Sophie Kinsella

Aga Saga

Judy Astley
Amanda Brookfield
Elizabeth Noble

Jean Saunders
Lou Wakefield
Amanda Eyre Ward

Sarah Willis
Meg Wolitzer
Grace Wynne-Jones

Ann Widdecombe   1947-

www.annwiddecombemp.com

Annabel Dilke
Margaret Forster
Libby Purves

Rebecca Shaw
Jane Urquhart

Amanda Eyre Ward
Marcia Willett

Marianne Wiggins   1947-   US

A S Byatt
William Golding

Michael Ondaatje
Salman Rushdie

Carol Shields
Barry Unsworth

John Wilcox

War: Historical - C19th
🏃 Capt Simon Fonthill & Sgt '352' Jenkins - Boer War

Roger Carpenter
Bernard Cornwell
Iain Gale

Richard Howard
C C Humphreys
Garry Kilworth

Allan Mallinson
Patrick Rambaud

Kim Wilkins   1970-   Aus

www.kimwilkins.com

Fantasy

Kelley Armstrong
Poppy Z Brite

Kim Harrison
Terry Pratchett

Anne Rice
Phil Rickman

Annie Wilkinson

Saga
early C20th - NE England

Catherine Cookson
Josephine Cox
Ken McCoy

Rebecca Shaw
Grace Thompson
Janet MacLeod Trotter

Marcia Willett
Dee Williams
Audrey Willsher

☺ also writes children's books

285

Marcia Willett

also writes as Willa Marsh
www.devonwriters.co.uk

Saga

⃛ Chadwick Family

Elizabeth Edmondson	Harriet Hudson	Santa Montefiore
Adèle Geras	Kate Long	Rosamunde Pilcher
Rebecca Gregson	Sara MacDonald	Ann Widdecombe
Julie Highmore	Joan Medlicott	Annie Wilkinson

Dee Williams

Saga

East End, London

Pip Granger	Connie Monk	Grace Thompson
Annie Groves	Sheila Newberry	Jeanne Whitmee
Gwen Madoc	Michael Taylor	Annie Wilkinson

John Williams   1961-   Wales

Crime: Hardboiled

Cardiff

Jake Arnott	James Ellroy	Jason Starr
Lorenzo Carcaterra	James Sallis	Jim Thompson

Liz Williams   1965-

Fantasy: Contemporary

⃛ DI Chen - Singapore

Marion Zimmer Bradley	Jim Butcher	Tanith Lee
Patricia Briggs	Barbara Hambly	Scott Lynch
Lois McMaster Bujold	Gwyneth Jones	Charles Stross

Niall Williams   1958-   Ire

www.niallwilliams.com

Dermot Bolger	Simon Mawer	Joseph O'Connor
Jennifer Johnston	Edna O'Brien	Colm Toibin
Bernard MacLaverty		

Nigel Williams   1948-

Humour

David Baddiel	Jonathan Coe	John Lanchester
Guy Bellamy	Stephen Fry	David Nobbs
Alan Bennett	Andrew Holmes	Henry Sutton
Mavis Cheek	Tom Holt	P G Wodehouse

Polly Williams

Mature Chick Lit

www.pollywilliams.com

Catherine Alliott	Sophie King	Lesley Pearse
Jane Green	Jill Mansell	Sarah Tucker

Sean Williams   1967-   Aus   Science Fiction: Space opera
www.seanwilliams.com

Greg Bear	Greg Egan	Robert Reed
Gregory Benford	Ursula K Le Guin	Charles Stross
Ben Counter	China Miéville	

Tad Williams   1957-   US   Fantasy: Epic
www.tadwilliams.com

David Bilsborough	David Eddings	Sean Russell
Terry Brooks	Greg Keyes	J R R Tolkien
David A Drake	Stan Nicholls	

Science Fiction: Near future

Steve Aylett	Nick Sagan	Michael Marshall Smith
Jon Courtenay Grimwood	Lucius Shepard	David Zindell

Connie Willis   1945-   US   Science Fiction: Space and time
www.sftv.org/cw

Harlan Ellison	Ian McDonald	Christopher Priest
Jasper Fforde	Diana Norman	Jules Verne
William Gibson	Tim Powers	Robert Charles Wilson

Sarah Willis   US
www.sarahwillis.net

Anita Diamant	Maggie O'Farrell	Rebecca Wells
Sue Miller	Nicholas Sparks	Madeleine Wickham
Laura Moriarty	Lisa Tucker	

Tim Willocks   1957-   Adventure/Thriller
www.timwillocks.com

Thomas Harris	Dean R Koontz
Andrew Klavan	James Twining

Audrey Willsher   Saga
London • Leicestershire

Harriet Hudson	Lynda Page	Annie Wilkinson
Meg Hutchinson	Mary Jane Staples	Sally Worboyes
Joan Medlicott	Elizabeth Waite	

Go to back for lists of
Pseudonyms • Authors by Genre • Characters and Series
Prize Winners • Crossover Authors • Further Reading • Websites

A N Wilson 1950-

♀ Lampitt Chronicles

♟ JLR 1978

Julian Barnes	Edward Docx	Anthony Powell
Malcolm Bradbury	Iris Murdoch	Bernice Rubens

Derek Wilson 1935-

Crime: Historical - C18th

also writes as Jonathan Kane   ♀ George Keene, Spy • Nathaniel Gye, Parapsychologist
www.derekwilson.com   Tim Lacy - Art world

Earlene Fowler	Roy Lewis	John Malcolm
Janet Gleeson	David Liss	Iain Pears
Daniel Hecht		

Laura Wilson

Crime: Psychological

www.laura-wilson.co.uk

Carol Anne Davis	Jeff Lindsay	Louis Sanders
Sarah Diamond	R N Morris	Chris Simms
Carol Goodman	Margaret Murphy	Carol Smith
Jane Hill	Ruth Rendell	Andrew Taylor

Robert Wilson 1957-

Adventure/Thriller

♀ Bruce Medway - West Africa
Insp Javier Falcon - Portugal

♟ CWA 1999

Ronan Bennett	Dan Fesperman	Joseph Kanon
Peter Corris	Alan Furst	J Wallis Martin
Charles Cumming	Reg Gadney	Henry Porter

Robert Charles Wilson 1953- Can Science Fiction: Space and time

www.robertcharleswilson.com

David Brin	Christopher Priest	Connie Willis
Wil McCarthy	Kristine Kathryn Rusch	David Zindell
Linda Nagata		

T R Wilson 1962-

Saga

also writes as Tim Wilson

East Anglia

Tessa Barclay	Mary Mackie	Alexandra Raife
Margaret Dickinson	Joan Medlicott	Graham Swift
Harriet Hudson		

R D Wingfield 1928-2007

Crime: Police work - UK

was Rodney David Wingfield

DI Jack Frost - 'Denton'

Kate Atkinson	Kate Ellis	M R D Meek
Robert Barnard	Andrew Holmes	Nick Oldham
Chris Collett	Katherine John	Mike Ripley
Deborah Crombie	Ken McCoy	Andrew Taylor

Don Winslow 1953- US

Crime: Amateur sleuth

www.donwinslow.com

Neal Carey - Nevada

Edward Bunker	Loren D Estleman	José Latour
Robert Crais	Dashiell Hammett	Shane Maloney
Jo Dereske	John Hart	Patrick Quinlan
John Dunning	Matthew Klein	Jim Thompson

Jacqueline Winspear 1955-

Crime: PI

www.jacquelinewinspear.com

Maisie Dobbs - WW1 & onwards, London & Kent

Conrad Allen	Robert Goddard	Susan Kandel
James Anderson	Ann Granger	Catriona McPherson
Rhys Bowen	Patricia Harwin	Robin Paige
Agatha Christie	Michael Innes	David Roberts

Jeanette Winterson ☺ 1959-

www.jeanettewinterson.com

🏆 Whitbread 1985   JLR 1987

Isabel Allende	Laura Esquivel	Bernice Rubens
Iain Banks	Niall Griffiths	Colin Thubron
Emma Donoghue	Michèle Roberts	Fay Weldon
Patricia Duncker	Meg Rosoff	Virginia Woolf

Tim Winton 1960- Aus

Murray Bail	Siri Hustvedt	Andrew McGahan
Peter Carey	Thomas Keneally	Brian Moore
Robert Drewe		

David Wishart 1952- Sco

Crime: Historical - Ancient

www.david-wishart.co.uk

Marcus Corvinus - Ancient Rome

Philip Boast	Lauren Haney	John Maddox Roberts
Lindsey Davis	Sophia McDougall	Rosemary Rowe
Margaret Doody	Allan Massie	Steven Saylor

---

may be suitable for young adults

Mary Withall   Sco   Saga
Eisdalsa Island Trilogy - Scotland

Maggie Craig	Gwen Kirkwood	Eileen Ramsay
Christine Marion Fraser	Elisabeth McNeill	Mary Stewart
Evelyn Hood	Frances Paige	Sally Stewart

P G Wodehouse   1881-1975   Humour
was Pelham (Plum) Grenville Wodehouse   Jeeves, Butler • Bertie Wooster

James Anderson	Stephen Fry	David Nobbs
Alan Bennett	Tom Holt	Nigel Williams
George Macdonald Fraser	John Mortimer	

Gene Wolfe   1931-   US   Fantasy: Literary
BSFA 1981

Robert Holdstock	Julian May	Adam Roberts
Stephen Hunt	Tim Powers	Geoff Ryman
Ursula K Le Guin		

Tom Wolfe   1931-   US
www.tomwolfe.com

Charles Dickens	John Irving	Anthony Trollope
Bret Easton Ellis	Norman Mailer	Gore Vidal
Colin Harrison	Curtis Sittenfeld	

Isabel Wolff   Humour
www.isabelwolff.com

Raffaella Barker	Wendy Holden	Sue Margolis
Claire Calman	India Knight	Lou Wakefield
Julie Highmore	Josie Lloyd & Emlyn Rees	

Tobias Wolff   1945-   US

Don DeLillo	Patrick McGrath	Tom Robbins
Richard Ford	Richard Powers	John Updike
John Irving		

Meg Wolitzer   1959-   US

Louise Doughty	Alison Lurie	Jane Smiley
Penelope Lively	Terry McMillan	Madeleine Wickham

Barbara Wood   1947-   Historical
www.barbarawood.com

Janet Dailey	Sarah Kate Lynch	Nicola Thorne
Iris Gower	Maureen Peters	Barbara Whitnell
Joanne Harris	E V Thompson	

Valerie Wood   Saga
www.valeriewood.co.uk

Jessica Blair	Rosie Harris	Wendy Robertson
Irene Carr	Evelyn Hood	Kay Stephens
Rosie Goodwin	Audrey Howard	

Cathy Woodman   Chick Lit
www.cathywoodman.com

Cecelia Ahern	Wendy Holden	Jill Mansell
Louise Bagshawe	Louise Kean	Fiona Walker
Irene Carr	Josie Lloyd & Emlyn Rees	Sally Worboyes

Daniel Woodrell   1953-   US
Ozark Mountains - Missouri

Nicholas Evans	Charles Frazier	Cormac McCarthy
William Faulkner	David Guterson	

Janet Woods   Aus   Saga
www.members.iinet.net.au/~woods   C19th Dorset

Tessa Barclay	Julia Bryant	Connie Monk
Anne Bennett	Claire Lorrimer	Pamela Oldfield
Rose Boucheron		

Stuart Woods   1938-   US   Adventure/Thriller
www.stuartwoods.com   ⚉ Stone Barrington, PI - New York
Chief Holly Barker, Police - Florida

John Gilstrap	Patricia Highsmith	Michael Malone
James Grippando	Douglas Kennedy	Joseph Wambaugh
Stuart Harrison	Andrew Klavan	

Gerard Woodward   1961

Jonathan Coe	Sarah Hall	Edward St Aubyn
Anne Enright	Lloyd Jones	Graham Swift
Tessa Hadley	Ian McEwan	Louisa Young

Virginia Woolf 1882-1941

Martin Amis	E M Forster	Iris Murdoch
Joseph Conrad	James Joyce	Michèle Roberts
Michael Cunningham	Jackie Kay	Jeanette Winterson

Sally Worboyes

Saga

London • Kent

Elizabeth Daish	Kitty Neale	Audrey Willsher
Pip Granger	Victor Pemberton	Cathy Woodman
Harriet Hudson	D M Purcell	

Elizabeth Wrenn

Aga Saga

www.elizabethwrenn.com

Cecelia Ahern	Elizabeth Edmondson	Lesley Pearse
Marika Cobbold	Rebecca Gregson	Eva Rice
Rose Doyle	Sara MacDonald	Jane Yardley

Deborah Wright 1975-

Chick Lit

Maggie Alderson	Wendy Holden	Rosy Thornton
Lucy Diamond	Freya North	Alison Weir
Alison Penton Harper	Victoria Routledge	Liz Young

T M Wright 1947- US

Horror

also writes as F W Armstrong
www.tmwrightonline.net

Ramsey Campbell	Richard Laymon	Dan Simmons
Stephen Gallagher	Brian Lumley	Peter Straub
Stephen King	Robert McCammon	Koji Suzuki

Janny Wurts 1953- US

Fantasy: Epic

www.paravia.com/JannyWurts

Jonathan Carroll	Katherine Kurtz	Mickey Zucker Reichert
Louise Cooper	L E Modesitt Jr	Steph Swainston
Robert Jordan	Elizabeth Moon	

John Wyndham 1903-69

Science Fiction: Near future

was John Wyndham Harris

Brian W Aldiss	Robert A Heinlein	Neal Stephenson
Isaac Asimov	Geoff Ryman	H G Wells
Philip K Dick	Michael Marshall Smith	

Grace Wynne-Jones   Ire

www.gracewynnejones.com

Sarah Harrison	Nisha Minhas	Penny Vincenzi
Marian Keyes	Melissa Nathan	Madeleine Wickham
Dorothy Koomson	Sarah Tucker	Laura Zigman

Xinran   1958-   China

is Xinran Xve

Alma Alexander	Anchee Min	Lisa See
Arthur Golden	Qiu Xiaolong	Su Tong
Xiaolu Guo		

Jane Yardley   Aga Saga

Sarah Challis	Preethi Nair	Lou Wakefield
Marika Cobbold	Nora Naish	Amanda Eyre Ward
Kate Jacobs	Elizabeth Noble	Elizabeth Wrenn

Margaret Yorke   1924-   Crime: Psychological

                                                                 ♁ Patrick Grant

🏆 CWA 1999

Jane Adams	Gerald Hammond	Danuta Reah
Louise Doughty	Julie Parsons	Louis Sanders
Elizabeth Ferrars		

Banana Yoshimoto   1964-   Ja

www.yoshimotobanana.com

Natsuo Kirino	Jane Smiley
David Mitchell	Gail Tsukiyama

Liz Young   Chick Lit

also writes as Elizabeth Young

Susannah Bates	Jill Mansell	Sarah Tucker
Wendy Holden	Sheila Norton	Deborah Wright
Lisa Jewell		

Louisa Young

                                ♁ Evangeline Gower, ex Belly Dancer

Anne Enright	Marge Piercy	Meera Syal
James Hawes	Zadie Smith	Gerard Woodward
Hanif Kureishi		

Robyn Young 1975- Historical Romance: Medieval
www.robynyoung.com ♣ Knights Templar

Bernard Cornwell	Christian Jacq	Tim Severin
Tom Harper	Valerio Massimo Manfredi	Pip Vaughan-Hughes
Richard Howard	Sharan Newman	Alison Weir
Conn Iggulden	Caroline Roe	Jack Whyte

Carlos Ruiz Zafón 🎧 1964- Spain Adventure/Thriller
www.carlosruizzafon.co.uk

Thalassa Ali	Khaled Hosseini	Audrey Niffenegger
Paulo Coelho	Yasmina Khadra	Orhan Pamuk
Umberto Eco	Marina Lewycka	Gail Tsukiyama
Leif Enger	Manuel Vázquez Montalbán	Markus Zusak

Sarah Zettel 1966- US Fantasy: Myth
www.sarahzettel.com

Ashok K Banker	C S Lewis	Judith Tarr
David Eddings	Caiseal Mor	J R R Tolkien
Ursula K Le Guin		

Laura Zigman US Chick Lit
www.laurazigman.com

Lisa Jewell	Freya North	Andrea Semple
Sophie Kinsella	Morag Prunty	Penny Vincenzi
Kathy Lette	Tina Reilly	Grace Wynne-Jones

David Zindell 1952- US Science Fiction: Space and time

Iain M Banks	China Miéville	Brian Stableford
Orson Scott Card	Christopher Priest	Jules Verne
Mark Chadbourn	Kristine Kathryn Rusch	Tad Williams
Harlan Ellison	Lucius Shepard	Robert Charles Wilson

Markus Zusak 🎧 ☺ Aus

Chinua Achebe	Yasmina Khadra	James Robertson
Thalassa Ali	Irene Nemirovsky	Meg Rosoff
Nadeem Aslam	Orhan Pamuk	Sarah Waters
G W Dahlquist	Elliot Perlman	Carlos Ruiz Zafón

☺ also writes children's books

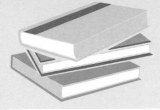

Pseudonyms

Many writers use pseudonyms, and some write under several different names. This section provides an index to some of the alternative names used by authors included in the main A-Z listing which do not have a separate entry.

A

Susan Wittig Albert and Bill Albert	Robin Paige
Peter Alding	Roderic Jeffries
Vanessa Alexander	Michael Clynes; Paul Doherty
Rupert Allason	Nigel West
Francis Amery	Brian Stableford
Alex Andrews	Mary Mackie
Johnny Angelo	Mark Timlin
Anna Apostolou	Michael Clynes; Paul Doherty
F W Armstrong	T M Wright
Andrew Arncliffe	Nicholas Rhea
Stephanie Ash	Chris Manby
William Ashbless	Tim Powers (with James P Blaylock)
Jeffrey Ashford	Roderic Jeffries
Robert Lynn Asprin	Robert Asprin
Margaret Astbury	Meg Hutchinson
Jonathan Aycliffe	Daniel Easterman
Catherine Aydy	Emma Tennant

B

Donna Baker	Lilian Harry
Alex Baldwin	W E B Griffin
Jim Ballantyne	Mark Timlin
David Bannerman	David Hagberg
Bernard Bastable	Robert Barnard
Ken Begg	Ken McClure
Morgan Benedict	Fidelis Morgan
Elizabeth Bennett	Cynthia Harrod-Eagles
Pauline Bentley	Kate Tremayne
Jane Bidder	Sophie King
Jessica Bird	J R Ward
Cleo Birdwell	Don DeLillo
Robert Black	Robert Holdstock
Veronica Black	Maureen Peters
Alan Blackwood	Graham Masterton
Ken Blake	Robert Holdstock
Patrick Blake	Clive Egleton
Sally Blake	Jean Saunders
Sterling Blake	Gregory Benford
Reginald Bliss	H G Wells
Judith Bordill	Marjorie Eccles
Jean Bowden	Tessa Barclay
Edgar Box	Gore Vidal

Felix Boyd	Harry Harrison
Steve Brackeen	John Farris
Edward P Bradbury	Michael Moorcock
Sally Bradford	Barbara Taylor Bradford
Jane Brindle	Josephine Cox
Morna Doris Brown	Elizabeth Ferrars
Francis Bryan	Frank Delaney
Marie Buchanan	Clare Curzon
Stephen Bury	Neal Stephenson
Richard Butler	Ted Allbeury

C

Patricia Cabot	Meg Cabot
Alison Cairns	M R D Meek
Ken & Christian Cameron	Gordon Kent
Curt Cannon	Ed McBain
Jack Cannon	Nelson DeMille
Chris Carlsen	Robert Holdstock
Claire Carmichael	Claire McNab
Alex Carr	Jenny Siler
Marion Carr	Freda Lightfoot
Philippa Carr	Victoria Holt; Jean Plaidy
Jenny Carroll	Meg Cabot
Jayne Castle	Jayne Ann Krentz; Amanda Quick
Grace Cavendish	Patricia Finney
Jessie Chambers	D H Lawrence
Caroline Charles	Mary Mackie
Emily Chase	Julie Garwood
Cathy Christopher	Mary Mackie
Kay Christopher	Grace Thompson
Mary Christopher	Mary Mackie
Brenda Clarke	Kate Sedley
Roy Clews	Sara Fraser
Tucker Coe	Donald Westlake
Brian Coffey	Dean R Koontz
Margaret M Coghlan (with Hugh C Rae)	Jessica Stirling
Emma Cole	Susanna Kearsley
Hunt Collins	Ed McBain
Peter Collinson	Dashiell Hammett
James Colvin	Michael Moorcock
Beatrice Coogan	Claire Lorrimer
Christopher Coram	Nicholas Rhea
Caroline Courtney	Penny Jordan
William Coyle	Thomas Keneally
Brian Craig	Brian Stableford
David Craig	Bill James
John Creed	Eoin McNamee
Caroline Crosby	Jessica Stirling
Susan Lynn Crose	Lisa Jackson

D

Laura Daniels	Amy Myers
Catherine Darby	Maureen Peters
Lawrence H Davison	D H Lawrence
Frank Dempsey	Harry Harrison
J M Dillard	Jeanne Kalogridis

James L Docherty	James Hadley Chase
Arthur Douglas	Gerald Hammond
Garry Douglas	Garry Kilworth
Billy Douglass	Barbara Delinsky
Bonnie Drake	Barbara Delinsky
Shannon Drake	Heather Graham
Emma Drummond	Elizabeth Darrell
Jack Drummond	Martin O'Brien
Ann Dukthas	Michael Clynes; Paul Doherty
Deanne Dwyer	Dean R Koontz
K R Dwyer	Dean R Koontz

E

James Eliot	John Case
Rosemary Ellerbeck	Nicola Thorne
Peter Beresford Ellis	Peter Tremayne
Phillip Emmons	Bentley Little
Jonathan Evans	Brian Freemantle

F

Ruth Fabian	Aileen Armitage
Lee N Falconer	Julian May
Martin Fallon	Jack Higgins
Robert Faulcon	Robert Holdstock
James Ferguson	Nicholas Rhea
Tom Ferris	Nicholas Rhea
Sean Flannery	David Hagberg
Georgina Fleming	Gillian White
Holly Fox	Elizabeth McGregor
Jane Fraser	Rosamunde Pilcher
Jonathan Freedland	Sam Bourne
Sean French (with Nicci Gerrard)	Nicci French

G

Elizabeth Gage	LaVyrle Spencer
W R Gallaher	Judith Gould
Esther Garber	Tanith Lee
Paul Garrison	Justin Scott
Peter Garrison	Craig Shaw Gardner
Peter Gethers	Russell Andrews
Frances Gordon	Sarah Rayne
C L Grace	Michael Clynes; Paul Doherty
Roderic Graeme	Roderic Jeffries
James Graham	Jack Higgins
Robert Graham	Joe Haldeman
Vanessa Graham	Anthea Fraser
Ambrose Grant	James Hadley Chase
David Grant	Craig Thomas
Jonathan Grant	Jonathan Gash
Lynn Granville	Linda Sole
Caroline Gray	Christopher Nicole
Kristine Grayson	Kristine Kathryn Rusch
Patricia Grey	Liz Evans

H

Ann Halam	Gwyneth Jones
Daniel Hall	Jonathan Lunn
Steffie Hall	Janet Evanovich
Dorothy Halliday	Dorothy Dunnett
Ralph Hammond-Innes	Hammond Innes

David Handler	Russell Andrews
Elizabeth Hankin	Elizabeth Gill
Paul Harding	Michael Clynes; Paul Doherty
Ross Harding	David Gemmell
Andrew Harper	Douglas Clegg
Elizabeth Harris	Alys Clare
Chip Harrison	Lawrence Block
David Harsent	David Lawrence
Christopher Hart	William Napier
Geraldine Hartnett	Geraldine Evans
Jemma Harvey	Amanda Hemingway
Graham Hastings	Roderic Jeffries
Kate Hatfield	Natasha Cooper
Alexandra Henry	Hilary Norman
Nancy Herndon	Elizabeth Chadwick
Evelyn Hervey	H R F Keating
Lydia Hitchcock	Penny Jordan
Dalby Holden	Gerald Hammond
Taylor Holden	Wendy Holden
Jim & Carolyn Hougan	John Case
Linda S Howington	Linda Howard
Alma Hromic	Alma Alexander
Jeffrey Hudson	Michael Crichton
Maggie Hudson	Margaret Pemberton
Ann Hulme	Ann Granger
Evan Hunter	Ed McBain
Gary Hunter	Gwen Hunter
Christopher Hyde	Paul Christopher
Jennifer Hyde	Marjorie Eccles

I

Martin Inigo	Conrad Allen; Keith Miles
Jean Innes	Jean Saunders
Eric G Iverson	Harry Turtledove

J

Everatt Jackson	Margaret Dickinson
Sherry-Anne Jacobs	Anna Jacobs
Judith James	Bill James
Stephanie James	Jayne Ann Krentz
Vanessa James	Sally Beauman
Shannah Jay	Anna Jacobs
Jane Johnson	Jude Fisher
Jessie Jones	Maria Beaumont
Laura Jordan	Sandra Brown
Jordan	Katie Price

K

Jonathan Kane	Derek Wilson
Dan Kavanagh	Julian Barnes
Paul Kavanagh	Lawrence Block
Susannah Kells	Bernard Cornwell
Lauren Kelly	Joyce Carol Oates
Patrick Kelly	Ted Allbeury
Richard Kelly	Richard Laymon
Samuel M Key	Charles de Lint
Gabriel King	Jude Fisher
Jancy King	Rosie Thomas

	Will Kingdom	Phil Rickman
	Richard Kirk	Robert Holdstock
	Calvin M Knox	Robert Silverberg
L	Kurt Ladner	Nelson DeMille
	Dinah Lampitt	Deryn Lake
	Frank Lane	Harold Robbins
	John Lange	Michael Crichton
	Elizabeth Law	Maureen Peters
	Carol Laymon	Richard Laymon
	Clare Layton	Natasha Cooper
	Peter Lear	Peter Lovesey
	Annie Leith	Anita Burgh
	Terry Lennox	John Harvey
	Isabelle Lewis	Kerry Greenwood
	J R Lewis	Roy Lewis
	Shannon Lewis	Morgan Llywelyn
	Megan Lindholm	Robin Hobb
	Rosina Lippi	Sara Donati
	J B Livingstone	Christian Jacq
	Jack Ludlow	David Donachie
	Thomas Luke	Graham Masterton
	Chang Lung	Robert Jordan
	Eric Lustbader	Eric Van Lustbader
M	Peter MacAlan	Peter Tremayne
	Dinah McCall	Sharon Sala
	Wendell McCall	Ridley Pearson
	Catriona McCloud	Catriona McPherson
	Anson MacDonald	Robert A Heinlein
	John Macdonald	Ross Macdonald
	Mark McGarrity	Bartholomew Gill
	Kinley MacGregor	Sherrilyn Kenyon
	Charlotte McKay	Charlotte Moore
	Duncan MacNeil	Philip McCutchan
	James Mann	John Harvey
	Catherine Marchant	Catherine Cookson
	Mac Marlow	Christopher Nicole
	Hugh Marlowe	Jack Higgins
	Willa Marsh	Marcia Willett
	Allan Marshall	Donald Westlake
	Raymond Marshall	James Hadley Chase
	Richard Marsten	Ed McBain
	Brad Matthews	Nelson DeMille
	John Maxwell	Brian Freemantle
	Susan Meadmore	Susan Sallis
	The Medieval Murderers	Susanna Gregory; Philip Gooden; Michael Jecks; Bernard Knight; Ian Morson; C J Sansom
	Jennie Melville	Gwendoline Butler
	Barbara Mertz	Elizabeth Peters
	Barbara Michaels	Elizabeth Peters
	David Michaels	Raymond Benson
	Kenneth Millar	Ross Macdonald

Martin Millar	Martin Scott
Sue Mongredien	Lucy Diamond
Rachel Moore	Jean Saunders
Clare Morgan	Patricia Highsmith
Philippa Morgan	Philip Gooden
Dick Morland	Reginald Hill
Mohammed Moulessehoul	Yasmina Khadra
Christopher Mountjoy	Edward Marston
James Munro	E V Thompson
Simon Myles	Ken Follett

N

Grant Naylor	Rob Grant & Doug Naylor
Kris Nelscott	Kristine Kathryn Rusch
Jodie Nicol	Jean Saunders
Leigh Nicols	Dean R Koontz

O

E G O'Brien	Arthur C Clarke
Regan O'Neal	Robert Jordan
Jackson O'Reilly	Robert Jordan
Regan O'Reilly	Robert Jordan
B J Oliphant	Sheri S Tepper
A J Orde	Sheri S Tepper
David Osborne	Robert Silverberg
Barbara Ovstedal	Rosalind Laker

P

Harry Patterson	Jack Higgins
Barbara Paul	Rosalind Laker
Keith Peterson	Andrew Klavan
Will Peterson	Mark Billingham
Rhona Petrie	Clare Curzon
Elizabeth Pewsey	Elizabeth Aston
Heather Graham Pozzessere	Heather Graham
Mary Monica Pulver	Margaret Frazer

Q

Aileen Quigley	Aileen Armitage
Emma Quincey	Linda Sole
Janet Quin-Harkin	Rhys Bowen
Martin Quinn	Martin Cruz Smith
Simon Quinn	Martin Cruz Smith

R

Hugh C Rae	Jessica Stirling
Richard Raine	Colin Forbes
Anne Rampling	Anne Rice
Mark Ramsay	John Maddox Roberts
Robert Randall	Robert Silverberg
Ellen Randolph	Melanie Rawn
Alis A Rasmussen	Kate Elliott
René Brabazon Raymond	James Hadley Chase
Joyce Reardon	Ridley Pearson
Matthew Reid	Quintin Jardine
Patricia Robins	Claire Lorrimer
Suzanne Robinson	Lynda S Robinson
Rosemary Rowe	Rosemary Aitken
Gillian Rubenstein	Lian Hearn
Patrick Ruell	Reginald Hill
Richard Patrick Russ	Patrick O'Brian
Alan Rustage	Sally Spencer

Rachel Ryan	Sandra Brown
Jonathan Ryder	Robert Ludlum
Andrew Saville	Andrew Taylor
Raymond Sawkins	Colin Forbes
Sandy Schofield	Kristine Kathryn Rusch
Alicia Scott	Lisa Gardner
Ariana Scott	Elizabeth Adler
Michael Shepherd	Robert Ludlum
Jan Siegel	Amanda Hemingway
James Sinclair	Mary Jane Staples
Ainslie Skinner	Paula Gosling
Rosamond Smith	Joyce Carol Oates
Jane Somers	Doris Lessing
Bill Spence	Jessica Blair
David Springfield	Roy Lewis
Erin St Claire	Sandra Brown
Reginald Staples	Mary Jane Staples
Richard Stark	Donald Westlake
Reed Stephens	Stephen Donaldson
Susan Stevens	Mary Mackie
John Innes Mackintosh Stewart	Michael Innes
Ian Stuart	Alistair MacLean
Logan Swanson	Richard Matheson
John Tarrant	Clive Egleton
John Robert Taylor	Andrew Taylor
Edwin Thomas	Tom Harper
Ian Thorne	Julian May
Nye Tredgold	Nigel Tranter
Judy Turner	Katie Flynn; Judith Saxton
N H Turtletaub	Harry Turtledove
Charles Underhill	Reginald Hill
Caroline Upcher	Hope McIntyre
Peter Norman Walker	Nicholas Rhea
Linda Watson-Brown	Grace Monroe (with Maria Thomson)
Nicola West	Lilian Harry
Owen West	Dean R Koontz
Mary Westmacott	Agatha Christie
Charles Whiting	Duncan Harding
Tony Williams	Mark Timlin
Charles Willis	Arthur C Clarke
Jack Winchester	Brian Freemantle
Aaron Wolfe	Dean R Koontz
Dave Wolverton	David Farland
Bridget Wood	Sarah Rayne
Emma Woodhouse	Cynthia Harrod-Eagles
James Garcia Woods	Sally Spencer
Daphne Wright	Natasha Cooper
Melinda Wright	Penny Jordan
Jack Yeovil	Kim Newman
Andrew York	Christopher Nicole
Katherine Yorke	Nicola Thorne

S

T

U

W

Y

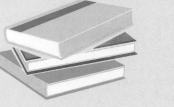

Authors listed by Genre

It is almost impossible to identify accurately individual authors with one particular section of genre fiction; often there is no 'cut off' point between, for instance, **War** and **Adventure**; between **Fantasy**, **Science Fiction** and **Horror**; or between **Historical** and **Saga**. So, although in the main sequence this Guide indicates under the names of each author the genre in which they usually write, and these names are repeated again in the lists that follow, it is suggested that readers also refer to linking genres — and in particular to the main list — to discover new names that could become firm favourites.

Some categories — **Adventure/Thriller**, **Crime**, **Fantasy**, **Science Fiction**, **Sea Stories** and **War** — have been sub-divided to help readers find novelists they will enjoy. Do remember that some authors use a different name when they write in another genre, and others will produce an occasional book which is quite different in character to their usual style. Always look at the book jacket and the introduction before you borrow or purchase.

Adventure/Thriller

Stories with fast moving plots, exotic settings and usually larger-than-life main characters and with the action full of thrilling and daring feats. Many of these authors specialised in stories set in the period of the cold war but increasingly now they have a political, financial industrial espionage or terrorist background.

Paul Adam	Tom Bradby	Murray Davies
Ted Allbeury	Dale Brown	Len Deighton
Russell Andrews	Dan Brown	Nelson DeMille
Geoffrey Archer	Robert Gregory Browne	Richard Doetsch
Jeffrey Archer	John Buchan	Brendan Dubois
Campbell Armstrong	Michael Byrnes	Daniel Easterman
Michael Asher	Stephen J Cannell	Clive Egleton
David Baldacci	Lorenzo Carcaterra	Barry Eisler
Carla Banks	John Case	Jon Evans
Alex Barclay	Lee Child	Duncan Falconer
Linwood Barclay	Lincoln Child	Dan Fesperman
James Barrington	Paul Christopher	Joseph Finder
Ronan Bennett	Tom Clancy	Ian Fleming
Raymond Benson	James Clavell	Vince Flynn
Alex Berenson	Frank Coates	James Follett
Steve Berry	Stephen Coonts	Ken Follett
Tim Binding	Michael Cordy	Colin Forbes
Alice Blanchard	Bryce Courtenay	Frederick Forsyth
Anna Blundy	Harold Coyle	Clare Francis
Sam Bourne	Charles Cumming	Brian Freemantle
	Clive Cussler	Scott Frost

Genre

Alexander Fullerton
John Fullerton
Alan Furst
Tom Gabbay
Joseph Garber
Lisa Gardner
David Gibbins
John Gilstrap
Robert Goddard
Jean-Christophe Grangé
Michael Gruber
David Hagberg
Brian Haig
Tom Harper
Robert Harris
Colin Harrison
Stuart Harrison
A J Hartley
Jack Harvey
John Twelve Hawks
Humphrey Hawksley
Paul Henke
Richard Herman
Jack Higgins
Tobias Hill
David Hosp
Gwen Hunter
Stephen Hunter
Graham Hurley
Gregg Hurwitz
Greg Iles
Hammond Innes
Alan Judd
Joseph Kanon
John Katzenbach
Judith Kelman

Douglas Kennedy
Gordon Kent
Philip Kerr
Michael Kimball
Natsuo Kirino
Dean R Koontz
Chris Kuzneski
John Le Carré
Stephen Leather
Patrick Lennon
Robert Littell
Sam Llewellyn
James Long
Greg Loomis
Robert Ludlum
Gayle Lynds
Amin Maalouf
Charles McCarry
Andy McDermott
Andrew McGahan
Alistair MacLean
Eoin McNamee
Michael Marshall
Glenn Meade
Deon Meyer
Kyle Mills
Grace Monroe
Richard Montanari
Chris Mooney
David Morrell
John J Nance
Bill Napier
Christopher Nicole
Hilary Norman
Gareth O'Callaghan
Chris Paling

James Pattinson
Chris Petit
Henry Porter
Stanley Pottinger
Douglas Preston
Julian Rathbone
Matthew Reilly
Stella Rimington
James Rollins
Nicholas Royle
Chris Ryan
Robert Ryan
Julian Jay Savarin
Alex Scarrow
Justin Scott
Tim Sebastian
Gerald Seymour
Sidney Sheldon
Nevil Shute
James Siegel
Daniel Silva
Paullina Simons
Scott Smith
Wilbur Smith
Nick Stone
Paul Sussman
Craig Thomas
Brad Thor
James Twining
Paul Watkins
Nigel West
Robin White
Tim Willocks
Robert Wilson
Stuart Woods
Carlos Ruiz Zafón

Historical

Stephen Baxter

Raymond Khoury

Arturo Pérez-Reverte

Legal/financial

Jeff Abbott
Harry Bingham
John Burdett

Alafair Burke
Linda Davies

Brad Meltzer
Michael Ridpath

Medical

Robin Cook

Michael Palmer

Psychological

Suzanne Berne
Mary Higgins Clark
Nicci French
Thomas Harris

Joanna Hines
Andrew Klavan
J Wallis Martin
Julie Parsons

Thomas Perry
Christina Schwarz
Claire Seeber
Gillian White

303

Aga Saga

A phrase that came into being in the early 1990s, the Aga Sagas are novels based upon the middle-class surroundings of the type of person that typically owns an Aga cooker, but who is not immune to the emotional dilemmas that can confront all classes of society.

Diana Appleyard
Trisha Ashley
Judy Astley
Maeve Binchy
Charlotte Bingham
Amanda Brookfield
Elizabeth Buchan
Claire Calman
Sarah Challis
Clare Chambers
Lucy Clare
Victoria Clayton
Marika Cobbold
Rowan Coleman
Amanda Craig
Domenica de Rosa
Barbara Delinsky
Annabel Dilke

Anne Doughty
Rose Doyle
Jessica Duchen
Elizabeth Edmondson
Patricia Fawcett
Kate Fenton
Patricia Gaffney
Adèle Geras
Rebecca Gregson
Sarah Harrison
Julie Highmore
Ann Hood
Rachel Hore
Sandra Howard
Kate Jacobs
Kate Long
Sara MacDonald
Santa Montefiore

Charlotte Moore
Nora Naish
Elizabeth Noble
Kate O'Riordan
Elizabeth Palmer
Robin Pilcher
Rosamunde Pilcher
Jean Saunders
Kate Saunders
Joanna Trollope
Jane Elizabeth Varley
Lou Wakefield
Amanda Eyre Ward
Mary Wesley
Madeleine Wickham
Elizabeth Wrenn
Jane Yardley

Chick Lit

Stories written by young women for other young women, usually with a central plot of boyfriend mishaps and the problems of staying in shape.

Jessica Adams
Cecelia Ahern
Maggie Alderson
Catherine Alliott
Sherry Ashworth
Louise Bagshawe
Tilly Bagshawe
Zoë Barnes
Emily Barr
Lynne Barrett-Lee
Susannah Bates
Maria Beaumont
Susie Boyt
Hester Browne
Meg Cabot
Colette Caddle
Rebecca Campbell
Louise Candlish
Claudia Carroll
Jenny Colgan
Lucy Dawson

Martina Devlin
Lucy Diamond
Clare Dowling
Anne Dunlop
Sabine Durrant
Imogen Edwards-Jones
Harriet Evans
Katie Fforde
Helen Fielding
Fiona Gibson
Jane Green
Sophie Hannah
Maeve Haran
Alison Penton Harper
Kate Harrison
Louise Harwood
Donna Hay
Veronica Henry
Melissa Hill
Julia Holden
Wendy Holden
Debby Holt

Lisa Jewell
Milly Johnson
Rachel Johnson
Belinda Jones
Christina Jones
Louise Kean
Cathy Kelly
Marian Keyes
Sophie King
Sophie Kinsella
India Knight
Dorothy Koomson
Kathy Lette
Julia Llewellyn
Josie Lloyd & Emlyn Rees
Shari Low
Monica McInerney
Serena Mackesy
Gil McNeil
Debbie Macomber
Chris Manby
Jill Mansell

Sue Margolis
Sarah Mason
Carole Matthews
Anna Maxted
Nisha Minhas
Jane Moore
Sinead Moriarty
Melissa Nathan
Clare Naylor
Freya North
Sheila Norton
Anita Notaro
Sheila O'Flanagan
Imogen Parker
Adele Parks

Alexandra Potter
Morag Prunty
Carmen Reid
Tina Reilly
Victoria Routledge
Olivia Ryan
Patricia Scanlan
Andrea Semple
Sara Shepard
Robyn Sisman
Bernadette Strachan
Plum Sykes
Kathleen Tessaro
Kate Thompson
Rosy Thornton

Paige Toon
Sarah Tucker
Fiona Walker
Daisy Waugh
Sarah Webb
Jennifer Weiner
Arabella Weir
Lauren Weisberger
Jane Wenham-Jones
Polly Williams
Cathy Woodman
Deborah Wright
Liz Young
Laura Zigman

Crime

This type of novel is usually characterised by the clues which gradually lead the reader to the final solution, often within an atmosphere of rising tension or danger. Although there are basically two types of detective, the private investigator (**PI**) and the official policeman, there are an increasing number of subgenres within these two broad headings. The style of crime writing has been divided, in the majority of cases, into separate headings, and under each is shown the list of authors who usually but not always write in that vein.

Amateur sleuth

Gilbert Adair
Marian Babson
Nevada Barr
Robert G Barrett
C J Box
Gyles Brandreth
Lilian Jackson Braun
Simon Brett
William Brodrick
Edna Buchanan
Jan Burke
Caroline Carver
Kate Charles
Agatha Christie
Harlan Coben
Natasha Cooper
Jo Dereske
John Dunning
Martin Edwards
Ruth Dudley Edwards
Elizabeth Ferrars
Earlene Fowler
Dick Francis

John Francome
Frances Fyfield
Jonathan Gash
Mark Gatiss
Andrew M Greeley
Denise Hamilton
Gerald Hammond
Janis Harrison
Carolyn G Hart
Patricia Harwin
Veronica Heley
Lauren Henderson
Joyce Holms
Hazel Holt
Lis Howell
Alison Joseph
Susan Kandel
Jim Kelly
Jonathon King
Roy Lewis
Marianne MacDonald
Hope McIntyre
Catriona McPherson

John Malcolm
Shane Maloney
Liza Marklund
Margaret Maron
Rosemary Martin
M R D Meek
Keith Miles
Denise Mina
Gwen Moffat
Fiona Mountain
Chris Niles
Iain Pears
Jenny Pitman
Richard Pitman
Ann Purser
Mike Ripley
Graeme Roe
Betty Rowlands
Catherine Sampson
Ian Sansom
Dorothy L Sayers
Zoë Sharp
Catherine Shaw

Amateur sleuth (continued)

Yrsa Sigurdardottir
Lyndon Stacey
Veronica Stallwood

Rebecca Tope
M J Trow
Jill Paton Walsh

Patricia Wentworth
Don Winslow

Forensic

Lin Anderson
Simon Beckett
Max Allan Collins
Patricia D Cornwell
Colin Cotterill

Jeffery Deaver
Aaron Elkins
Kathryn Fox
Leonard Goldberg
Iris Johansen

Keith McCarthy
Nigel McCrery
Kathy Reichs
Karin Slaughter

Hardboiled

Jake Arnott
Lawrence Block
Ken Bruen
Edward Bunker
James Lee Burke
Massimo Carlotto
James Hadley Chase
Martina Cole
Alan Dunn
James Ellroy
Robert Ferrigno
G M Ford

Heather Graham
Allan Guthrie
June Hampson
Mandasue Heller
Bill James
Simon Kernick
Matthew Klein
Roberta Kray
Elmore Leonard
Kevin Lewis
Walter Mosley

Chuck Palahniuk
David Peace
George P Pelecanos
Sheila Quigley
Patrick Quinlan
James Sallis
Jason Starr
Boston Teran
Martyn Waites
Louise Welsh
John Williams

Historical

Paul Doherty
Amy Myers
Orhan Pamuk
Matthew Pearl
Philip Boast Ancient
Lindsey Davis Ancient
Margaret Doody Ancient
Lauren Haney Ancient
Mary Reed and Eric Mayer Ancient
John Maddox Roberts Ancient
Lynda S Robinson Ancient
Rosemary Rowe Ancient
Steven Saylor Ancient
Marilyn Todd Ancient
David Wishart Ancient
Simon Beaufort Medieval
Alys Clare Medieval
Ariana Franklin Medieval
Margaret Frazer Medieval
Susanna Gregory Medieval
Michael Jecks Medieval
Bernard Knight Medieval

Edward Marston Medieval
Pat McIntosh Medieval
Ellis Peters Medieval
Candace Robb Medieval
Kate Sedley Medieval
Peter Tremayne Medieval
Sharan Newman C12th
Ian Morson C13th
Pip Vaughan-Hughes C13th
Caroline Roe C14th
P F Chisholm C16th
Michael Clynes C16th
Patricia Finney C16th
Philip Gooden C16th
Cora Harrison C16th
Simon Levack C16th
John Pilkington C16th
C J Sansom C16th
Peter Tonkin C16th
Fidelis Morgan C17th
Laura Joh Rowland C17th
Martin Stephen C17th
Janet Gleeson C18th
Deryn Lake C18th
David Liss C18th

Derek Wilson C18th
Boris Akunin C19th
David Ashton C19th
Sara Fraser C19th
Jason Goodwin C19th
John Maclachlan Gray C19th
Michael Gregorio C19th
John Harwood C19th
Peter J Heck C19th
Lee Jackson C19th
Alanna Knight C19th
Joan Lock C19th
Peter Lovesey C19th
Andrew Martin C19th
James McGee C19th
Robin Paige C19th
Andrew Pepper C19th
Elizabeth Peters C19th
David Pirie C19th
Barrie Roberts C19th
Norman Russell C19th
Rosemary Stevens C19th
Anne Perry C19th/C20th
Conrad Allen C20th
Barbara Cleverly C20th

Historical (continued)

David Dickinson C20th
Carola Dunn C20th
Stuart M Kaminsky C20th

Laurie R King C20th
Rebecca Pawel C20th
Michael Pearce C20th

David Roberts C20th
Frank Tallis C20th
Charles Todd C20th

Genre

Humour

Christopher Brookmyre
Tim Dorsey
Janet Evanovich
Jasper Fforde
Christopher Fowler
Kinky Friedman
Peter Guttridge

Sparkle Hayter
Carl Hiaasen
Danny King
Andrey Kurkov
Joe R Lansdale
Robert Lewis

Douglas Lindsay
Pauline McLynn
Malcolm Pryce
Zane Radcliffe
Sarah Strohmeyer
Donald Westlake

Legal/financial

William Bernhardt
Stephen L Carter
Linda Fairstein
Mark Gimenez
James Grippando
John Grisham
John Hart
Jilliane Hoffman

Craig Holden
John T Lescroart
John McLaren
Phillip Margolin
Steve Martini
Perri O'Shaughnessy
Barbara Parker
Richard North Patterson

Christopher Reich
Nancy Taylor Rosenberg
Lisa Scottoline
Susan R Sloan
Peter Spiegelman
Robert K Tanenbaum
Scott Turow

Medical

Paul Carson

Tess Gerritsen

Ken McClure

PI

Kate Atkinson
Linda Barnes
Cara Black
Victoria Blake
Raymond Chandler
Carol Higgins Clark
Peter Corris
Robert Crais
James Crumley
Stephen Donaldson
Arthur Conan Doyle
Stella Duffy
Robert Edric
Loren D Estleman
Liz Evans
Reg Gadney

Meg Gardiner
Sue Grafton
Kerry Greenwood
James W Hall
Steve Hamilton
Dashiell Hammett
Paul Johnston
Laura Lippman
Gabrielle Lord
Ken McCoy
Ross Macdonald
Manuel Vázquez Montalbán
Marcia Muller
Reggie Nadelson
Sara Paretsky
Robert B Parker

Eliot Pattison
Rick Riordan
S J Rozan
John Shannon
Alexander McCall Smith
Michelle Spring
Dana Stabenow
Cath Staincliffe
Peter Temple
Ronald Tierney
Mark Timlin
Eric Van Lustbader
Ayelet Waldman
Valerie Wilson Wesley
Stella Whitelaw
Jacqueline Winspear

Police work - UK

Catherine Aird
James Anderson
David Armstrong
Vivien Armstrong
Jeffrey Ashford
Jo Bannister
Robert Barnard

M C Beaton
Pauline Bell
Mark Billingham
Rhys Bowen
W J Burley
Gwendoline Butler
Karen Campbell

Glenn Chandler
Paul Charles
Ann Cleeves
Chris Collett
John Connor
Brian Cooper
Elizabeth Corley

Crime

Police work - UK (continued)

Deborah Crombie
Clare Curzon
Judith Cutler
Colin Dexter
Margaret Duffy
Marjorie Eccles
Kate Ellis
Geraldine Evans
Anthea Fraser
Gillian Galbraith
Elizabeth George
Caroline Graham
Ann Granger
Alex Gray
J M Gregson
Martha Grimes
Georgie Hale
Patricia Hall
Cynthia Harrod-Eagles
John Harvey
Reginald Hill

Susan Hill
Lesley Horton
Graham Hurley
Michael Innes
Graham Ison
P D James
Peter James
Quintin Jardine
Katherine John
H R F Keating
Susan B Kelly
John Lawton
Frederic Lindsay
Peter Lovesey
Stuart MacBride
Iain McDowall
Brian McGilloway
Adrian Magson
Barry Maitland
Ngaio Marsh

Priscilla Masters
Maureen O'Brien
Nick Oldham
Stuart Pawson
Ian Rankin
Ruth Rendell
Nicholas Rhea
Peter Robinson
Pauline Rowson
Roger Silverwood
Dorothy Simpson
Sally Spencer
Andrew Taylor
Aline Templeton
Leslie Thomas
June Thomson
Peter Turnbull
Camilla Way
Neil White
R D Wingfield

Police work - US

Chelsea Cain
Jodi Compton
Michael Connelly
Robert Ellis
Brian Freeman
Paula Gosling
W E B Griffin
Donald Harstad
Lynn Hightower
Tony Hillerman

J A Jance
Faye Kellerman
Jesse Kellerman
Jonathan Kellerman
J A Kerley
Lynda La Plante
Thomas Laird
Dennis Lehane
Ed McBain
Michael McGarrity

Michael Malone
Archer Mayor
Theresa Monsour
Carol O'Connell
Jefferson Parker
Ridley Pearson
J D Robb
John Sandford
Jess Walter
Joseph Wambaugh

Police work - other foreign

Jon Cleary Australia
Garry Disher Australia
Claire McNab Australia
Luiz Alfredo Garcia-Roza Brazil
Giles Blunt Canada
Louise Penny Canada
Medora Sale Canada
Peter May China
Andy Oakes China
Lisa See China
Qiu Xiaolong China
José Latour Cuba
Matti Joensuu Finland
Martin O'Brien France
Georges Simenon France

Fred Vargas France
Craig Russell Germany
Arnaldur Indridason Iceland
Bartholomew Gill Ireland
Brian McGilloway Ireland
Andrea Camilleri Italy
Michael Dibdin Italy
David Hewson Italy
Donna Leon Italy
Carlo Lucarelli Italy
Magdalen Nabb Italy
A C Baantjer Netherlands
Janwillem van de Wetering
Netherlands
K O Dahl Norway

Karin Fossum Norway
Anne Holt Norway
Jo Nesbo Norway
R N Morris Russia
Martin Cruz Smith Russia
Roderic Jeffries Spain
Ake Edwardson Sweden
Kjell Eriksson Sweden
Mari Jungstedt Sweden
Åsa Larsson Sweden
Henning Mankell Sweden
Hakan Nesser Sweden
Maj Sjöwall & Per Wahlöö
Sweden
Barbara Nadel Turkey

Genre

Psychological

Jane Adams	Tami Hoag	Patrick Redmond
Karin Alvtegen	Babs Horton	John Rickards
Lindsay Ashford	Elisabeth Hyde	Liz Rigbey
Ingrid Black	Morag Joss	Michael Robotham
Hilary Bonner	Alex Kava	Louis Sanders
Stephen Booth	David Lawrence	Manda Scott
Gianrico Carofiglio	Jeff Lindsay	Jenny Siler
John Connolly	Sharyn McCrumb	Chris Simms
Thomas H Cook	Val McDermid	Carol Smith
Carol Anne Davis	Cody McFadyen	Sally Spedding
Sarah Diamond	Elizabeth McGregor	Erica Spindler
R J Ellory	Guillermo Martinez	Boris Starling
Joy Fielding	Steve Mosby	Tony Strong
Carol Goodman	Margaret Murphy	Jim Thompson
Gregory Hall	Jonathan Nasaw	P J Tracy
Sophie Hannah	Meg O'Brien	Barbara Vine
Mo Hayder	Ed O'Connor	Sue Walker
Daniel Hecht	James Patterson	Minette Walters
Frances Hegarty	Andrew Pyper	Stephen White
Patricia Highsmith	Sarah Rayne	Laura Wilson
Jane Hill	Danuta Reah	Margaret Yorke

Romantic suspense

Elizabeth Adler	Heather Graham	Nora Roberts
Beverly Barton	Christiane Heggan	Karen Rose
Allison Brennan	Linda Howard	Sharon Sala
Suzanne Brockmann	Lisa Jackson	Madge Swindells

Fantasy

Fantasy novels – as distinct from Science Fiction – deal with the impossible, being based on magic or the supernatural. They follow no scientific 'rules', only the whim of the author. While there are many sub-divisions in the world of Fantasy, we have used six sub-genres to help readers find the kind of book they most enjoy: **Contemporary** – the intrusion of the fantastic into modern life; **Dark** – Fantasy which incorporates a sense of horror; **Epic** – books in which heroes and heroines wage epic combat with forces of evil; **Myth** – authors who place their stories in worlds of myth, saga and legend, particularly Celtic; **Humour** – not all fantasy is dark, and these authors write light and humorous stories, often including elements of familiar folk tales; **Literary** – the characters of fiction and literature in general take on reality in a fantasy world rich in literary allusion.

Susanna Clarke	Amanda Hemingway	Scarlett Thomas
G W Dahlquist	Philip Pullman	Kim Wilkins

Contemporary

Mark Chadbourn	Neil Gaiman	Tim Powers
Charles de Lint	Sergei Lukyanenko	Liz Williams
Hal Duncan		

Fantasy

Genre

Dark

Jonathan Carroll
Storm Constantine

Graham Joyce
Tim Lebbon

Tanith Lee

Epic

Joe Abercrombie
Sarah Ash
Robert Asprin
R Scott Bakker
James Barclay
Carol Berg
David Bilsborough
Marion Zimmer Bradley
Chaz Brenchley
Terry Brooks
Trudi Canavan
James Clemens
Eoin Colfer
Louise Cooper
Stephen Donaldson
Sara Douglass
David A Drake
David Eddings
Kate Elliott
Steven Erikson
David Farland
Raymond E Feist
Jude Fisher
Maggie Furey
David Gemmell

Mary Gentle
Terry Goodkind
Simon Green
Elizabeth Haydon
Lian Hearn
Robin Hobb
Ian Irvine
J V Jones
Robert Jordan
Guy Gavriel Kay
Paul Kearney
Greg Keyes
Katherine Kurtz
Mercedes Lackey
Ursula K Le Guin
Holly Lisle
Tom Lloyd
Scott Lynch
Fiona McIntosh
Juliet E McKenna
John Marco
George R R Martin
Julian May
Karen Miller

L E Modesitt Jr
Elizabeth Moon
Michael Moorcock
Robert Newcomb
Stan Nicholls
William Nicholson
Christopher Paolini
K J Parker
Melanie Rawn
Mickey Zucker Reichert
Patrick Rothfuss
J K Rowling
Brian Ruckley
Sean Russell
R A Salvatore
Steph Swainston
Sheri S Tepper
J R R Tolkien
Harry Turtledove
Freda Warrington
Margaret Weis
Jane Welch
Tad Williams
Janny Wurts

Humour

Craig Shaw Gardner
Tom Holt

Christopher Moore
Terry Pratchett

Martin Scott

Literary

Robert Holdstock

C S Lewis

Gene Wolfe

Myth

Alma Alexander
Ashok K Banker
C J Cherryh
Cecilia Dart-Thornton
Barbara Hambly

Stephen Hunt
Katharine Kerr
Stephen R Lawhead
Gregory Maguire
Juliet Marillier

Caiseal Mor
Garth Nix
Judith Tarr
Sarah Zettel

Glitz & Glamour

This genre features the modern world of big business and entertainment, with generous proportions of sex, violence and avarice.

Sally Beauman
Celia Brayfield
Sandra Brown
Candace Bushnell
Jackie Collins
Jilly Cooper
Jude Deveraux

Olivia Goldsmith
Eileen Goudge
Judith Gould
Jayne Ann Krentz
Susan Lewis
Johanna Lindsey
Lesley Lokko

Judith Michael
Fern Michaels
Una-Mary Parker
Tasmina Perry
Katie Price
Harold Robbins
Penny Vincenzi

Historical

Another very popular category, where fictional characters are set against an actual historical perspective, with close and realistic links between fiction and fact. Some are based on real people and events, while others are purely imaginary.

Thalassa Ali
Elizabeth Aston
Jean M Auel
Vanora Bennett
Geraldine Brooks
Tracy Chevalier
Gloria Cook
Bernard Cornwell
Will Davenport
Sara Donati
Jennifer Donnelly
Dorothy Dunnett
Robert Edric
Margaret Elphinstone
Barbara Erskine
Barbara Ewing
Ken Follett
Diana Gabaldon
Julie Garwood
Kathleen O'Neal Gear
Margaret George
Amitav Ghosh
Melanie Gifford
Posie Graeme-Evans
Winston Graham
Philippa Gregory
Sandra Gulland
Jane Harris
Cynthia Harrod-Eagles
Caroline Harvey

Anne Haverty
Anne Herries
Joanna Hines
Linda Holeman
Helen Hollick
C C Humphreys
Jeanne Kalogridis
Matthew Kneale
Rosalind Laker
Morgan Llywelyn
Colleen McCullough
Sophia McDougall
Katharine McMahon
Valerio Massimo Manfredi
Robin Maxwell
Anchee Min
Kate Mosse
Diana Norman
Edith Pargeter
Margaret Pemberton
Sharon Penman
Maureen Peters
Jean Plaidy
Steven Pressfield
Julian Rathbone
Mary Renault
James Robertson
James Runcie
Edward Rutherfurd
Simon Scarrow

Manda Scott
Tim Severin
Patricia Shaw
Jane Stevenson
Reay Tannahill
E V Thompson
Nigel Tranter
Barry Unsworth
Susan Vreeland
Peter Watt
Barbara Wood
Michael Curtis Ford Ancient
Robert Harris Ancient
Conn Iggulden Ancient
Christian Jacq Ancient
Allan Massie Ancient
William Napier Ancient
Scott Oden Ancient
Wilbur Smith Ancient
Elizabeth Chadwick Medieval
Tom Harper Medieval
Jack Whyte C12th
Suzannah Dunn C16th
Alison Weir C16th
Christie Dickason C17th
Clare Clark C18th & C19th
Victoria Holt Romantic
suspense

Historical Romance

These novels have a history-dependent plot with the authors frequently setting their stories during periods of change and general unrest. Settings are usually based in historical reality while characters may be real or imaginary, Romance plays a strong role in the story line.

Elizabeth Bailey	Fenella-Jane Miller	Mary Balogh C19th
Marion Chesney	Amanda Quick	Anne Barbour C19th
Catherine Coulter	Julia Quinn	Georgette Heyer C19th
Elizabeth Darrell	Kate Tremayne	Stephanie Laurens C19th
Emily Hendrickson	Robyn Young Medieval	

Horror

This section includes authors who frequently write suspense and horror, where the storyline involves pursuit and eventual escape – often from the supernatural, demonic or the occult.

Richard Bachman	James Herbert	Graham Masterton
Clive Barker	Tanya Huff	Richard Matheson
Poppy Z Brite	Shaun Hutson	Mark Morris
Ramsey Campbell	Peter James	Scott Nicholson
Jonathan Carroll	Stephen King	Christopher Pike
Simon Clark	Stephen Laws	Phil Rickman
Douglas Clegg	Richard Laymon	John Saul
Jeremy Dyson	Bentley Little	Dan Simmons
Bret Easton Ellis	Brian Lumley	Peter Straub
John Farris	Robert McCammon	Whitley Strieber
Christopher Fowler	Paul Magrs	Koji Suzuki
Stephen Gallagher	David Martin	T M Wright

Humour

A select group of authors whose novels are mainly written to amuse.

Guy Bellamy	Tom Holt	Alexei Sayle
Alan Bennett	Garrison Keillor	Tom Sharpe
Mavis Cheek	Marina Lewycka	William Sutcliffe
Jonathan Coe	Sue Limb	Linda Taylor
Joseph Connolly	Laura Marney	Alan Titchmarsh
Roddy Doyle	Magnus Mills	Sue Townsend
Michael Frayn	John Mortimer	Lynne Truss
Stephen Fry	Geoff Nicholson	Keith Waterhouse
James Hawes	David Nobbs	Nigel Williams
Charles Higson	Allison Pearson	P G Wodehouse
Andrew Holmes	Lily Prior	Isabel Wolff

Lad Lit

Nick Hornby and Tony Parsons began the male equivalent to Chick Lit. Written about men in the same age range who have trouble expressing their emotions.

Mark Barrowcliffe	Sam Holden	Kevin Sampson
Matt Beaumont	Nick Hornby	Matt Thorne
Matt Dunn	David Nicholls	Matt Whyman
Mike Gayle	Tony Parsons	

Humour

Paul Burke	John Harding	John O'Farrell
James Delingpole	Mil Millington	

Mature Chick Lit

The books portray a world where slightly older women juggle the demands of career and relationships in new and non-traditional ways and the stories have an emphasis on friendship but not necessarily on romance.

Susie Boyt	Debby Holt	Sinead Moriarty
Louise Candlish	Rachel Johnson	Imogen Parker
Harriet Evans	Sophie King	Adele Parks
Katie Fforde	India Knight	Tina Reilly
Fiona Gibson	Julia Llewellyn	Victoria Routledge
Maeve Haran	Monica McInerney	Robyn Sisman
Alison Penton Harper	Gil McNeil	Kate Thompson
Kate Harrison	Debbie Macomber	Sarah Tucker
Veronica Henry	Jill Mansell	Polly Williams
Julia Holden		

Paranormal

Almost anything paranormal or unexplained by natural causes is included in this genre, especially vampires and werewolves. Settings can be either historical or contemporary and the beings can be the embodiment of good and evil.

Lara Adrian	Christine Feehan	Sherrilyn Kenyon
Kelley Armstrong	Lori Handeland	Kim Newman
Keri Arthur	Laurell K Hamilton	Sara Reinke
Patricia Briggs	Charlaine Harris	Anne Rice
Jim Butcher	Kim Harrison	J R Ward
Mary Janice Davidson		

Saga

A popular genre, frequently set against an historical background, telling the story of two or more generations of a family, with the plot often revolving around the purchase of property or the development of a family business.

Genre

Rosemary Aitken
Lyn Andrews
Aileen Armitage
Anne Baker
Tessa Barclay
Anne Bennett
Maggie Bennett
Emma Blair
Jessica Blair
Philip Boast
Rose Boucheron
Harry Bowling
Clare Boylan
Barbara Taylor Bradford
Rita Bradshaw
Benita Brown
Julia Bryant
Anita Burgh
Helen Cannam
Irene Carr
Jean Chapman
Catrin Collier
Alexandra Connor
Catherine Cookson
Dilly Court
Josephine Cox
Maggie Craig
Glenice Crossland
Janet Dailey
Elizabeth Daish
Doris Davidson
Margaret Thomson Davis
Frank Delaney
R F Delderfield
Margaret Dickinson
Elizabeth Elgin
Pamela Evans
Katie Flynn
June Francis
Christine Marion Fraser
Sara Fraser
Elizabeth Gill
Rosie Goodwin
Iris Gower
Pip Granger
Hilary Green
Annie Groves

Ruth Hamilton
Rosie Harris
Lilian Harry
Meg Henderson
Elizabeth Ann Hill
Evelyn Hood
Billy Hopkins
Una Horne
Audrey Howard
Susan Howatch
Harriet Hudson
Meg Hutchinson
Sara Hylton
Anna Jacobs
Elizabeth Jeffrey
Jeannie Johnson
Joan Jonker
Penny Jordan
Margaret Kaine
Sheelagh Kelly
Beryl Kingston
Gwen Kirkwood
Mary A Larkin
Maureen Lee
Judith Lennox
Freda Lightfoot
Elizabeth Lord
Claire Lorrimer
Ken McCoy
Mary Mackie
Tamara McKinley
Elisabeth McNeill
Gwen Madoc
Beryl Matthews
Margaret Mayhew
Joan Medlicott
Connie Monk
Di Morrissey
Elizabeth Murphy
Annie Murray
Kitty Neale
Sheila Newberry
Judy Nunn
Geraldine O'Neill
Gilda O'Neill
Joan O'Neill
Pamela Oldfield

Sharon Owens
Lynda Page
Frances Paige
Victor Pemberton
Belva Plain
D M Purcell
Alexandra Raife
Eileen Ramsay
Miss Read
Elvi Rhodes
Carol Rivers
Denise Robertson
Wendy Robertson
Liz Ryan
Susan Sallis
Judith Saxton
Rebecca Shaw
Anne Rivers Siddons
Linda Sole
LaVyrle Spencer
Mary Jane Staples
Danielle Steel
Kay Stephens
Sally Stewart
Jessica Stirling
Sue Sully
Rowena Summers
Janet Tanner
June Tate
Michael Taylor
Rosie Thomas
Grace Thompson
Nicola Thorne
Margaret Thornton
Adriana Trigiani
Janet MacLeod Trotter
Elizabeth Waite
Jeanne Whitmee
Barbara Whitnell
Annie Wilkinson
Marcia Willett
Dee Williams
Audrey Willsher
T R Wilson
Mary Withall
Valerie Wood
Janet Woods
Sally Worboyes

Although Science Fiction (SF) and Fantasy are often mixed, SF deals with the possible, and is based (often tenuously) on scientific knowledge obeying the laws of nature in the universe — however fantastic some of the stories may seem. The literature of SF is substantial and we have used five subgenres to help you find the type of author you want to read: **Near future** – stories concerning all pervasive technologies, their use and misuse, normally set within the next hundred years; **Space opera** – space adventure stories of extravagant dimensions, often involving galactic empires and space battles; **Space and time** – travel into either the past or the future, exploring history as it might have been, or the future as the author sees it; **Technical** – SF novels with an overriding emphasis on the technical and scientific achievement, usually involving flight into outer space; **Humour** – authors whose books highlight the humorous aspects of SF.

Humour

Douglas Adams	Harry Harrison	Robert Rankin
Rob Grant		

Near future

Neal Asher	Gwyneth Jones	Nick Sagan
Steve Aylett	James Lovegrove	Andrzej Sapkowski
John Birmingham	Richard Morgan	Lucius Shepard
Eric Brown	Jeff Noon	Michael Marshall Smith
Greg Egan	Richard Powers	Neal Stephenson
William Gibson	Kim Stanley Robinson	Tad Williams
Steven Gould	Justina Robson	John Wyndham
Jon Courtenay Grimwood	Geoff Ryman	

Space and time

Brian W Aldiss	Jack McDevitt	Robert Silverberg
Isaac Asimov	Ian McDonald	Jules Verne
Ben Bova	Ken MacLeod	Kurt Vonnegut
Ray Bradbury	China Miéville	H G Wells
Philip K Dick	Audrey Niffenegger	Connie Willis
Harlan Ellison	Larry Niven	Robert Charles Wilson
Robert A Heinlein	Christopher Priest	David Zindell
Anne McCaffrey	Kristine Kathryn Rusch	

Space opera

Dan Abnett	Ben Counter	Frank Herbert
Kevin J Anderson	Alan Dean Foster	Robert Reed
Poul Anderson	Michael Jan Friedman	Alastair Reynolds
Iain M Banks	Colin Greenland	Adam Roberts
David Brin	Joe Haldeman	Dan Simmons
Lois McMaster Bujold	Peter F Hamilton	Charles Stross
Orson Scott Card	Brian Herbert	Sean Williams
C J Cherryh		

Technical

J G Ballard	Arthur C Clarke	John Meaney
Stephen Baxter	Paul J McAuley	Linda Nagata
Greg Bear	Wil McCarthy	Brian Stableford
Gregory Benford		

Sea

A popular category where many authors have made a well-deserved reputation for writing about the sea either in an historical or a modern setting. Many novelists in this genre will also be found under **Adventure/Thriller** and also under **War stories**.

Historical

Tom Connery	Jonathan Lunn	Julian Stockwin
David Donachie	James L Nelson	Peter Smalley C18th
C S Forester	Patrick O'Brian	G S Beard C19th
Alexander Kent		

Historical & Modern

Philip McCutchan   Dudley Pope

Modern

Brian Callison	Nicholas Monsarrat	Patrick Robinson
James H Cobb	Douglas Reeman	Peter Tonkin
Duncan Harding		

War

Authors who have written widely but not exclusively about war, generally within the 19th and 20th centuries. Many books about war will also be found under **Adventure/Thriller** and also under **Sea stories**. Some **General** novelists have also written individual books about war.

Guy Walters   James Webb

Historical

Roger Carpenter	Iain Gale	Patrick Rambaud
Joy Chambers	Richard Howard	Garry Kilworth C19th
Bernard Cornwell	Allan Mallinson	John Wilcox C19th
George Macdonald Fraser		

Modern

Frank Barnard	W E B Griffin	David L Robbins
F G Cottam	James Holland	Derek Robinson
Elizabeth Darrell	Andy McNab	Alan Savage
David Fiddimore	Robert Radcliffe	Terence Strong

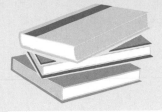

Characters and Series

This section lists all the Characters, Series and Family names which appear in the main A-Z sequence of the guide.

A

Bea Abbot	Veronica Heley
Ben Abbott	Justin Scott
Abdouf	Jean-Christophe Grangé
Jack Absolute	C C Humphreys
Laura Ackroyd	Patricia Hall
The Hon Barnaby Adair	Stephanie Laurens
Adams Family	Mary Jane Staples
Commissaire Adamsberg	Fred Vargas
Adelia Aguiler	Ariana Franklin
Captain Alatriste	Arturo Pérez-Reverte
Alexander the Great	Paul Doherty
Alexander the Great	Valerio Massimo Manfredi
Alfred the Great	Bernard Cornwell
DS Khalid Ali	Lesley Horton
DI Roderick Alleyn	Ngaio Marsh
Alligator	Massimo Carlotto
Gabriel Allon	Daniel Silva
Alpiew	Fidelis Morgan
DI Enrique Alvarez	Roderic Jeffries
Amerotke	Paul Doherty
Simon Ames	Patricia Finney
Robert Amiss	Ruth Dudley Edwards
Fitzroy Maclean Angel	Mike Ripley
DI Michael Angel	Roger Silverwood
Anno Dracula Series	Kim Newman
Father Anselm	William Brodrick
Callie Anson	Kate Charles
DI John Appleby	Michael Innes
April Grove Series	Lilian Harry
Lew Archer	Ross Macdonald
Owen Archer	Candace Robb
Kate Ardleigh	Robin Paige
Comm Jan Argand	Julian Rathbone
Jonathan Argyll	Iain Pears
Aristotle	Margaret Doody
Israel Armstrong	Ian Sansom
Sheriff Spenser Arrowood	Sharyn McCrumb
King Arthur	Bernard Cornwell
Arthurian Trilogy	Helen Hollick
Countess Ashby-de-la-Zouche	Fidelis Morgan
DI Carol Ashton	Claire McNab
Peter Ashton	Clive Egleton

B

Askham Family	Nicola Thorne
Demetrios Askiates	Tom Harper
Brother Athelstan	Paul Doherty
Attila the Hun	William Napier
Jack Aubrey	Patrick O'Brian
Kurt Austin	Clive Cussler
Mick Axbrewder	Stephen Donaldson
Badge of Honour Series	W E B Griffin
Bill Bailey	Catherine Cookson
DS Geoffrey Bailey	Frances Fyfield
Lt Bak	Lauren Haney
Jonathan Bale	Edward Marston
Robin Ballantyne	Catherine Sampson
Jessica Balzano	Richard Montanari
CI Alan Banks	Peter Robinson
Chief Holly Barker	Stuart Woods
Barleybridge Series	Rebecca Shaw
Alexandra Barnaby	Janet Evanovich
DCI Tom Barnaby	Caroline Graham
Harry Barnett	Robert Goddard
Smokey Barrett	Cody McFadyen
Stone Barrington	Stuart Woods
Lee Bartholomew	Hope McIntyre
Matthew Bartholomew	Susanna Gregory
Frank Bascombe	Richard Ford
Andrew Basnett	Elizabeth Ferrars
Charlie Bassett	David Fiddimore
Mark Beamon	Kyle Mills
Det J P Beaumont	J A Jance
Martin Beck	Maj Sjöwall & Per Wahlöö
David Becket	Patricia Finney
Holly Beckman	Jessica Stirling
Dr Joseph Bell	David Pirie
Beloved People Trilogy	Denise Robertson
Alex Benedict	Jack McDevitt
Annika Bengtzon	Liza Marklund
Bebe Bennett	Rosemary Martin
Sgt Francis Benton-Smith	P D James
DI Ernest Best	Joan Lock
Ashraf Bey	Jon Courtenay Grimwood
Big Stone Gap Series	Adriana Trigiani
Jim Bishop	Andrew Klavan
Lucrezia 'Cree' Black	Daniel Hecht
Tom Black	Elizabeth Darrell
Oz Blackstone	Quintin Jardine
Insp Sam Blackstone	Sally Spencer
Mike Blackwood	Douglas Reeman
Det Sonora Blair	Lynn Hightower
Anita Blake	Laurell K Hamilton
DS Lucy Blake	J M Gregson
Naomi Blake	Jane Adams
Natasha Blake	Fiona Mountain

Joanna Blalock	Leonard Goldberg
Sgt Lou Boldt	Ridley Pearson
Myron Bolitar	Harlan Coben
Adam Bolitho	Alexander Kent
Richard Bolitho	Alexander Kent
Bonaparte Series	Richard Howard
Josephine Bonaparte	Sandra Gulland
Napoleon Bonaparte	Simon Scarrow
James Bond	Ian Fleming
James Bond	Raymond Benson
Harry Bosch	Michael Connelly
Sgt Bottomley	Norman Russell
Boudica	Manda Scott
Sister Agnes Bourdillon	Alison Joseph
Jason Bourne	Robert Ludlum
Samuel Bowater	James L Nelson
Eva Bower	Aileen Armitage
Lucifer Box	Mark Gatiss
DS Tina Boyd	Simon Kernick
Nicholas Bracewell	Edward Marston
Sheriff Joanna Brady	J A Jance
Kate Brannigan	Val McDermid
DS Brant	Ken Bruen
Andy Brazil	Patricia D Cornwell
Breadmakers Series	Margaret Thomson Davis
Dr Temperance Brennan	Kathy Reichs
Gervase Bret	Edward Marston
Brethren of the Coast Trilogy	James L Nelson
Insp John Bright	Maureen O'Brien
Dr Solomon Brightman	Alex Gray
DI Brock	Graham Ison
DCI David Brock	Barry Maitland
Det Jackson Brodie	Kate Atkinson
Kat Bronsky	John J Nance
Brotherhood of War Series	W E B Griffin
CI Browne	Pauline Bell
Verity Browne	David Roberts
Richard Browning	Peter Corris
Beau Brummell	Rosemary Stevens
Commissario Guido Brunetti	Donna Leon
Arthur Bryant	Christopher Fowler
Tam Buchanan	Joyce Holms
DI Kate Burrows	Martina Cole
Dr Clare Burtonall	Jonathan Gash
Kevin Byrne	Richard Montanari
Brother Cadfael	Ellis Peters
Julius Caesar	Conn Iggulden
DI Jack Caffery	Mo Hayder
Calder Family	Janet Dailey
Alex Calder	Michael Ridpath
Keith Calder	Gerald Hammond
Sgt Anna Cameron	Karen Campbell

C

Donald Cameron	Philip McCutchan
Fiona Cameron	Val McDermid
Sgt Liam Campbell	Dana Stabenow
Margaret Campbell	Peter May
Caper Court Series	Caro Fraser
Det John Cardinal	Giles Blunt
Det Steve Carella	Ed McBain
Sam 'Mad' Carew	Ken McCoy
Neal Carey	Don Winslow
Sir Robert Carey	P F Chisholm
Carlotta Carlyle	Linda Barnes
Liz Carlyle	Stella Rimington
Tommy Carmellini	Stephen Coonts
Insp James Carrick	Margaret Duffy
Cece Caruso	Susan Kandel
Pepe Carvalho	Manuel Vázquez Montalbán
DCI Casey	Geraldine Evans
Quintus Licinus Cato	Simon Scarrow
Thomas Catt	Geraldine Evans
Chadwick Family	Marcia Willett
Insp Hal Challis	Garry Disher
Thomas Chaloner	Susanna Gregory
Champagne Series	Nicola Thorne
Cardinal Chang	G W Dahlquist
Det Mike Chapman	Linda Fairstein
Eddie Chase	Andy McDermott
Tom Chatto	Philip McCutchan
Jim Chee	Tony Hillerman
DI Chen	Liz Williams
Insp Chen	Qiu Xiaolong
Lydia Chin	S J Rozan
DCI Henry Christie	Nick Oldham
Paul Christopher	Charles McCarry
Church of England Series	Susan Howatch
Winston Churchill	Michael Dobbs
Cicero	Robert Harris
Robert Clark	Lis Howell
DC Siobhan Clarke	Ian Rankin
Denise Cleever	Claire McNab
Frank Clemons	Thomas H Cook
Com John Coffin	Gwendoline Butler
Artie Cohen	Reggie Nadelson
Insp Robert Colbeck	Edward Marston
Elvis Cole	Robert Crais
Lewis Cole	Brendan Dubois
Hap Collins	Joe R Lansdale
Gail Connor	Barbara Parker
The Continental Op	Dashiell Hammett
Conway Family	Jessica Stirling
Alexandra Cooper	Linda Fairstein
DC Ben Cooper	Stephen Booth
PC Den Cooper	Rebecca Tope

Coppins Bridge Series	Elizabeth Daish
Sir Hugh Corbett	Paul Doherty
Cordwainer Series	Iris Gower
Det John Corey	Nelson DeMille
Lord Edward Corinth	David Roberts
Corps Series	W E B Griffin
Frank Corso	G M Ford
Corvill Family	Tessa Barclay
Marcus Corvinus	David Wishart
Det Nic Costa	David Hewson
Thomas Covenant	Stephen Donaldson
Covert-One Series	Robert Ludlum
Ladies of Covington Series	Joan Medlicott
Dick Coward	James Delingpole
Craddock Family	R F Delderfield
Melissa Craig	Betty Rowlands
Craigallan Family	Tessa Barclay
Alan Craik	Gordon Kent
Francis Crawford of Lymond	Dorothy Dunnett
Tildy Crawford	Sara Fraser
Ray Crawley	Peter Corris
Sgt Cribb	Peter Lovesey
Dr Anya Crichton	Kathryn Fox
DI Mike Croft	Jane Adams
DS Crosby	Catherine Aird
Det Alex Cross	James Patterson
Sgt 'Fancy' Jack Crossman	Garry Kilworth
DI John Crow	Roy Lewis
Crowner John	Bernard Knight
Gil Cunningham	Pat McIntosh
John Cunningham	Gerald Hammond
Kit Curtis	Frank Barnard
Richard Cypher	Terry Goodkind
D Josse D'Acquin	Alys Clare
Supt Adam Dalgleish	P D James
Isabel Dalhousie	Alexander McCall Smith
Eve Dallas	J D Robb
Daisy Dalrymple	Carola Dunn
Quintilian Dalrymple	Paul Johnston
DI Dalziel	Reginald Hill
Kathryn Dance	Jeffery Deaver
Darcy Family	Elizabeth Aston
The Dark Tower Series	Stephen King
Annie Darling and Max Darling	Carolyn G Hart
Lucas Davenport	John Sandford
'Dangerous' Davies	Leslie Thomas
Leo Davies	Caro Fraser
Sgt de Gier	Janwillem van de Wetering
Hugh de Lac	James Patterson
Justin de Quincey	Sharon Penman
Sir John de Wolfe	Bernard Knight
DeBeers Family Series	Virginia Andrews

Officer Cindy Decker	Faye Kellerman
Lt Pete Decker	Faye Kellerman
Insp DeKok	A C Baantjer
Evan Delaney	Meg Gardiner
Alex Delaware	Jonathan Kellerman
Ralph Delchard	Edward Marston
Det Alex Delillo	Scott Frost
John Delmas	Raymond Chandler
Det Lisa Delorme	Giles Blunt
Frank Dempsey	Paul Burke
Sgt Denny	Gwendoline Butler
Deravenel Series	Barbara Taylor Bradford
Insp Benedict Devlin	Brian McGilloway
Harry Devlin	Martin Edwards
Georgia Dew	Amy Myers
DI Alison Dexter	Ed O'Connor
Det Serena Dial	Brian Freeman
Eve Diamond	Denise Hamilton
Peter Diamond	Peter Lovesey
Auguste Didier	Amy Myers
George Porter Dillman	Conrad Allen
Sean Dillon	Jack Higgins
Discworld	Terry Pratchett
Jim Dixon	Kingsley Amis
Maisie Dobbs	Jacqueline Winspear
Trixie Dolan	Marian Babson
DS Cal Donovan	Jo Bannister
Joe Donovan	Martyn Waites
John Dortmunder	Donald Westlake
Arthur Conan Doyle	David Pirie
Harry Dresden	Jim Butcher
Drovers Series	Iris Gower
Drummond Family	Emma Blair
Sean Drummond	Brian Haig
Philip Dryden	Jim Kelly
Mike Dukas	Gordon Kent
Steven Dunbar	Ken McClure
Eve Duncan	Iris Johansen
Vanessa Duncan	Catherine Shaw
Dune Saga	Brian Herbert
Easter Empire	Beryl Kingston
Tam Eildor	Alanna Knight
Eisdalsa Island Trilogy	Mary Withall
John Eisenmenger	Keith McCarthy
DC Frank Elder	John Harvey
Emma	Elizabeth Daish
Insp Espinosa	Luiz Alfredo Garcia-Roza
Elena Estes	Tami Hoag
Lady Victoria Georgiana Charlotte Eugenie	Rhys Bowen
Constable Evan Evans	Rhys Bowen
Nicholas Everard	Alexander Fullerton

E

Det Jan Fabel	Craig Russell
Fairacre	Miss Read
Marcus Didius Falco	Lindsey Davis
Insp Javier Falcon	Robert Wilson
Sam Falconer	Victoria Blake
Erast Fandorin	Boris Akunin
DI Joe Faraday	Graham Hurley
DI Jeremy Faro	Alanna Knight
Brodie Farrell	Jo Bannister
Feeney Family	Sheelagh Kelly
CI George Felse	Ellis Peters
Dave Fenner	James Hadley Chase
DCI Andrew Fenwick	Elizabeth Corley
'Fiarlyden' Series	Gwen Kirkwood
Sister Fidelma	Peter Tremayne
Kit Fielding	Dick Francis
DCI Jack Finch	June Thomson
Scott Finn	David Hosp
Firebird Series	Iris Gower
First North American Series	Kathleen O'Neal Gear
Hon Phryne Fisher	Kerry Greenwood
Ginny Fistoulari	Stephen Donaldson
Fizz Fitzgerald	Joyce Holms
Henry Fitzroy	Tanya Huff
William Falconer	Ian Morson
Sir Harry Flashman	George Macdonald Fraser
DI Marjory Fleming	Aline Templeton
Helena Flemming	Keith McCarthy
PI Tom Fletcher	Patrick Lennon
DS Ray Flowers	Jane Adams
Zelda Fluck	Pip Granger
Capt Simon Fonthill	John Wilcox
Forrest Family	Julia Bryant
Lily Forrester	Nancy Taylor Rosenberg
Forsyte Saga	John Galsworthy
Socrates Fortlow	Walter Mosley
Sarah Fortune	Frances Fyfield
Artemis Fowl	Eoin Colfer
Charlie Fox	Zoë Sharp
Foxearth Trilogy	Pamela Oldfield
Jill Francis	Andrew Taylor
Max Freeman	Jonathon King
Felix & Virginia Freer	Elizabeth Ferrars
Sister Frevisse	Margaret Frazer
Kinky Friedman	Kinky Friedman
DI Frank Frølick	K O Dahl
DI Jack Frost	R D Wingfield
DS Diane Fry	Stephen Booth
Sir Baldwin Furnshill	Michael Jecks
John Fury	G S Beard
Sheriff Matt Gabriel	Paula Gosling
Jimmy Gage	Robert Ferrigno

Characters & Series

H

Jan Hardy	Jenny Pitman
Sgt Timo Harjunpaa	Matti Joensuu
Robert Harland	Henry Porter
DS Frances Harman	Judith Cutler
Steve Harmas	James Hadley Chase
Benni Harper	Earlene Fowler
DCI Colin Harpur	Bill James
Emma Harte	Barbara Taylor Bradford
Scot Harvath	Brad Thor
Harvey Series	Gloria Cook
DS Barbara Havers	Elizabeth George
Det Al Hawkin	Laurie R King
Hawksmoor Series	Aileen Armitage
Matthew Hawkwood	James McGee
DS Roger Hayes	Vivien Armstrong
Tamara Hayle	Valerie Wilson Wesley
Heart of Gold Series	Catrin Collier
Abbess Helewise	Alys Clare
DCI Hennessy	Peter Turnbull
Heron Saga	Pamela Oldfield
Matthew Hervey	Allan Mallinson
Dr Tony Hill	Val McDermid
Hillsbridge Family	Janet Tanner
Kate Hilton	Margaret Dickinson
Hitch-Hikers Guide to the Galaxy Series	Douglas Adams
Dido Hoare	Marianne MacDonald
DI Harry Hole	Jo Nesbo
Billy-Bob Holland	James Lee Burke
Sebastian Holmes	Brian Freemantle
Sherlock Holmes	Arthur Conan Doyle
Sherlock Holmes	Barrie Roberts
Sherlock Holmes	Laurie R King
Max Holt	Janet Evanovich
Det Bert Hook	J M Gregson
Sam Hooker	Janet Evanovich
Alison Hope	Susan B Kelly
DS Lloyd Hopkins	James Ellroy
Ward Hopkins	Michael Marshall
Horatio Hornblower	C S Forester
DI Andy Horton	Pauline Rowson
Dep Sheriff Carl Houseman	Donald Harstad
Jack Howard	David Gibbins
Robin Hudson	Sparkle Hayter
Insp Liu Hulan	Lisa See
DI Lorraine Hunt	Sheila Quigley
Dr David Hunter	Simon Beckett
Sano Ichiro	Laura Joh Rowland
Cetin Ikmen	Barbara Nadel
ACC Desmond Iles	Bill James
Jack Irish	Peter Temple
Isaac of Gerona	Caroline Roe
Dr Maura Isles	Tess Gerritsen

I

	Kate Ivory	Veronica Stallwood
J	DS Ken Jackson	Anthea Fraser
	DI Saul Jackson	Norman Russell
	DCI Jacobson	Iain McDowall
	Det Karin Jacobsson	Mari Jungstedt
	CI Daniel Jacquot	Martin O'Brien
	DI Gemma James	Deborah Crombie
	Jesse James	Meg O'Brien
	Cliff Janeway	John Dunning
	Jeeves	P G Wodehouse
	Harriet Jeffries	Medora Sale
	Sgt '352' Jenkins	John Wilcox
	Riley Jensen	Keri Arthur
	Sarah Jensen	Linda Davies
	Jay Jessup	Graeme Roe
	Sonchai Jitpleecheep	John Burdett
	John the Eunuch	Mary Reed and Eric Mayer
	Joliffe Players Series	Margaret Frazer
	Bridget Jones	Helen Fielding
	D J Jones	Chris Kuzneski
	Fearless Jones	Walter Mosley
	Sam Jones	Lauren Henderson
	Constable Sunset Jones	Joe R Lansdale
	DCI Carol Jordan	Val McDermid
	Sgt Trevor Joseph	Katherine John
	Judge of Egypt	Christian Jacq
	DCI Richard Jury	Martha Grimes
K	Dmitri Kameron	Michael Pearce
	Kane Family	Frank Delaney
	India Kane	Caroline Carver
	Roger 'Butch' Karp	Robert K Tanenbaum
	DI Frank Kavanagh	David Armstrong
	George Keene	Derek Wilson
	John Keller	Lawrence Block
	Irene Kelly	Jan Burke
	Clare Kelso	Jessica Stirling
	Commodore Kemp	Philip McCutchan
	Lennox Kemp	M R D Meek
	Kylie Kendall	Claire McNab
	DI Christy Kennedy	Paul Charles
	Patrick Kenzie	Dennis Lehane
	Harry Keogh	Brian Lumley
	Kevin Kerney	Michael McGarrity
	DS Kerr	Iain McDowall
	Margaret Kerr	Candace Robb
	Kershaw Sisters	Anna Jacobs
	Insp Khalifa	Paul Sussman
	Genghis Khan	Conn Iggulden
	Kidd	John Sandford
	Sal Kilkenny	Cath Staincliffe
	Kit Killigrew	Jonathan Lunn
	Ben Kincaid	William Bernhardt

Sup Duncan Kincaid	Deborah Crombie
DDA Samantha Kincaid	Alafair Burke
Sean King	David Baldacci
Willow King	Natasha Cooper
Kings Series	Christine Marion Fraser
Tom Kirk	James Twining
Louie Knight	Malcolm Pryce
Knights Templar	Robyn Young
Deborah Knott	Margaret Maron
CI Anders Knutas	Mari Jungstedt
Koko (Siamese cat)	Lilian Jackson Braun
DS Kathy Kolla	Barry Maitland
DS Mike Korpanski	Priscilla Masters
Det Sam Kovac	Tami Hoag
Takeshi Kovacs	Richard Morgan
Thomas Paine Kydd	Julian Stockwin
Jordan Lacey	Stella Whitelaw
Tim Lacy	Derek Wilson
Det John Lambert	J M Gregson
Locke Lamora	Scott Lynch
Lampitt Chronicles	A N Wilson
Arnold Landon	Roy Lewis
Daisy Lane	June Hampson
Professor Robert Langdon	Dan Brown
Ingrid Langley	Margaret Duffy
DCI James Langton	Lynda La Plante
Lilac Larkin	Katie Flynn
Stephen Larkin	Martyn Waites
Dr Samantha Laschen	Nicci French
Sgt Alain Lausard	Richard Howard
Rina Lazarus	Faye Kellerman
Joe Leaphorn	Tony Hillerman
Dr Hannibal Lecter	Thomas Harris
Aimée Leduc	Cara Black
Thorgils Leiffson	Tim Severin
Det Supt Sholto Lestrade	M J Trow
Catherine LeVendeur	Sharan Newman
Libertus	Rosemary Rowe
Abe Lieberman	Stuart M Kaminsky
Dr Max Liebermann	Frank Tallis
Jack Liffey	John Shannon
PI Gemma Lincoln	Gabrielle Lord
Insp Ann Lindell	Kjell Eriksson
DS Lineham	Dorothy Simpson
Nicholas Linnear	Eric Van Lustbader
Sara Linton	Karin Slaughter
Tinks Liska	Tami Hoag
Sgt D Llewellyn	Geraldine Evans
Robin Llewellyn	Robert Lewis
London Sequence	Margaret Pemberton
Ben London	Philip Boast
DCI William Lorimer	Alex Gray

L

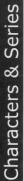

George Markham	Tom Connery
Philip Marlowe	Raymond Chandler
Thomas Marlowe	James L Nelson
Miss Marple	Agatha Christie
DS Charles Marriott	Graham Ison
Peter Marsh	Amy Myers
DS Harriet Martens	H R F Keating
Saz Martin	Stella Duffy
Det Kate Martinelli	Laurie R King
Rebecka Martinsson	Åsa Larsson
DS Mary Mary	Jasper Fforde
Genevieve Masefield	Conrad Allen
Mathilde of Westminster	Paul Doherty
Daphne Matthews	Ridley Pearson
Stephen Maturin	Patrick O'Brian
Alex Mavros	Paul Johnston
Michelle Maxwell	David Baldacci
Peter Maxwell	M J Trow
John May	Christopher Fowler
Caroline Maybry	Jess Walter
Kate Mayfield	Nelson DeMille
Supt Gil Mayo	Marjorie Eccles
Lois Meade	Ann Purser
Major Mearns	Gwendoline Butler
Bruce Medway	Robert Wilson
Paddy Meehan	Denise Mina
DI Jim Meldrum	Frederic Lindsay
Patrick Melrose	Edward St Aubyn
Lord Meren	Lynda S Robinson
Decius Caecilius Metellus the younger	John Maddox Roberts
David Middleton-Brown	Kate Charles
Alec Milius	Charles Cumming
Kinsey Millhone	Sue Grafton
Milo Milodragovitch	James Crumley
Det Minami	David Peace
PI Max Mingus	Nick Stone
Paris MInton	Walter Mosley
DI Kate Miskin	P D James
DCI Benny Mitchell	Pauline Bell
Meredith Mitchell	Ann Granger
Mitford Series	Jan Karon
Tess Monaghan	Laura Lippman
Insp William Monk & Hester Monk	Anne Perry
Monkton Family	Margaret Thomson Davis
Insp Salvo Montalbano	Andrea Camilleri
Britt Montero	Edna Buchanan
Dr Laurie Montgomery	Robin Cook
Monty (dog)	Iris Johansen
DI Abigail Moon	Marjorie Eccles
DS Stella Mooney	David Lawrence
Admiral Arnold Morgan	Patrick Robinson
Dexter Morgan	Jeff Lindsay

Rachel Morgan	Kim Harrison
Morland Dynasty	Cynthia Harrod-Eagles
DI Morse	Colin Dexter
Whit Mosley	Jeff Abbott
DS Angus Mott	Clare Curzon
Evadne Mount	Gilbert Adair
Charlie Muffin	Brian Freemantle
Molly Murphy	Rhys Bowen
Det Paris Murphy	Theresa Monsour
Tom Musgrave	Peter Tonkin

N

Tres Navarre	Rick Riordan
Insp Grazia Negro	Carlo Lucarelli
Vicki Nelson	Tanya Huff
Net Force Explorers	Tom Clancy
Bob Newman	Colin Forbes
Thursday Next	Jasper Fforde
Neyler Family	Judith Saxton
Nicholson Family	Jessica Stirling
Pierre Niemans	Jean-Christophe Grangé
Noble Series	Christine Marion Fraser
Chris Norgren	Aaron Elkins
Les Norton	Robert G Barrett

O

Det Petra O'Connor	Jonathan Kellerman
Maggie O'Dell	Alex Kava
Maureen O'Donnell	Denise Mina
Joseph O'Loughlin	Michael Robotham
Det Supt Oddie	Robert Barnard
Capt James Ogilvie	Philip McCutchan
Sigurdur Oli	Arnaldur Indridason
Billy Oliphant	Alan Dunn
Dr Gideon Oliver	Aaron Elkins
Michael Osbourne	Daniel Silva
Mysteries of Osiris	Christian Jacq
Outlander Series	Diana Gabaldon
Gareth Owen (The Mamur Zapt)	Michael Pearce

P

P Division	Peter Turnbull
Sam Packer	Geoffrey Archer
Lorraine Page	Lynda La Plante
Christopher Paget	Richard North Patterson
Dr Siri Paiboun	Colin Cotterill
Palace Theatre Series	Iris Gower
Frank Palmer	Adrian Magson
George & Molly Palmer-Jones	Ann Cleeves
Mrs Pargeter	Simon Brett
Charles Paris	Simon Brett
Jack Paris	Richard Montanari
PC Nick Parish	Nicholas Rhea
Rona Parish	Anthea Fraser
Det Jimmy Parisi	Thomas Laird
Charlie 'Bird' Parker	John Connolly
Ruby Parker	Rowan Coleman
Jack Parlabane	Christopher Brookmyre

DS Pascoe	Reginald Hill
Sarah Patrick	Iris Johansen
Patterson Family	Jessica Stirling
Jonathon Payne	Chris Kuzneski
Jimmy Paz	Michael Gruber
Amelia Peabody	Elizabeth Peters
DC Charlie Peace	Robert Barnard
DCI Percy Peach	J M Gregson
Pearce	Allan Guthrie
John Pearce	David Donachie
Sister Pelagia	Boris Akunin
John Pellam	Jeffery Deaver
DS Mark Pemberton	Nicholas Rhea
Agent E L Pender	Jonathan Nasaw
Pendragon Island Series	Grace Thompson
Pengarron Series	Gloria Cook
Catherine Penny	Patricia Harwin
Det Jimmy Perez	Ann Cleeves
Douglas Perkins	Marian Babson
DS Lou Perlman	Campbell Armstrong
Gianni Peroni	David Hewson
Reginald Perrin	David Nobbs
Toby Peters	Stuart M Kaminsky
DS Wesley Peterson	Kate Ellis
Vlado Petric	Dan Fesperman
Brother Petroc	Pip Vaughan-Hughes
Det Porfiry Petrovich	R N Morris
Primavera Phillips	Quintin Jardine
Sun Piao	Andy Oakes
Joe Pickett	C J Box
Connie Pickles	Sabine Durrant
DI Joanna Piercy	Priscilla Masters
Anna Pigeon	Nevada Barr
Leonard Pine	Joe R Lansdale
Melinda Pink	Gwen Moffat
DCI Rose Piper	Hilary Bonner
Dirk Pitt	Clive Cussler
Insp Thomas Pitt & Charlotte Pitt	Anne Perry
DI Montague Pluke	Nicholas Rhea
Stephanie Plum	Janet Evanovich
DS Romulus Poe	Faye Kellerman
Hercule Poirot	Agatha Christie
Poldark Series	Winston Graham
DS Poole	Graham Ison
Harry Potter	J K Rowling
Thomas Potts	Sara Fraser
DS Kate Power	Judith Cutler
Lord Francis Powerscourt	David Dickinson
Sgt Prentice	Vivien Armstrong
DI Ian Preston	Vivien Armstrong
Prey Series	John Sandford
Det Sarah Pribeck	Jodi Compton

Pride Family	Annie Groves
DI Charlie Priest	Stuart Pawson
Prince Family	Sheelagh Kelly
Princess Mia Diaries Series	Meg Cabot
Laura Principal	Michelle Spring
DS Judith Pullen	Vivien Armstrong
Simon Puttock	Michael Jecks
Pyke	Andrew Pepper

Q

Queen of Freedom Trilogy	Christian Jacq
Ellie Quicke	Veronica Heley
Kimberly Quincy	Lisa Gardner
Pierce Quincy	Lisa Gardner
Quinn Family	Nora Roberts
Terry Quinn	George P Pelecanos
Anthony Quintana	Barbara Parker
Quirke	Benjamin Black
Septimus Severus Quistus	Philip Boast
Francis Quoynt	Christie Dickason
Imogen Quy	Jill Paton Walsh
Jim Qwilleran	Lilian Jackson Braun

R

Alexandra Rafferty	James W Hall
DI Joe Rafferty	Geraldine Evans
John Rain	Barry Eisler
Agatha Raisin	M C Beaton
Rambo	David Morrell
Precious Ramotswe	Alexander McCall Smith
DI Stephen Ramsay	Ann Cleeves
Ramses	Christian Jacq
Sunny Randall	Robert B Parker
Mitch Rapp	Vince Flynn
Ravenscar Series	Barbara Taylor Bradford
John Rawlings	Deryn Lake
Easy Rawlins	Walter Mosley
Jack Reacher	Lee Child
DI John Rebus	Ian Rankin
Red Riding Quartet	David Peace
Christopher Redmayne	Edward Marston
Clio Rees	Jo Bannister
Nina Reilly	Perri O'Shaughnessy
Regan Reilly	Carol Higgins Clark
Insp Arkady Renko	Martin Cruz Smith
Capt William Rennie	Peter Smalley
DI Charlie Resnick	John Harvey
Retallick Family	E V Thompson
Nick Revill	Philip Gooden
Revolution at Sea Saga	James L Nelson
Alison Reynolds	J A Jance
Sukey Reynolds	Betty Rowlands
Rhanna Series	Christine Marion Fraser
DI Oscar Rheinhardt	Frank Tallis
Bernie Rhodenbarr	Lawrence Block
Lincoln Rhyme	Jeffery Deaver

Megan Rhys	Lindsay Ashford
Alice Rice	Gillian Galbraith
Merlin Richards	Keith Miles
DI Tom Richmonds	Marjorie Eccles
Major Jason Richter	Dale Brown
Paul Richter	James Barrington
Sam Ridley	Chris Niles
Tom Ripley	Patricia Highsmith
Rising Family	Susan Sallis
Leo Rivers	Robert Edric
Sophie Rivers	Judith Cutler
Det Jane Rizzoli	Tess Gerritsen
DCI Roberts	Ken Bruen
Dave Robicheaux	James Lee Burke
Rochford Family	Claire Lorrimer
Roger of Durham	Simon Beaufort
Roger the Chapman	Kate Sedley
Helga Rolfe	James Hadley Chase
Jean Rombaud	C C Humphreys
Melissa Romney-Jones	Hester Browne
Rosato & Associates	Lisa Scottoline
Rose Saga	Linda Sole
Alan Rosslyn	Reg Gadney
Insp Porfiry Rostnikov	Stuart M Kaminsky
Roth Trilogy	Andrew Taylor
PI Alex Rourke	John Rickards
Horace Rumpole	John Mortimer
Rune	Jeffery Deaver
Mary Russell	Laurie R King
Peter Rutland	Roger Carpenter
Insp Ian Rutledge	Charles Todd
Blackie Ryan	Andrew M Greeley
Finn Ryan	Paul Christopher
Jack Ryan	Tom Clancy
Sam Ryan	Nigel McCrery
Max Rydal	Elizabeth Darrell
Det Carson Ryder	J A Kerley
DC Jane Salt	David Armstrong
Gerald Samper	James Hamilton-Paterson
Bernard Samson	Len Deighton
DI John Sanders	Medora Sale
Insp Joe Sandilands	Barbara Cleverly
Det Justin Savile	Michael Malone
Saxon	Ingrid Black
Alan Saxton	Keith Miles
Kay Scarpetta	Patricia D Cornwell
Capt Shane Schofield	Matthew Reilly
44 Scotland Street Series	Alexander McCall Smith
Matthew Scudder	Lawrence Block
Det Shane Scully	Stephen J Cannell
Carole Seddon	Simon Brett
Lucy Sedgwick	Clare Curzon

S

Claudia Seferius	Marilyn Todd
Insp Konrad Sejer	Karin Fossum
Sara Selkirk	Morag Joss
DCI Simon Serrailler	Susan Hill
Seymour	Michael Pearce
Holden Shadbolt	Murray Bail
Sir Roger Shallot	Michael Clynes
Deets Shanahan	Ronald Tierney
DCI Frank Shapiro	Jo Bannister
Dr Matthew Shardlake	C J Sansom
Nick Sharman	Mark Timlin
DC Karen Sharpe	John Connor
Richard Sharpe	Bernard Cornwell
Mary Ann Shaughnessy	Catherine Cookson
DI Dave Shenfield	Georgie Hale
Dan 'Spider' Shepherd	Stephen Leather
Sheridan Family	Elizabeth Darrell
Archie Sheridan	Chelsea Cain
Sir Charles Sheridan	Robin Paige
Kate Shugak	Dana Stabenow
Sigma Force	James Rollins
Miss Maud Silver	Patricia Wentworth
Tim Simpson	John Malcolm
Evangeline Sinclair	Marian Babson
Det Jake Sinclair	Leonard Goldberg
Joe Sixsmith	Reginald Hill
Jacob Skarre	Karin Fossum
DCC Bob Skinner	Quintin Jardine
DI Bill Slider	Cynthia Harrod-Eagles
DI Sloan	Catherine Aird
Drew Slocombe	Rebecca Tope
Lieut Viktor Slutsky	Andrey Kurkov
Henry Smart	Roddy Doyle
George Smiley	John Le Carré
Bill Smith	S J Rozan
Grace Smith	Liz Evans
Bretta Solomon	Janis Harrison
Sam Spade	Dashiell Hammett
Suzy Spencer	Lis Howell
Spenser	Robert B Parker
DI Jon Spicer	Chris Simms
DI Jack Spratt	Jasper Fforde
St Benet's Trilogy	Susan Howatch
Michael St Pierre	Richard Doetsch
Sookie Stackhouse	Charlaine Harris
DI Vera Stanhope	Ann Cleeves
Staples Family	Mary Jane Staples
Dr Jack Stapleton	Robin Cook
Star Trek Series	Michael Jan Friedman
Nathaniel Starbuck	Bernard Cornwell
David Stark	Lisa See
Dan Starkey	Colin Bateman

Clarice Starling	Thomas Harris
Insp Starrett	Paul Charles
Lt Jack Steele	Iain Gale
Nick Stefanos	George P Pelecanos
Stephanos	Margaret Doody
Kellen Stewart	Manda Scott
Hanno Stiffeniis	Michael Gregorio
Stone of Light Trilogy	Christian Jacq
Chief Jesse Stone	Robert B Parker
Nick Stone	Andy McNab
Stonemoor Series	Kay Stephens
Serge Storms	Tim Dorsey
Derek Strange	George P Pelecanos
Leo Street	Pauline McLynn
Pearl Street	Maureen Lee
Det Jonathan Stride	Brian Freeman
Jim Stringer	Andrew Martin
Lt Jack Stryker	Paula Gosling
Supt Yngvar Stubo	Anne Holt
Det Milo Sturgis	Jonathan Kellerman
C W Sughrue	James Crumley
Sheriff John Victor Sully	Boston Teran
Supt Gregory Summers	Susan B Kelly
Sutton Family	Elizabeth Elgin
Insp Erlendur Sveinsson	Arnaldur Indridason
Dr Svenson	G W Dahlquist
Swann Family	R F Delderfield
Sweet Rosie Series	Iris Gower
Jack Swyteck	James Grippando
Yashim Tagalu	Jason Goodwin
Tanner Trilogy	Harry Bowling
Sgt Jack Tanner	James Holland
Gerry Tate	Marian Babson
Betsy Taylor	Mary Janice Davidson
Jack Taylor	Ken Bruen
DC Jennie Taylor	Pauline Bell
Carlos Tejada	Rebecca Pawel
Telamon	Paul Doherty
Jack Teller	Tom Gabbay
The Templars	Paul Doherty
Miss Temple	G W Dahlquist
CI Mark Tench	Brian Cooper
DCI Jane Tennison	Lynda La Plante
Frank Terrell	James Hadley Chase
PC Thackeray	Peter Lovesey
DCI Michael Thackeray	Patricia Hall
DI Luke Thanet	Dorothy Simpson
Thomas the Falconer	John Pilkington
Mercy Thompson	Patricia Briggs
Barney Thomson	Douglas Lindsay
Thorn	James W Hall
DI Tom Thorne	Mark Billingham

T

U

V

W

Characters & Series

John Wells	Alex Berenson
Matt Wells	Paul Johnston
Werner Family	Belva Plain
Helen West	Frances Fyfield
CI George Wexford	Ruth Rendell
Murray Whelan	Shane Maloney
Jane Whitefield	Thomas Perry
DI Ray Whitelaw	Georgie Hale
Edmund Whitty	John Maclachlan Gray
Wideacre Trilogy	Philippa Gregory
Nina Wilde	Andy McDermott
Oscar Wilde	Gyles Brandreth
CI Wilkins	James Anderson
Terry Williams	Tony Strong
Lord Peter Wimsey	Dorothy L Sayers
Erik Winter	Ake Edwardson
' Women's Murder Club'	James Patterson
DCI Charlie Woodend	Sally Spencer
Bertie Wooster	P G Wodehouse
World War 1 Series	Anne Perry
Supt Wycliffe	W J Burley
Bubbles Yablonsky	Sarah Strohmeyer
Det Li Yan	Peter May
Yaotl	Simon Levack
Supt Mike Yeadings	Clare Curzon
DS Yellich	Peter Turnbull
Yum Yum (Siamese cat)	Lilian Jackson Braun
Insp Shan Tao Yun	Eliot Pattison
Charlie Zailer	Sophie Hannah
Faith Zanetti	Anna Blundy
The Mamur Zapt (Gareth Owen)	Michael Pearce
Aurelio Zen	Michael Dibdin
Miss Zukas	Jo Dereske
Nick Zuliani	Ian Morson

Y

Z

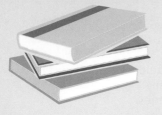

Literary Prizes and Awards

There are over 250 literary prizes and awards available in the United Kingdom of which some 30 relate to fiction. These are listed in this section with a brief description of each award followed by the names of the winning authors and titles, generally from 2000 or when the award commenced. Earlier winners and discontinued prizes can be found in previous editions of this guide.

Authors' Club First Novel Award

This is awarded to the most promising First Novel written by a British author and published in the UK during the calendar year preceding the year in which the award is presented.

2000	Ann Harries	*Manly Pursuits*
2001	Brian Clarke	*The Stream*
2002	Carl Tighe	*Burning Worm*
2003	Dan Rhodes	*Timoleon Vieta Come Home*
2004	Susan Fletcher	*Eve Green*
2005	Henry Shukman	*Sandstorm*
2006	Neil Griffiths	*Betrayal in Naples*
2007	Nicola Monaghan	*The Killing Jar*
2008	Segun Afolabi	*Goodbye Lucille*

James Tait Black Memorial Prizes

The James Tait Black Memorial Prizes, founded in memory of a partner in the publishing house A & C Black Ltd, were instituted in 1919. Two prizes are awarded annually; one for the best biography or work of that type and the other for the best work of fiction published during the calendar year. The prizes are the UK's oldest continuous book awards.

2000	Zadie Smith	*White Teeth*
2001	Sid Smith	*Something Like a House*
2002	Jonathan Franzen	*The Corrections*
2003	Andrew O'Hagan	*Personality*
2004	David Peace	*GB 84*
2005	Ian McEwan	*Saturday*
2006	Cormac McCarthy	*The Road*
2007	Rosalind Belben	*Our Horses in Egypt*

British Fantasy Awards

www.britishfantasysociety.org/awards.html

The British Fantasy Society, founded in 1971, sponsors a number of awards including the August Derleth Award for the best novel of the year. Winners are selected by members of the Society at their annual Fantasy Convention.

2000	Graham Joyce	*Indigo*
2001	China Miéville	*Perdido Street Station*
2002	Simon Clark	*The Night of the Triffids*
2003	China Miéville	*The Scar*
2004	Christopher Fowler	*Full Dark House*
2005	Stephen King	*Dark Tower VII, the Dark Tower*
2006	Neil Gaiman	*Anansi Boys*
2007	Tim Lebbon	*Dusk*

British Science Fiction Association Awards

www.bsfa.co.uk/bsfa/website/awards.aspx

Awarded annually after a ballot of members, by the British Science Fiction Association (BSFA). Winners of the Best Novel prize are listed below.

2000	Mary Gentle	*Ash: A Secret History*
2001	Alastair Reynolds	*Chasm City*
2002	Christopher Priest	*The Separation*
2003	Jon Courtenay Grimwood	*Felaheen*
2004	Ian McDonald	*River of Gods*
2005	Geoff Ryman	*Air*
2006	Jon Courtenay Grimwood	*End of the World Blues*
2007	Ian McDonald	*Brasyl*

Arthur C Clarke Award

www.clarkeaward.com

Established in 1986 the Arthur C Clarke Award is supported and judged jointly by the British Science Fiction Association, the Science Fiction Foundation and the Science Museum. It is for a Science Fiction novel receiving its first British publication. Horror and Fantasy are excluded unless there is a strong Science Fiction element in the book.

2000	Bruce Sterling	*Distraction*
2001	China Miéville	*Perdido Street Station*
2002	Gwyneth Jones	*Bold as Love*
2003	Christopher Priest	*The Separation*
2004	Neal Stephenson	*Quicksilver*
2005	China Miéville	*Iron Council*
2006	Geoff Ryman	*Air*
2007	M John Harrison	*Nova Swing*
2008	Richard Morgan	*Black Man*

Prizes

Commonwealth Writers' Prize

www.commonwealthfoundation.com/culturediversity/writersprize

Established in 1987 by the Commonwealth Foundation in association with the Book Trust and the Royal Overseas League, the award is administered annually within one of four regions of the Commonwealth. Entries submitted by publishers must be novels or short stories in English.

2000	J M Coetzee	*Disgrace*
2001	Peter Carey	*True History of the Kelly Gang*
2002	Richard Flanagan	*Gould's Book of Fish*
2003	Austin Clarke	*The Polished Hoe*
2004	Caryl Phillips	*A Distant Shore*
2005	Andrea Levy	*Small Island*
2006	Kate Grenville	*The Secret River*
2007	Lloyd Jones	*Mister Pip*
2008	Lawrence Hill	*The Book of Negroes*

Costa Book Awards

(formerly the Whitbread Book of the Year and Literary Awards)
www.costabookawards.com

Established in 1971, the Whitbread plc prizes were ultimately awarded to five categories: Novel; First Novel; Children's Novel; Poetry and Biography. From 2006 sponsorship passed to the Costa Coffee Co, a subsidiary of Whitbread plc with the format of the awards unchanged.

Whitbread

2000	First Novel	Zadie Smith	*White Teeth*
	Novel & 'Book of The Year'	Matthew Kneale	*English Passengers*
2001	First Novel	Sid Smith	*Something Like a House*
	Novel	Patrick Neate	*Twelve Bar Blues*
	Book of the Year	Philip Pullman	*The Amber Spyglass*
2002	First Novel	Norman Lebrecht	*The Song of Names*
	Novel	Michael Frayn	*Spies*
2003	First Novel	D B C Pierre	*Vernon God Little*
	Novel & 'Book of the Year'	Mark Haddon	*The Curious Incident of the Dog in the Night-Time*
2004	First Novel	Susan Fletcher	*Eve Green*
	Novel & 'Book of the Year'	Andrea Levy	*Small Island*
2005	First Novel	Tash Aw	*The Harmony Silk Factory*
	Novel	Ali Smith	*The Accidental*

Costa

2006	First Novel & 'Book of the Year'	Stef Penney	*The Tenderness of Wolves*
	Novel	William Boyd	*Restless*
2007	First Novel	Catherine O'Flynn	*What Was Lost*
	Novel & 'Book of the Year'	A L Kennedy	*Day*

Prizes

The first meeting of the Association was convened by John Creasey in November 1953 and awards have been presented since 1955. From 2006 the principal awards have been sponsored by Duncan Lawrie Private Bank.

Gold Dagger	for the best thriller, suspense novel or spy fiction published in the UK in the English language
Silver Dagger	for the runner-up
JCMA	John Creasey Memorial Dagger, for the best crime novel by an author who has not previously published a full-length work of fiction
Historical Dagger	the Ellis Peters Historical Dagger
Cartier Diamond Dagger	for outstanding contribution to the genre of crime writing
Steel Dagger	the Ian Fleming Steel Dagger for thrillers
Dagger in the Library	for "the author of crime fiction whose work has given most pleasure to readers" as nominated by UK libraries
Duncan Lawrie Dagger	formerly Gold Dagger
Duncan Lawrie International Dagger	for the best crime novel translated into English
New Blood Dagger	formerly JCMA

2000	Gold Dagger	Jonathan Lethem	*Motherless Brooklyn*
	Silver Dagger	Donna Leon	*Friends in High Places*
	JCMA	Boston Teran	*God is a Bullet*
	Historical Dagger	Gillian Linscott	*Absent Friends*
	Cartier Diamond Dagger	Peter Lovesey	
2001	Gold Dagger	Henning Mankell	*Sidetracked*
	Silver Dagger	Giles Blunt	*Forty Words for Sorrow*
	JCMA	Susanna Jones	*The Earthquake Bird*
	Historical Dagger	Andrew Taylor	*The Office of the Dead*
	Cartier Diamond Dagger	Lionel Davidson	
2002	Gold Dagger	José C Samoza	*The Athenian Murders*
	Silver Dagger	James Crumley	*The Final Country*
	JCMA	Louise Welsh	*The Cutting Room*
	Historical Dagger	Sarah Waters	*Fingersmith*
	Steel Dagger	John Creed	*The Sirius Crossing*
	Cartier Diamond Dagger	Sara Paretsky	
2003	Gold Dagger	Minette Walters	*Fox Evil*
	Silver Dagger	Morag Joss	*Half Broken Things*
	JCMA	William Landay	*Mission Flats*
	Historical Dagger	Andrew Taylor	*The American Boy*
	Steel Dagger	Dan Fesperman	*The Small Boat of Great Sorrows*
	Cartier Diamond Dagger	Robert Barnard	

2004	Gold Dagger	Sara Paretsky	*Blacklist*
	Silver Dagger	John Harvey	*Flesh and Blood*
	JCMA	Mark Mills	*Amagansett*
	Historical Dagger	Barbara Cleverly	*The Damascened Blade*
	Steel Dagger	Jeffrey Deaver	*Garden of Beasts*
	Cartier Diamond Dagger	Lawrence Block	
2005	Dagger of Daggers - Golden Jubilee	John Le Carré	*The Spy Who Came in From the Cold*
	Gold Dagger	Arnaldur Indridason	*Silence of the Grave*
	Silver Dagger	Barbara Nadel	*Deadly Web*
	JCMA	Dreda Say Mitchell	*Running Hot*
	Historical Dagger	C J Sansom	*Dark Fire*
	Steel Dagger	Henry Porter	*Brandenburg*
	Dagger in the Library	Jake Arnott	
	Cartier Diamond Dagger	Ian Rankin	
2006	Duncan Lawrie Dagger	Ann Cleeves	*Raven Black*
	Duncan Lawrie Int'l Dagger	Fred Vargas	*The Three Evangelists*
	Ellis Peters Award	Edward Wright	*Red Sky Lament*
	Steel Dagger	Nick Stone	*Mr Clarinet*
	New Blood Dagger	Louise Penny	*Still Life*
	Dagger in the Library	Jim Kelly	
	Cartier Diamond Dagger	Elmore Leonard	
2007	Duncan Lawrie Dagger	Peter Temple	*The Broken Shore*
	Duncan Lawrie Int'l Dagger	Fred Vargas	*Wash This Blood Clean From My Hand*
	Ellis Peters Award	Ariana Franklin	*Mistress of the Art of Death*
	Steel Dagger	Gillian Flynn	*Sharp Objects*
	New Blood Dagger	Gillian Flynn	*Sharp Objects*
	Dagger in the Library	Stuart MacBride	
	Cartier Diamond Dagger	John Harvey	
2008	Duncan Lawrie Dagger	Frances Fyfield	*Blood From Stone*
	Duncan Lawrie Int'l Dagger	Dominique Manotti	*Lorraine Connection*
	Steel Dagger	Tom Robb Smith	*Child 44*
	New Blood Dagger	Matt Rees	*The Bethlehem Murders*
	Dagger in the Library	Craig Russell	
	Cartier Diamond Dagger	Sue Grafton	

www.societyofauthors.org/prizes_grants_and_awards

Awarded to the best second novel of the year published in that calendar year. The winner is chosen by a panel of judges from entries submitted by publishers. The award is administered by the Society of Authors and since 2005 has been awarded biennially.

joint winners 2000	John Burnside	*The Mercy Boys*
	Claire Messud	*The Last Life*
	Matt Thorne	*Eight Minutes Idle*
	Phil Whitaker	*Triangulation*
2001	Anne Enright	*What Are You Like?*
2002	Ali Smith	*Hotel World*
2003	Jeremy Gavron	*The Book of Israel*
2004	Michelle de Kretser	*The Hamilton Case*
2005	Nadeem Aslam	*Maps For Lost Lovers*
2007	M J Hyland	*Carry Me Down*

Geoffrey Faber Memorial Prize

As a memorial to the founder and first Chairman of the firm, Faber and Faber Limited established the prize in 1963. Awarded annually, it is given in alternate years for a volume of verse and for a volume of prose fiction published originally in this country by writers who are under 40 years of age.

2001	Trezza Azzopardi	*The Hiding Place*
2003	Justin Hill	*The Drink and Dream Teahouse*
2005	David Mitchell	*Cloud Atlas*
2007	Edward Docx	*Self Help*

Prizes

Foster Grant Romantic Novel of the Year

See Romantic Novel of the Year (page 349)

Guardian First Book Award

This award succeeded the Guardian Fiction Prize from the year 1999 onwards. It now recognises and rewards new writing by honouring an author's first book, which may be fiction or non-fiction.

2000	Zadie Smith	*White Teeth*
2001	Chris Ware	*Jimmy Corrigan: The Smartest Kid on Earth*
2002	Jonathan Safran Foer	*Everything is Illuminated*
2003–2004	No award to fiction	
2005	Alexander Masters	*Stuart: a Life Backwards*
2006–2007	No award to fiction	

Hawthornden Prize

Founded in 1919 by Miss Alice Warrender and along with the James Tait Black Award, it is one of the UK's oldest literary prizes. Awarded annually to an English writer for the best work of imaginative literature, it is especially designed to encourage young authors, and the word 'imaginative' is given a broad interpretation.

The following dates are the years for which the award was given to a work of fiction:

2001	Helen Simpson	*Hey Yeah Right Get a Life*
2005	Justin Cartwright	*The Promise of Happiness*
2006	Alexander Masters	*Stuart: a Life Backwards*
2007	M J Hyland	*Carry Me Down, Carry Me Down*
2008	Nicola Barker	*Darkmans*

Independent Foreign Fiction Award

Funded by the Arts Council & Champagne Taittinger and promoted by *The Independent* newspaper, an annual prize for the best contemporary work of prose fiction translated into English from any other tongue and published between 1 January and 31 December each year, since 2001.

2001	Marta Morazzoni translated from the Italian by Emma Rose	*The Alphonse Courriér Affair*
2002	W G Sebald translated from the German by Anthea Bell	*Austerlitz*
2003	Per Olov Enquist translated from the Swedish by Tiina Nunnally	*The Visit of the Royal Physician*
2004	Javier Cercas translated from the Spanish by Anne McLean	*Soldiers of Salamis*
2005	Frédéric Beigbeder translated from the French by Frank Wynne	*Windows on the World*
2006	Per Petterson translated from the Norwegian by Anne Born	*Out Stealing Horses*
2007	José Eduardo Agualusa translated from the Portuguese by Daniel Hahn	*The Book of Chameleons*
2008	Paul Verhaeghen translated from the Dutch by the author	*Omega Minor*

International IMPAC Dublin Literary Award

www.impacdublinaward.ie

Established in 1996 and awarded to a work of fiction written and published in the English language or written in a language other than English and published in English translation. The winner is chosen by nominations from 150 public libraries in 40 countries.

2000	Nicola Barker	*Wide Open*
2001	Alistair MacLeod	*No Great Mischief*
2002	Michel Housellebecq	*Atomised*
2003	Orhan Pamuk	*My Name is Red*
2004	Taher Ben Jelloun	*This Blinding Absence of Light*
2005	Edward P Jones	*The Known World*
2006	Colm Toibin	*The Master*
2007	Per Petterson	*Out Stealing Horses*
2008	Rawi Hage	*De Niro's Game*

Irish Times International Fiction Prize

As this prize was discontinued after 2001, please see the 5th edition of this guide for prize winners.

Jewish Quarterly/Wingate Literary Prize for Fiction

www.jewishquarterly.org/wingateprize.shtml

Established in 1977 by the late Harold Hyman Wingate, this prize is the only award in the UK to recognise major works by Jewish or non-Jewish authors that stimulate an interest in and awareness of themes of Jewish concern among a wider reading public.

2000	Howard Jacobson	*The Mighty Walzer*
2001	Mona Yahia	*When the Grey Beetles Took Over Baghdad*
2002	W G Sebald	*Austerlitz*
2003	Zadie Smith	*The Autograph Man*
2004	David Grossman	*Someone to Run With*
2005	David Besmozgis	*Natasha and Other Stories*
2006	Imre Kertesz	*Fatelessness*
2007	Howard Jacobson	*Katooki Nights*
2008	Etgar Keret	*Missing Kissinger*

Prizes

John Llewellyn Rhys Prize

www.booktrust.org.uk/Prizes-and-awards/John-Llewellyn-Rhys-Prize

This prize is awarded in honour of the writer John Llewellyn Rhys, who was killed in action in World War II. It was founded by his young widow to honour and celebrate his life. It rewards the best work of literature (fiction, non-fiction, poetry, drama) by a UK or Commonwealth writer aged 35 or under. From 1987 to 2003 it was funded by *The Mail on Sunday* but after the 2002 prize was awarded *The Mail on Sunday* withdrew and the prize is now run by Booktrust.

2000	Edward Platt	*Leadville*
2001	Susanna Jones	*The Earthquake Bird*
2002	No Award for Fiction	
2003	Charlotte Mendelson	*Daughters of Jerusalem*
2004	Jonathan Trigell	*Boy A*
2005	Uzodinma Iweala	*Beasts of No Nation*
2006/7	Sarah Hall	*The Carhullan Army*

Man Booker Prize for Fiction

www.themanbookerprize.com/prize

Established in 1968 by Booker McConnell Ltd. Eligible novels must be written in English by a citizen of Britain, the Commonwealth or the Republic of Ireland. Since 2002 sponsorship has been by the Man Group and the prize is now known as the Man Booker Prize.

2000	Margaret Atwood	*The Blind Assassin*
2001	Peter Carey	*True History of the Kelly Gang*
2002	Yann Martel	*Life of Pi*
2003	D B C Pierre	*Vernon God Little*
2004	Alan Hollinghurst	*The Line of Beauty*
2005	John Banville	*The Sea*
2006	Kiran Desai	*The Inheritance of Loss*
2007	Anne Enright	*The Gathering*

To celebrate the 40th anniversary of this award, Salman Rushdie's *Midnight's Children* was crowned the Best of the Booker.

Man Booker International Prize

www.themanbookerprize.com/prize

Awarded every two years from 2005 to an author writing fiction in the English language or whose work is widely translated into English. It will celebrate English language fiction as a major cultural force in the modern world.

2005	Ismail Kadare
2007	Chinua Achebe

Somerset Maugham Awards

www.societyofauthors.org/prizes_grants_and_awards

The purpose of these annual awards is to encourage young writers to travel, and the emphasis of the founder is on originality and promise. Authors must be under 35 years of age, a British subject by birth, and ordinarily resident in the United Kingdom. Poetry, fiction and non-fiction are all eligible.

	2000	Sarah Waters	*Affinity*
	2001	Ben Rice	*Pobby and Dingan*
joint winners	2002	Charlotte Hobson	*Black Earth City*
		Marcel Theroux	*The Paperchase*
	2003	Hari Kunzru	*The Impressionist*
joint winners	2004	Charlotte Mendelson	*Daughters of Jerusalem*
		Mark Blayney	*Two Kinds of Silence*
joint winners	2005	Justin Hill	*Passing Under Heaven*
		Maggie O'Farrell	*The Distance Between Us*
joint winners	2006	Chris Cleave	*Incendiary*
		Zadie Smith	*On Beauty*
	2007	James Scudamore	*The Amnesia Clinic*
joint winners	2008	Gwendoline Riley	*Joshua Spassky*
		Steven Hall	*The Raw Shark Texts*

McKitterick Prize

www.societyofauthors.org/prizes_grants_and_awards

Endowed by the late Tom McKitterick the award is made to a first novel (published or unpublished) by an author over the age of 40.

2000	Chris Dolan	*Ascension Day*
2001	Giles Waterfield	*The Long Afternoon*
2002	Manil Suri	*The Death of Vishnu*
2003	Mary Lawson	*Crow Lake*
2004	Mark Haddon	*The Curious Incident of the Dog in the Night-Time*
2005	Lloyd Jones	*Mr Vogel*
2006	Peter Pouncey	*Rules for Old Men Waiting*
2007	Reina James	*This Time of Dying*
2008	Jennie Walker	*24 for 3*

Melissa Nathan Award for Comedy Romance

www.melissanathan.com/Award/Index.asp

This award was set up by Melissa's husband in 2007 honouring the criteria that she drew up herself very shortly before she died of cancer in 2006. She wanted to encourage and reward writers who can combine in a novel the magical, life-enhancing elements of humour and love.

| 2007 | Marian Keyes | *Anybody Out There* |
| 2008 | Lisa Jewell | *31 Dream Street* |

Ondaatje Prize

www.rslit.org/pmwiki.php?n=Awards.Ondaatje

The Royal Society of Literature launched in 2004 this new award for writing 'that evokes the spirit of a place'. It has been funded by business man and philanthropist Christopher Ondaatje with extra backing from *Conde Nast Traveller* magazine. It is open to fiction and non-fiction works and was presented for the first time in May 2004. This award is a successor to the Winifred Holtby prize for regional fiction which has been discontinued.

Winifred Holtby

2000	Donna Morrissey	*Kit's Law*
2001	Anna Burns	*No Bones*
2002	Alexandra Fuller	*Don't Let's Go to the Dogs Tonight*

Ondaatje

2004–2005	No award for fiction	
2006	James Meek	*The People's Act of Love*
2007	Hisham Matar	*In the Country of Men*
2008	No award for fiction	

Orange Broadband Award for New Writers

www.orangeprize.co.uk/Award-for-New-Writers

This prize was created in 2005. Open to any first work of fiction by a woman of any nationality and published in the UK in the preceding year. Novels can be entered for both the new Award and the main Orange Prize.

2005	Diana Evans	*26a*
2006	Naomi Alderman	*Disobedience*
2007	Karen Connelly	*The Lizard Cage*
2008	Joanna Kavenna	*Inglorious*

Prizes

Orange Broadband Prize

www.orangeprize.co.uk

Founded in 1996, this award is open to women authors of any nationality, provided that entries have been published in the United Kingdom. Administered by Booktrust.

2000	Linda Grant	*When I Lived in Modern Times*
2001	Kate Grenville	*The Idea of Perfection*
2002	Ann Patchett	*Bel Canto*
2003	Valerie Martin	*Property*
2004	Andrea Levy	*Small Island*
2005	Lionel Shriver	*We Need to Talk About Kevin*
2006	Zadie Smith	*On Beauty*
2007	Chimamanda Ngozi Adichie	*Half of a Yellow Sun*
2008	Rose Tremain	*The Road Home*

Pulitzer Prize for Fiction

www.pulitzer.org/bycat/Fiction

Joseph Pulitzer, reporter, editor, publisher and a founder of the Graduate School of Journalism at Columbia University, established in 1903 a system of prizes to encourage 'public service, public morals, American literature and the advancement of education'. The Fiction Prize was first awarded in 1948.

2000	Jhumpa Lahiri	*Interpreter of Maladies*
2001	Michael Chabon	*The Amazing Adventures of Kavalier and Clay*
2002	Richard Russo	*Empire Falls*
2003	Jeffrey Eugenides	*Middlesex*
2004	Edward P Jones	*The Known World*
2005	Marilynne Robinson	*Gilead*
2006	Geraldine Brooks	*March*
2007	Cormac McCarthy	*The Road*
2008	Junot Diaz	*The Brief Wondrous Life of Oscar Wao*

Prizes

Romantic Novel of the Year

www.rna-uk.org/index.php?page=rnoty_award

Established in 1960 and administered by The Romantic Novelists Association, the award is for the best romantic novel of the year by a United Kingdom citizen.

2000	Maureen Lee	*Dancing in the Dark*
2001	Cathy Kelly	*Someone Like You*
2002	Philippa Gregory	*The Other Boleyn Girl*
2003	Sarah Mason	*Playing James*
2004	Jojo Moyes	*Foreign Fruit*
2005	Katharine Davies	*A Good Voyage*
2006	Erica James	*Gardens of Delight*
2007	Rosie Thomas	*Iris & Ruby*
2008	Freya North	*Pillow Talk*

Saga Award for Wit

The Award, sponsored by *Saga Magazine*, was for humorous writing, whether fiction or non-fiction, by authors aged 50 or over.

2003	Alexander McCall Smith	*The Full Cupboard of Life*
2004	No Award for Fiction	
2005	Marina Lewycka	*A Short History of Tractors in Ukrainian*

This prize was first awarded in 2003 and has now been discontinued.

Sagittarius Prize

Awarded to a first novel by a writer over 60 years of age, first published in the United Kingdom during the year preceding the year in which the award was presented. Administered by the Society of Authors.

2000	David Crackanthorpe	*Stolen Marches*
2001	Michael Richardson	*The Pig Bin*
2002	Zvi Jagendorf	*Wolfy and the Strudelbakers*
2003	Margaret Kaine	*Ring of Clay*
2004	William Newton	*The Two Pound Tram*
2005	Lauro Martines	*Loredana*

This prize has now been discontinued.

WHSmith Literary Award

Awarded from 1959 to the book that, in the opinion of the judges, has made the most outstanding contribution to literature in the year under review. There are no age limits for the author and the award is open to all types of literature including foreign works in translation.

2000	Melvyn Bragg	*The Soldier's Return*
2001	Philip Roth	*The Human Stain*
2002	Ian McEwan	*Atonement*
2003	Donna Tartt	*The Little Friend*
2004	Richard Powers	*The Time of our Singing*
2005	Philip Roth	*The Plot Against America*
2006	J K Rowling	*Harry Potter and the Half-Blood Prince*

Sunday Times Young Writer of the Year Award

www.societyofauthors.org/prizes_grants_and_awards

Awarded to a writer who is under the age of 35 on the strength of the promise shown by a full-length published work of fiction, non-fiction or poetry.

2000	Sarah Waters	*Affinity*
2001	Zadie Smith	*White Teeth*
2002–2006	No award for fiction	
2007	Naomi Alderman	*Disobedience*
2008	Adam Foulds	*The Truth About These Strange Times*

Theakston's Old Peculiar Crime Novel of the Year

www.harrogate-festival.org.uk/crime/prize.html

The Award is open to any British Crime Fiction published for the first time in paperback and is sponsored by Theakston's Old Peculiar and promoted nationwide by Waterstone's book shops. The winner is selected from a short list issued in March and the prize is presented in July at the Harrogate Crime Writing Festival. First awarded in 2005.

2005	Mark Billingham	*Lazy Bones*
2006	Val McDermid	*The Torment of Others*
2007	Allan Guthrie	*Two-Way Split*
2008	Stef Penney	*The Tenderness of Wolves*

Thumping Good Read Book Award

Awarded to a novel that is judged by a panel of WHSmith's customers to be an "accessible and page-turning good read".

2000	Boris Starling	*Storm*
2001	Jeffery Deaver	*The Empty Chair*
2002	Mo Hayder	*The Treatment*
2003	Harlan Coben	*Gone For Good*

This prize has now been discontinued.

Betty Trask Awards

www.societyofauthors.org/prizes_grants_and_awards

Started in 1984 and administered by the Society of Authors, the awards are for the benefit of young authors (under 35), and are given on the strength of the manuscript of a first novel of a romantic or traditional — rather than experimental — nature. The winners are required to use the money for foreign travel. The principal winners are:

2000	Jonathan Tulloch	*The Season Ticket*
2001	Zadie Smith	*White Teeth*
2002	Hari Kunzru	*The Impressionist*
2003	Jon McGregor	*If Nobody Speaks of Remarkable Things*
2004	Louise Dean	*Becoming Strangers*
2005	Susan Fletcher	*Eve Green*
2006	Nick Laird	*Utterly Monkey*
2007	Will Davis	*My Side of the Story*
2008	David Szalay	*London & the South East*

Whitbread Book of the Year and Literary Prizes

See Costa Book Awards (page 340)

Wingate Literary Prize for Fiction

See Jewish Quarterly/Wingate (page 345)

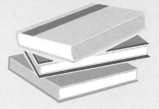

Crossover Authors

Selecting suitable books for Young Adults, i.e. the 16+ age group is not easy. The right book for the right person at this stage can vary enormously. One author may write just one title which appeals or maybe every book by that author will be devoured. Where authors have written books for children these are indicated with a ☺ as the children's books are written for a much younger age range. The list is certainly not exhaustive for several other authors in *Who Else Writes Like ...?* will be enjoyed by young adults. The suggestions here are subjective but, in our opinion, offer a reliable selection of authors to introduce older teenagers to adult fiction.

Recommended authors are indicated by ⌒ in the main listing.

Viv Green and Mary Yardley

Chinua Achebe
Peter Ackroyd
Douglas Adams
Cecelia Ahern
Brian W Aldiss
Monica Ali
Isabel Allende
Kingsley Amis
Martin Amis
James Anderson
Virginia Andrews
Jeffrey Archer
Sherry Ashworth ☺
Isaac Asimov
Kate Atkinson
Margaret Atwood
Jean M Auel
Jane Austen
Beryl Bainbridge
David Baldacci
J G Ballard
Iain Banks
Iain M Banks
Clive Barker
Pat Barker
Raffaella Barker ☺
Colin Bateman
Greg Bear

Alan Bennett
Maeve Binchy
Sam Bourne
William Boyd
Malcolm Bradbury
Ray Bradbury
Marion Zimmer Bradley
Anita Brookner
Terry Brooks
Dan Brown
John Buchan
Candace Bushnell
A S Byatt
Meg Cabot ☺
Trudi Canavan ☺
Orson Scott Card
Peter Carey
Raymond Chandler
Tracy Chevalier
Lee Child ☺
Agatha Christie
Tom Clancy
Mary Higgins Clark
Arthur C Clarke
Susanna Clarke
Harlan Coben
Jonathan Coe
Paulo Coelho

J M Coetzee
Martina Cole
Eoin Colfer ☺
Jenny Colgan
Max Allan Collins
Michael Connelly
Joseph Conrad
Jilly Cooper
Louise Cooper ☺
Bernard Cornwell
Patricia D Cornwell
Douglas Coupland
Michael Crichton
Michael Cunningham
Clive Cussler
Mary Janice Davidson
Lindsey Davis
Louis de Bernières
Jeffery Deaver
Len Deighton
Anita Desai
Colin Dexter
Philip K Dick
Charles Dickens
Garry Disher
Stephen Donaldson
Jennifer Donnelly ☺
Sara Douglass

Arthur Conan Doyle
Roddy Doyle ☺
Margaret Drabble
Daphne Du Maurier
Helen Dunmore ☺
David Eddings
Imogen Edwards-Jones
Clive Egleton
Ben Elton
Barbara Erskine
Janet Evanovich
William Faulkner
Sebastian Faulks
Christine Feehan
Jasper Fforde
Helen Fielding
Anne Fine ☺
F Scott Fitzgerald
Ian Fleming ☺
James Follett
Ken Follett
C S Forester
E M Forster
Margaret Forster
Frederick Forsyth
John Fowles
Clare Francis
Dick Francis
Michael Frayn
Nicci French
Esther Freud
Stephen Fry
Carlos Fuentes
Alexander Fullerton
Jostein Gaarder ☺
Neil Gaiman ☺
Patrick Gale
Gabriel Garcia Márquez
Jane Gardam ☺
Alex Garland
Elizabeth Gaskell
David Gemmell
Elizabeth George
Adèle Geras ☺
Tess Gerritsen
Robert Goddard
William Golding
Terry Goodkind
Sue Grafton
Caroline Graham

Winston Graham
Rob Grant
Robert Graves
Jane Green
Graham Greene
Philippa Gregory
Niall Griffiths
John Grisham
David Guterson
Mark Haddon ☺
Laurell K Hamilton
Thomas Hardy
Joanne Harris
Robert Harris
Thomas Harris
Lian Hearn ☺
Joseph Heller
Zoë Heller
Ernest Hemingway
Frank Herbert
Georgette Heyer
Carl Hiaasen ☺
Jack Higgins ☺
Patricia Highsmith
Charles Higson ☺
Reginald Hill
Susan Hill
Robin Hobb
Peter Hoeg
Alice Hoffman
Wendy Holden
Tom Holt
Nick Hornby ☺
Khaled Hosseini
Elizabeth Jane Howard
Aldous Huxley
Conn Iggulden
Hammond Innes
John Irving
Kazuo Ishiguro
Henry James
P D James
Peter James
Lisa Jewell
Ruth Prawer Jhabvala
Robert Jordan
James Joyce
Cathy Kelly
Thomas Keneally
Alexander Kent ☺

Sherrilyn Kenyon
Jack Kerouac
Katharine Kerr
Marian Keyes
Garry Kilworth ☺
Stephen King
Sophie Kinsella
Hanif Kureishi
Lynda La Plante
Stephen R Lawhead
D H Lawrence
John Le Carré
Ursula K Le Guin ☺
Stephen Leather
Harper Lee
Tanith Lee ☺
Elmore Leonard
Doris Lessing
Andrea Levy
C S Lewis ☺
Sue Limb ☺
Joan Lingard ☺
Toby Litt
Penelope Lively ☺
Sam Llewellyn ☺
David Lodge
Robert Ludlum
Sergei Lukyanenko
Alison Lurie
Anne McCaffrey
Ian McEwan
Alistair MacLean
Larry McMurtry
Andy McNab ☺
Henning Mankell ☺
Jill Mansell
Yann Martel
W Somerset Maugham
Armistead Maupin
Santa Montefiore
Toni Morrison
John Mortimer
Kate Mosse
Iris Murdoch
David Nicholls
William Nicholson ☺
Garth Nix ☺
Patrick O'Brian
Joseph O'Connor
Joan O'Neill ☺

Joyce Carol Oates ☺
George Orwell
Christopher Paolini ☺
Tony Parsons
James Patterson ☺
Elizabeth Peters
Ellis Peters
Jodi Picoult
Christopher Pike ☺
Terry Pratchett ☺
Philip Pullman ☺
Mario Puzo
Ian Rankin
Robert Rankin
Kathy Reichs
Erich Maria Remarque
Ruth Rendell
Anne Rice
J K Rowling ☺
Chris Ryan ☺
J D Salinger

Dorothy L Sayers
Simon Scarrow
Alice Sebold
Will Self
Tom Sharpe
Lionel Shriver
Nevil Shute
Georges Simenon
Alexander McCall Smith ☺
Ali Smith
Zadie Smith
Muriel Spark
John Steinbeck
Robert Louis Stevenson
Mary Stewart
Patrick Suskind
Meera Syal
Donna Tartt
Kate Thompson ☺
J R R Tolkien ☺
Sue Townsend ☺

P J Tracy
Anthony Trollope
Joanna Trollope
Barry Unsworth
Jules Verne
Alice Walker
Fiona Walker
Minette Walters
Evelyn Waugh
H G Wells
Irvine Welsh
Edith Wharton
Matt Whyman ☺
Kim Wilkins
R D Wingfield
Jeanette Winterson ☺
P G Wodehouse
Virginia Woolf
John Wyndham
Carlos Ruiz Zafón
Markus Zusak ☺

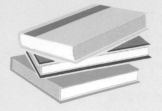

Further Reading

This short list contains books which should be readily available in most public library systems. They form an additional complement to *Who Else Writes Like ...?* and will help the reader explore a particular genre, pursue the reading of a series or follow up a more detailed path from one specific author and title to another.

Bloomsbury Essential Guide for Reading Groups
Edited by Susan Osborne, A & C Black, 2nd edition 2008
Offers up-to-date advice on finding, joining or setting up a reading group plus a list of 75 of the very best reads to stimulate discussion by including a summary of the book, a brief author biography and a set of titles for further reading that deal with similar themes.

Bloomsbury Good Reading Guide
Edited by Nick Rennison, A & C Black, 7th revised edition, 2006
A greatly expanded edition which includes the latest contemporary authors and landmark novels as well as prize winner and book club lists. An accessible and easy-to-read guide.

Bloomsbury Good Reading Guide to Crime Fiction
Edited by Nick Rennison, Bloomsbury Publishing plc, 2003
A complementary guide, arranged in a similar format and featuring over 200 authors covering many subgenres of crime fiction.

Bloomsbury Good Reading Guide to World Fiction
Edited by Vincent Cassar and Nik Kalinowski, A & C Black, 2007
Arranged geographically by continent and then by country the guide highlights the best modern novels that reflect the culture of a particular location. It features hundreds of authors and over a thousand novels.

Chambers Dictionary of Literary Characters
Chambers, 2nd edition, 2004
First published in 1994 this greatly enlarged second edition contains entries for more than 6,500 of the most famous and influential characters from novels, plays and poetry.

100 Must-read Classic Novels
By Nick Rennison, A & C Black, 2006
A selection of writing that has made an everlasting impression on our literary heritage. 100 of the best titles are fully reviewed and a further 500 recommended.

100 Must-read Crime Novels

By Nick Rennison and Richard Shephard, A & C Black, 2006
Following the same format as the Classic Novels it also includes a browsing by theme approach as well as listing the top ten crime characters and their creators.

100 Must-read Science Fiction Novels

By Stephen E Andrews and Nick Rennison, A & C Black, 2006
It is arranged by theme including a reader's fast guide to the world of science fiction as well as listing award winners of prizes and book club recommendations. Also included is a special category covering science fiction and film adaptations.

One Thousand and One (1001) Books You Must Read Before You Die

General editor Peter Boxall, Cassell, 2008
An authoritative selection of novels reviewed by an international team of critics. Arranged chronologically and with a plentiful supply of illustrations, both coloured and black and white.

The Rough Guide to Classic Novels

Edited by Simon Mason, Rough Guides 2008
Covers 229 novels or sequences of novels by novelists from 36 different countries published between the 17th and 21st century with information on translations, screen adaptations and suggestions for further reading.

The Rough Guide to Crime Fiction

By Barry Forshaw, Rough Guides, 2007
Recommends over 200 classic crime novels and mystery authors written over the past century. It also includes screen adaptations and ideas for further reading.

Sequels Vol 1: Adult Books

Compiled by Mandy Hicken, Career Development Group, CILIP, 13th ed 2004
Lists novels in which the same characters appear; sequences of novels connected by theme; sequences of novels with a geographical or historical connection; and non-fiction, mainly autobiographical, which is intended to be read in sequence. The arrangement is primarily under the author, with an index of series and characters. Invaluable if you want to read a series in order.

The Ultimate Teen Book Guide

Edited by Daniel Hahn & Leonie Flynn, A & C Black, 2006
Contains reviews to over 700 books and suggestions for what to read next, The ultimate reference for anyone aged 12 and over.

Who Next...? A Guide to Children's Authors

Edited by Viv Warren and Mary Yardley, LISU, Loughborough University, 3rd edition, 2007.
It is designed as a tool to help parents, teachers and librarians in schools and public libraries to guide children to find authors they will enjoy reading. Arranged in three age groups with the oldest section covering the 12-14 age range.

Whodunit? A Who's Who in Crime & Mystery Writing
Edited by Rosemary Herbert, OUP, 2003
Containing 380 short essays telling readers whodunit by identifying fictional people who perpetrate and solve crimes. It also answers the question "who's done it?" by helping readers to get to know the writers as well.

Who's Who of Twentieth Century Novelists
Edited by Tim Woods, Routledge, 2001
Contains 1,000 biographical entries of novelists who have influenced 20th century fiction. Drawn from a broad range of countries, genres and styles including writers of popular genre fiction. The emphasis is on post 1945 writers.

Who Wrote What? A Dictionary of Writers and their Works
Edited by Michael Cox, OUP, 2002
A selective listing of over 25,000 titles from nearly 3,000 well known British, American & Commonwealth authors including major European and Classical figures.

An American Company, Libraries Unlimited, a member of The Greenwood Publishing Group, publish a whole range of material that serves the needs of the profession through quality publications. Two ranges especially worth considering are the **Genreflecting Advisory Series** and **Read On Series; Reading Lists for Every Taste**. (www.lu.com)

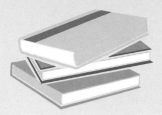

Websites

With the growth of the Internet there is now a bewildering range of websites which can assist both the professional librarian and the reader to expand their interest in particular authors and their works. Here are a few selected sites which should prove useful but do please note that although they were accurate at the time of going to press, they may very well change during the life of this edition.

General Interest
www.bookstoread.com
www.contemporarywriters.com
www.fantasticfiction.co.uk
www.meettheauthor.co.uk/home.html
www.whatshouldireadnext.com
www.whichbook.net

Chick Lit
www.chicklit.co.uk

Crime
www.thecwa.co.uk
www.thrillingdetective.com
www.ex.ac.uk/~RDavies/bankfiction
   (financial thrillers)
www.eurocrime.co.uk
www.reviewingtheevidence.com
www.twbooks.co.uk

Historical Fiction
www.histfiction.net
www.historicalnovelsociety.org

Horror
www.horrorworld.org

Romance
www.likesbooks.com
www.rna-uk.org
www.theromancereader.com

Science Fiction and Fantasy
www.britishfantasysociety.org/news
www.infinityplus.co.uk
www.sfrt.com
www.sfwa.org

Western
www.readwest.com

Bookshops
All primarily book selling sites but with useful information on authors

www.amazon.co.uk
www.bookdepository.co.uk
www.bookfinder.com
   (for second-hand books)
www.borders.co.uk
www.murderone.co.uk
www.waterstones.com

Reading Groups
www.bookgroup.info
www.encompassculture.com (British
   Council worldwide reading group)
www.reader2reader.net
www.readinggroupguides.com